Study Guide
Psychology
Second Edition

D1065567

Study Guide

GLEITMAN
Psychology
Second Edition

JOHN JONIDES
UNIVERSITY OF MICHIGAN

PAUL ROZIN
UNIVERSITY OF PENNSYLVANIA

W · W · NORTON & COMPANY · NEW YORK · LONDON

Permissions and credits, constituting an extension of the copyright page, are located on pages 293–294.

W. W. Norton & Company, Inc., 500 Fifth Avenue,
New York, N.Y. 10110
W. W. Norton & Company Ltd., 37 Great Russell Street,
London WC1B 3NU

ISBN 0-393-95381-5

2 3 4 5 6 7 8 9 0

CONTENTS

ACKNOWLEDGMENTS

The authors would like to thank Georgia Larounis and Deborah Reyher for having devoted so many hours to reviewing and editing this study guide. We also thank David Bauer, Elizabeth Gross, Georgia Larounis, Linda Millman, Deborah Reyher, and Barbara Zeeff for their contributions and valuable suggestions.

In the course of developing the sections entitled "investigating psychological phenomena" for each chapter, we have had occasion to seek the advice of colleagues and students who have particular expertise in the areas in question. We would like to acknowledge the help of Lyn Abramson, Henry Gleitman, Aaron Katcher, Charles G. Morris, Lorraine Nadelman, Harriet Oster, Christopher Peterson, Martin E. P. Seligman, W. John Smith, Marjorie Speers, and Edward Stricker. We also thank Richard Day for his suggestions on parts of the manuscript. In addition, we thank Walter Love and Jeannie Morrow for special assistance in field testing a number of the activities that we have included.

We also gratefully acknowledge the help provided by Amanda Adams, Nancy Palmquist, and Donna Seldin in the final preparation of all the material in this study guide.

Finally, we thank Donald Fusting for his encouragement and advice throughout the development of the text. In his role as editor, he reviewed the entire manuscript with great care, suggesting many improvements and clarifications in the behavioral objectives, questions, and experiments.

The authors of this guide are listed in alphabetical order on the title page.

TO THE STUDENT

This study guide is designed to help you to understand and apply the material presented in *Psychology*, Second Edition, by Henry Gleitman. Each chapter in the study guide corresponds to one in the textbook. There are four sections in each study guide chapter: Learning Objectives, Programmed Exercises, Self Test, and Investigating Psychological Phenomena. The first three sections will help you determine the essential ideas of the chapter, as well as give you experience with possible test questions. The fourth section, Investigating Psychological Phenomena allows you to extend your knowledge of some issues raised in the text. This section will also give you a feeling for how the data used by psychologists are collected, and how theories are tested in psychology. Let us briefly review the function of each of these sections.

LEARNING OBJECTIVES

We have provided an outline of the key issues discussed in each chapter. Each entry in the outline refers to a basic fact, theory, or relationship that you should have learned from the chapter. These entries are listed in order of occurrence in the chapter and are arranged under the same headings used in the chapter. It may be useful to read the learning objectives before reading the chapter, as well as after. They will help to orient you to the major issues, or the "big picture," of the chapter.

PROGRAMMED EXERCISES

For each chapter of the text, we have provided fill-in-the-blank questions. These questions test your basic knowledge of the key words and concepts of the chapter. These questions are very straightforward and can be looked up and verified in the text. So that you will know whether you are correct, the answer has been provided on the right side of the page. Be sure to cover that side of the page with your hand or a piece of paper as you do the exercises.

To facilitate locating the answers in the text, the programmed exercises are also arranged under the major headings of the textbook, and they follow the order of presentation in the text. This allows you to see which fact or theory pertains to which major point of the chapter.

SELF TEST

For each chapter in the text, we have prepared a self test composed of multiple-choice questions. They also follow the order of the text. In general, these questions are more difficult than the fill-ins, though both types of questions cover the range of materials presented in the text. The multiple choices sometimes highlight subtle distinctions, ask for some amount of integration, or test your ability to apply some of the material in the text.

Since multiple-choice questions are commonly used in examinations, and since they can also be very instructive, we will spend some time in this section discussing how to answer them. We will also describe and illustrate some different types of multiple-choice questions used in this manual.

First, some basic strategies. Most multiple-choice questions on examinations, and in this manual, have four or five choices. On most examinations there is a penalty of $-1/3$ point for wrong answers of four-choice questions, and $-1/4$ point for wrong answers on five-choice questions. This would mean that wild guessing should net a score of zero. But if you can eliminate even one choice, it pays to guess among the remaining alternatives.

Read each question carefully. Try to understand the *point* of the question. Read through the alternatives. The answer may be obvious to you. If not, try to eliminate some of the choices. You may be able to eliminate choices on the following grounds:

1. The choice is inherently inconsistent, illogical, or actual nonsense (e.g., word salad: a bunch of usually relevant terms combined in a meaningless way).

2. The choice makes sense and may even be true, but it is not an *answer* to the question.

3. On the basis of your knowledge, the choice is just the wrong answer to the question.

Get used to sorting out sense from nonsense and relevant from irrelevant answers. These skills will stand you in good stead in many of your activities outside of this course. Work with the remaining choices (if more than one choice remains), and do the best you can to determine the best fit between the question and the answer.

We will illustrate a number of different types of multiple-choice questions, all represented in this manual. For each example we will indicate the correct answer and add comments on some of the incorrect choices.

Straight factual questions. Many multiple-choice questions simply ask for your knowledge of facts: names, definitions, and basic concepts.

1. The Prime Minister of Great Britain at the end of World War II was:
   a. Neville Chamberlain
   b. Winston Churchill
   c. Harold Wilson
   d. Sir D. Winter
   e. Anthony Eden

Comment. This is a very straightforward question. You know it or you don't. The answer is *b*, Winston Churchill. The other names were selected to make the question somewhat difficult: Three of the other choices were prime ministers of Great Britain at the beginning or after the war, and one, Sir D. Winter, is a fictitious name.

2. The best way to describe inflation is:
   a. increase in the gross national product not accompanied by increased unemployment
   b. a general increase in prices
   c. a decrease in the money supply
   d. a decrease in the value of the monetary system, when associated with a gross national product
   e. another form of recession

Comment. This question is more difficult than 1. This is in part because the choices are more difficult. The correct answer is *b*. Answers *a, c,* and *e* are just wrong. Though *a* is consistent with inflation, it does not define it. Item *d* is inherently wrong, that is, it is sort of nonsense. What does it mean to decrease the value of the monetary *system* as opposed to money? And everything is associated with some gross national product. Keep your eyes open for nonsense. There is a lot of it in the world.

Evaluating evidence for a theory. In this type of question you are asked to judge whether particular results (real or hypothetical) support a particular theory (or which theory would be supported or opposed by a particular result). The theory and/or results may have been presented in the text, or they may be introduced in the question. The question tests both your knowledge of the materials, and your progress in understanding how to evaluate evidence. This type of question is often formulated in the negative—"Which of the following would be evidence against theory X?"—simply because it is usually easier to come up with results supporting major theories than results opposing them. We will assume, for the next sample question, that you have read in some text or other that Yentzel claimed that the crime rate increases as population mass and density increase. (Yentzel is a fictitious name.)

3. Which of the following would be evidence against Yentzel's theory? (Note: We assume that New York is larger than Philadelphia, which is larger than Tucson).
   a. Philadelphia has a crime rate higher than Tucson
   b. a few cities with increasing population also have increasing crime rates
   c. a few cities with decreasing population have an increase in crime rate
   d. Philadelphia has a lower crime rate than New York
   e. the ratio of murders to robberies is lower in New York than in Tucson

Comment. The correct answer is *c*, because this result is opposite to what would be predicted by Yentzel's theory. Answers *a, b,* and *c* are supporting evidence for the theory. Answer *e* is irrelevant: The theory says nothing about the type of crime, and *e* says nothing about the overall crime rate. (Note another clue to the right answer: *b* and *c* are opposites, so it is likely that one is evidence against the theory. However, clever exam writers know about this and sometimes put in opposites that are irrelevant to the question, to keep you on your toes).

Extending a principle or theory to a new situation. This type of question tests your understanding of a principle, theory, or concept by asking you to apply it in a situation other than those presented in the text.

4. If the saying "a stitch in time saves nine" were applied to medicine, one would recommend:
   a. reducing the amount of sewing in surgery
   b. increasing the cost of medical insurance
   c. increasing the frequency of checkups
   d. increasing the number of physicians
   e. making prescription drugs available over the counter

Comment: The correct answer is *c*. To answer the question, one must understand the saying and translate it into medical terms. This translation would be something like: Medical precautions can lead to avoidance of major illnesses. Alternative *a* is irrelevant to the *real* meaning of the saying and simply follows the *literal* meaning. Answer *b* would not lead, in any direct way, to avoidance of illness. But *b* is a sort of correct answer, since one might assume that increasing the cost of medical insurance would lead to increased coverage. The answer says increasing the cost, not the amount of insurance. Answer *c* relates directly to the saying: More checkups should lead to early discovery of illnesses that might prove harmful if allowed to develop. While *d* might well cut down the rate of illnesses, it is not a direct way of arriving at prevention. Lastly, *e* is irrelevant to the issue raised in the saying.

Relating different ideas or facts, or integrating materials. This type of question often involves materials from different sections of a chapter, or perhaps from different chapters (we have refrained from the latter, since we don't know the order in which you will be reading the chapters in the book).

5. The President of the United States is related to the electoral college as a U.S. Senator is related to:*
   a. his own college faculty
   b. the voters of his state
   c. the members of the House of Representatives
   d. the state of his electors
   e. the state of his voters

Comment: The correct answer is *b*. The electoral college is the group of people who actually elect the president. The voters of a senator's state are the people who elect the senator. Item *a* is totally wrong and simply a play on the word college. Item *c* is factually wrong. Item *d* is wrong and doesn't make too much sense, and item *e* is a

*This type of relation is often stated as "President of the U.S. : electoral college :: U.S. Senator : _____"

reversal of the correct answer and has no relation to the question.

INVESTIGATING PSYCHOLOGICAL PHENOMENA

For each chapter of the text, we have presented one or two activities or experiments. These activities build upon concepts or theories presented in the chapter and extend and deepen your knowledge and understanding of these concepts or theories.

The activities give you an opportunity to understand something about the progress of psychology as a science. While the text emphasizes our current understanding of psychology, the activities emphasize the process through which we arrive at this understanding. How is a theory tested? How do psychologists get data to describe basic relations or test theories? How do they analyze the data? We hope to give you a feeling for how progress is made, while at the same time indicating the problems and difficulties associated with the serious study of something as complex as the human mind.

We have attempted to provide you with a variety of activities. Some emphasize the generation or testing of theories, others data collection or analysis. We have tried to cover the major methods of data collection used by psychologists: Among all the activities are included examples of the experiment, the questionnaire, direct observation, and the interview. In many cases we provide data from studies we have done with introductory psychology students as a base for comparison with the data that you collect. In each activity in which you collect data, we guide you through some analysis of the data and get you to try to interpret the data and relate it to issues raised in the text. If your instructor wishes to include the activities as part of the course, he or she may ask you to tear out the report (data) sheet pages, and hand them in. These sheets are duplicated at the end of the book in Appendix B. Otherwise, you may consider these activities as a less formal extension of your education in psychology.

We have tried out all of these activities on undergraduate students like yourselves. We have only included studies that work out for the great majority of students. Of course, with people as variable as they are, all the studies that you do on one or a few students will not show the same results. But we expect that most of you will get most of the predicted results.

Many of the most important phenomena in psychology cannot be included in these activities because they must be measured under controlled conditions, which you could not easily arrange. Some involve expensive equipment, like timers that can time thousandths of a second, or panels of lights and switches. Some important relations are not striking enough to be seen in one or a few subjects. We have tried to find, for each chapter, at least one activity that can be appreciated within the limits that you will be working under. We require no equipment other than pencil, paper, some sort of second indicator (stopwatch, digital watch with second indicator, or a watch with a second hand), and materials presented within this manual. We have limited the time demands on you for any activity to less than one hour. In all but a few cases, we have limited the number of subjects to a very few. At the beginning of each activity, we indicate the equipment involved and the time demands it will make on you and the subjects.

These activities are designed to be both educational and entertaining. We hope that you find that they meet these goals.

CHAPTER 1

Introduction

Learning Objectives

THE SCOPE OF PSYCHOLOGY

Electrically triggered images
1. What do experiments on electrical stimulation of memory tell us about the relationship between psychology and physiology?

Ambiguous sights and sounds
2. What determines the interpretation of an ambiguous stimulus?

Automatization
3. What is the importance of automatization? How can it be measured?

The perceptual world of infants
4. How does the study of infants suggest that some abilities may be innate?

Displays
5. How does social interaction in animals differ from that in humans? Give an example to prove the point.

Complex social behavior in humans
6. Be aware of the characteristics of social interactions in humans. How are panic phenomena related to social causes?

A SCIENCE OF MANY FACES

7. Discuss the range of phenomena studied by psychologists.

Dreams as mental experiences
8. How are private mental experiences, like dreams, studied by psychologists?
9. What does anecdotal evidence tell us about the makeup of dream content?

Dreams as behavior
10. What behaviors are indicative of dreams? How do they aid the study of this mental phenomenon?

Dreams as cognition
11. What is meant by "cognition" and how is it related to dreaming?
12. What factors make for better dream recall?

Dreams and social behavior
13. How do dreams incorporate social factors?
14. How are dreams culturally influenced?
15. Discuss Freud's theory of dreams.

Dreams and human development
16. Trace the development of the concept of a "dream" in children.

Dreams and individual differences
17. How are dreams representative of individual makeup?

THE TASK OF PSYCHOLOGY

18. What is, and what is not, the main purpose of psychology? What is its approach to the study of the individual?

Programmed Exercises

THE SCOPE OF PSYCHOLOGY

1. Psychology involves not only the study of the mind, but also the study of _behaviour_

behavior

2. Electrical stimulation of the brain sometimes results in reports of _memories_

memories

3. _Context_ is an important determinant of how we perceive an ambiguous figure.

Context

4. The study of automatization and perceptual skills in infants shows us that some skills are _learned_ while others are

learned

innate .

innate

5. In animals, many social interactions depend largely on

innate forms of communication.

innate

6. The behavior of panicky crowds is determined not only by each individual, but also by individuals' _social_ interactions.

social (group)

A SCIENCE OF MANY FACES

7. According to Aristotle, dreams are mental _re-evocations_ of events that occurred during the dreamer's waking life.

re-evocations

8. A waking experience is most likely to appear in a dream if the experience was highly _emotional_

emotional

9. The stage of sleep that is characterized by dreaming and rapid movement of the eyes is termed _REM_ sleep.

REM

10. The term "_Subject_" is used by psychologists to designate the person or animal whose behavior is being studied.

subject

11. According to Freud, dreams represent the individual's inner

conflict

conflict

12. In Freud's view, urges are represented in dreams in the form

of _symbols_

symbols

13. Children have a hard time distinguishing _subjective_ from

subjective

objective events.

objective

14. _Schizophrenic_ people often report dreams that are far more bizarre than those of other people.

Schizophrenic

THE TASK OF PSYCHOLOGY

15. Psychology can be studied from perspectives emphasizing

action (overt behavior), _cognition_ (human knowledge),

action, cognition

social interaction (the influence of others on individual

social interaction

action), and _individual_ differences (how people are alike or

individual

different.

Self Test

1. Psychology is the:
   a. science of the mind
   b. science of behavior
   c. both of the above
   d. none of the above

2. When the brain is stimulated electrically:
   a. visual experiences may occur
   b. previous memories may be blocked
   c. new memories are blocked
   d. none of the above

3. If we are first shown a picture of a rat, and then the ambiguous figure below, we will most likely see:

   a. the man
   b. the rat
   c. the rat or man, depending on other factors
   d. neither the rat nor man

4. Taken together, the Stroop effect and the visual cliff results suggest that:
   a. skills could be learned
   b. skills could be innate
   c. either a or b
   d. neither a nor b

5. According to Aristotle, dreams:
   a. were outlets for creative energies
   b. were manifestations of physical discomfort during sleep
   c. were of telepathic origin
   d. were reoccurrences of events in the real world

6. Outside stimuli:
   a. always find their way into dreams
   b. never find their way into dreams
   c. sometimes find their way into dreams
   d. are all that dreams are made of

7. Subjects dream during:
   a. all types of sleep
   b. quiet sleep
   c. the end of the night only
   d. REM sleep

8. Culture:
   a. has influence only on dream content
   b. determines only how people interpret dreams
   c. influences both dream content and interpretation
   d. may or may not influence our dreams at all depending on the particular culture

9. In Freud's view, dreams:
   a. are a result of physical discomfort during sleep
   b. represent a compromise between biological urges and societal constraints
   c. serve as reminders of the events of the day
   d. pertain mostly to current conflicts in real life

10. According to Freud, dreams contain:
    a. symbolic fulfillment of forbidden wishes
    b. prophesies of the future
    c. undisguised urges
    d. all of the above

11. Young children think of dreams as:
    a. physical objects
    b. a special reality sent from outside
    c. purely subjective experiences
    d. both a and b

12. The dreams of schizophrenic individuals are often:
    a. more sedate than those of others
    b. more exciting than those of others
    c. more bizarre than those of others
    d. are not substantially different from those of others

13. Psychology consists of the study of:
    a. action
    b. cognition
    c. social processes
    d. individual differences
    e. all of the above

Answer Key for Self Test

1. c p. 1
2. a p. 2
3. b p. 3
4. c p. 4
5. d p. 7
6. c p. 8
7. d p. 9
8. c p. 10
9. b p. 11
10. a p. 11
11. d p. 12
12. c p. 13
13. e p. 13

Investigating Psychological Phenomena

THE CONSISTENCY OF DREAMS

Equipment: None
Number of subjects: One, yourself
Time per subject: Ten to twenty minutes
Time for experimenter: Ten to twenty minutes

Although Chapter 1 is meant as a general introduction to psychology, it also provides us with an opportunity to illustrate how a particular phenomenon can be studied scientifically. The text outlines various approaches that have been used to study the phenomenon of dreams. These approaches entail different kinds of experimentation to study dreaming. Let us illustrate one kind of experimental approach that is useful. The technique used in this approach involves collecting ratings or categorizations of various stimuli. Here are the specifics:

One of the fundamental issues in dream research concerns the extent to which dreams represent the realization of basic problems, wishes, needs, or areas of concern to the dreamer. Freud's theory of dreams, for example, claims that the content of dreams is determined primarily by these factors. This suggests that the dreams of any one dreamer ought to be identifiably more similar to one another than the dreams of several dreamers. The question then arises: Is there consistency in a dreamer's dreams?

To test this idea, nine dream reports have been transcribed below. These reports were collected from three individuals, with three reports collected per individual. Your task is to select which three dreams were produced by each of the three individuals who were sampled.

There are several criteria that you could use to classify the dreams. One caution: You might think to use the language characteristics, that is, the use of certain consistent phrases, but don't be led astray by such a strategy. Language characteristics would not be appropriate criteria, since the purpose of the exercise is to assess whether there is evidence of consistency in dream *content*. So you should concentrate on the content of the dreams as a basis for classification.

DREAM 1

A girl and I were being chased through a woods. We entered a log cabin. We were hiding when two people came in after us. One of the men who entered was tall with a thick dark beard. He looked like a typical backwoodsman. His assistant, by contrast, was short and fat. I decided to outsmart them. I crawled into a back room and began to make some noise. I stood on a box holding a milk bottle in my hand. The man entered. I hit him over the head several times, but the bottle did not break and he only laughed. The next thing I knew, the man was pointing a two-barrelled shotgun at me. I noticed that the ends of the barrels seemed magnified. He shot me in the lower right stomach. I looked down at the hole, saw the blood, and felt very weak. Then I was driving in my car by some railroad tracks. The wheels of my car became stuck on the tracks; my car would only move backward. I saw a train approaching rapidly and somehow managed to move off the tracks. I watched a huge train go past. My car continued moving in reverse. I had to keep the car moving perfectly straight, which was a very difficult task, and the train only missed me by inches. As I sped backward, I noticed a fence alongside the tracks. I saw a spot where the fence had been pushed down. I got out, picked up my car, and climbed over the fence. As I did this, I noticed two wounds, the one from the shotgun and a similar mark on the other side of my body. I began to look for a girl, not sure if I was looking for the one who had been with me in the cabin. I searched through a series of backyards, hiding behind bushes. I felt guilty about something. I found the girl I was looking for; she helped me attempt an escape. She led me back over to the fence, which was on a hill above the tracks. I started to climb the fence, which resembled a baseball backstop, but I was too weak from my wounds to be successful. The girl climbed on ahead and offered to hold my shirt as I climbed. Suddenly, two men on the railroad tracks below caught my eye. They were shooting at me with a bow and arrow. I told the girl not to worry; I thought I would be safe because the wind would deflect the arrows. Three or four of the arrows missed, but I was finally hit in my left front pocket. Luckily, the arrow had pierced my wallet instead of going into my leg. (In real life I keep my wallet in another pocket.)

DREAM 2

New York was being attacked by Germans. My mother told me not to worry. She told me that the last time the Germans attacked, only three persons who were in a cemetery had been killed. I went to warn my grandmother, who was at my uncle's basement apartment. My aunt was standing outside of the building. She also told me not to worry; she said she would wait outside for me. I walked down two flights of stairs. Strangely, the walls were made of dirt. I saw several of my relatives. Suddenly, I heard a loud noise. Water poured out of one of the walls. My uncle and cousin were covered with dirt. I dug them out just before they would have suffocated. I left with my grandmother. Then, things changed to a cemetery; I saw people walking behind a coffin. I was looking down from an aerial view. (I have had this kind of dream once before, several years ago).

DREAM 3

I was with a group of people in the church I attended as a child. I knew most of the people there. I saw Paul Newman among the group. Guns appeared from somewhere; everyone grabbed one. Two groups formed; shooting started. I watched Newman fight a burly man. It seemed I became Newman—I could hear and feel everything he felt and heard. We threw "ourself" out into the open to try for a clear shot, but had no time to shoot before we were shot by the burly man. We felt the searing pain; I was sure death was imminent. Suddenly, the pain cleared. We shot the burly man, killing him. The fighting ended. We went inside, once again having our own identities. I saw Newman shaking his head, saying that it was only supposed to have been a game.

DREAM 4

I was on a highway, walking instead of driving. There were no cars, and everyone was walking, but I felt as if I were in a car. I saw someone I knew; we started talking. I got off at the exit to the beach. I walked up a circular ramp. The end of the ramp resembled a manhole. I had a bathing suit on under my clothes, but I had no towel. I started looking for one. I found two that looked as if they did not belong to anyone, so I took them. A woman approached me while I was lying on the sand. She said they were her towels. I told her I had taken them by mistake; she said she was going to call the police. I stayed; the police never came.

DREAM 5

I was in a restaurant or a cafeteria. I picked up some food. I thought it was a dessert and expected it to be sweet and delicious. Instead, I found that it tasted terrible. I thought someone had substi-

tuted salt for sugar in the recipe. I felt as though the salty taste grew and grew; I was now alone in a vast, dry wasteland with no relief in sight. (I woke up with the taste of salt still parching my mouth.)

DREAM 6

First, I was seated on the top bunk of my bed. I was with some friends. Then I found myself walking around piles of boards. My house had been destroyed—either it had collapsed or burned down—and my belongings were covered with rubble. Then I was outside the house digging a ditch longer than it was deep. Building materials lay nearby. While I dug, I got dirt in my hair. I wanted a hat, so I went to the part of the house where the boards were. After finding a hat, I started out of the rubble. Some of the boards fell out of place; they knocked my father's car, our dog, and a chair over a steep cliff. I did not look over the cliff. I could hear my father's car smash into pieces. Then I saw a large field below the cliff. The dog and the chair also broke into pieces. The pieces began moving end over end to the other side of the field. When they stopped rolling, they were reassembled. I felt very unhappy about all this. I returned to the ditch and saw my father. I told him not to worry as he would soon be getting a company car. Then things changed and I was driving in my convertible with three friends. We had a case of beer with us. The road was covered with snow, although it was only snowing lightly at that moment. We stopped at a house where I walked around to the yard. It was twenty-three minutes to six, and I had to be home at five, but I felt that I could not tell my friends this. I saw my roommate swinging on a pole in the backyard. He said he wanted to swing up onto a window ledge. I offered to help; he refused my offer. Eventually we both got up on the ledge. I looked in through the window. A lady was in the kitchen. By now it was almost six, so I jumped down from the ledge, saying I had to go. I was alone.

DREAM 7

I was in a room I am familiar with but cannot now identify. A girl I work with was also there. The room made me think of Patricia Hearst; perhaps she had lived there. I thought she might be close by. I searched for clues. I wanted to find the clue that would solve the kidnapping case. I found something small lying on the floor; it was thin and cylindrical with screwlike threads at one end. I felt that this might be the clue to the kidnapping that I was looking for, but when I showed it to the girl she said it was something of hers. She took it.

DREAM 8

My brother and I were standing on a patio waiting
for something. Four or five large jet planes passed
the yard. The planes were a few feet above the
ground. As my brother went to get a better look,
another plane came by and snatched him up. He
was strapped into a seat like a baby's car seat.
Next, I was inside a house. I was handed a tube
about a foot long. The tube was clear; it had white
caps at either end. Something was inside—something red and jellylike. It reminded me of lobster. I
was shocked when they told me it was my brother. I
wanted to let him out of the tube; I was also
afraid of what might happen. The organism was
fighting violently; it was my brother. A strange-
looking person entered the room then. He said
he was my brother. I thought the person was
wearing a disguise. I grabbed him; we started to
fight. Somehow I was convinced it was my
brother. I said, "I hate to do this, but it's for your
own good." Next I found myself walking with
two friends towards a building. I had books in my
hand. I then noticed that all of the lights in the
town were off, so that there was no sense in continuing to go where I had intended. I crossed the
bridge and left my friends, telling them I was going back for something. I returned to the patio.
People were coming towards me. My brother was
standing beside me. A group of girls I knew walked
out of the building; I then recognized it to be a
movie theater. I walked over to one of the girls,
who said that she had seen an "awfully strange
movie." I was very relieved that everything that
had just happened to me was only a movie, and
that my brother was safe beside me.

DREAM 9

I was going to school in Paris. I did not feel that I
was really in Paris, however. I received a letter
from a friend. He had just spent two weeks in Lorraine. He thought I should also travel. I decided to
go to Geneva.

Write your answers in the spaces below:

Dreamer A ____ ____ ____

Dreamer B ____ ____ ____

Dreamer C ____ ____ ____

After you have made your judgments, check
the correct answers on the bottom of this page.
How correct were you? Based on our results, what
would you conclude about the consistency of people's dreams? What is the implication of these
conclusions for a theory of dreams? You may
want to come back to these results after you have
read Chapter 12, which provides much more
detail about the topic of dreams. In this chapter
you will discover that certain theories of dreams
claim that the overt content of a dream may be
different from its true (but hidden) meaning. Certain events in dreams are supposed to symbolize
other events that are not directly present. Once
you have read this section, you should return to
these nine dreams to check whether you might be
able to discover some "latent" content in them
that could provide a new basis for your
judgments.

ANSWERS TO DREAM EXPERIMENT

Dreamer A   1,9,8

Dreamer B   2,4,6

Dreamer C   3,5,7

Biological Bases of Behavior

Learning Objectives

THE ORGANISM AS MACHINE

Descartes and the reflex concept
1. Be familiar with Descartes's conception of the reflex, and how, in part, it still forms the basis of animal and human action.

The basic nervous functions: reception, integration, reaction
2. Be able to describe fully the action sequence: reception, integration, reaction.
3. What functions do the following serve: stimulus, receptors, afferent nerves, efferent nerves, effectors, interneurons?

NERVE CELL AND NERVE IMPULSE

From animal spirits to nerve impulse
4. What led to the rejection of the notion of animal spirits?

The neuron
5. What are dendrites, the axon, and the synapse?
6. What purpose do the sensory neurons and motor neurons serve?
7. Be able to describe the electrical activity of the neuron; know the difference between resting potential and action potential.
8. What is the all-or-none law?
9. What effect does stimulus intensity have on the number of neurons stimulated and on the frequency of impulses?

INTERACTION AMONG NERVE CELLS

The reflex
10. Describe the reflex arc.

Inferring the synapse
11. How did Sherrington infer the existence of the synapse? Describe spatial and temporal summation.
12. Be able to explain central excitatory state, inhibition, and disinhibition.

The synaptic mechanism
13. Know the anatomy of the synaptic mechanism (pre- and postsynaptic neurons, synaptic cleft, vesicles, and neurotransmitters), and the way that neural excitation (the nerve impulse) is transmitted across the synapse.
14. Be able to explain how inhibition and excitation occur at synapses, and how the postsynaptic neuron integrates the various inhibitory and excitatory effects on it.
15. What are the basic differences between action potentials and synaptic transmission?
16. What is a neurotransmitter? What are the effects of some major neurotransmitters (acetylcholine, dopamine, and norepinephrine), and how are these effects modified by (respectively) the drugs curare, chlorpromazine, and amphetamine?
17. What are the endorphins and how are they related to the perception of pain?

INTERACTION THROUGH THE BLOODSTREAM: THE ENDOCRINE SYSTEM

18. Explain the mode of action of the endocrine system, and know the similarities and differences between the types of interaction and transmission in the nervous and endocrine systems.

**THE MAIN STRUCTURES OF
THE NERVOUS SYSTEM**

The evolution of central control
19. Describe the tendency toward increasing centralization in the evolution of the nervous system.

The peripheral and central nervous systems
20. Be able to distinguish the peripheral and the central nervous system, and the somatic and autonomic nervous system.
21. Describe the basic anatomy of the brain; what functions do the hindbrain, midbrain, and forebrain serve?
22. Know the structure of the cerebral cortex, including the four lobes, the corpus callosum, and the limbic system.

Hierarchical function in the nervous system
23. Explain the hierarchical function of the nervous system.

THE CEREBRAL CORTEX

Projection areas
24. Describe the function of projection areas of the brain, and indicate what determines how much space in these areas is devoted to different parts of the body.

Association areas
25. What are apraxia, agnosia, and aphasia? What types of brain lesions produce each?

One brain or two?
26. Explain the meaning of lateralization, and how the brain organization of left-handers differs from that of right-handers.
27. What does research on people with split brains tell us about the differences between the cerebral hemispheres?
28. Be able to explain how measures of reaction time and brain blood flow indicate which hemisphere of normal people is more activated.
29. What are the two modes of mental functioning that some believe are associated with the left and right hemispheres?

Some problems in localizing brain function
30. What problems, in both our understanding of behavior and of the organization of the nervous system, make it difficult to assign psychological functions to particular parts of the brain?

Programmed Exercises

THE ORGANISM AS MACHINE

1. The conception of man as a machine can be traced to the

   great French philosopher _Descartes_   Descartes

2. According to Descartes, excitation from the senses leads to

   muscle contraction, in what we now call a _reflex_ .   reflex

3. The three basic components of an action sequence are

   reception, _conduction-integration_, and _reaction_.   reception, conduction-integration, reaction

4. Nerves that connect receptors to the central nervous system

   are called _afferent_ nerves.   afferent (sensory)

5. Nerves carrying excitation from the central nervous system to

   muscles and glands are called _efferent_ nerves.   efferent (motor)

6. Afferent neurons usually produce effects in efferent neurons

   via _inter_ neurons.   inter-

NERVE CELL AND NERVE IMPULSE

7. The basic building block of the nervous system is the nerve

   cell, or _neuron_.   neuron

8. When Swammerdam found that a muscle did not expand in volume during contraction, he provided evidence against the notion of _animal spirits_ as the medium of nervous excitation.

animal spirits

9. Label the following diagram of the neuron.

A. _dendrites_   B. _Cell body_   C. _axon._

dendrites, cell body, axon

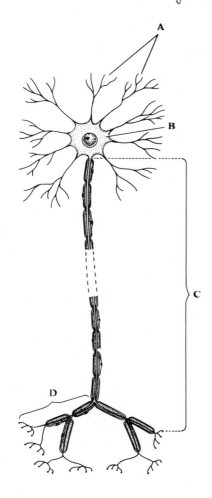

10. The gap between the axon terminals of one neuron and the denditric processes of another is called the _synapse_

synapse

11. Receptor cells _transduce_ stimulus energy into nerve impulses.

transduce

12. The axons of _motor neurons_ terminate in effector cells and activate the _skeletal musculature_

motor neurons

skeletal musculature

13. In complex organisms, the vast majority of neurons are neither sensory nor motor, but rather _interneurons_ .

interneurons

14. The device used to record nerve impulses on a fluorescent

    screen is called an ~oscilloscope~   oscilloscope

15. The ~resting potential~ of the neuron is about —70 millivolts.   resting potential

16. The reversal of polarization that passes along a nerve fiber

    when it is stimulated is called the ~action potential~   action potential

17. When the cell membrane is depolarized past a certin threshold

    value, the ~nerve impulse~ results.   action potential or
                                                                        nerve impulse

18. The ~all or none~ law states that the size of the action potential   all-or-none
    and its speed are independent of the intensity of the stimulus,
    provided the stimulus is above threshold intensity.

19. The above-mentioned law does not apply to the stimulation of

    nerves since there is much variation in the ~thresholds~ of the   thresholds
    neurons in the nerve.

INTERACTION AMONG NERVE CELLS

20. The fact that a chicken may run around for a while after its
    head has been cut off shows that some movements and re-

    flexes are controlled by the ~spinal cord~ .   spinal cord

21. The ~reflex~ represents the simplest level of integration.   reflex (arc)

22. The existence of the synapse was inferred from evidence at the

    level of ~behavior~ by the great English physiologist ~Sherrington~ . behavior
                                                                        Sir Charles Sherrington

23. Subthreshold stimulation at two adjacent points, when applied
    simultaneously, may lead to a response. This illustrates the

    phenomenon of ~spatial summation~   spatial summation

24. Subthreshold stimulation, when applied a few times in rapid
    succession, may lead to a response. This illustrates the phe-

    nomenon of ~temporal summation~   temporal summation

25. According to Sherrington, temporal summation occurs because

    of integration at the ~synapse~, which is accomplished by   synapse
    "storage" of excitation from previous stimulation. This results

    in an increase in the ~central excitatory state~   central excitatory state

26. Sherrington observed that when a flexor muscle contracts, the
    corresponding extensor relaxes. This is an example of

    ~reciprocal inhibition~   reciprocal inhibition

27. Whether a neuron fires or not is determined by the net result

    of its integration of ~excitatory~ and ~inhibitory~ stimulation.   excitatory, inhibitory

28. An increase in the strength of a reflex when higher brain

    centers are removed is called ~disinhibition~ .   disinhibition

29. Electrical activity is transmitted across the synapse by neuro-

    transmitters, from the ~presynaptic~ neuron to the ~postsynaptic~   presynaptic, postsynaptic
    neuron.

30. The synaptic vesicles contain chemical substances called

neurotransmitters   neurotransmitters

31. Label this diagram of a synapse.

A. _Pre synaptic mem_   D. _neuro transmitter_

B. _Post   "   "_   E. _synaptic clef._

C. _vessicl_

A. presynaptic membrane

B. postsynaptic membrane

C. vesicle

D. neurotransmitter

E. synaptic cleft

32. The summation of neural impulses at the level of the synapse
is actually the summation of _inhibitory_ and _excitatory_ poten-   inhibitory, excitatory
tials. These are produced by _neurotransmitter_ liberated by firing of   neurotransmitters
the presynaptic neuron.

33. While action potentials are all-or-none, synaptic potentials are

graded   graded

34. The idea that neurotransmitters only affect the postsynaptic
membrane if their shape fits the shape of the certain receptor
sites on that membrane is called the _lock A Key_   lock-and-key
model.

35. Acetylcholine, dopamine, and norepinephrine are all _neurotransmitters_.   neurotransmitters

36. Curare, chlorpromazine, and amphetamine are _drugs_ that   drugs
affect synaptic transmission.

37. The action of the neurotransmitter _acetylcholine_ that causes   acetylcholine
muscles to contract is blocked by the drug _curare_.   curare

38. The arousing effects of the neurotransmitter _dopamine_ are   dopamine
blocked by the drug _chlorpro_, which is used to treat the   chlorpromazine
major mental disorder _schiz_.   schizophrenia

39. The arousing effects of the neurotransmitter _norepinephrine_ are   norepinephrine
enhanced by the drug _amphetamine_.   amphetamine

40. Neurotransmitters similar to the drug morphine that seem to
reduce pain are called _endorphins_   endorphins

41. A drug, _naloxone_, that blocks the effect of endorphins also   naloxone
blocks the lessening of pain produced by the Chinese technique
of _acupuncture_   acupuncture

INTERACTION THROUGH THE BLOODSTREAM:
THE ENDOCRINE SYSTEM

42. The _____ glands secrete _____ into the bloodstream.   endocrine, hormones

THE MAIN STRUCTURES OF THE NERVOUS SYSTEM

43. Early in evolutionary history the cell bodies of many inter-
    neurons began to clump together to form _____ .   ganglia

44. The brain and spinal cord together comprise the

    _____ _____ _____.   central nervous system

45. The two divisions of the peripheral nervous system are the

    _____ and the _____ .   somatic, autonomic

46. The portion of the hindbrain concerned with controlling some
    critical body processes, such as respiration and heartbeat, is

    called the _____ .   medulla

47. The portion of the hindbrain that controls bodily balance and

    motor coordination is called the _____ .   cerebellum

48. The general activating system that extends from the hindbrain
    through the midbrain and into the forebrain is called the

    _____ _____ .   reticular formation

49. The _____ is a part of the forebrain involved in the   hypothalamus
    control of behavior patterns that stem from basic biological
    urges such as feeding.

50. Label the four major lobes of the human cerebral cortex.

    A. _____   C. _____   A. frontal

    B. _____   D. _____   B. parietal

                                                                          C. occipital

                                                                          D. temporal

51. Label the following structures on the sketch of the human
    brain (at the top of the next page).

    A. _____   C. _____ _____   A. hindbrain (medulla)

    B. _____   D. _____ _____   B. cerebellum

                                                                          C. cerebral cortex

                                                                          D. corpus callosum

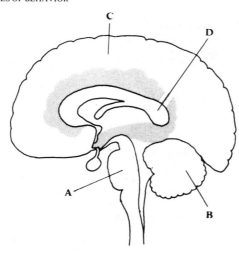

52. An older portion of the cerebral hemispheres with particular importance in the mediation of emotional and motivational activities is called the _____ _____ .

limbic system

53. The structure connecting the two cerebral hemispheres is called the _____ _____ .

corpus callosum

54. The nervous system is organized in layers of control, such that higher centers control those centers below them. This pattern of organization is called _____ .

hierarchical

THE CEREBRAL CORTEX

55. Excitation of the left _____ _____ _____ will lead to movements of the right side of the body.

motor projection area (motor homunculus)

56. In man, the greatest amount of cortical space for motor functions is assigned to the _____ and _____ .

fingers, tongue

57. Each portion of the body surface is represented in the sensory homunculus, located in the _____ _____ of the _____ lobes.

somatosensory area
parietal

58. The projection areas for vision and hearing are located in the _____ and _____ lobes, respectively.

occipital, temporal

59. The portion of the cerebral cortex that is part of neither the motor nor sensory areas is described as the _____ _____ .

association areas

60. _____ is a serious disturbance in the organization of voluntary action.

Apraxia

61. A disorganization of aspects of the sensory world, without loss of basic sensory capacities is termed _____ .

agnosia

62. A patient with a primary disorder in the expression of speech can be described as suffering from language apraxia, or an

   _____ _____ . This disorder is commonly caused by   expressive aphasia

   lesions in _____ _____ .   Broca's area

63. In right-handed persons, aphasia usually results from lesions

   in the _____ hemisphere.   left

64. A language defect reflected primarily by an inability to comprehend language, or a language agnosia, is described as a

   _____ _____ . The lesions responsible for this disorder receptive aphasia

   commonly occur in _____ _____ .   Wernicke's area

65. The asymmetry of function in the human cerebral hemispheres

   is described as _____ .   lateralization (of function)

66. In terms of differences in function between left and right

   cerebral hemispheres, left-handers are generally less _____ lateralized
   than right-handers.

67. A right-hander who, following a stroke, has great difficulty with spatial representation, maps, and the perception of complex forms, probably has a lesion in the _____ hemisphere.   right

68. A split-brain patient is someone whose _____ _____   corpus callosum
   has been surgically severed.

69. A right-handed split-brain patient would probably not be able

   to name a common object placed in his _____ hand.   left

70. Composite pictures, differing in their left and right halves, are

   identified verbally as whatever is on the _____ by split-   right
   brain patients.

71. Lateralization can be demonstrated in normal subjects by

   showing that right-handers show a longer _____ _____   reaction time
   to name objects flashed to their left as opposed to their right
   visual field.

72. Studies show that more _____ goes to the left as opposed   blood
   to the right hemisphere of normals when normals are speaking
   or solving a verbal task.

73. Many psychologists believe that _____ and _____ pro-   verbal, spatial
   cesses represent radically different modes of thought which
   reflect different clusters of intellectual functioning.

74. Some psychologists believe that the left hemisphere is specialized for the organization of _____ since such a function   time

   would be relevant to both _____ and _____ _____ .   language, motor dexterity

75. It is hard to assign a particular brain area to a particular psychological function, because more than one part of the brain is involved in any psychological function. This is true, in part,

   because of the _____ organization of the nervous system.   hierarchical

Self Test

1. Which of the following commonly observed characteristics of human or animal behavior goes counter to Descartes's reflex notion?
   a. the withdrawal response upon touching a hot object
   b. the appearance of a behavior (e.g., running) in the absence of any obvious stimulus
   c. the existence of nerves connecting receptors and effectors to the brain
   d. the repeatability of reflexes
   e. none of the above

2. By viewing animal behavior as the result of a machine's responding to external stimuli, Descartes made the claim that:
   a. animal behavior is governed by physical laws and is therefore predictable
   b. animal behavior can only be understood in terms of the hierarchical organization of the nervous system
   c. animals must have souls
   d. neither humans nor animals have free will
   e. introductory psychology is *the* fundamental science

3. The course of excitation through the nervous system following a stimulus is:
   a. interneuron, efferent nerve, afferent nerve
   b. efferent nerve, interneuron, afferent nerve
   c. afferent nerve, interneuron, efferent nerve
   d. integration, reception, reaction
   e. conarium, stimulus, action

4. The tripartite view of an action sequence—reception, conduction and integration, reaction—is clearly represented by the sequence of:
   a. afferent nerve, efferent nerve, interneuron
   b. axon, cell body, dendrites
   c. push, fall, hurt
   d. none of the above

5. Under normal circumstances the path of excitation in the nervous system would follow which of the following sequences:
   a. axon → synapse → dendrite → cell body
   b. axon → dendrite → synapse → cell body
   c. dendrite → cell body → synapse → axon
   d. dendrite → axon → cell body → synapse
   e. synapse → dendrite → axon → cell body

6. Receptors:
   a. are always a specialized part of sensory neurons
   b. transduce physical stimuli into neural impulses
   c. are responsible for the conduction of optic stimuli
   d. a and b
   e. b and c

7. Which of the following properties are characteristic of interneurons?
   a. they usually show much branching of dendrites
   b. they perform the integration function of the action sequence
   c. they comprise the majority of neurons
   d. all of the above

8. When graphed over time, the complex electrical event known as the action potential looks something like:

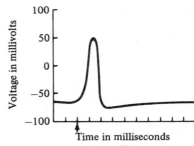

A

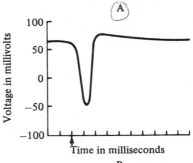

B

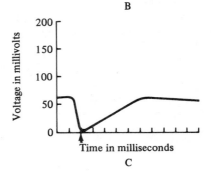

C

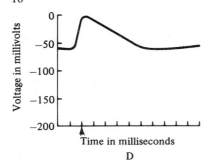

Time in milliseconds

D

9. The all-or-none law states that:
   a. the threshold of a single neuron is a property which alternates between two extreme values but never has any of the values in between
   b. reflexes cannot involve just the spinal cord; the entire nervous system must respond by generating a central excitatory state
   c. an axon terminal releases a chemical substance, called a neurotransmitter, when an action potential arrives
   d. the frequency of spikes in an individual nerve fiber increases with the number of action potentials per unit time
   e. once a stimulus exceeds the threshold of an individual neuron, further increases in stimulation intensity make no difference in the height and form of the action potential generated

10. How can the nervous system represent increases in the intensity of a *stimulus*?
    a. by an increase in the size of the action potential in every neuron fired by the stimulus
    b. by an increase in the number of neurons being fired by the stimulus
    c. by an increase in the frequency of firing in the neurons fired by the stimulus
    d. b and c
    e. a and c

11. Sherrington used a spinal animal in order to:
    a. eliminate inhibition
    b. simplify the system he was studying
    c. take advantage of brain modulation of neural activity in the spinal cord
    d. study the irreversibility of conduction
    e. cut expenses

12. From his observations of temporal and spatial summation in reflexes, Sherrington inferred the existence of:
    a. receptors
    b. inhibition
    c. the synapse
    d. disinhibition
    e. the simple reflex

13. A subthreshold stimulus will evoke a spinal reflex if it is repeated within a reasonable interval, say 1/2 second. This temporal summation is caused by:
    a. increased frequency of neural firing
    b. enhanced central excitatory state
    c. the spinal cord
    d. the release of neurotransmitters from motoneurons to interneurons
    e. inhibition

14. Consider this example: Brief strong stimulation of a receptor produces no movement, but a longer period of stimulation causes a particular muscle to stop contracting. These results could most easily be explained by the principles of:
    a. excitation and inhibition
    b. inhibition and disinhibition
    c. all-or-none law and inhibition
    d. temporal summation, spatial summation, and the all-or-none law
    e. inhibition and temporal summation

15. The phenomenon of disinhibition:
    a. exists only in insects
    b. depends on reflex interaction, especially in the spinal cord
    c. reveals the presence of inhibition
    d. takes place entirely within a single neuron
    e. all of the above

16. Many neurons fire action potentials at a moderate rate even when they are not receiving synaptic excitation from presynaptic neurons. This is called spontaneous activity. Which plot on the next page indicates what would happen to the firing rate of such a neuron if it was first exposed to synaptic inhibition and then synaptic excitation?

17. Sherrington reported that the time (reflex latency) between stimulation of a reflex and the reflex response was much longer than the time it would take for an action potential to go from the receptor to the muscle. This

Inhibition   Excitation

→ Time

a.

b.

c.

d.

e.

"delay" could be accounted for in terms of:
a. inhibition
b. excitation
c. the time for disinhibition to occur
d. the time for depolarization of the axon membrane
e. the time for the neurotransmitter to cross the synaptic cleft and stimulate the postsynaptic neuron

18. Axon conduction resembles synaptic transmission in that:
a. both involve neurotransmitters
b. both are about the same speed
c. both are all-or-none
d. none of the above

19. The lock-and-key model accounts for:
a. the existence of neurotransmitters
b. the summation of excitation and inhibition in postsynaptic neurons
c. the fact that specific neurotransmitters stimulate specific postsynaptic neurons
d. the release of neurotransmitters from vesicles
e. the all-or-none law

20. Chlorpromazine and curare have in common the fact that they:
a. block the action of specific neurotransmitters
b. enhance the action of specific neurotransmitters
c. produce postsynaptic inhibition
d. produce postsynaptic excitation
e. relieve the symptoms of schizophrenia

21. Many researchers now believe that in at least some cases of depression, the cause is low levels of dopamine or norepinephrine in the brain. If this were true, then we would expect chlorpromazine to _____ depression, and amphetamine to _____ depression.
a. increase, decrease
b. decrease, increase
c. increase, increase
d. decrease, decrease
e. have no effect on, have no effect on

22. The relation between acetylcholine and curare is like the relation between:
a. acetylcholine and dopamine
b. norepinephrine and amphetamine
c. endorphins and naloxone
d. endorphins and placebo
e. axon and synapse

23. A dentist finds that when she gives her patient what is actually a sugar pill, and tells the patient that it will relieve his pain, all of the patient's pain disappears. This is an example of:
a. an effect of naloxone
b. a placebo effect
c. an endocrine effect
d. the all-or-none law
e. synaptic interaction

24. Hormones and neurotransmitters are both:
a. secreted only by endocrine glands
b. secreted into the bloodstream
c. chemical messengers
d. all of the above
e. none of the above

25. In which of the following sequences are the main divisions of the central nervous system arranged in ascending order?
    a. peripheral, somatic, autonomic
    b. cerebellum, integration centers, transmission tracts
    c. spinal cord, autonomic system, brain
    d. spinal cord, motor areas, sensory areas
    e. spinal cord, brain stem, cerebral hemispheres

26. Match the structure on the left with its associated function on the right.
    i. medulla   a. sleep
    ii. cerebellum   b. respiration and
    iii. reticular formation   heartbeat
    iv. hypothalamus   c. basic biological
                             urges
                          d. balance and
                             motor coordination

    i. _____

    ii. _____

    iii. _____

    iv. _____

27. The lobes of the cerebral hemisphere are:
    a. frontal, parietal, occipital, temporal
    b. hindbrain, midbrain, forebrain
    c. limbic system, corpus callosum, cerebral cortex
    d. each cerebral hemisphere is a single lobe of the cerebral cortex

28. Which of the following statements is *not* true of the limbic system?
    a. it is a subcortical structure
    b. it is anatomically associated with the hypothalamus
    c. it integrates the functions of the cerebral hemispheres
    d. it is involved in the control of emotional and motivational activities
    e. it is present on both sides of the brain

29. A rat with its brain transected above the hindbrain will chew food placed in its mouth, but this chewing is not affected by its state of food deprivation. If the transection is made above the hypothalamus, its acceptance of food will depend on its state of deprivation, but unlike a fully intact rat, it will not search for food. This is an example of:
    a. the projection areas
    b. disinhibition

    c. the function of the corpus callosum
    d. hierarchical organization
    e. none of the above

30. What part of an elephant might you expect to have a particularly large representation in the motor homunculus?
    a. the ears
    b. the front legs
    c. the back legs
    d. the trunk
    e. the eyes

31. Following a stroke, a patient shows grossly diminishing sensitivity to touch and other stimulation in the right hand and arm. The probable site of the lesion is:
    a. the motor homunculus
    b. the left somatosensory area
    c. the right somatosensory area
    d. the left frontal area
    e. the right frontal area

32. A disorder in the organization of voluntary movement is called:
    a. agnosia
    b. aphasia
    c. apraxia
    d. amenorrhea
    e. none of the above

33. Seriously apraxic patients can sometimes perform actions as part of automatic routines in the face of an inability to perform these acts on command. This suggests:
    a. hierarchical organization of motor function
    b. a disorganization of the sensory world
    c. a lesion in Broca's area
    d. a disorder in function of the brain stem

34. A person exhibiting "psychic blindness," or the inability to coordinate the separate details of the visual world into a whole, suffers from:
    a. visual agnosia
    b. receptive aphasia
    c. a lesion in Broca's area
    d. a lesion in Wernicke's area
    e. visual apraxia

35. Damage to a left-handed person in the language center often has less drastic consequences than in a right-handed person because:
    a. left-handers are slower to develop language functions
    b. recovery is more rapid in the left hemisphere in left-handers

c. the hemispheres are not as functionally lateralized in left-handers
d. highly developed visual-spatial abilities compensate for language loss
e. a and d

36. Afferent input from the right hand projects primarily to the left hemisphere while the left hand projects primarily to the right hemisphere. In an average right-handed, split-brain patient, which hand would the subject use to handle an unseen object if he wished to name it:
   a. the left hand
   b. the right hand
   c. neither hand could do it
   d. both hands could do it equally well
   e. a split-brain patient cannot name any objects

37. A right-handed subject has lost the entire projection area of his left occipital cortex, as shown below, but is otherwise normal. Which of the following deficits would you expect?

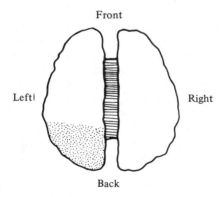

Front

Left| Right

Back

   a. loss of the right side of his visual field
   b. loss of the left side of his visual field
   c. inability to produce speech despite ability to understand it
   d. inability to understand speech despite the ability to produce it
   e. inability to read

38. The same subject referred to in the previous question suffers an additional defect: His corpus callosum is completely cut. What is the extent of his deficit?
   a. inability to produce or understand speech
   b. inability to produce speech despite understanding it

c. inability to understand speech despite the ability to produce it
d. inability to read
e. visual agnosia

39. For a normal right-handed subject, which of the following findings would be expected?
   a. a shorter reaction time to respond to a spatial problem presented in the left visual field
   b. greater blood flow to the left hemisphere while solving a verbal problem
   c. a shorter reaction time to respond to a verbal problem presented in the right visual field
   d. all of the above
   e. none of the above

40. In which of the following tasks would you expect superior performance from the left hemisphere of a right-hander?
   a. matching paint colors
   b. recognizing faces
   c. remembering a series of movements to be performed in a specific order
   d. drawing the floor plan of a familiar house
   e. all of the above

41. Localizing psychological functions in specific parts of the brain is difficult because:
   a. many psychological functions are represented in more than one part of the brain
   b. we are not certain as to what meaningful psychological functions are
   c. we have no way of determining what part of the brain is damaged
   d. a and b
   e. all of the above

Answer Key for Self Test

1. b p. 16
2. a p. 16
3. c p. 17
4. d p. 17
5. a pp.18–19
6. b p. 17
7. d pp. 17, 19
8. a p. 21
9. e p. 21
10. d pp. 21–22
11. b p. 23
12. c p. 24
13. b p. 24
14. e pp. 24–25
15. c pp. 25–26

16. d pp. 22–25
17. e pp. 26–27
18. d pp. 21, 26–27
19. c p. 28
20. a pp. 28–29
21. a pp. 28–29
22. c pp. 28–29
23. b p. 29
24. c p. 30
25. e p. 33
26.   i. b pp. 33–34
    ii. d
    iii. a
    iv. c
27. a p. 34

28. c p. 35
29. d p. 35
30. d p. 37
31. b pp. 37–38
32. c p. 38
33. a pp. 38–39
34. a p. 39

35. c p. 41
36. b pp. 41–42
37. a pp. 39–40
38. d pp. 39–42
39. d pp. 41–45
40. c pp. 45–46
41. d pp. 46–47

Investigating Psychological Phenomena

SPEED OF THE NERVE IMPULSE: THE USE OF REACTION TIME IN THE MEASUREMENT OF A PSYCHOLOGICAL PROCESS

Equipment: A stopwatch, or a watch that indicates seconds.
Number of subjects: Five
Time per subject: Fifteen minutes (all subjects are involved at the same time)
Time for experimenter: Twenty-five minutes

One of the great stumbling blocks to advances in theory about psychological processes was the belief that thought, and hence nervous impulses, occurred instantaneously or nearly so. In fact the German physiologist Johannes P. Mueller (1801–1858) once estimated that the speed of the nerve impulse was eleven million miles per second. Naturally, this claim that nerve impulses travel at an immeasurably fast rate discouraged scientific research on the physiology of the nervous system and encouraged mystical or dualistic interpretation of mind. It also discouraged study of the speed of various mental activities, research that is today an important cornerstone of the field of cognitive psychology.

In 1850, Herman Ludwig Ferdinand von Helmholtz (1821–1894) succeeded in measuring the speed of the nerve impulse and found it to be much slower than previously believed, between fifty and one hundred meters per second in humans. This finding was followed by intensive investigation of the nervous system within the framework of the physical and biological sciences. It also opened the door to the use of reaction time as a tool in the study of thought processes. This experiment is an attempt to familiarize you with the general logic used by a psychologist who is interested in measuring the speed of a psychological event that cannot be directly observed. To ac-

complish this, you must first understand the experiment that Helmholtz performed and also how his experimental technique can be applied to the measurement of the speed of the nerve impulse in humans.

Helmholtz's technique was quite simple. He first dissected out a muscle and an attached nerve fiber from a frog's leg. The experiment then consisted of stimulating the nerve at various distances from the muscle and measuring the length of time between nerve stimulation and muscle contraction. First, he electrically stimulated the nerve close to the point at which it was attached to the muscle, then he stimulated the nerve farther from this point of attachment. He found that the second reaction time (that is, the time between stimulation and contraction) was longer than the first. To obtain an estimate of nerve impulse speed, he used a simple bit of reasoning: The difference in time between the two measurements must correspond to the time it takes the impulse to travel the distance between the two points of stimulation (See figure). Hence, the distance between the point of stimulation divided by the time *difference* between the conditions of stimulating close to the muscle versus stimulating farther away should yield an estimate of nerve impulse speed. This is how he obtained his estimate of fifty to one hundred meters per second. Let A and B be two points of stimulation, M be the point at which the nerve connects to the muscle, t_A be the time to contraction from stimulation at A and t_B the time to contraction from stimulation at B.

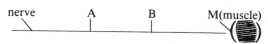

Then $\dfrac{(A \text{ to } M) - (B \text{ to } M)}{t_A - t_B}$ = speed of nerve impulse.

Happily, Helmholtz's estimate can be demonstrated in humans without resorting to dissection. You might suppose that the simplest way to do this would be to perform the following sort of experiment: Stimulate someone on the ankle (by pinching him, for example) and have him respond by pushing a button as soon as he feels the stimulation. With a good timer, you could then measure the time between stimulation and depression of the button. To estimate nerve conduction time, you would then measure the total distance between ankle and brain, and between brain and finger and divide this number by the subject's reaction time. But there are complications which make this procedure unsuitable. Part of the reaction time, for example, would be due to the length of time it took the subject to decide to press the button, a figure which is obviously more than simply nerve impulse time. From the point of view of processes in the nervous system, the reaction time includes the time to cross synapses as well as axon conduction time. In short, total reaction time is a confounded measure.

Thus, the experiment must be made more complicated. Using Helmholtz's logic, one could measure not only the time between ankle stimulation and response, but also between, say, upper arm stimulation and response. The ankle condition should result in a longer reaction time than the upper arm condition. The difference between these reaction times corresponds to the time it takes for the nerve impulse to travel a distance equal to the difference between the ankle and the finger, and the upper arm and the finger. Notice that this difference excludes any time due to such things as decision-making processes. So the nerve conduction time can be estimated by subtracting the distance of the upper arm to the brain from the distance of the ankle to the brain (the distance from the brain to the finger is constant) and dividing by the reaction time difference.

In practice, the reaction time for either stimulating the ankle or stimulating the upper arm is quite small, and hence a clock that measures time in hundredths of a second would be needed to measure it. This problem can be solved by adding together the reaction times of several people; after obtaining the total time, simply dividing this by the number of people would give the average individual time. This general mass reaction time technique will be used to measure the speed of the nerve impulse. Perform the nerve impulse speed experiment in the following way:

Get five people to participate. Have them form a circle with each person very loosely clasping the ankle of his neighbor to the right. Tell each person to squeeze the ankle he is holding when he feels his ankle squeezed. Be sure the subjects' eyes are closed during all trials. You can then start the experiment by squeezing one person's ankle and simultaneously noting the time on a second hand of a watch. Now watch the ankle that you squeezed. When you see it squeezed for the fifth time (excluding your initial squeeze) note the time that elapsed. Repeat this procedure for a total of five times, each time recording the time in the spaces provided in part I of the answer sheet on the next page (record results to an accuracy of .1 second).

Next have each person in the circle release the ankle he is holding and grasp the upper arm, just below the shoulder of the person to his right. You run another five trials exactly as you did for the ankle trials, each time recording the time in part II of the answer sheet.

You will probably note that the total reaction time dropped within each set of five trials. Why? Hopefully, the last two to three trials yielded about the same values.

These ten trials serve as practice: The group of five subjects and the measurer "learn" in some general way, to do this task efficiently. Having completed practice, you are now ready to begin the measurement of the speed of the nerve impulse. Run four more trials as before, the first and fourth with ankle stimulation, the second and third with upper arm. This will generate two ankle and two upper arm mass reaction times (record these in part III of the data sheet).

Each reaction time represents the sum of twenty-five reaction times (five subjects, five times each). Obtain the average individual reaction time by dividing the total reaction times by twenty-five. Now average the two ankle reaction times and, separately, the two upper arm reaction times. Subtract the averaged arm time from the averaged ankle time. This is the amount of time it takes the impulse to go the extra distance from the ankle to the level of the shoulder. To calculate the speed of the nerve impulse, you must estimate the magnitude of this distance (in meters).

Measure the distance for the third tallest person in your group of five subjects. Measure the distance from ankle to the base of the neck and from the upper arm to the base of the neck. Take the difference between the numbers, divide by the time difference, and you will have an estimate of the speed of the nerve impulse. How does it compare with Helmholtz's estimate? (Helmholtz estimated a speed of from 50 to 100 meters per second. Modern measurements range from 6 to 122 meters per second, depending on the type of nerve fiber). *(If your instructor collects the data, fill out the report sheet in Appendix B.)*

FURTHER EXPERIMENTS

Now that you have calculated an estimate of the speed of the nerve impulse, you might want to test whether some fairly common variables will affect this speed. Consider fatigue for instance. If a person is tired, does his nerve impulse speed slow down? To test this, design your own experiment, using the same measurement technique you used to get your main estimate of nerve impulse speed. To test whether fatigue has an effect, measure the speed both at a time when subjects are well rested and at a time when they are tired (for example, in the morning and at night, or before and after exercise). Does fatigue affect nerve impulse speed? Note, by the way, that given the way the estimate is obtained, it is possible to find that fatigue may well slow down reaction time in general, yet have no effect on the speed of the nerve impulse.

Can you think of other variables which you think might affect (speed up or slow down) nerve impulse speed? If so, design experiments to test your hypotheses.

Report Sheet

Practice   Time in seconds*

Part I   Trial 1 ankle = _____

             Trial 2 ankle = _____

             Trial 3 ankle = _____

             Trial 4 ankle = _____

             Trial 5 ankle = _____

Part II   Trial 1 upper arm = _____

             Trial 2 upper arm = _____

             Trial 3 upper arm = _____

             Trial 4 upper arm = _____

             Trial 5 upper arm = _____

Test

Part III   Trial 1 ankle time = _____

             ÷ 25 = _____ (a)

             Trial 2 upper arm time = _____

             ÷ 25 = _____ (b)

             Trial 3 upper arm time = _____

             ÷ 25 = _____ (c)

             Trial 4 ankle time = _____

             ÷ 25 = _____ (d)

$\dfrac{a + d}{2}$ = _____ (average ankle time)

$\dfrac{b + c}{2}$ = _____ (average upper arm time)

Average ankle time − average upper arm time = _____ (difference 1)

(1) Distance of ankle to brain (for third tallest person) = _____

(2) Distance of upper arm to brain (for third tallest person) = _____

    Distance 1 − distance 2 = _____ (difference 2)

$\dfrac{\text{difference 2}}{\text{difference 1}}$ = _____ (speed of nerve impulse)

*Record time accurate to .1 second.

CHAPTER 3

Motivation

Learning Objectives

MOTIVATION AS DIRECTION

1. Can directed action be reconciled with Descartes's notion of humans and animals as reflex machines?

Control systems
2. Describe the action of negative and positive feedback systems. Give examples of negative and positive feedback systems from modern technology.

SELF-REGULATION

Homeostasis
3. What is homeostasis?

Temperature regulation
4. Know how reflexes and behavior function to maintain body temperature.
5. Describe the way the two branches of the autonomic nervous system function in temperature regulation, and the role of the hypothalamus.

THIRST

6. Describe how the brain is informed about the body's need for water.

HUNGER

The signals for feeding
7. Indicate the internal and external signals that influence hunger and satiety.
8. What evidence makes it likely that animals stop eating in anticipation of the arrival of sufficient nutrients in the cells?

Hypothalamic control centers
9. Describe the role of the hypothalamus in feeding.
10. What is the dual-center theory? How do the phenomena of aphagia and hyperphagia support this theory?
11. How does the idea of set-point help account for the regulation of temperature and food intake, and how does it account for the behavior of hyperphagic rats?

Food selection
12. Indicate how different species with different ranges of acceptable foods (carnivores, omnivores, etc.) have different solutions to the problem of identifying foods.
13. Describe the roles of innate preferences, learning, and neophobia in omnivore food selection.
14. What are cuisines, what is their function, and how are they related to the determinants of food selection mentioned in item 13?

Obesity
15. Distinguish between behavioral and bodily factors as causes of obesity. Explain two possible bodily factors that have been suggested as causes: oversecretion of insulin and excess number of fat cells.
16. What behavioral factors may be involved in obesity? Describe the externality hypothesis and the restrained-eating hypothesis.
17. How can restrained eating be explained in terms of set-point?
18. Is overweight a disorder? What are its health and social consequences? Which are more important?

FEAR AND RAGE

Threat and the autonomic nervous system

19. What are the functions of the parasympathetic and sympathetic systems?
20. Describe the emergency reaction. What role does the sympathetic arousal system play in the flight-or-fight response? Understand the biological survival value of the emergency reaction.
21. How are fear and rage responses organized in the central nervous system? What is the role of the limbic system?
22. Indicate how stimulus intensity and novelty are related to fear and counterattack.

Disruptive effects of autonomic arousal

23. Describe the immediate disruptive effects of sympathetic arousal, and the phenomenon of parasympathetic overshoot. How is weeping an example of parasympathetic overshoot?

SLEEP AND WAKING

Waking

24. Describe the action of the reticular activating system. Where is it located? How do brain lesion and stimulation studies demonstrate that it is involved with wakefulness?

Sleep

25. Be able to describe the stages of sleep and the two kinds of sleep.

26. What is the relation between REM sleep and dreaming?
27. What are the effects of sleep deprivation? What is known about the functions of sleep?

WHAT DIFFERENT MOTIVES HAVE IN COMMON

Level of stimulation

28. Describe Hull's theory of drive reduction. Be able to criticize this theory.
29. What is meant by optimal arousal level, and how does it relate to drive reduction? What is the evidence for an optimal arousal level above zero?
30. Describe drug addiction and the phenomena of tolerance and withdrawal.

The opponent-process theory of motivation

31. Describe the opponent-process theory of motivation. How do studies of drug addiction and skydiving support this theory?

Are there pleasure centers in the brain?

32. What do studies of electrical stimulation of the brain tell us about motivation? Are there both general and motivation-specific pleasure centers in the brain?

The nature of motives

33. Review the evidence for and against the idea that all motives come together at some place in the brain.
34. Indicate how the biological basis for motives interacts with individual experience (learning) and culture.

Programmed Exercises

MOTIVATION AS DIRECTION

1. In _____ _____ systems, the feedback strengthens the initial behavior.

positive feedback

2. In a _____ _____ system, the feedback stops, or even reverses, the original behavior.

negative feedback

3. _____ are man-made devices which operate according to the principles of negative feedback.

Servomechanisms

SELF-REGULATION

4. The maintenance of a stable equilibrium in the body is called

_____ .

homeostasis

5. Vasoconstriction and piloerection are two forms of _____

responses to _____ in body temperature.

reflexive

decreases

6. Voluntary and reflexive heat-loss responses are brought into play when the body temperature drops below a temperature standard determined internally, which is called the _____.   set-point

7. The autonomic nervous system sends its commands to

_____ and _____ _____ .   glands, smooth muscles

8. The _____ and _____ divisions of the autonomic nervous system work in opposite directions to control tempera-   sympathetic, parasympathetic

ture. The _____ division acts to generate heat, to counter-   sympathetic
act low temperatures.

9. The activation of the divisions of the autonomic nervous

system is determined by _____ located in the part of the   (thermo)receptors

brain that controls these divisions, the _____ .   hypothalamus

THIRST

10. The brain detects the body's need for water from _____   volume
receptors located in the brain and some bood vessels, and

_____ receptors, which detect the concentration of min-   osmo-
erals in the body fluids. These latter receptors are located in

the _____ .   hypothalamus

HUNGER

11. Experiments which dilute food with nonnutritive substances

indicate that it is the _____ _____ rather than the   caloric value

_____ _____ of food that is regulated.   total volume

12. Receptors sensitive to the metabolic state (energy need) of the

organism have been postulated to exist in the _____ and   liver

_____ .   brain

13. The dual-center theory is supported by the fact that lesions in

the lateral hypothalamus produce _____ , while lesions in   aphagia

the ventromedial hypothalamus produce _____ .   hyperphagia

14. According to dual-center theory, "on" and "off" feeding

centers in the hypothalamus are mutually _____ .   inhibitory

15. The fact that hyperphagic rats gain weight and then maintain themselves at the new, higher weight suggests that they are

regulating their body weight around an elevated _____.   set-point

16. The human infant has a few innate preferences, including an

avoidance of _____ tastes and an attraction to _____   bitter, sweet
tastes.

17. Because nutritive quality and toxicity vary widely from one type of food to another, animals that eat a wide variety of foods, or _____ , have to _____ about what is edible and what is not.

omnivores (generalists), learn

18. The tendency to be suspicious of new foods is called _____ .

neophobia

19. The food preferences and aversions of a culture are generally represented in a cultural institution called a _____ .

cuisine

20. Recent studies suggest that some obesity may be caused by bodily factors. Excess feeding early in life may permanently increase the _____ of _____ cells in the body.

number, fat

21. Another bodily factor may be a disorder in which some people store too much food as fat, as a result of oversecretion of _____ .

insulin

22. According to the _____ _____ , obese people are relatively unresponsive to their own internal hunger signals and more susceptible to signals from the outside, like taste.

externality hypothesis

23. According to the _____ _____ _____ , externality is a feature of people who go on diets.

restrained-eating hypothesis

24. Restrained eaters and obese people may have, on the average, higher _____ than the rest of the population.

set-points

25. The justification of getting treatment for obesity is that thinner people are more attractive, and hence are more _____ successful. There are probably also _____ benefits for not being obese.

socially

health (medical)

FEAR AND RAGE

26. The parasympathetic system handles the _____ functions of the body.

vegetative

27. The sympathetic system has an _____ function.

activating

28. The sympathetic nervous system accelerates the conversion of _____ to _____ , in part, by _____ insulin secretion.

glycogen, glucose, inhibiting

29. Sympathetic action is supported or amplified by the secretion of the hormone _____ (or _____).

adrenaline, epinephrine

30. The emergency reaction results from activation of the _____ nervous system.

sympathetic

31. Decreased electrical resistance of the skin, or the _____ _____ _____ , is sometimes used as an index of autonomic arousal, as in lie detector tests.

galvanic

skin response

32. The portion of the brain that governs the autonomic system and is responsible for the control of emotional reactions is called the _____ system.

limbic

33. In general, organisms tend to fear stimuli that are _____   novel

and _____ .   intense (strong)

34. Loss of bladder control under conditions of great stress is an

example of the phenomenon of _____ _____ .   parasympathetic overshoot

SLEEP AND WAKING

35. The arousal of the brain is the function of the _____   reticular

_____ system.   activating

36. The reticular activating system can be aroused either by

_____ stimulation or internally, via connections with the   sensory

_____ .   cortex

37. The record of the voltage changes occurring in the brain over

time is called the _____ (   ).   electroencephalogram (EEG)

38. An EEG associated with waking relaxation shows _____   alpha
waves.

39. Rapid eye movements (REM), a waking EEG, relaxed muscles,
and low sensitivity to external stimulation all characterize

_____ sleep.   active

40. The average person dreams (exhibits REM sleep) for about

_____ hour(s) each night.   1−2

41. The specific need for both REM and non-REM sleep has been

shown through experiments in selective _____ _____ .   sleep deprivation

WHAT DIFFERENT MOTIVES HAVE IN COMMON

42. Hull believed that all built-in rewards produce some decrease

in tension, or _____ _____ .   drive reduction

43. The fact that animals will learn to press a lever to engage in

sexually arousing behavior argues for an_____ _____   optimal level

_____ _____ that is greater than zero.   of arousal

44. Addiction is associated with decreased sensitivity to a drug.

This effect is called _____ .   tolerance

45. According to _____ _____ theory, withdrawal symp-   opponent-process
toms can be explained as a result of action by the nervous
system to neutralize the effects of the drug.

46. Hot peppers produce unpleasant pain in people who try them
for the first time. Yet many come to like the "burn" after
many experiences. This could be accounted for by _____   opponent-

_____ _____ , which might hold that the body counter-   process theory
acts this pain by generating pleasure internally. This pleasure

response might result from _____ , neurotransmitters   endorphins
known to be secreted in response to pain.

47. Rats will learn an instrumental response if it is followed by

    _____ _____ of certain _____ _____ in the   electrical stimulation, pleasure
    brain.   centers

48. Rats are more likely to press a lever to stimulate their brain
    electrically if their brain has recently been stimulated. This is

    called a _____ effect, and is an example of _____   priming, positive
    feedback.

Self Test

1. Motivated behavior presents a serious problem to some machine models of behavior,
   because:
   a. motivated behavior involves a whole set
      of different reactions, any of which may
      lead toward the same goal
   b. motivated behavior involves direction,
      and this assumes a type of feedback that
      cannot be incorporated into machines
   c. motivated behavior assumes the opera-
      tion of at least one type of servomech-
      anism
   d. all of the above
   e. none of the above

2. In human sexual behavior, sexual foreplay
   seems to gradually increase sexual arousal of
   the partners. This would be an example of:
   a. homeostasis
   b. negative feedback
   c. a servomechanism
   d. positive feedback
   e. none of the above

3. Which of the following is a reflexive thermo-
   regulatory response to high temperature?
   a. shivering
   b. constriction of the blood vessels in the
      skin
   c. sweating
   d. piloerection (ruffling of fur)
   e. moving to a colder place

4. The word pair reflexive-voluntary, represents a relationship paralleled by which of the
   following pairs?
   a. homeostasis-whole organism
   b. vasoconstriction-vasodilation
   c. sweating-panting
   d. vasoconstriction-building a shelter
   e. none of the above

5. A dog is in a room comfortably heated to
   75°F. His hypothalamus is cooled experimentally. The result will be:

   a. he will shiver and his body temperature
      will go up
   b. he will shiver and his body temperature
      will go down
   c. he will pant and his body temperature will
      go up
   d. he will pant and his body temperature will
      go down
   e. no change in temperature, because his
      skin temperature remains unchanged

6. A rat's hypothalamus is cooled, and it learns
   to settle down over a warm air current in one
   part of its cage. This behavior illustrates:
   a. the operation of hypothalamic thermo-
      receptors
   b. the mobilization of voluntary behavior by
      the hypothalamic thermoregulatory system
   c. that directly manipulating hypothalamic
      temperature can cause an animal to make
      a response that is inappropriate to its
      actual body temperature
   d. all of the above
   e. none of the above

7. Maintenance of the body's water supply is
   affected by all except:
   a. regulation of the volume and concentra-
      tion of body fluids
   b. changes in reabsorption of water and
      minerals by the kidneys
   c. drinking in response to signals from in-
      ternal receptors
   d. a substance secreted by the kidneys and
      sensed in the hypothalamus
   e. extent of piloerection

8. In both thermoregulation and thirst:
   a. receptors in the hypothalamus sense im-
      portant aspects of bodily needs
   b. homeostasis occurs
   c. there is both reflexive and voluntary
      control
   d. all of the above
   e. none of the above

9. When rats are given a great deal of exercise, their intake of food increases, that is, they eat a larger amount of food. Rats also decrease their intake of a food if it is enriched, so that it contains more calories per gram. These findings suggest that:
   a. stomach fullness must be critical in regulating the rat's food intake
   b. the rat is regulating the volume of food consumed
   c. the rat is regulating the caloric or energy value of the food consumed
   d. all of the above
   e. a and c

10. Which of the following statements best summarizes the way that internal and external signals influence food intake?
    a. signals from various internal structures (brain receptors, liver, etc.) determine the amount eaten; external factors have almost no effect
    b. metabolic information from receptors in the brain controls about half of food intake, and external stimulation the other half
    c. metabolic information from receptors in the liver, brain, and possibly other locations interacts with external stimulation to determine the amount eaten
    d. palatability is the main determinant of amount eaten, as shown by the experiments in which ice cream was diluted with quinine
    e. hypothalamic receptors for internal and external events have a dual role in maintaining caloric intake

11. Two rats (or people) differ greatly in weight and fatness, but each of them holds its weight rather constant over a period of months. These results suggest that the two differ in:
    a. set-point
    b. stomach size
    c. ability to regulate body weight
    d. ability to regulate food intake
    e. size of hypothalamus

12. Food intake usually ceases before significant amounts of food have been absorbed from the bloodstream. This suggests that:
    a. the stomach may play an important role in satiety
    b. learning may play an important role in satiety

c. oral factors (e.g., monitoring how much has gone into the mouth) may play a role in satiety
    d. a and c
    e. all of the above

13. Initiation of eating is most likely to be associated with:
    a. high blood glucose
    b. excitation of the lateral hypothalamus
    c. inhibition of the lateral hypothalamus
    d. high liver glycogen
    e. excitation of the ventromedial hypothalamus

14. Dual-center theory makes all but one of the following assumptions or predictions. Which assumption is not a necessary part of the theory?
    a. information from internal and external receptors is integrated in the hypothalamus
    b. the relation between the two hypothalamic feeding centers is one of mutual inhibition
    c. the liver is the primary source of information concerning the metabolic state of the organism
    d. damage to the "on" center should produce aphagia
    e. damage to the "off" center should produce hyperphagia

15. Consider three types of animals: those that eat only one narrow type of food ("univores"), those that eat a variety of animal foods (carnivores), and those that eat a variety of plant foods (general herbivores). Which of the following arranges these types in terms of the increasing importance of learning in their food selection?
    a. univore, general herbivore, carnivore
    b. general herbivore, carnivore, univore
    c. carnivore, univore, general herbivore
    d. univore, carnivore, general herbivore
    e. b or d

16. Which of the following is *not* a likely example of neophobia?
    a. the rejection of corn, when it came from the Americas, by most cultures in Europe
    b. the avoidance of a new food by a wild rat
    c. the avoidance of a food by a rat after it consumed that food and became ill
    d. the tendency of many young children to accept only a few foods
    e. the tendency of many cultures to put a familiar flavoring on a new food

17. Pure sugar (as an additive) and artificial sweeteners are popular among most people, and are part of most cuisines. This fact suggests that:
    a. some of our innate features appear in cuisine
    b. pleasure, as well as nutrition, is an important aspect of cuisine
    c. cuisine is basically utilitarian
    d. a and b
    e. all of the above

18. Which one of the following has *not* been suggested as a cause of obesity?
    a. oversecretion of insulin
    b. damage to the lateral zone of the hypothalamus
    c. an excessive number of fat cells
    d. a high set-point
    e. overresponsiveness to palatability of food

19. This figure provides support for:

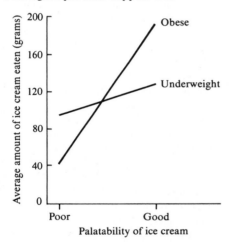

Poor   Good
Palatability of ice cream

    a. the dual-center theory of feeding
    b. the idea that obese people are metabolically different from underweight people
    c. the drive-reduction theory of motivation
    d. the externality hypothesis
    e. all of the above

20. The results in the figure for question 19 can also be explained by the restrained-eating hypothesis, since:
    a. not eating is disinhibited because of the high palatability of the food
    b. good palatability ice cream is not restrained
    c. highly palatable ice cream is more fattening than ice cream of poor palatability
    d. ice cream is external to the eater

    e. obese subjects have a higher set-point than underweight subjects only when ice cream is palatable

21. When dieters break their diets, they often go on an eating binge. This can be accounted for as:
    a. dropping of set-point
    b. raising of set-point
    c. externality
    d. activation of the ventromedial hypothalamus
    e. disinhibition

22. The externality and restrained-eating hypotheses make many similar predictions. Which of the following outcomes supports restrained eating as opposed to externality?
    a. overweight people eat relatively more of tasty foods
    b. most overweight people do not differ from normal-weight people in hormones or number of fat cells
    c. dieters eat relatively more of tasty foods
    d. most overweight people have higher set-points than normal-weight people
    e. overweight people who are not dieting are not as external as those who are dieting

23. Which of the following best describes the relations among externality, restrained eating, and set-point?
    a. people with higher set-points are likely to be both more external and restrained eaters
    b. anyone with a high set-point will be external and a restrained eater
    c. restrained eating probably causes a higher set-point, which in turn leads to externality
    d. a and c
    e. none of the above

24. The sympathetic branch of the autonomic nervous system is responsible for which of the following?
    a. the paleness of a flounder when its pigment spots change color
    b. crying after a sad movie
    c. vegetative functions, such as digestion
    d. emptying of the colon and bladder
    e. none of the above

25. The responses of a cat about to do battle with a dog are mediated by:
    a. the parasympathetic system
    b. the sympathetic system

c. vegetative functions
d. the galvanic skin response
e. b and c

26. Which of the following is *not* associated with activity of the sympathetic system?
    a. the emergency reaction
    b. epinephrine
    c. secretion by the adrenal medulla
    d. increased heart rate
    e. secretion of digestive enzymes

27. The shaded area of this cross-section of the brain represents a part of the brain that is involved in motivation and emotion. It is called the:
    a. hypothalamus
    b. limbic system
    c. cerebrum
    d. pituitary gland
    e. corpus callosum

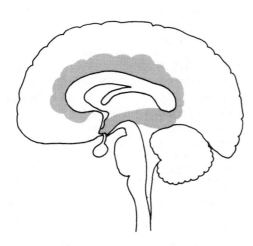

28. Which of the following stimuli should cause the least fear?
    a. a novel and very strong stimulus
    b. a familiar and weak stimulus
    c. a familiar but strong stimulus
    d. a novel and weak stimulus
    e. all will cause about equal fear

29. Which of the following reactions to an emergency situation does *not* suggest parasympathetic overshoot?
    a. crying
    b. urination
    c. piloerection
    d. cardiac relaxation
    e. secretion of digestive juices

30. Richter's studies on sudden death in animals suggest that the phenomenon of sudden and mysterious death in humans may be explained in terms of parasympathetic overshoot. If this were true, all but one of the following would be characteristic of sudden death. Which would *not* be expected in a case of sudden death?
    a. at the time of death, the heart would be beating rapidly and digestion would be inhibited
    b. a drug which opposed the effects of norepinephrine would not postpone death
    c. a low level of norepinephrine in the blood at the time of death
    d. a switch from an inactive to an actively functioning digestive system before death
    e. inability to produce an emergency reaction near the point of death

31. The sympathetic system is to the reticular activating system as:
    a. diffuse is to focused
    b. excitation is to inhibition
    c. body arousal is to brain arousal
    d. vasoconstriction is to vasodilatation

32. The involvement of the reticular activating system in wakefulness is demonstrated by all but one of the following results. Which result does not clearly support the RAS-wakefulness linkage?
    a. stimulation of the RAS leads to wakefulness
    b. removal of the RAS leads to somnolence
    c. external stimuli can arouse an animal even when the direct sensory pathways to the cortex are destroyed
    d. transmitter substances are involved in the operation of the RAS

33. Active sleep is sometimes called paradoxical sleep because:
    a. behaviorally the person seems to be sleeping, but his brain waves show a pattern of activity usually associated with a waking EEG
    b. it occurs at unexpected times, e.g., in a noisy environment or during the day
    c. the person is easily roused, yet his EEG consists of slow, large amplitude, synchronous waves
    d. all of the above
    e. a and b

34. Which of the following pairings represents a contrast between active sleep and quiet sleep?
   a. rapid eye movements—no rapid eye movements
   b. dreaming—lack of dreaming
   c. EEG waking activity—EEG slow waves
   d. all of the above
   e. a and c

35. When subjects are awakened after fifteen minutes of REM they relate longer dreams than when they are awakened after five minutes of REM. This result is evidence that:
   a. dreams are not only better remembered during REM, but actually unfold during REM
   b. dreams are rarely influenced by external sensory stimulation
   c. as dreams progress, they are related to memories of waking life
   d. dreams are mediated by the cerebral cortex and the RAS

36. Restorative functions for both active and quiet sleep are suggested by:
   a. increased duration of quiet sleep after quiet sleep deprivation
   b. increased duration of active sleep after active sleep deprivation
   c. increased duration of quiet sleep after bodily exhaustion
   d. increased duration of active sleep after mental exhaustion
   e. all of the above

37. The fact that nonnutritive saccharine serves as a reward for rats, and that solving a puzzle seems to be its own reward for monkeys and humans, suggests that:
   a. drive reduction is not the only mechanism of reward
   b. Hull's conception of reward was correct
   c. drive reduction does not depend on electrical stimulation of the brain
   d. organisms seek to diminish their arousal levels
   e. a and d

38. The mechanical puzzle at the top of the next column is used to demonstrate that monkeys:
   a. will be motivated by drive reduction
   b. will perform some acts as ends in themselves
   c. will only work for drive reduction
   d. can be stimulated

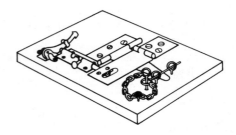

39. A person addicted to a specific euphoria-producing drug suddenly stops using this drug. He goes into a deep depression. This reaction is an example of:
   a. the effects of tolerance
   b. the effects of addiction
   c. a withdrawal symptom
   d. drive reduction

40. Withdrawal results from the same forces that produce tolerance to drugs, according to:
   a. opponent-process theory
   b. optimal arousal theory
   c. studies on electrical stimulation of the brain
   d. drive-reduction theory

41. According to which formulation is pleasure simply the absence of pain?
   a. opponent-process theory
   b. Hull's theory of drive reduction
   c. the externality hypothesis
   d. the dual-center theory
   e. none of the above

42. Studies on electrical stimulation of the brain have indicated:
   a. the existence of motivation-specific "pleasure centers" in the brain
   b. the possible presence of general "pleasure centers"
   c. priming, a positive feedback of stimulation on responding for further stimulation
   d. all of the above
   e. none of the above

43. Food sometimes tastes better after the first few bites, and then gradually becomes less tasty as we consume substantial amounts. This sequence can be accounted for as:
   a. an effect of brain stimulation
   b. priming
   c. positive feedback followed by negative feedback

d. opponent processes, in which endorphins are secreted more and more during a meal

e. an instance of drive-reduction theory

44. Which of the following can be considered a homeostatic motive?

a. hunger

b. sex

c. curiosity

d. a and b

e. none of the above

Answer Key for Self Test

1. a pp. 50–51	23. a pp. 59, 64–65
2. d p. 51	24. a p. 69
3. c p. 53	25. b p. 69
4. d p. 53	26. e p. 68
5. a pp. 54–55	27. b p. 70
6. d pp. 54–55	28. b pp. 71–73
7. e pp. 53, 55–56	29. c p. 72
8. d pp. 53–56	30. a pp. 72–73
9. c p. 57	31. c pp. 68, 74
10. c pp. 57–58	32. d p. 74
11. a p. 59	33. a p. 76
12. e pp. 57–58	34. d p. 76
13. b p. 59	35. a p. 77
14. c p. 58	36. e p. 78
15. d p. 61	37. a pp. 79–80
16. c pp. 61–62	38. b p. 80
17. d pp. 62–63	39. c p. 81
18. b pp. 64–65	40. a p. 81
19. d p. 65	41. b p. 79
20. a p. 65	42. d p. 83
21. e p. 65	43. c pp. 51, 82
22. e pp. 64–65	44. a p. 52

Investigating Psychological Phenomena

EFFECTS OF MENTAL PROCESSES ON AUTONOMIC ACTIVITY

Equipment: Stopwatch or watch with second indicator

Number of subjects: Three

Time per subject: Ten minutes

Time for experimenter: Forty minutes

As part of its role in the control of bodily functions, the autonomic nervous system (ANS) controls heart rate. In this way it can influence the rate of delivery of oxygen and nutrients to the cells of the body. In times when the body is stressed, increased heart rate (and other changes) increases the delivery of nutrients to cells, as well as increasing the rate of disposal of waste products. The changes in heart rate are produced directly by nerve impulses sent to the heart. They are also produced indirectly by stimulation, through autonomic pathways, of the release of epinephrine (adrenaline) and related substances from the adrenal glands.

Arousal of the sympathetic system, and hence increased heart rate, occurs when the organism is undergoing physical exertion. But it can also be produced by mental events. Such a pathway would allow an organism to mobilize its physiological resources in anticipation of a physical stress. On the other hand, it also allows for high and ultimately damaging levels of sympathetic arousal based on chronic anxiety or mental tension.

In this study we will demonstrate the effectiveness of the sympathetic nervous system link between mental activity and heart rate. Subjects will be asked to increase their heart rate by thinking either about a strenuous physical activity or something that is mentally exciting.

Make sure that your subject is seated comfortably, has been relaxing for at least ten minutes, and did not engage in any strenuous exercise in the last half hour. Before reading the instructions make sure you can find the subject's pulse on his or her wrist. The unit of recording for heart rate will be a thirty-second interval. You will record the number of beats every thirty seconds on the data sheet below. Allow fifteen seconds to pass between each thirty-second interval of recording so that you will have enough time to record the pulse and give the instruction. If you have an instruction to give the subject (e.g. "Relax," "Increase Mental") give the instruction as soon as you have recorded the pulse rate, but wait the full fifteen seconds before counting heartbeats.

Instructions to read to the subject:

This is a short, ten-minute experiment to determine whether you can control the rate of beating of your heart. When I say "Begin," you should close your eyes and relax while I take your pulse. After a minute I will say "Increase physical activity," and you should try to increase your heart rate by thinking about some physical activity in which you are personally engaged and which requires a lot of exertion. After I record your pulse I will say, "Relax," and you should stop trying to increase your heart rate and relax again. I will take your pulse for another minute and then I will say "Increase, mental." This time you should try to increase your heart rate by thinking of something that is exciting but that does not involve a lot of physical activity. This could be a fearful experience that you have had, the excitement from watching a sports event, preexamination anxiety, and so on. Following this one-minute episode I will say, "Relax," and you should stop trying to increase your heart rate and relax. I will take your pulse for one final minute. Before you begin the experiment decide on each image you will think about for the physical activity and the mental activity. After you have decided, stop thinking about the images until I give you the instruction during the actual experiment.

Give the subject a few minutes to decide on the images and then to stop thinking about them before you begin the experiment. Wait one minute after the subject has selected the two images, to allow any excitation that this may have produced to go away.

DATA FROM THREE SUBJECTS (A, B, AND C)

Instruction and time	A	B	C
"Begin and Relax"			
00:00–0:30			
0:45–1:15			
"Increase, physical activity"			
1:30–2:00			
2:15–2:45			
"Relax"			
3:00–3:30			
3:45–4:15			
"Increase, mental"			
4:30–5:00			
5:15–5:45			

"Relax"			
6:00–6:30			
6:45–7:15			

List for each subject the basic situation that they imagined in the "increase" minutes.

	Physical	Mental
A	_____	_____
B	_____	_____
C	_____	_____

Plot the data for each subject on the graph below. Use a different symbol for each subject, and connect the symbols for each subject by lines. Since heart rate is usually expressed as beats per minute, double each of the numbers you have recorded (since you recorded beats per thirty seconds) before plotting. We have plotted the results from ten undergraduates (mean). In our study nine of the ten undergraduates showed the increased heart rate effect.

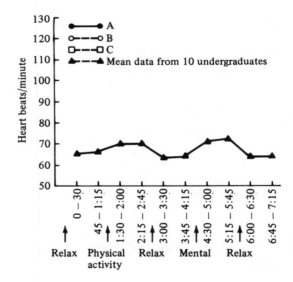

Do all of your subjects show an ability to increase heart rate by mental activity? Which procedure, thinking of physical activity or something mentally exciting, is more effective? *(If your instructor collects the data, fill out the report sheet in Appendix B.)*

FURTHER PROJECTS

Lowering heart rate is much more difficult than raising it. You might see if you can get some subjects to do that.

Some people have great difficulty in raising their heart rate. If one of your subjects is such a person, you could try to get an increase by having the subject *talk* about physical activity or something exciting during a one-minute period.

You could also explore whether certain kinds of "exciting thoughts" (e.g. fear, excitement of a spectator at a sports event) are more effective in raising heart rate.

CHAPTER 4

Learning

Learning Objectives

1. Describe the point of view of behavior theorists.

HABITUATION

2. Define habituation and discuss its adaptive significance.

CLASSICAL CONDITIONING

Pavlov and the conditioned reflex
3. Explain the basic procedure (paradigm) of classical conditioning, and define conditioned and unconditioned stimuli and responses.
4. Distinguish among conditioned and unconditioned reflexes and habituation.

The major phenomena of classical conditioning
5. Draw a curve to represent the acquisition, extinction, and reconditioning of a conditioned response.
6. Be able to define: reinforcement, higher-order conditioning, extinction, and reconditioning.
7. Describe generalization and discrimination, and contrast the two processes.

The scope of classical conditioning
8. Indicate how classical conditioning can account for acquired fears and phobias.
9. Show that the conditioned response often functions to prepare the organism for the unconditioned stimulus, and illustrate this with the example of conditioned compensatory responses.

What is learned in classical conditioning?
10. Discuss the effects of different times of onset of the conditioned and unconditioned stimuli. What is the most effective CS-UCS interval, and why is this adaptive?
11. Distinguish contiguity and contingency, and explain the studies that indicate that contingency is a critical factor in the formation of conditioned responses.
12. Describe the phenomena of overshadowing and blocking.
13. Explain the analogy between scientific thinking (the amateur scientist) and classical conditioning.

INSTRUMENTAL CONDITIONING

14. Review the major similarities and differences between classical conditioning and instrumental learning.

Thorndike and the law of effect
15. Explain the law of effect and indicate the evidence that supports it.
16. What is the relation between the law of effect and the evolutionary principle of survival of the fittest? How did the law change thinking about the problem of mental continuity between animals and humans?

Skinner and operant behavior
17. What additions and modifications did Skinner propose to Thorndike's view of instrumental learning?

The major phenomena of instrumental conditioning
18. How do the phenomena of instrumental learning parallel those of classical conditioning?

19. Define negative and positive reinforcers, and describe the processes of generalization, discrimination, and shaping in instrumental learning.
20. Give examples of conditioned and primary reinforcers, and describe how a conditioned reinforcer can be produced or eliminated.
21. Describe the effect of delay of reinforcement, and the properties of different schedules of reinforcement.
22. Define and describe schedules of reinforcement, and indicate the effect of the schedule on resistance to extinction.
23. Indicate the ways in which aversive stimuli influence learning, by describing punishment, escape, and avoidance learning.
24. Why does avoidance learning present a problem for behavior theory, and why is it hard to extinguish?

What is learned in instrumental conditioning
25. Explain the role of contingency in instrumental conditioning, and its relation to learned helplessness.
26. How has learned helplessness been used to explain some types of depression in humans?

BEHAVIOR THEORY AND HUMAN DISORDERS

Behavior therapy
27. Indicate the learning principles involved in flooding and systematic desensitization therapies, and describe how both are used to treat phobias.
28. Describe how principles of reinforcement are used therapeutically to eliminate or strengthen behaviors, and indicate a possible shortcoming of these procedures.

Behavior theory and medicine
29. Explain the role of learning in psychophysiological disorders and, in particular, in resistance to cancer.

SOME LIMITATIONS OF BEHAVIOR THEORY

Biological constraints on learning
30. What is the basic criticism of behavior theory that is described as biological constraints? In what sense can animals and humans learn arbitrary relationships?
31. Describe the phenomenon of taste aversion learning, and indicate why it illustrates biological constraints.
32. Discuss belongingness in response-outcome relations in instrumental learning.
33. Discuss the senses in which humans can be considered both intellectual generalists and specialists.

Cognitive learning
34. Distinguish between the positions of cognitive and behavior theorists.
35. Describe the evidence that supports the idea that animals learn about things and relations, i.e., that they have cognitions. What is the relation of latent learning to this argument?
36. Describe the phenomenon of insight in animals, and indicate why it presents problems for behavior theory.
37. How do we determine whether insight or trial and error is a better way of describing a particular behavior? What is the role of transfer in making this distinction?
38. What are learning sets?
39. Explain what a higher-order relationship is, and illustrate this with results from matching to sample and same-different symbol studies. Distinguish between generalization and transfer.
40. What is meant by "access" to intellectual operations?

The generality of behavior theory
41. Describe both qualifications of general laws of learning that have been suggested, and the problems with using such laws to explain the acquisition of knowledge.
42. Evaluate the strengths and shortcomings of behavior theory.

Programmed Exercises

1. _____ _____ believe that a few simple laws of learning can account for most of human and animal behavior.   Behavior theorists

HABITUATION

2. _____ is a decline in the tendency to respond to stimuli that have become familiar due to repeated exposure.   Habituation

CLASSICAL CONDITIONING

3. Unlike habituation, classical conditioning involves the formation of _____ between events.

associations

4. Classical conditioning was first demonstrated in the laboratory by _____ _____ .

Ivan Pavlov

5. After classical conditioning, the salivation of a dog upon presentation of a previously neutral bell would be called a

_____ _____ .

conditioned response

6. Salivation to meat powder in the mouth is a(n) _____

_____ _____ . Salivation to a tone paired with meat

powder in the mouth is a(n) _____ _____ _____ .

unconditioned

reflex (response)

conditioned reflex (response)

7. According to Pavlov, when the CS is followed by the UCS, the connection between them is _____ .

reinforced

8. Response strength in conditioning can be measured as the

amount of response, that is, the _____ , or the time from

onset of the CS to the onset of the CR, called the _____ .

amplitude

latency

9. A light is paired with shock. Subsequently, a tone paired with

the light comes to elicit fear. This is an example of _____

_____ _____ .

higher-

order conditioning

10. If after a CR has been established, the CS is presented, but not

followed by the UCS, the result will be _____ of the CR.

extinction

11. Reconditioning usually requires _____ trials than did the original conditioning.

fewer

12. Horizontal stripes on a card (CS) are paired with a puff of air to the eye (US), resulting in a conditioned eye blink response. Now, the first time vertical stripes are presented, a condi-

tioned eye blink is observed. This is an example of _____

_____ .

stimulus

generalization

13. The greater the difference between a conditioned stimulus and another test stimulus, the weaker the conditioned response to

this test stimulus. This relationship is described as a _____

_____ .

generalization

gradient

14. Reinforcement (US presentation) after CS^+, and nonreinforce-

ment (No UCS) after a CS^- leads to _____ .

discrimination

15. According to a classical conditioning analysis, the object of a

phobia or fetish can be considered to be a _____ _____ .

conditioned stimulus

16. In many instances, the CR does not duplicate the UCR, but

rather _____ the animal to deal with the UCS.

prepares

17. Sometimes, the CR has the opposite effect from the UCR. In

this case, the CR is called a conditioned _____ response.

compensatory

18. Learning of a conditioned response (CR) occurs most efficiently

    when the _____ precedes the _____ by a small time   CS, UCS

    interval. This is called _____ pairing.   forward

19. Pavlov and others claimed that togetherness in time, pairing,

    or _____ forms the basis for classical conditioning.   contiguity

20. Later research suggests that what is critical for conditioning is

    that the CS predicts the UCS, so that there is a _____   contingency
    between CS and UCS.

21.

    The pattern of shock and signals shown in A above is most

    likely to give rise to the state of _____ , whereas the   fear

    _____ shock shown in B is likely to give rise to the state   unsignaled (uncontingent)

    of _____ .   anxiety

22. When two stimuli both predict an important event (UCS),
    only one of these stimuli may show classical conditioning. This

    phenomenon is called _____ .   overshadowing

23. A stimulus (CS-1) is presented contingently with a UCS. Then,
    a second stimulus (CS-2) is also presented at the same time as
    CS-1, and both are followed by the UCS. Often, only CS-1
    will show classical conditioning. This phenomenon is called

    _____ .   blocking

24. Two conditions that seem necessary for classical conditioning

    to occur are that the CS must show a _____ relation to   contingent

    the UCS, and the CS must provide _____ that the   information
    organism did not have before.

INSTRUMENTAL CONDITIONING

25. In classical conditioning, a relation between two stimuli is
    learned. In instrumental conditioning, however, the relation

    that is learned exists between a _____ and a _____ .   response, reward

26. The experimental study of instrumental learning was begun by

    _____ in the context of a debate over the mental conti-   (Edward L.) Thorndike
    nuity of man and animals which was stimulated by the evolu-

    tionary theories of _____ .   (Charles) Darwin

27. Thorndike's _____ _____ _____ states that the   law of effect
    consequences of a response determine whether it becomes
    strengthened or weakened.

28. The most prominent figure in modern behavior theory is

_____ . (B. F.) Skinner

29. Skinner emphasized distinctions between classical conditioning and instrumental learning. In the former, responses are

_____ , while in instrumental learning they are _____ . elicited, emitted

30. Skinner used the term "_____ " to describe the "voluntary" or "emitted" responses that are studied in instrumental operants

learning. He preferred to measure _____ _____ as a measure of response strength. response rate

31. In instrumental learning, the delivery of some preferred substance (e.g., food) or situation following a particular response

is called _____ _____ . positive reinforcement

32. Although operants are not elicited by external stimuli, the

stimuli can control behavior as _____ _____ . discriminative stimuli

33. Animals can be trained to perform difficult responses by the

method of _____ _____ . successive approximation (shaping)

34. Presentation of food or water, or termination of a painful

stimulus are examples of _____ _____ , in contrast to primary reinforcement
presentation of a light paired with one of these, or

"approval," which are examples of _____ _____ . secondary reinforcement

35. Conditioned reinforcement is established by a procedure that

seems to be the same as _____ conditioning. classical

36. Reinforcements become less effective the longer the _____ delay (time)
between the response and the reinforcement.

37. The rule set up by the experimenter (or society) which determines the occasions on which a response is reinforced is called

a _____ _____ _____ . schedule of reinforcement

38. An animal that is reinforced for every five responses is on a

_____ _____ schedule. fixed ratio

39. Responses acquired with intermittent reinforcement exhibit

greater resistance to extinction. This is termed the _____ partial

_____ _____ . reinforcement effect

40. Loud noises, painful stimuli, bitter tastes, and social rejection

are examples of _____ stimuli. aversive

41. In _____ training, an aversive stimulus follows a particular punishment
response.

42. _____ learning is a type of instrumental learning in which Escape
the organism is required to perform a response which terminates or reduces an unpleasant stimulus.

43. Avoidance learning presents problems for behavior theory be

cause it is not easy to identify the _____ for the avoidance reinforcer
response.

44. Avoidance responses are particularly resistant to _____ .   extinction
    This may account for the persistence in humans of certain

    intense fears, or _____ .   phobias

45.

Trials

    This graph illustrates the transition from _____ to   escape

    _____ learning.   avoidance

46. Just as is the case with classical conditioning, what is learned

    in instrumental learning is a _____ .   contingency

47. Dogs given inescapable shocks are then placed in an avoidance
    situation shuttlebox where they could learn a jumping response
    to escape and avoid shock. Instead, they lie quietly and take
    the shocks. Their behavior has been interpreted as learning
    that the presence or absence of shocks is not contingent on

    their behavior, a state called _____ _____ .   learned helplessness

48. The symptoms shown by helpless dogs resemble those seen in

    the human disorder of _____ .   depression

BEHAVIOR THEORY AND HUMAN DISORDERS

49. Psychologists who treat certain disorders by applying principles

    of learning are called _____ _____ .   behavior therapists

50. Two behavior therapy techniques used to treat phobias are
    flooding
    _____ and _____ .   systematic desensitization

51. Treatment of a phobia by pairing the avoided CS with a new
    CR that is incompatible with the phobic response is called

    _____ .   counterconditioning

52. A child loves a particular type of candy bar and eats too many
    of them. A behavior therapist treats this "problem" by giving
    the child hundreds of candy bars of this type. The approach is

    called _____ .   satiation

53. Token economies have been set up to regulate behavior among
    chronic mental patients. In these economies, the token func-

    tions as a _____ _____ .   conditioned reinforcement

54. Psychological factors may be part of the cause of diseases like peptic ulcer, colitis, or hypertension, which are called

    _____ disorders.   psychophysiological

55. In some cases, individuals have been taught to gain voluntary control over normally involuntary bodily responses, through

    the technique of _____ .   biofeedback

56. There is evidence that learned helplessness training can depress

    the function of the _____ system.   immune

SOME LIMITATIONS OF BEHAVIOR THEORY

57. Behavior theory assumes that the relation between stimuli in classical conditioning, or between response and outcome in

    instrumental learning, is _____ .   arbitrary

58. One criticism of behavior theory holds that there are certain

    built-in limitations called _____ _____ that determine   biological constraints
    what a given animal can easily learn.

59. Belongingness in animal learning, as illustrated by taste aversion learning, seems to fit well with the survival needs of

    animals. Thus, rats, who rely heavily on _____ in feeding,   taste
    tend to associate that with the aftereffects of eating, while

    birds, which rely on _____ in feeding, tend to associate   vision (sight)
    this type of stimulus with the aftereffects of eating.

60. The fact that it is easier to train a pigeon to flap its wings to

    escape shock than to receive food is an instance of _____   belongingness

    in _____-_____ relations in instrumental learning.   response-outcome (act)

61. It can be argued that humans and some other animals seem relatively good at learning arbitrary relationships. In this sense,

    they can be seen as _____ as opposed to _____ .   generalists, specialists

62. Köhler claimed that animals can acquire _____ , as well as   cognitions
    responses.

63. A child ambles down the same street a few times on the way to a ballfield. One day she is asked to get a key made and remembers that there was a key store on the way to the ball-

    field. This could be considered an example of _____   latent

    _____ .   learning

64. The figure on the next page represents a situation studied by

    Köhler in which he demonstrated the phenomenon of _____ .   insight

65. A chimpanzee solves the problem of knocking down a piece of fruit hung above the cage by throwing a ball at it. When the ball is taken away, it throws a piece of fruit. This demonstrates

    _____ .   transfer

66. Behavior theory interprets transfer effects as instances of

    _____ _____ , but transfer often seems to be based on   stimulus generalization

    abstract _____ relationships.   conceptual

67. Successive improvement across a series of unrelated discrimin-

    ation problems demonstrates the acquisition of a _____   learning

    _____ .   set

68. An animal is shown one stimulus and, below it, two other
    stimuli. One of these two is identical to the upper stimulus.
    The correct response is to indicate this stimulus. This pro-

    cedure is called _____ _____ _____ .   matching to sample

69. The idea of "sameness" developed by Sarah, the chimpanzee,

    is an example of a _____ _____ relationship.   second-order

70. A creature that knows what it knows, or can use specific

    capacities in new situations, is said to have _____ to its   access
    own intellectual operations. This can be considered an aspect

    of _____ .   intelligence

71. A major criticism of behavior theory that emerges from recent
    work is that we must explore not only what animals (and

    humans) *do*, but also what they _____ .   know

Self Test

1. Behavior theorists share with Descartes the conviction that:
   a. one must study the nervous system to understand behavior
   b. learning is the most important aspect of animal behavior
   c. complex behavior can be analyzed into simpler, more elementary processes
   d. almost all behavior can be described as prewired

2. An animal startles when it is exposed to the sound of either a door slamming or a gong ringing. It is then exposed, about ten times, to the gong ringing followed by the door slamming. Now, when the gong rings, the animal does *not* show startle. This is an example of:
   a. habituation
   b. classical conditioning
   c. extinction
   d. associations
   e. a learning curve

3. Classical conditioning and habituation have in common the fact that both:
   a. involve associations
   b. require a conditioned stimulus
   c. are built-in responses that animals show in laboratory situations
   d. involve a change in response to a stimulus
   e. occur primarily in dogs, though they may occur in some other species

4. In a classical conditioning experiment in which a tone is paired with meat in the mouth, a dog comes to salivate to the sound of the tone. The tone is called the:
   a. conditioned stimulus
   b. unconditioned stimulus
   c. unconditioned response
   d. orientation reflex
   e. reinforcer

5. Ivan Pilaff developed a fear of German shepherds because on a few occasions, he was bitten by them. Some weeks later, he became friendly with someone who had a German shepherd as a pet. After a few visits to this friend plus shepherd, he became fearful of the friend, even though this particular German shepherd never bit him. This is an example of:
   a. discrimination
   b. extinction
   c. reinforcement
   d. learning with a long delay
   e. higher-order conditioning

6. A dog is first classically conditioned to seven stimuli (A-G) until he responds equally to all. He then gets some further training. At the end he produces the unusual generalization curve shown below. What was the further training the dog received?

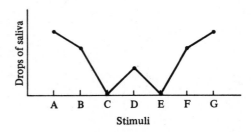

   a. extinguish stimuli A, B, D, F, and G
   b. extinguish B, D, and F; further condition A and G
   c. extinguish C and E
   d. extinguish C, D, and E
   e. extinguish C and E; further condition D

7. This figure illustrated the phenomenon of:

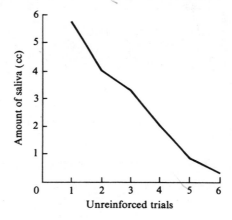

   a. conditioning
   b. generalization
   c. extinction
   d. reconditioning

8. Classical conditioning has been:
   a. shown to occur only with salivation
   b. used to explain responses to music, in conjunction with Romantic conditioning
   c. demonstrated only in vertebrates
   d. suggested as an explanation for phobias
   e. a and c

9. During World War II, air raid sirens preceded bombing raids. A person who, as a result of fear, stopped her ongoing activity (e.g., eating, working) shows:

a. response suppression
b. a siren phobia
c. extinction
d. compensatory conditioning
e. a generalization gradient

10. An experienced sky diver does not show nearly as much arousal, on entering the plane from which he will jump, as does a novice sky diver. Consider an experienced sky diver who is just about to enter the plane, but is called back at the last minute. If he shows a conditioned compensatory response, we would expect that:
a. his arousal would be about the same as that of the novice
b. he would show a bigger increase in arousal than the novice
c. he would show the same decrease in arousal as the novice
d. he would show the same increase in arousal as the novice
e. he would become less aroused than he normally is in daily life

11. The relation between a UCR and a conditioned compensatory response is like the relation between excitation and:
a. conditioning
b. reconditioning
c. extinction
d. response suppression
e. inhibition

12. This figure demonstrates that it is very difficult to produce conditioning with:

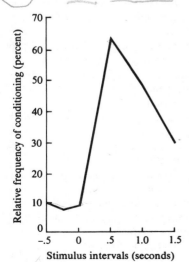

a. forward pairing
b. higher-order conditioning

c. extinction
d. simultaneous pairing
e. all of the above

13. Consider the following table of probabilities of CS and UCS. What predictions would the contiguity and contingency accounts make of whether conditioning would occur in this case?

	UCS	No UCS
CS	9	1
No CS	9	1

a. both predict conditioning
b. both predict no conditioning
c. only contingency predicts conditioning
d. only contiguity predicts conditioning

14. Consider the following table of occurrences of CS and UCS. What predictions would the contiguity and contingency accounts make of whether conditioning would occur in this case?

	UCS	No UCS
CS	7	3
No CS	3	7

a. both predict conditioning
b. both predict no conditioning
c. only contingency predicts conditioning
d. only contiguity predicts conditioning

15. In the case of unsignaled shock (a random relation between a signal and shock), the relation between a signal and the shock is one of:
a. anxiety
b. absence of contingency
c. contingency
d. contiguity
e. overshadowing

16. Some properties of classical conditioning suggest that it functions to make predictions about events in the world, somewhat like a scientist. Which feature(s) of classical conditioning has (have) this property?
a. sensitivity to contingency
b. forward pairing
c. overshadowing
d. blocking
e. all of the above

17. Harriet gets very excited whenever she approaches the house of her boyfriend, Milton. She notices that her heart starts beating when she turns his corner and sees the name of his street on the corner sign. But she is surprised one day to note that the sign is down, and that she does not get excited on turning the corner, nor on passing Milton's street mailbox, just twenty feet from the corner. Why doesn't the

mailbox cause her heart to increase beating?
a. blocking
b. conditioned compensatory response
c. Harriet is an amateur scientist
d. the mailbox doesn't have a contingent
   relation with Milton
e. fear suppresses her response

18. Instrumental learning differs from classical
    conditioning in that:
    a. in instrumental learning, a response-
       reward association is learned, while in
       classical conditioning, a relation between
       stimuli is learned
    b. associations are formed only in classical
       conditioning
    c. responses are never involved in classical
       conditioning
    d. instrumental learning always occurs grad-
       ually, in trial-and-error fashion, whereas
       classical conditioning occurs very rapidly
    e. a and c

19. According to the law of effect, responses
    followed by reward:
    a. increase in latency
    b. are not always reinforced
    c. become trials or errors
    d. are strengthened
    e. all of the above

20. The parallel between Darwin's theory of
    evolution and instrumental conditioning is
    between:
    a. mental continuity and trial-and-error
       learning
    b. learning and extinction
    c. survival of the fittest and the law of effect
    d. a and b
    e. all of the above

21. As described by Thorndike, instrumental
    learning:
    a. is gradual
    b. involves no complex, uniquely human
       processes
    c. is accomplished on a trial-and-error basis
    d. is a means of strengthening particular
       responses
    e. all of the above

22. This device for the study of instrumental
    learning was designed by and named after
    _____ , one of the major figures in the
    field.
    a. Thorndike
    b. Skinner
    c. Watson
    d. Pavlov

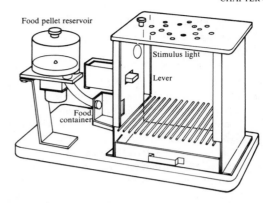

Food pellet reservoir
Stimulus light
Lever
Food container

23. Skinner added to Thorndike's conception(s)
    the idea that the responses conditioned in
    instrumental learning were:
    a. emitted or voluntary, as opposed to
       elicited as in classical conditioning
    b. increased in strength by the process of
       reinforcement
    c. selected from all responses emitted on the
       basis of the law of effect
    d. a and c
    e. all of the above

24. The desire for good grades illustrates the
    phenomenon of:
    a. stimulus generalization
    b. simultaneous discrimination
    c. secondary reinforcement
    d. association by contiguity

25. A rat is placed in a chamber and is given a
    number of pellets of food, each preceded by a
    clicking sound. It is later trained to lever
    press, with the reinforcement only the sound-
    ing of the click, but no food. Every other
    day the rat receives pairings of click and food,
    and on the alternate days, it presses only for
    the click. Eventually, it stops pressing the
    lever on the "click" days. This cessation
    could be explained as:
    a. generalization
    b. loss of secondary reinforcement proper-
       ties by the click
    c. discrimination between clicks in two dif-
       ferent situations
    d. an illustration of the importance of delay
       of reinforcement

26. In order to shape an animal to perform a
    difficult response, all but one of the follow-
    ing procedures should be followed. Which
    procedure is *not* appropriate?
    a. provide a clear signal for the arrival of
       reinforcement
    b. present the reinforcement immediately
       after the response is performed

c. initially reinforce approximations to the desired response

d. at first, reinforce those parts of the desired response sequence that come at the end of the sequence

e. work with the most difficult component in the response sequence first

27. Skinner and Thorndike share in common a belief in:

a. the importance of schedules of reinforcement

b. the law of effect

c. the idea that instrumental behavior is emitted

d. the superiority of instrumental training with discrete trials

28. A hippopotamus is placed in a puzzle box. On the first trial he performs a series of responses: R1 (ramming at the doors), R2 (bellowing), R3 (stamping on the floor), and finally, R4 (stepping on a pedal which opens a door and lets him out and gives him access to mountains of hippopotamus food). According to the law of effect, any response which is followed by reinforcement will be connected to the stimulus situation. This being so, there should be a strengthening of R1, R2, and R3, but, in fact, we notice that these responses decline in probability. How would Thorndike explain this?

a. by referring to the importance of conditioned reinforcement

b. by invoking schedules of reinforcement

c. by referring to the role of delay of reinforcement

d. by referring to disinhibition

e. by referring to generalization

29. Consider each swing by a baseball player as an operant response, and every successful hit (single, double, etc.) as a reinforced swing. Then what schedule of reinforcement is a baseball batter on?

a. continuous reinforcement (fixed ratio 1)

b. fixed ratio

c. variable ratio

d. extinction

30. Paradoxically, when an operant is reinforced on a schedule (e.g., every third response is reinforced), the response shows a greater resistance to extinction than when it receives an equal number of reinforced responses on *every trial*. This effect (partial reinforcement effect) is paradoxical because:

a. the nonreinforced trials in partial reinforcement training are extinction trials and should weaken the response

b. CS-US contingencies must be precisely controlled in order for good conditioning to occur

c. the animal on partial reinforcement performs more responses in training

d. the organism is learning a discrimination during training

e. all of the above

31. Avoidance learning presents a problem for behavior theory because:

a. it is not clear what reinforces the avoidance response

b. it is particularly resistant to extinction

c. it occurs after the animal learns to escape

d. a and b

e. none of the above

32. Studies on learned helplessness in dogs and infants' responses to mobiles that they could or could not control are evidence for the importance of:

a. the law of effect

b. contiguity

c. contingency

d. belongingness

p. 114 – 15 read.

33. Animals exposed to lights randomly paired with shock (hence, unsignaled shock) sometimes develop pathologies related to stress. The relation of this finding to learned helplessness is the same as the relationship of:

a. conditioning to extinction

b. the optimum CS-UCS interval to contingency

c. generalization in classical conditioning to generalization in instrumental conditioning

d. behavior therapy to the partial reinforcement effect

e. extinction of instrumental conditioning to establishment of classical conditioning

34.

Stimuli	Anxiety Level
snakes	20
worms	15
spaghetti	10
water hoses	5
rubber bands	0

A person with a snake phobia is tested for the extent to which this phobia generalizes to four stimuli: worms, spaghetti, water hoses, and rubber bands. The table above indicates the

relative amount of anxiety produced by each stimulus. The therapist has to decide which of the four stimuli he shall choose to begin desensitization training. Which is it to be?
a. worms
b. spaghetti
c. water hoses
d. rubber bands
e. it doesn't matter which he chooses

35. Both flooding and systematic desensitization rely heavily on the learning principle of:
a. extinction
b. generalization
c. discrimination
d. helplessness
e. partial reinforcement effect

36. A concern with some types of behavior therapy is that by rewarding certain activities, they may make those activities less inherently rewarding to the person in question. Which type of behavior therapy is most susceptible to this criticism?
a. flooding
b. token economies
c. satiation
d. systematic desensitization

37. There is evidence that learned helplessness depresses the function of the immune system, resulting in greater susceptibility to cancer. What experience other than learned helplessness would also be likely to have these effects?
a. avoidance learning
b. unsignaled shock
c. escape learning
d. systematic desensitization
e. punishment

38. A simplified version of John Garcia's belongingness experiment would present bright-noisy tasty water to rats, followed by X-ray produced illness. The rats would show an aversion only to the taste (one of the groups in the experiment described in the text). However, without the use of a second group in which shock is the UCS, this experiment could be criticized by a behavior theorist, because:
a. bright-noisy type of stimuli don't associate well with UCS's like those induced by X rays
b. the bright-noisy stimuli might have been generally less effective as CS's than the taste stimulus

c. this result would contradict the bird studies, showing selective association of visual stimuli and gastrointestinal effects
d. the selective association could have been previously learned by the rats

39. Rats have a special ability to associate tastes with illness. Pigeons learn to peck a key for food, but have difficulty learning to peck a key to avoid shock. Both of these phenomena demonstrate belongingness. However, they differ in that the belongingness in the case of learned taste aversions occurs between _____ while in the pigeon example it occurs between _____.
a. species specific stimuli, general stimuli
b. stimuli, responses
c. responses, stimuli
d. stimuli, responses and outcomes
e. stimulus and response, responses

40. Which of the following instances of human learning most clearly represents arbitrary, as opposed to biologically specialized or prepared, learning?
a. acquisition of grammar
b. learning to catch a ball
c. learning the rules of chess
d. learning to judge distance

41. Which of the following phenomena does *not* present a serious problem to behavior theory?
a. latent learning
b. taste aversion learning
c. insight learning
d. phobias
e. transfer

42. Which of the following statements describes a fundamental difference between behavior and cognitive theorists?
a. behavior theorists think a response is necessary for learning, while cognitive theorists think responses may be merely an index of learning
b. behavior theorists believe in reinforcement, and cognitive theorists deny its existence
c. behavior theorists believe in belongingness, while cognitive theorists believe in latent learning
d. all of the above
e. none of the above

43. In his attempts to demonstrate higher mental processes in animals, Köhler's experiments differed from those of Thorndike in that:

a. Köhler used an animal which might have greater reasoning power
b. Köhler used situations in which it was possible to "reason" a solution
c. Köhler used problems which could be gradually understood
d. a and c
e. a and b

44. Köhler suggested that a way to distinguish insightful from trial-and-error learning is that only insightful learning would:
a. generalize
b. show transfer
c. be arbitrary
d. be accomplished by apes
e. show belongingness

45. Primates seem superior to other mammals or invertebrates tested in learning situations in that they show:
a. more rapid learning of initial discriminations
b. more rapid instrumental conditioning
c. more rapid classical conditioning
d. clearer learning sets

46. Learning sets are a challenge to behavior theory because they imply that:
a. learning can be very rapid
b. monkeys respond to perceptual relationships
c. the particular form of the response is not important
d. monkeys can employ "strategies" (e.g., win-stay, lose-shift)

47. The figure at the top of the next column sets out a problem used frequently in studies with primates. The problem is called:
a. discrimination
b. symbol manipulation
c. learning to learn
d. matching to sample

48. Critical evidence for a *concept* of "sameness" in chimpanzees comes from the demonstration of:
a. discrimination
b. generalization
c. belongingness
d. matching to sample
e. transfer

49. A relationship like "same," which holds regardless of the specific objects that are used to illustrate it, can be described as:

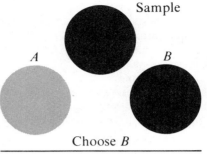

Sample

A   *B*

Choose *B*

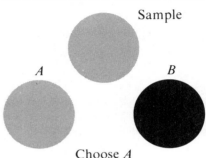

Sample

A   *B*

Choose *A*

a. a good relationship
b. a higher-order relationship
c. latent
d. insightful
e. matching to sample

50. Which of the following pairs best expresses a distinction between behavior theory and cognitive theory?
a. discrimination versus generalization
b. same versus different
c. biological constraints versus higher-order relationships
d. insight versus out of sight
e. doing versus knowing

51. Cognitive theorists criticize behavior theorists on the grounds that behavior theorists:
a. assume animals are able to learn any arbitrary relationship
b. underestimate the ability of some animals to show sophisticated learning in some specific situations
c. rely too much on the response as a necessary part of learning
d. a and c
e. all of the above

52–54. For the following three questions, the same set of answer alternatives are relevant.

Each question describes a major principle of behavior theory. For each one, choose the answer that describes a finding that casts doubt on this principle. The possible answers are listed below.

  a. latent learning
  b. random pairing of CS and UCS leads to no conditioning
  c. insight learning
  d. learned helplessness
  e. taste-aversion learning

52. contiguity in time of two stimuli is sufficient grounds for conditioning

53. any CS can be associated equally well with any UCS

54. learning will only occur if there is reinforcement

Answer Key for Self Test

1.	c p. 88	28.	c p. 109
2.	a p. 88	29.	c p. 110
3.	d pp. 88–90	30.	a pp. 110–11
4.	a p. 90	31.	d p. 112
5.	e p. 91	32.	c pp. 114–15
6.	c p. 92	33.	c pp. 114–15
7.	c p. 92	34.	c p. 117
8.	d p. 94	35.	a pp. 116–18
9.	a p. 94	36.	b p. 118
10.	e p. 95	37.	b pp. 120–21
11.	e p. 95	38.	b pp. 122–23
12.	d p. 96	39.	d pp. 122–23
13.	d pp. 97–98	40.	c pp. 121–25
14.	a p. 98	41.	d pp. 94, 122, 123, 127–29
15.	b pp. 98–99	42.	a p. 126
16.	e pp. 96, 97, 100	43.	e pp. 127–29
17.	a p. 100	44.	b p. 129
18.	a p. 102	45.	d p. 130
19.	d pp. 102–103	46.	d p. 130
20.	c pp. 102–103	47.	d p. 131
21.	e pp. 103–105	48.	e pp. 129, 131
22.	b p. 106	49.	b p. 131
23.	a p. 105	50.	e p. 126
24.	c pp. 108–109	51.	e p. 126
25.	c p. 107	52.	b p. 101
26.	e pp. 107–108	53.	e pp. 122–23
27.	b pp. 103–106	54.	a p. 127

Investigating Psychological Phenomena

MAZE LEARNING

Equipment: Stopwatch or watch with second indicator

Number of subjects: One (yourself)

Time per subject: Twenty to thirty-five minutes

Time for experimenter: Twenty to thirty-five minutes

This experiment illustrates a basic feature of learning: the acquisition curve, or the gradual acquisition of a skill or task. It employs a technique that was commonly used with animals in the earlier part of this century. The task is to find a way through a maze, presumably through learning a series of correct choices at the various choice-points. In the experiment you will proceed through the same maze four times: each time, a record will be kept of both your total time to completion and the number of errors (false entries). Learning would be demonstrated by a drop in either time to completion or the number of errors, as the number of trials increases.

Beginning on page 53, a maze is reprinted 4 times. In each case, using the second indicator on a wrist watch or a stopwatch, time yourself from the time you begin with a pencil at the starting point to the time you leave the maze. You should never pick your pencil off the paper until the maze is completed. If you make an error, simply retrace your steps with the pencil. Upon completion of the maze, record the total time taken at the bottom of the page. Do not record the number of errors until you have finished all the mazes, since calculation of errors would be like another trial (you would have to work through the maze again).

Finish all four trials and then calculate errors for each trial. An error is defined as the crossing of the imaginary line at the mouth of an "alley" that leads to a dead end. One such entry can only count for one error, no matter how far you go up the blind alley before realizing that it is blind. In other words, once you have entered an alley which will ultimately be blind, you can only score one error, even if there is a further choice-point along this path (both of these choices would of course have to be blind alleys). The only way you can score two errors for the same blind alley is if you enter it twice.

Plot the time/trial and errors/trial on the two graphs provided below. Do you show evidence for gradual mastery of the maze? Compare your results with those from a group of undergraduate students that we have plotted on the same graph. We have plotted the mean (the average) scores. Individuals vary a lot; not all individuals show smooth curves like these averaged curves. In the graph, •———• represents the mean for eight subjects. H and L represent the range. H is the highest value of eight subjects; L is the lowest score of eight subjects.

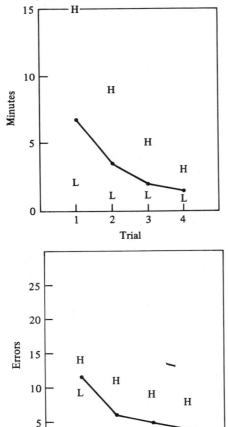

In the earlier part of this century, psychologists speculated about what exactly is learned when a rat or human learns a maze. Some, like John B. Watson, took a "molecular" position and claimed that a sequence of responses is learned. The most critical responses would be those at the choice-points: From this point of view, the learning would be represented as a series of turning instructions (e.g. left, right, right) one for each successive choice-point. Others, such as Edward Chace Tolman, argued that the subject, rat or human, developed a spatial representation of the maze in his head, a "cognitive map," rather than a sequence of responses. What do you think you actually learned in this task?

You should realize that this type of maze differs markedly from the mazes used for rats, or the life-size mazes for humans. In these cases, the subject does not get a direct picture of the whole layout; rather, the subject can only see the part of the maze in the immediate vicinity of the choice-point. This, of course, would make it much harder for the subject to build up a map of the maze. To get a feeling for the difference, cut out a hole about 1/2″ square from the center of a full-sized piece of paper. Place it at the beginning of the fifth duplication of the maze, and attempt to move through the maze with the pencil again, moving the hole along as you move the pencil. If you had learned a series of turns or choices, this procedure should not seriously affect your performance. On the other hand, insofar as you used a "map," or some sort of larger view of the shape of the maze and your path through it, this procedure should seriously affect your performance. *(If your instructor collects the data, fill out the report sheet in Appendix B.)*

FURTHER ACTIVITIES

We have included one extra copy of the maze. You can use this copy for further experiments: If you need more than one maze, you can make a copy of this unused maze.

You might wish to test the idea of a map of the maze versus a set of turning responses, by trying to run the maze backward (start at finish and end at start). What predictions would you make? A cognitive map view would hold that the backward run would be a lot easier than the first run in the "proper" direction, since the same maze map would work in both directions. But a response-learning view would not predict that having learned the maze in the original order would aid in the learning of the reversed maze. The sequence of turns (e.g., left, left, right, left, etc.) would be entirely different when running the maze backward.

Of course, there is a problem here. How do you know how long it would have taken to run the maze backward if you did that on your first trial? You don't. One possibility would be to run a few people on one trial forward and a few others on one trial backward. One could then see if one direction was harder than the other. Another possiblity, not as satisfying, is just to assume that it should be about as easy forward as backward, since it wasn't designed to be more difficult one way than another.

Another activity would be to look at forgetting. Do the final maze in a few days or a week and compare your time and errors to your performance today. Would you expect your performance to be about the same as trial 4? Better than trial 1?

On the following three pages, cover the top (completed) maze while doing the bottom one.

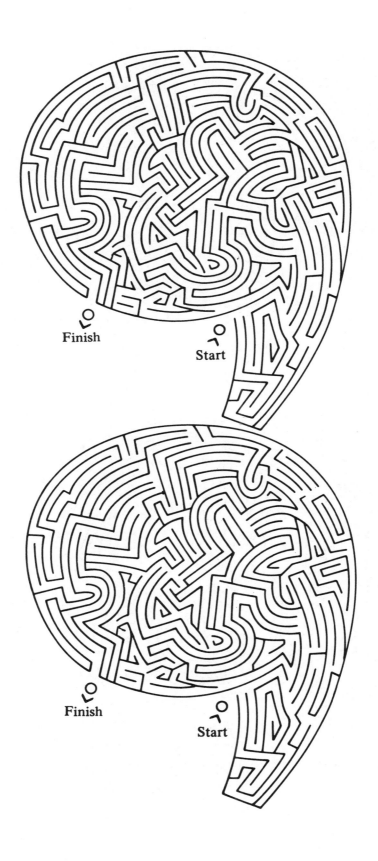

Finish

Start

Finish

Start

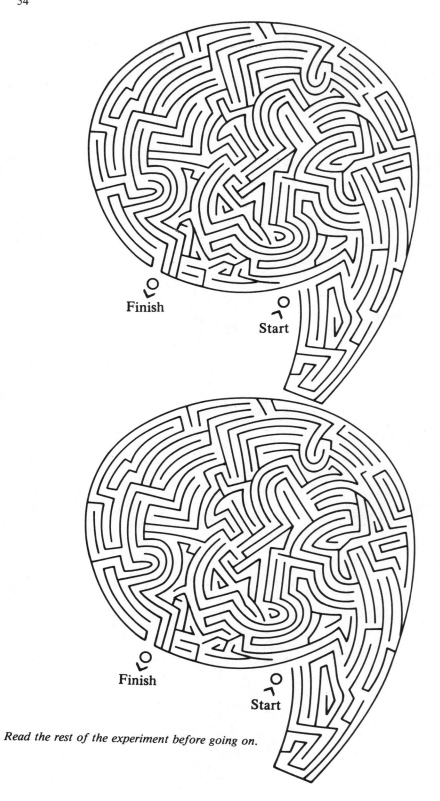

Read the rest of the experiment before going on.

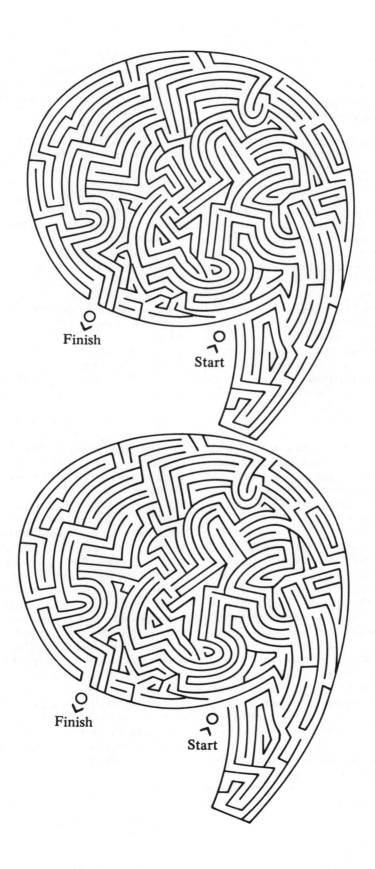

LEARNED TASTE AVERSIONS

Equipment: None
Subjects: Five to eight
Time per Subject: Five minutes
Time for Experimenter: Sixty minutes

One of the basic assumptions of behavior theory is that any conditioned stimulus (CS) could become associated with any unconditioned stimulus (UCS). That is, it is assumed that the relation of the CS to the UCS is arbitrary. This assumption has been seriously challenged by the discovery of the phenomenon of learned taste aversions in rats. As first demonstrated by John Garcia and his colleagues, rats can learn in one trial to associate a taste (CS) with illness (UCS). They will subsequently avoid the taste. This learned taste aversion was of particular importance because Garcia and his colleagues showed that this rapid learning would only occur with tastes as the CS and certain types of illness as the UCS. This specificity of association between tastes and illness is an illustration of belongingness, the nonarbitrariness of associations.

Because learned taste aversions differ from most of the frequently studied types of learning, they were investigated in some detail. We now know that:

1. The specificity (belongingness) is between tastes and specific types of illness: symptoms from the upper gastrointestinal system, especially nausea, seem by far the most effective.

2. The learning typically occurs in one trial (thus allowing rats to avoid poisons without too many life-threatening trials).

3. The rat can accomplish this learning even if the illness follows the taste by more than one hour. This challenges the view that two stimuli must occur close together in time in order to be associated. CS-UCS intervals of more than an hour rarely, if ever, support conditioning in traditional classical conditioning, using salivation or startle responses, and tones, bells, and lights.

4. Novel tastes show much more conditioning than familiar ones. This makes sense: if eating of the familiar food has not been followed by illness, it is reasonable to associate the illness with the new food. This is true in other types of classical conditioning as well: there is generally more conditioning to novel stimuli.

It often happens that after a new phenomenon is described, it is found to be common, and one wonders how it could have escaped notice before. So it was with learned taste aversions. A phenomenon similar to that described by Garcia in the rat seems to occur in humans. Most commonly, someone eats a (usually new) food and gets ill within a few hours. Nausea and vomiting are particularly common symptoms. After this one experience, a person finds the food distasteful. Garb and Stunkard (1974) distributed a questionnaire about such experiences to about 700 people. They found that somewhat over one-third of people have had at least one such experience. The analysis of the results of their questionnaire confirmed the presence of the basic properties of learned taste aversions in humans:

1. Belongingness. Aversions were almost always limited to the food and its taste. Rarely were there reports of aversion to the restaurant, tablecloth, accompanying people, or other stimuli that were also associated, in time, with the illness. Furthermore, the illness in question almost always (87 percent of time) involved the gastrointestinal system.

2. One trial learning. The aversions usually occurred after one food-illness pairing.

3. Long CS-UCS intervals. There was often an interval measured in hours between food ingestion and illness.

4. Novelty. Novel foods (tastes) seem more effective. In spite of the fact that almost everything eaten on any given day would be familiar, 45 percent of the aversions involved foods that had been eaten no more than twice before the pairing with illness.

5. "Irrationality." In many cases, a subject knew that the food did not cause the illness (e.g., other people eating the same food did not get ill, and/or other friends not at the meal came down with the same viral illness at about the same time). Yet, this knowledge that the food did not cause the illness did not weaken the aversion.

We will attempt to confirm the phenomenon of learned taste aversion in humans and highlight its unusual properties. Since, according to Garb and Stunkard, about one-third of people show this phenomenon, we will ask you to interview five to eight people, in the hope that you will find one to four subjects with aversions. We will use an interview protocol that asks many of the same questions covered in Garb and Stunkard's questionnaire. Read the introduction, below, to each subject. If the subject has an aversion, ask each of the questions indicated and record the answers.

LEARNED TASTE AVERSIONS: INTERVIEW PROTOCOL

If a person becomes sick after eating a particular food, he may develop an intense dislike, called an aversion, for that food, whether or not it was responsible for the illness. For example, one person developed a high fever after eating pizza in a restaurant, and found that he did not like pizza any more. Another person became very nauseous after eating a breakfast with hash-brown potatoes, and found the potatoes distasteful after this experience. She also found she did not want to eat from the plate that the potatoes were on. Have you ever come to dislike a food because you became ill after eating it? If so, please answer the following questions:

1. Your current age.

   (Subject A) _____ (B) _____

   (C) _____ (D) _____

2. Age when the aversion experience occurred.

   (A) _____ (B) _____ (C) _____

   (D) _____

3. What is the food? (A) _____

   (B) _____ (C) _____

   (D) _____

4. Describe the experience, in terms of what and where you were eating, and the symptoms of the illness. *(Use extra sheet of paper if necessary.)*

   (A) _____

   _____

   _____

   (B)_____

   _____

   _____

   (C) _____

   _____

   _____

   (D) _____

   _____

   _____

5. Did this happen only once? If more than once, how many times? (A) _____,

   _____ (B) _____, _____

   (C) _____, _____ (D) _____,

   _____

6. What was the most important symptom you had? (A) _____ (B) _____

   (C) _____ (D) _____

7. Were you nauseous? Did you vomit (if not mentioned in answer above)? (A) _____,

   _____ (B) _____, _____

   (C) _____, _____ (D) _____,

   _____

8. About how long after you ate the food did the symptoms appear? (A) _____

   (B) _____ (C) _____ (D) _____

9. Do you believe that the food actually caused your illness? (A) _____ (B) _____

   (C) _____ (D) _____

10. List all the foods that you can remember at the meal before you got sick. Indicate for each food whether it was relatively unfamiliar (you ate it no more than three times in your life). Indicate if you developed an aversion to any of these foods:

	Food	Unfamiliar	Aversion
(A)			
	_____	_____	_____
	_____	_____	_____
	_____	_____	_____
	_____	_____	_____
(B)			
	_____	_____	_____
	_____	_____	_____
	_____	_____	_____
	_____	_____	_____
(C)			
	_____	_____	_____
	_____	_____	_____
	_____	_____	_____
	_____	_____	_____
(D)			
	_____	_____	_____
	_____	_____	_____
	_____	_____	_____

11. List all the other things or events that you can remember at this same meal and in the time after the meal and before the illness (e.g., the restaurant, table settings, people with you, books read, and so on). Indicate if you acquired an aversion to any of these items.

(A) _____

_____

(B) _____

_____

(C) _____

_____

(D) _____

_____

12. Do you still have this aversion?

(A) _____ (B) _____ (C) _____

(D) _____

13. Was (Is) the aversion to the taste, smell, and/or sight of the food?

	Taste	Smell	Sight
(A)	_____	_____	_____
(B)	_____	_____	_____
(C)	_____	_____	_____
(D)	_____	_____	_____

Summarize the results from all of your subjects below. You decide which questions are relevant to each feature of learned taste aversion, and summarize your results with respect to each of the features listed below.

BELONGINGNESS Relevant questions (Nos.)

_____

_____

_____

ONE TRIAL LEARNING Relevant questions (Nos.)

_____

_____

_____

LONG CS-UCS INTERVAL Relevant questions (Nos.)

_____

_____

_____

NOVELTY EFFECT Relevant questions (Nos.)

_____

_____

_____

"IRRATIONALITY" Relevant questions (Nos.)

_____

_____

_____

OTHER INTERESTING RESULTS:

_____

_____

_____

Do your data confirm the basic properties of learned taste aversions?

Comment: Interview protocols like this are quite common in psychological research. They are essentially questionnaires, but they are administered by a researcher or someone on his or her staff. In a way they are more subjective than questionnaires because the interviewer could influence the answers of the subject, especially if there is embarrassing material in the protocol. On the other hand, the interview allows for an interaction between the researcher and the subject: if a subject misunderstands a question, he or she can be corrected. If the subject says something that is ambiguous, it can be expanded. Similarly, if the subject says something of unusual interest, it can be followed up.

The introductory statement in the interview is critical. We tried to write it so as not to guarantee that subjects would only describe specific food aversions based on gastrointestinal illness. Note that we gave one example of another sort of illness and also suggested the possibility of an aversion to items other than tastes. This certainly does not guarantee an "unbiased" sample of aversions, but it allows for exceptions to the phenomena as described by Garcia and, later, by Garb and Stunkard. Garb and Stunkard's introductory paragraph was more suggestive of gastrointestinal illness than is the paragraph we use here. *(If your instructor collects the data, fill out the report sheet in Appendix B.)*

PROBLEMS AND FURTHER ACTIVITIES

Garb and Stunkard's questionnaire and our interview are not experiments. They can demonstrate that one-trial taste-illness aversions occur in humans. But by themselves they cannot demonstrate belongingness. Remember that Garcia's experiments with rats showed that although lights and tastes were equally paired with both illness and electric shock, the taste was much more strongly associated with illness and the lights with shock. Our introduction for the subjects (and more so Garb and Stunkard's) pointed the subject toward taste-illness associations. We did not ask the subjects if they ever got to dislike a restaurant or a person because they were "followed by" illness or whether they ever got to dislike a food because it was followed by pain or a variety of other unpleasant events. On the contrary, we could ask whether, as a consequence of a very unpleasant event such as a death in the family or painful injury, a subject developed an aversion to any object, event, or food. Such questions have not been asked systematically. Do you have any such aversion? Do any of your friends? If there are many aversions linking food with unpleasant events "outside of the body" or outside of the gastrointestinal system, or if there are aversions to visual or other objects paired with illness, then there is little evidence for the belongingness effects in humans. We don't think there *are* many such effects, but we are not sure at this time.

We have suggested that nausea and vomiting are especially important in generating taste aversion. See if you can get evidence for this. If you know anyone (including yourself) with a food allergy, interview him, using a protocol like the one we have used for aversions. (You will have to make a few modifications.) The critical question is whether people with food allergies develop aversions to these foods. In particular, if the allergy produces no symptoms in the gastrointestinal system, is there an aversion? There is some recent data (Pelchat and Rozin, 1982) that suggest that people with food allergies outside of the gastrointestinal system do not have aversions to these foods—that is, they don't dislike these allergenic foods.

References

Garb, F., and Stunkard, A. Taste aversions in man. *American Journal of Psychiatry*, 1974, *131*, 1204–1207.

Logue, A. W., Ophir, I., and Strauss, K. E. The acquisition of taste aversion in humans. *Behavior Research and Therapy*, 1981, *19*, 319–33.

Pelchat, M. L., and Rozin, P. The special role of nausea in the acquisition of food dislikes by humans. *Appetite*, 1982, *3*, 341–51.

CHAPTER 5

Sensory Processes

Learning Objectives

THE ORIGINS OF KNOWLEDGE

The empiricist view
1. Be familiar with the viewpoint of the British empiricists.
2. What is the distinction drawn between proximal and distal stimuli?
3. Understand the difference between sensation and perception.
4. Understand the role of association in the empiricists' view of perception.
5. What is the relevance of visual convergence and of linear perspective in a discussion of association?

The nativist rejoinder
6. How does nativism differ from empiricism? Are the two reconcilable?

PSYCHOPHYSICS

7. What is the sequence of events leading from the stimulus to the reported sensation? Differentiate between the neurophysiological and psychological approaches.

Sensory quality
8. Explain the doctrine of specific nerve energies as it applies both within and between sensory modalities.

Sensory intensity
9. Why is the just-noticeable difference (j.n.d.) important in measuring sensory intensity? What is the implication for absolute threshold?
10. What is Weber's law? How is Weber's fraction used to compare the sensitivities of different sensory modalities?

11. What is the biological rationale for Fechner's law?

Detection and decision
12. What are the various types of errors possible in a detection experiment? How do payoff manipulations affect response bias?
13. What are the characteristics of ROC curves, and how are they used to measure the separate effects of sensitivity and response bias?

AN OVERVIEW OF THE SENSES

Kinesthesis and the vestibular senses
14. Define kinesthesis.
15. Describe the function of the semicircular canals.

The sense of taste
16. What are the four basic taste qualities? How is sensitivity to these distributed on the tongue?
17. Be aware of the different types of sensory interactions, both within and between sensory systems.

The skin senses
18. Be familiar with the four basic skin sensations. How is sensitivity to these distributed over the skin?
19. What is the biological value of pain?

The sense of smell
20. List the primary smell sensations. What underlying principle is responsible for their elicitation?
21. Why is olfaction a minor sense in humans?
22. Be familiar with the various functions of pheromones.

Hearing
23. Sound waves are auditory stimuli. Be aware of their physical and psychological dimensions.

24. Describe the mechanisms by which the ear conducts and amplifies sound waves en route to the auditory receptors.
25. What are the auditory receptors, and how are they stimulated?
26. Compare and contrast the place and frequency theories of pitch perception. What is the evidence for each?

The senses: some common principles
27. What four phenomena are found throughout the sensory system? What are some examples of these phenomena?

VISION

The stimulus: light
28. Visual sensations register the emission and reflection of light. What are the characteristics of light, and what are their visual consequences? `

Gathering the stimulus: the eye
29. How is the eye like a camera?
30. Describe the retinal image.

The visual receptors
31. Be familiar with the following terms: rods, cones, bipolar cells, ganglion cells, optic nerve, and blind spot.
32. Understand the nature of the two types of receptors. What is the evidence for these receptors, and why are they needed?
33. Where is visual acuity greatest and why?
34. Explain the duplexity theory of vision. Refer to spectral sensitivity in discussing the evidence.
35. How are visual pigments similar to and different from the emulsions on film?

Interaction in time
36. What is sensory adaptation? What does the organism gain by sensory adaptation?
37. Explain the technique used to show that stabilization of the retinal image leads to visual adaptation.

38. What is the biological significance of involuntary eye movements?

Interaction in space
39. Recall that brightness contrast increases with progressive intensity difference between two regions and with decreasing distance between them. How is this phenomenon important in visual perception? How do Mach bands illustrate this?
40. Be familiar with the characteristics of receptive fields and the effects of lateral inhibition.

Color
41. Remember that color is a qualitative, rather than quantitative, psychological dimension.
42. What are the dimensions of color?
43. Describe the "unique" colors. What does it mean to refer to a unique color as extraspectral?
44. Are differences in brightness best observed in chromatic or in achromatic colors?
45. Be aware of the role of saturation in distinguishing between chromatic and achromatic colors.
46. Describe the color solid. How are different dimensions of color represented in it? What is its relationship to the color circle?
47. Differentiate between additive and subtractive mixture of colors. Give examples illustrating each.
48. What are complementary colors? How do their antagonistic characters account for simultaneous color contrast and negative afterimages?
49. Explain the difference among the three cone types in human color vision.

Color coding
50. It is important to understand the opponent-process theory thoroughly. Be aware of the relevance of primary colors, color antagonists, and inhibition in the perception of hue and brightness.
51. What is the physiological evidence for the opponent-process theory?

Programmed Exercises

THE ORIGINS OF KNOWLEDGE

1. John Locke postulated that all knowledge comes by way of experience. This school of thought is known as _____.　　　　empiricism

2. Locke used the metaphor of a _____ _____ in describing the human mind at birth.　　　　tabula rasa (blank slate)

3. An object in the real world is known as a _____ stimulus.   distal

4. When the energy from an object impinges on a sensory
   surface, we say that this pattern of energy has become a

   _____ stimulus.   proximal

5. According to the empiricists, complex ideas are perceived by

   the linking together, or _____, of two or more sensations.   association

6. According to the empiricists, one association between sensation

   and motor movement is _____, which is the angular   convergence
   motion of the two eyes as they focus on an object.

7. Two identical objects have different retinal sizes. This clue
   that one object is closer than the other is known as

   _____ _____.   linear perspective

8. Kant believed that a number of aspects of perception are in-

   nate. This view has since been labeled _____.   nativism

PSYCHOPHYSICS

9. The study of the relationship between properties of the stimu-

   lus and sensory experience is known as _____.   psychophysics

10. The _____ _____ is the minimal stimulus energy needed   absolute threshold
    to produce a sensation.

11. There clearly are qualitative differences in sensations. Smells
    are different from sounds. These differences are due to dif-

    ferences in sensory _____.   modality

12. According to the doctrine of _____ _____ _____,   specific nerve energies
    differences in subjective quality are caused by differences in
    associated nervous structures rather than by differences in-
    herent in the stimuli.

13. You find that you are unable to tell the difference between a
    25-lb. weight and a 28-lb. weight, but you can differentiate the
    25-lb. weight from any other weight over 28 lbs. Something

    slightly over 3 lbs. is your _____ _____. It will produce   difference threshold

    a _____ _____ _____ in this weight range.   just-noticeable difference
                                                                        (j.n.d.)
14. A difference threshold is 2 lbs. when the standard is 40 lbs.,

    _____ law predicts that the difference threshold with a   Weber's

    20-lb. standard would be _____ lb.   1

15. The j.n.d. divided by the standard stimulus is known as

    _____ _____ and, in general, seems to be constant.   Weber's fraction

16. Imagine that for a certain psychophysical task we found that
    sensation grew as a function of the logarithm of the physical

    stimulus intensity. This would be support for _____ law.   Fechner's

17. Imagine that we toss a coin 100 times, each time asking a sub-
    ject to predict the outcome (heads or tails). We find that 73

times he predicts heads. We also find that he knows that on the average, 100 tosses will result in approximately 50 heads. We can then attribute his deviation from this figure to a

_____ _____.   response bias

18. One duty of an air traffic controller is to watch a radar screen and determine what planes are in the area. There are two kinds of errors he might make in this task. First, he may not

    see a small dot on the screen, thus committing a _____, as   miss
    it is often called in signal-detection theory. On the other hand, he may report a plane when there is none there. This is called

    a _____ _____. Considering the costs of these two   false alarm

    errors, the _____ _____ error is probably more common   false alarm

    than the _____.   miss

19. Corresponding to the two types of errors, there are also two kinds of correct responses. When an event occurs in the world and we say that the event occurred, that is known as a

    _____. When an event hasn't occurred in the world and we   hit

    say that it hasn't, we have given a _____ _____.   correct negative

20. We have looked at response bias that is caused by the costs of making various types of errors and response bias due to unspecified internal preferences. In a detection experiment, re-

    sponse bias can be altered by varying the _____ _____.   payoff matrix

21. Imagine the following payoff matrix.

Subject says:	yes	no
stimulus present	+$5.00	−$1.00
stimulus absent	−$10.00	+$5.00

    Assuming that the subject would have no response bias if a payoff matrix was used which rewarded "yes" and "no" responses equally, it is most likely that the subject will pro-

    duce more _____ responses with the above matrix.   no

22. If we were to plot proportion of hits against proportion of false alarms, the resulting function would be called an

    _____ _____.   ROC curve

23. The distance of the ROC curve from the diagonal is a measure

    of _____.   sensitivity

24. The main diagonal represents total _____.   insensitivity

25. According to proponents of signal-detection theory, the reason that subjects have trouble telling whether a low intensity stim-

    ulus was presented or not is due to _____ _____.   background noise

AN OVERVIEW OF THE SENSES

26. The _____ _____ indicate rotation of the head. They   semicircular canals

    are located in the _____ _____.   inner ear

27. The taste threshold for _____ is lowest at the tip of the   sweet

    tongue, while that for _____ is at the back; the sides of   bitter

    the tongue best sense _____.   sour

28. Sensory interaction in taste is manifested in _____ to   adaptation
    continually presented stimuli as well as in the influence of

    _____ on taste.   smell

29. The four basic skin sensations are: _____, _____,   pressure, warmth

    _____, and _____.   cold, pain

30. The technical term for smell is _____.   olfaction

31. The sense of smell can be valuable in communication for

    organisms employing _____.   pheromones

32. Light intensity is to vision as _____ is to hearing.   amplitude

33. Hue is to vision as _____ is to audition.   pitch

34. Many different _____ _____, differing in both frequency   sine waves

    and amplitude, combine to form a _____ _____.   complex wave

35. The purpose of the middle ear, oval window, and inner ear is

    to _____ and _____ sound waves.   conduct, amplify

36. The structure which actually contains the auditory receptors is

    known as the _____.   cochlea

37. The actual auditory receptors are the _____ _____   hair cells

    which are stimulated by deformation of the _____ _____.   basilar membrane

38. Pitch perception seems to be based on two mechanisms. High

    frequencies are coded using _____ of excitation, while   place

    lower frequencies are coded by _____ firing rate.   neural

39. The _____ _____ would account for the perception of   volley theory
    tones above 1,000 hertz.

40. For all modalities, stimulus energy must be converted into a
    form which can be used by the senses. The translation is

    termed _____.   transduction

41. Higher neural centers process all sensory input and _____   translate
    this input into various quantitative and qualitative dimensions.

42. Any part of a sensory system is in _____ with the rest of   interaction
    that system.

VISION

43. Light energy can vary in _____, thus giving rise to per-   intensity

    ceived brightness, and in _____, which determines perceived   wavelength
    hue.

44. The visible spectrum extends from roughly _____ to roughly   400

    _____ nanometers.   750

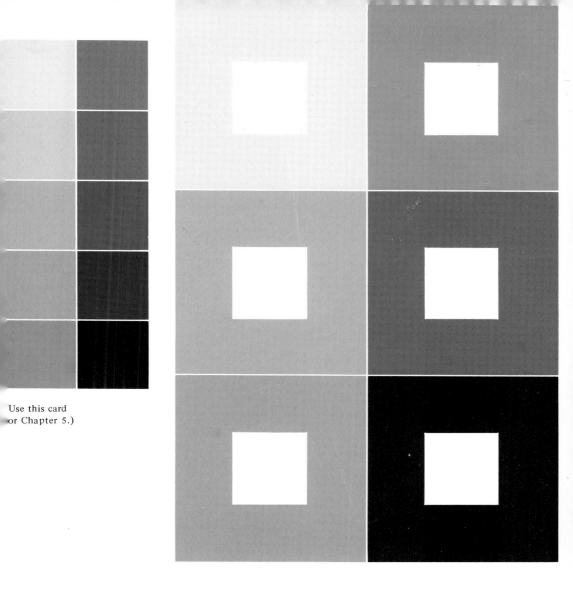

Use this card
or Chapter 5.)

5

1

6   1

7   2

7   3   8   3

9   4

10   5

10   4

6

45. The first place at which light energy from the world interacts with the senses is at the _____.

retina

46. The focusing of the eye is effected by _____ of the lens.

accommodation

47. _____ are most densely packed in the fovea, while _____ are most frequent in the periphery.

Cones, rods

48. The first cells to be stimulated by light are the _____,

receptors

which activate the _____ cells, which in turn stimulate the

bipolar

_____ cells.

ganglion

49. The axons of the ganglion cells form a bundle which is known

as the _____ _____.

optic nerve

50. One person is able to distinguish a one-inch "F" from a one-inch "E" at a distance of 300 feet. Another person is only able to make the same discrimination at 200 feet. These two

people have different _____ _____.

visual acuity

51. The fact that primarily nocturnal animals have no cones and rods, while animals that operate in daylight have many cones

and few rods, is evidence for a _____ theory of vision.

duplexity

52. The fact that sensitivity to dim light is greater in the periphery of the visual field (where rods are) than in the fovea (where

cones are) supports the _____ _____ of vision.

duplexity theory

53. The chemical reaction in which the visual pigment rhodopsin breaks down and then reforms into rhodopsin takes place in

the _____.

rods

54. _____ _____, as examples of visual adaptation, illustrate the role of temporal interaction in vision.

Stabilized images

55. _____ _____, a phenomenon of brightness contrast, are examples of spatial interaction.

Mach bands

56. In doing a single-cell recording, you find that light stimulation of certain places in the retina elicits an increased neural firing rate, stimulation of some places results in decreased firing, and stimulation of others has no effect. The areas that do affect the firing rate, either positively or negatively, are collec-

tively termed the _____ _____ of that cell.

receptive field

57. The physical resolution of the eye is not that good. In terms of physics, we shouldn't be able to see as clearly as we do. However, the exaggeration of contrast through

_____ _____ enhances the visual message.

lateral inhibition

58. The three attributes used to describe color are _____,

hue

_____, and _____.

brightness, saturation

59. _____ colors cannot be distinguished on the basis of hue.

Achromatic

60. Unique red is that red which appears to have neither any

_____ nor any _____ in it.

blue, yellow

61. Only _____ colors can differ in saturation.

chromatic

62. The _____ _____ equates spatial relationships along three dimensions with the three dimensions of color.   color solid

63. Colored filters placed over two different lights which are focused on the same spot produce an _____ color mixture.   additive

64. A _____ hue is one which, when mixed with another hue in the correct proportion, will produce the color gray.   complementary

65. A gray color, when surrounded by green, appears reddish. This is known as _____ _____ _____ and is evidence for antagonistic pairing of colors.   simultaneous color contrast

66. _____ _____ have the complementary hue and the opposite brightness of the original stimulus.   Negative afterimages

67. Human vision is termed _____, since there are three cone types.   trichromatic

68. According to the opponent-process theory of color vision, it should never be possible to see a red hue with a trace of _____ in it.   green

69. Color blindness is most common in _____ and apparently   males

entails the _____ of one of the opponent-process pairs.   absence

Self Test

1. John Locke, the British empiricist, would most likely agree with which of the following statements?
   a. "All knowledge is determined by innate mechanisms."
   b. "We are born with a fair amount of innate knowledge, with experience playing a small role."
   c. "Knowledge arrives through the senses."
   d. John Locke was not an empiricist and would not have agreed with any of the above statements

2. The metaphor which best describes the empiricists' view of the human mind at birth is:
   a. a camera
   b. an encyclopedia
   c. a pad and pencil
   d. a blank slate

3. An example of a distal stimulus would be:
   a. the patterns of light energy hitting the retina
   b. a Chevrolet
   c. the sensation (or perception) produced by a distant mountain
   d. a hallucination

4. An example of a proximal visual stimulus is:
   a. the array of photons that hit the retina
   b. an object situated very close to the retina
   c. a distant object which appears closer than it really is
   d. all of the above

5. The associationists explained depth perception as a result of the association of _____ and _____.
   a. learning, innate knowledge
   b. innate knowledge, body movement
   c. convergence, body movement
   d. convergence, linear perspective

6. Linear perspective serves as a depth cue because:
   a. it produces a memory of the associated experience of depth
   b. it mitigates the effect of convergence
   c. its use by painters has familiarized us with its symbolic representation of depth
   d. we are classically conditioned to accept it as such

7. Immanuel Kant believed:
   a. in innately determined categories of perception

b. that all knowledge came through the senses

c. that associations of sensations determined perception

d. in none of the above

8. The following is an example of transduction:

a. sound waves in the air being translated into electrical energy by a microphone

b. electrical waves being translated into sound waves by a loudspeaker

c. light energy being converted into nerve energy by the retina

d. all of the above

9. Psychophysics studies the relationship between:

a. the distal and proximal stimulus

b. the distal stimulus and sensory experience

c. sensation and perception

d. the proximal stimulus and sensory experience

10. The absolute threshold depends on:

a. the magnitude of the difference threshold

b. the neurophysiological hierarchy of modalities

c. the critical stimulus energy level required by the sensory system

d. differences in experience quality

11. Differences among the taste of a cold beer, the sound of a Mozart quartet, and the sight of a fireworks display are due to:

a. our past experiences with these stimuli

b. differences in the sense organs which respond to the stimuli

c. physiological differences in the conduction velocities of the neurons attached to the various sense organs

d. all of the above

12. If, by some freak of nature, the optic and olfactory nerves were crossed and led each to the opposite sense organ, the law of specific nerve energies would predict the following result:

a. smelling red

b. normal sensations

c. the law of specific nerve energies makes no predictions in such a case

d. any of the above

13. It can be argued that sensations cannot be measured directly. It should be possible, though, to compare sensations. For instance, we should be able to determine whether one sensation is the same as or different from another. This viewpoint would most likely be expressed by:

a. Kant

b. Locke

c. Fechner

d. Müller

14. You are shopping for a new car. You have test-driven a number of cars to determine which models have the best performance. You discover that you cannot tell the difference between models A and C. The difference (however measured) between cars A and C is below your:

a. difference threshold

b. response bias

c. criterion

d. sensitivity

15. Which of the following involves a search for an absolute threshold?

a. trying to determine whether drink A or drink B has more sugar in it

b. trying to determine which instrument in an orchestra is playing the loudest

c. trying to determine whether you were cheated on your Irish coffee (i.e., whether there is really any whiskey in it or not)

d. trying to determine if you detect any difference in your strength after three months of weight lifting

16. Which of the following agrees with Weber's law? (In each case, the first number represents the weight needed to produce a j.n.d., and the absolute stimulus energy is specified by the second number. Two pairs are provided for each possible answer.)

a. 1,10/2,100

b. 20,50/1,2.5

c. 5,100/5,50

d. all of the above are in agreement with Weber's law

17. As in 16 above, each of the pairs of numbers below represents a hypothetical Weber fraction with its associated stimulus energy value. Which of these fractions represents the greatest sensitivity?

a. 1,100

b. 1,10

c. 100,1000

d. 50,1000

18. Fechner's law states that the strength of the sensation increases _____ with stimulus intensity.
    a. inversely
    b. exponentially
    c. logarithmically
    d. linearly

19. A doctor is scanning a lung X ray. He sees something which may be either the beginnings of a tumor or harmless scar tissue. It is likely that response bias will come into play when the doctor decides whether to operate or not. Which of the following factors might influence this response bias?
    a. probability that it is a tumor
    b. risks associated with surgery
    c. risks associated with an untreated tumor
    d. all of the above
    e. none of the above; response bias is constant and cannot be easily changed

20. In the above example, what type of error is worse to make?
    a. false alarm
    b. miss
    c. a and b are equally important
    d. cannot be determined without knowing associated costs and benefits

21. Still considering the example in question 19, imagine that there are five different types of tumors such that each is associated with a different death rate when left untreated. Type I has the highest death rate, and type V has the lowest rate (with the others falling between one and five, in order). Imagine further that these five tumors can be distinguished from each other with X rays, but none of them can be distinguished from scar tissue (which is harmless). Assuming that everything else is constant from one tumor type to another, under which condition would the doctor be most likely to operate and risk putting the patient under the dangers of surgery?
    a. the patient has either scar tissue or type III tumor
    b. the patient has either scar tissue or type V tumor
    c. the patient has either scar tissue or type I tumor
    d. if the doctor was good, the probability of his operating would be constant, despite the type of tumor

22. The ROC curve:
    a. plots proportion of hits against proportion of false alarms

b. represents a subject's sensitivity
    c. separates response bias from pure sensitivity
    d. all of the above
    e. none of the above

23. If, under certain circumstances, a subject's hit rate went up while his false alarm rate stayed the same, we could conclude that his:
    a. response bias changed
    b. sensitivity decreased
    c. sensitivity increased
    d. sensitivity and response bias both changed

24. In which of the situations represented by the following graphs would a subject produce the highest ratio of hits to false alarms?

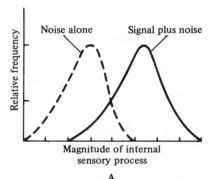

A

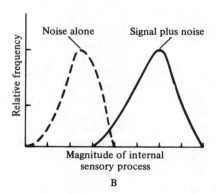

B

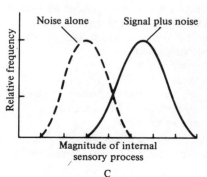

C

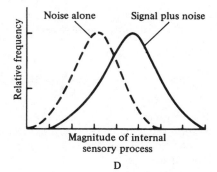

Magnitude of internal
sensory process

D

25. Kinesthesis is:
   a. information from the muscles, tendons, and joints
   b. a function of the ossicles in the inner ear
   c. the movement of hair cells in the cochlea
   d. the crystallization of the viscous liquid in the semicircular canals

26. Head rotation is sensed via:
   a. the pressure of crystals on hair cells in the vestibular sacs
   b. the deformation of hair cells in the semicircular canals
   c. dynamic tension of the relevant musculature
   d. the movement of the world relative to ourselves as we walk through it

27. A little sucrose and quinine are placed simultaneously on opposite sides of the tongue. What will be the primary result?
   a. the bitter taste produced by the quinine will make the sucrose taste sweeter
   b. sensitivity to taste will decline rapidly as the taste buds adapt
   c. the sweet taste produced by the sucrose will enhance the bitterness of the quinine
   d. since the sense of smell was not employed, both the quinine and the sucrose will be tasted equally

28. Pressure:
   a. is assessed via the two-point threshold
   b. is one of the four basic skin sensations
   c. depends on the allocation of cortical space
   d. is the sensation elicited by stimulation of capsule receptors

29. The sense of smell, or olfaction, exhibits which of the following characteristics?
   a. it could classify odors as fragrant, spicy, and putrid
   b. it could classify odors as aromatic, acrid, and rancid
   c. detects chemicals suspended in air
   d. b and c

30. Rats working in a Skinner box are exposed to air taken from the vicinity of a group of rats which suffered electric shock. What will be the probable result?
   a. the rats will exhibit aggressive behaviors
   b. there is no effect
   c. the rats' bar-pressing performance will be disrupted
   d. the pheromone present in the air will render the rats immobile

31. The physical stimulus for hearing is described in terms of amplitude and frequency. The corresponding psychological dimensions are:
   a. loudness and tone
   b. amplitude and pitch
   c. loudness and timbre
   d. loudness and pitch

32. Which pair of the following representative sound waves includes both a simple and a complex wave?

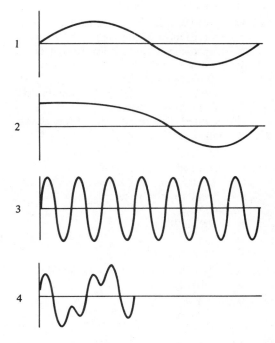

   a. 1 and 3
   b. 2 and 4
   c. 2 and either 3 or 4
   d. either 1 or 2 and 3

33. The correct ordering of anatomical structures in the ear (from outside in) is:
   a. eardrum, middle ear, oval window, cochlea
   b. oval window, middle ear, eardrum, cochlea

c. eardrum, oval window, middle ear, cochlea
d. none of the above

34. For low frequency tones (below 400 hz), pitch is detected by:
    a. a volley response
    b. localization on the basilar membranes
    c. firing frequency of the auditory nerve
    d. none of the above

35. For frequencies between 400 and 1000 hz, pitch is detected by:
    a. a volley response
    b. localization on the basilar membranes
    c. firing frequency of the auditory nerve
    d. none of the above

36. High frequencies are responded to by employing:
    a. a volley response
    b. localization on the basilar membranes
    c. firing frequency of the auditory nerve
    d. none of the above

37. Which of the following are characteristics common to most of the senses?
    a. the presence of anatomical structures
    b. the transduction of the physical stimulus to a neural impulse
    c. the translation of the neural impulse to a dimension of sensation
    d. the interaction of all parts of the sensory system
    e. all of the above

38. One light source appears bluish and another appears greenish. This difference in appearance is due to differences in:
    a. intensity
    b. wavelength
    c. opponent processes
    d. none of the above

39. Intensity is to brightness as wavelength is to:
    a. sensitivity
    b. darkness
    c. wattage
    d. hue

40. Which of the following wavelengths is not considered to be part of the visible spectrum?
    a. 650
    b. 400
    c. 300
    d. 575

41. The structure that bends light rays so that they are projected onto a light-sensitive surface is the:
    a. retina
    b. iris
    c. lens
    d. all of the above

42. During the process of accommodation, a close object will result in _____ of the lens.
    a. thickening
    b. flattening
    c. no change
    d. increased transparency

43. You arrive late to a movie theater and are forced to sit in the far right-hand seat of the first row. You must then look to your left to see the rectangular screen. What is the image of the screen that is projected onto your retina?

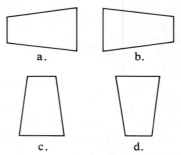

44. The two types of receptors in the human eye are known as _____ and _____.
    a. bipolars, horizontals
    b. ganglions, bipolars
    c. rods, cones
    d. bipolars, cones

45. An area near the center of the retina has virtually no rods, consisting entirely of cones. It is approximately two degrees in diameter and is known as the:
    a. periphery
    b. optic nerve
    c. optic chiasm
    d. fovea

46. In order to maximize visual acuity you should:
    a. stare slightly away from the thing which you are trying to see
    b. use only one eye at a time (to reduce interocular rivalry)

EXPERIMENT 2   STIMULUS LISTS

2	4	6	8	10
RED	BLUE	RED	RED	BLUE
GREEN	BLUE	GREEN	YELLOW	YELLOW
RED	YELLOW	GREEN	YELLOW	GREEN
BLUE	RED	YELLOW	BLUE	YELLOW
YELLOW	GREEN	BLUE	GREEN	BLUE
GREEN	RED	GREEN	RED	RED
YELLOW	BLUE	RED	YELLOW	RED
RED	YELLOW	YELLOW	GREEN	BLUE
BLUE	GREEN	RED	BLUE	YELLOW
GREEN	RED	GREEN	YELLOW	BLUE
YELLOW	RED	RED	YELLOW	RED
GREEN	RED	YELLOW	BLUE	GREEN
GREEN	BLUE	YELLOW	GREEN	RED
GREEN	BLUE	BLUE	RED	GREEN
BLUE	YELLOW	GREEN	BLUE	RED
YELLOW	GREEN	BLUE	BLUE	GREEN

EXPERIMENT 3   STIMULUS LISTS

1	3	5	7	9
STOVE	BOTTLE	STOVE	BOTTLE	ART
ART	STOVE	BOTTLE	ART	BOTTLE
BOTTLE	CAVE	CAVE	CAVE	CAVE
CAVE	BOTTLE	STOVE	STOVE	ART
STOVE	ART	CAVE	BOTTLE	CAVE
CAVE	BOTTLE	ART	CAVE	STOVE
BOTTLE	STOVE	BOTTLE	ART	BOTTLE
ART	CAVE	ART	BOTTLE	STOVE
STOVE	ART	CAVE	CAVE	CAVE
BOTTLE	CAVE	BOTTLE	STOVE	ART
CAVE	STOVE	BOTTLE	CAVE	BOTTLE
BOTTLE	BOTTLE	ART	STOVE	ART
ART	ART	STOVE	CAVE	BOTTLE
CAVE	CAVE	ART	ART	STOVE
STOVE	ART	STOVE	ART	CAVE
ART	STOVE	CAVE	STOVE	BOTTLE

EXPERIMENT 3   STIMULUS LISTS

2	4	6	8	10
GRASS	TOMATO	GRASS	TOMATO	SKY
SKY	GRASS	TOMATO	SKY	TOMATO
TOMATO	FIRE	FIRE	FIRE	FIRE
FIRE	TOMATO	GRASS	GRASS	SKY
GRASS	SKY	FIRE	SKY	FIRE
FIRE	TOMATO	SKY	FIRE	GRASS
TOMATO	GRASS	TOMATO	SKY	TOMATO
SKY	FIRE	SKY	TOMATO	GRASS
GRASS	SKY	FIRE	FIRE	FIRE
TOMATO	FIRE	TOMATO	GRASS	TOMATO
FIRE	GRASS	TOMATO	TOMATO	GRASS
TOMATO	TOMATO	SKY	GRASS	SKY
SKY	SKY	GRASS	FIRE	TOMATO
FIRE	FIRE	SKY	SKY	GRASS
GRASS	SKY	GRASS	SKY	FIRE
SKY	GRASS	FIRE	GRASS	TOMATO

EXPERIMENT 1   STIMULUS LISTS

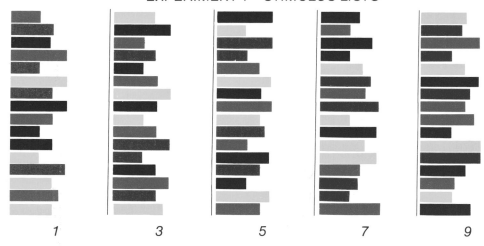

1	3	5	7	9

EXPERIMENT 1   STIMULUS LISTS

SLB	HLMG	SPRNDT	HLMG	CFLTK
CFLTK	SPRNDT	SLB	SLB	HLMG
HLMG	SLB	SPRNDT	CFLTK	SPRNDT
SPRNDT	CFLTK	SLB	SLB	SLB
SLB	SLB	HLMG	HLMG	HLMG
SPRNDT	CFLTK	SPRNDT	CFLTK	SPRNDT
HLMG	SPRNDT	CFLTK	CFLTK	CFLTK
SPRNDT	HLMG	SPRNDT	SPRNDT	HLMG
CFLTK	SLB	HLMG	SLB	CFLTK
SLB	HLMG	CFLTK	SPRNDT	SLB
CFLTK	SPRNDT	SLB	CFLTK	SPRNDT
SLB	SLB	HLMG	SPRNDT	SPRNDT
SPRNDT	CFLTK	HLMG	HLMG	HLMG
CFLTK	SPRNDT	SLB	HLMG	SLB
HLMG	HLMG	CFLTK	SLB	SLB
HLMG	CFLTK	CFLTK	SPRNDT	CFLTK

2	4	6	8	10

EXPERIMENT 2   STIMULUS LISTS

ART	CAVE	ART	ART	CAVE
STOVE	STOVE	BOTTLE	CAVE	BOTTLE
ART	BOTTLE	STOVE	BOTTLE	CAVE
CAVE	ART	BOTTLE	CAVE	BOTTLE
BOTTLE	STOVE	CAVE	STOVE	CAVE
STOVE	ART	STOVE	ART	BOTTLE
STOVE	CAVE	ART	BOTTLE	STOVE
ART	BOTTLE	BOTTLE	STOVE	ART
CAVE	STOVE	ART	CAVE	BOTTLE
ART	CAVE	STOVE	BOTTLE	CAVE
BOTTLE	ART	CAVE	ART	ART
CAVE	BOTTLE	BOTTLE	BOTTLE	STOVE
STOVE	ART	STOVE	STOVE	STOVE
BOTTLE	CAVE	CAVE	ART	ART
CAVE	BOTTLE	ART	CAVE	ART
BOTTLE	STOVE	CAVE	STOVE	STOVE

1	3	5	7	9

c. reduce the luminance of the area, in order to engage the more sensitive rod system
d. look directly at the object

47. Which of the following is not in agreement with the duplexity theory of vision?
    a. the rods are the receptors for night vision, while cones serve day vision
    b. rods respond to low light levels, cones to high levels
    c. rod vision provides good acuity, cones provide poor acuity
    d. rods result in achromatic vision, cones provide color vision

48. In a psychophysical task, we ask a subject to tell us when he can see a dim light. We vary the intensity until he reports that he sees it. We then record the luminance level. Now we change the wavelength against sensitivity. This figure is known as the:
    a. dark adaptation curve
    b. spectral sensitivity curve
    c. receiver operating characteristic (ROC)
    d. sensory adaptation curve

49. What happens when light hits a visual receptor?
    a. silver bromide molecules combine with light to release silver
    b. light strikes the retina and generates rhodopsin
    c. energy is converted to nervous impulses via a photochemical process which bleaches rhodopsin
    d. the reflected light from the receptor causes a photochemical alteration leading to neural excitation

50. Which of the following is an example of sensory adaptation?
    a. the cold ocean feels warmer after we've been in it for a while
    b. being able to see in a dark room after a period of adjustment
    c. increasing sensitivity to salt with continued exposure
    d. all of the above
    e. a and b

51. The first time you see a friend's new car, it is parked against a black wall. Later you see that same car parked against a white backdrop (at the same time of day) and comment that you remember the car as being much brighter.

This is an example of:
    a. brightness contrast
    b. adaptation
    c. temporal interaction
    d. none of the above

52. Using single-cell recordings in the retina, it was found that the firing rate of a cell was affected only when certain areas of the retina were stimulated. This gave rise to the term:
    a. "receptive field"
    b. "visual angle"
    c. "temporal interaction"
    d. "spatial interaction"

53. Lateral inhibition is responsible for which phenomenon?
    a. color vision
    b. Mach bands
    c. Purkinje shift
    d. all of the above

54. Which of the following is not used to classify colors?
    a. brightness
    b. hue
    c. wavelength
    d. saturation

55. White and black can be distinguished only on the basis of which dimension?
    a. brightness
    b. hue
    c. wavelength
    d. saturation

56. Red and green must differ on which dimension (at least)?
    a. brightness
    b. hue
    c. wavelength
    d. saturation

57. White and black cannot possibly differ on which dimension?
    a. hue
    b. saturation
    c. both of the above
    d. none of the above

58. The extent to which a color of some fixed hue is mixed with an achromatic color is represented by a value on the _____ dimension.
    a. brightness
    b. hue
    c. intensity
    d. saturation

59. Which of the following is true of the color
    solid?
    a. the central hoop consists of the colors red,
       green, yellow, blue, orange, purple, in
       that order
    b. horizontal distance from the central axis
       represents brightness
    c. the tilt of the central hoop reflects satura-
       tion
    d. none of the above

60. An example of a subtractive color mixture is:
    a. two spotlights, each with a different filter,
       trained on the same location
    b. the use of two filters on one spotlight
    c. the light as it enters the human eye
    d. all of the above

61. All of the following are examples of additive
    color mixtures except:
    a. color printing
    b. color TV
    c. human color vision
    d. mixing of paints

62. In an additive color mixture, equal amounts
    of complementary hues mixed together will
    produce:
    a. a unique hue
    b. a color with a hue intermediate to the two
       original hues
    c. a hueless color
    d. could be any of the above, depending on
       the choice of hues

63. All of the following are used as evidence for
    color antagonism except:
    a. complementary colors
    b. retinal bleaching
    c. simultaneous color contrast
    d. negative afterimages

64. Any wavelength will stimulate:
    a. all three receptor types, but unequally
    b. all three receptor types, and equally
    c. only one or two receptor types
    d. from one to three receptors, depending on
       the intensity and wavelength

65. In the opponent-process theory, the three
    pairs of receptors are:
    a. red-blue, green-yellow, black-white
    b. red-yellow, blue-green, black-white
    c. red-green, blue-yellow, black-white
    d. never specified

66. An achromatic color results when which
    system(s) is(are) in balance?
    a. red-green
    b. blue-yellow

c. red-green and blue-yellow
d. black-white

67. Which of the following would be predicted
    by the opponent-process theory?
    a. the dark gray appearance of black pepper
       placed against a gray background
    b. chromatic contrast
    c. negative afterimages
    d. all of the above

68. A person who is color-blind will probably:
    a. use color names appropriately
    b. be female
    c. be unable to distinguish any hues at all
    d. be unable to imagine how ultraviolet
       looks to a bee

Answer Key for Self Test

1. c p. 135	35. b p. 154−55
2. d p. 135	36. a p. 155
3. b p. 136	37. e p. 156
4. a p. 136	38. b p. 157
5. c p. 138	39. d p. 157
6. a p. 138	40. c p. 157
7. a pp.138−39	41. c p. 157
8. d p. 140	42. a p. 157
9. b p. 140	43. a p. 157
10. c p. 140	44. c p. 158
11. b p. 140	45. d p. 158
12. a p. 140	46. d p. 158
13. c p. 140	47. c p. 158
14. a p. 141	48. b p. 159
15. c p. 141	49. c p. 159−60
16. b p. 141	50. e p. 160
17. a p. 141	51. a p. 161
18. c p. 142	52. a p. 164
19. d p. 143	53. b p. 163
20. d pp. 143−45	54. c p. 165
21. c pp. 143−45	55. a p. 166
22. d p. 145	56. b p. 165
23. c p. 145	57. c pp. 165−66
24. b p. 146	58. d p. 166
25. a p. 147	59. d p. 167
26. b p. 147	60. b p. 168
27. c p. 148	61. d p. 169
28. d p. 149	62. c p. 169
29. c p. 149	63. b p. 170
30. c p. 150	64. a p. 171
31. d p. 151	65. c p. 171
32. b p. 152	66. c p. 172
33. a p. 153	67. d pp. 171−72
34. c p. 155	68. a p. 173

Investigating Psychological Phenomena

MEASURING BRIGHTNESS CONTRAST

Equipment: Stimuli are included; one sheet of black construction paper needed
Number of subjects: One or more
Time per subject: Ten minutes
Time for experimenter: Twenty minutes

In the "Sensory Processes" chapter, Professor Gleitman describes a phenomenon that clearly illustrates the effect of context on perception. The phenomenon is brightness contrast. Examine Figure 5.21 in the text once again. Note how sharply different in brightness the four central gray squares appear to be; yet they are identical. (You can prove this to yourself by laying a sheet of paper over the figure with holes cut out where the squares are located.) The difference in brightness is apparently a result of interaction between each central square and its surrounding light or dark border. As the text explains, the surrounding border induces a contrast effect such that a patch will appear lighter when surrounded by a dark border, and darker when surrounded by a light border. The greater the difference in lightness between the center and its surroundings, the greater the illusion.

Of course, as you have probably already suspected, brightness contrast has limits. That is, there is just so much illusion that can be produced by a surrounding context, no matter how great the difference between the center and its surroundings. The present experiment provides an opportunity to examine the extent to which the visual system can be fooled by context. More importantly, however, in this exercise you will have a chance to conduct an actual psychophysical experiment to measure quantitatively the relationship between physical stimuli and psychological experience.

The purpose of the experiment is to measure the magnitude of brightness contrast for a particular test patch of a given, fixed lightness. This test patch will be surrounded by several borders that differ in their lightness, one from another. With this arrangement, we should be able to produce different degrees of brightness contrast. But how do we measure the extent of the effect? You might think that we could simply ask a subject to assign numbers to the test patch corresponding to how bright he thought it was. But we shall use a more accurate technique: each

time we present a border around the test patch, we shall ask the subject to match the apparent brightness of the test patch by choosing another patch that seems to match it. The matching patch that is chosen, having been carefully measured for its lightness, will then serve as an index of how light the subject perceived the test patch to be.

First, cut out the matching patches and the borders on the insert for Chapter 5. The matching patches are the ten squares on the left. Note that there is a number on the back of each that corresponds to its lightness. (The units for these numbers have to do with how various lightnesses are actually created by printers, and it is not necessary to know them for this exercise. It is sufficient that the patches are ordered correctly.) Now cut out the six borders on the right side of the insert, and cut out the central square area of each. Note that the borders are also marked with a lightness code on the back. Be very careful with both matching patches and borders to trim away any gray from the adjoining figures so that each cutout is an even gray. On the bottom of the insert is the test patch that has already been placed on a white surrounding region. The test patch has a lightness value of 6. Do not cut out the test figure! Leave it on its background and place this in turn on a sheet of black construction paper.

Now you are ready to run the experiment. The procedure is to select one background, place it over the test patch, and ask your subject to select a matching patch from among his ten choices that appears to match the test patch in brightness. (Be sure that he lays down the matching patch on the black area to the right of the background to be certain of his choice.) Be careful to tell the subject not to hesitate to select different matching patches with different backgrounds if he feels this is appropriate. Subjects may think that because the test patch remains the same, they should always select the same matching patch. Do not let the subject see the test patch without a border between trials, as this may also cause a bias toward a particular matching patch.

Place the matching patches at the top of the black construction paper haphazardly. Run the subject through eighteen trials of the experiment, three trials with each background. In order to have the backgrounds presented in a random order in each set of six, here are three random orders that you may use to determine the order in which the backgrounds are presented: 5, 10, 3, 1, 4, 7; 4, 3, 10, 7, 1, 5; 10, 4, 1, 5, 7, 3 (the numbers refer to the lightness codes on the back of each background).

After you have presented a background over the test patch and the subject has chosen his matching patch, place the value of the matching patch in the appropriate space in the table below. After the experiment is complete, add up the values in each column and divide by three to get an average matching patch value for each background.

Now you can plot these data in the graph provided. Along the x-axis are the six values of background that you used. Above each find the average value of matching patch that you cal-

culated from the table, and place a dot at the value (as determined from the y-axis). Now connect the dots and note the shape of the function.

Recall that the test patch has a lightness value of 6. Given this, what shape should the function have? How much of a brightness contrast were you able to obtain? How could you improve the experiment to get an even larger effect?

Reference

Heinemann, E. G. Simultaneous brightness induction as a function of inducing- and test-field luminance. *Journal of Experimental Psychology*, 1955, *50,* 89–96.

Background values:	1	3	4	5	7	10
matching value 1:	____	____	____	____	____	____
matching value 2:	____	____	____	____	____	____
matching value 3:	____	____	____	____	____	____
Total matching value:	____	____	____	____	____	____
Average matching value:	____	____	____	____	____	____

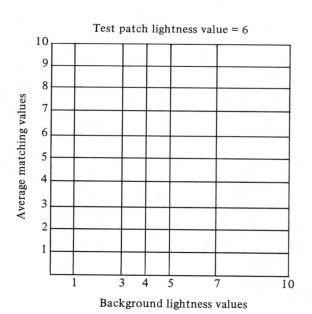

Test patch lightness value = 6

Perception

Learning Objectives

THE PROBLEM OF PERCEPTION

Going beyond the proximal stimulus
1. Keep in mind the characteristics of the proximal stimulus in comparison with the distal stimulus.

Empiricism and nativism revisited
2. How do the empiricists explain the discrepancy between the proximal stimulus and the perceived image?
3. What is the nativists' answer?
4. Regarding perceptual organization, understand the difference between the concept of unconscious inference (based on past experience) and the concept of direct response to the complex characteristics and invariant relationships of stimulus patterns.

PERCEPTUAL ORGANIZATION

The perception of form: what is it?
5. What is the significance of our ability to separate figure from ground? What phenomenon illustrates this ability?
6. What are the laws of perceptual grouping and how do they relate to each other?
7. Be familiar with the arguments and demonstrations in support of a Gestalt viewpoint of form perception. What is the significance of the perception of relationships among component parts of forms?

The perception of depth: where is it?
8. Be aware of the significance of binocular disparity in depth perception.
9. What are the monocular cues to depth perception? What is the evidence that suggests that we must learn to attend to these cues? In what sense are they artificial?

The perception of movement: what is it doing?
10. Be familiar with the explanations proposed to explain stroboscopic and induced movement, and the relevance of these phenomena to the study of real movement.
11. How are we able to distinguish between a moving world with a stationary self (e.g., watching a car go by) and a stationary world with a moving self (e.g., looking out the window of a moving train)?
12. Understand the difference between relative displacement and absolute displacement in perceived stability as it relates to an automatic compensation system in the brain.

PERCEPTUAL SELECTION: ATTENTION

Selection by physical orientation
13. How can the study of orienting movements tell us about attention?

Central selection
14. Be familiar with the concept of central selection and its manifestations in the auditory and visual modes.
15. What evidence suggests that attention is not an "all-or-none" phenomenon? What evidence is there for and against the filter theory of attention?

INNATE FACTORS IN PERCEPTUAL ORGANIZATION

Evidence for innate factors
16. What evidence indicates that young infants have at least a rudimentary ability to perceive various aspects of form and space?
17. How have studies of sensory deprivation in humans and in other animals enlightened us about the innate basis of form perception?

18. What do feature detector cells do? What are two examples of features that these cells detect?

19. How have adaptation studies shed light on the nature of feature detectors?

20. Given the existence of "prewired" systems in feature detection and the actual perception of organized wholes, what can be concluded about the empiricist/nativist debate concerning form perception?

LEARNED FACTORS IN PERCEPTUAL ORGANIZATION

Perceptual adaptation

21. What is the effect of wearing distorting lenses for a significant period of time? What does this tell us about perceptual plasticity?

22. Recount the evidence for the importance of active movement in perceptual adaptation.

23. Compare and contrast adaptation in visual receptors and feature detectors. What role does adaptation play in perceptual organization?

Perceptual differentiation

24. Discuss perceptual differentiation in terms of discrimination and distinctive features and in relation to the empiricist/nativist controversy over form perception.

Perceptual problem solving

25. Describe feature analysis as an approach to pattern recognition. What evidence leads scientists to believe that humans use a feature analysis approach to recognize forms?

26. How is context related to top-down processing? Give examples of context effects.

27. What roles do bottom-up and top-down processes have in perceptual processing? Explain how they work hand in hand.

28. Be able to state the goal of perceptual problem solving. Explain why and how impossible figures pose a perceptual problem for us.

THE PERCEPTION OF REALITY

The perceptual constancies

29. Understand lightness constancy and relevant terms such as reflectance, luminance, and illumination. What is the brightness ratio?

30. Recall Helmholtz's point of view regarding size constancy. What evidence suggests that size constancy is, to some extent, innately given?

31. Be familiar with what an illusion is. What are the reasons for the moon illusion and the Ponzo and Müller-Lyer illusions? Of what benefit is the study of illusions?

Programmed Exercises

THE PROBLEM OF PERCEPTION

1. The properties of a three-dimensional distal stimulus are perceived as constant despite continuing variation of the _____ stimulus.

proximal

2. According to the empiricists, prior learning of the rules relating retinal image and depth cues leads to the _____ inference of true size.

unconscious

3. Nativists stress the importance of _____ relationships within a stimulus pattern in explaining perceptual organization.

invariant

PERCEPTUAL ORGANIZATION

4. Contour looks very different depending upon the figure-ground organization; it is always seen as part of the _____ and never as belonging to the _____.

figure

ground

5. _____ figures (like the one at the top of the next page) are ones in which either of two figure-ground organizations is possible.

Reversible (ambiguous)

Royalist print from the French Revolution in which can
be seen the profiles of Marie Antoinette and Louis XVI
and their children.

6. Proximity, similarity, and closure are examples of the laws of

    _____ _____ .   perceptual grouping
                           (organization)

7. Contours that continue smoothly along their original course

    follow the law of _____ _____ .   good continuation

8. A melody can be recognized even when played in different
   keys. This indicates that we can recognize patterns even after

    _____ .   transposition

9. The _____ psychologists were a group who are identified   Gestalt
   with the phrase "The whole is different from the sum of its
   parts."

10. The two eyes look out on the world from slightly different
    positions and thus obtain a somewhat different view of any
    solid object on which they converge. This is called

    _____ _____ .   binocular disparity

11. Relative size is an example of a _____ depth cue.   monocular

12. Abrupt change in a _____ _____ produces the impres-   texture gradient
    sion of a sharp drop, a "visual cliff."

13. Far-off objects are blocked from view by other opaque objects
    that obstruct their optical path to the eye. This is a depth cue

    called _____ .   interposition

14. As we move our head or body from right to left, the images
    projected by the objects outside will move across the retina.
    The direction and speed of this motion is an enormously effec-

    tive monocular depth cue called _____ _____ .   motion parallax

15. Suppose we briefly turn on a light in one location in the visual
    field, then turn it off, and after an appropriate period of time
    (somewhere between 30 and 200 msec), turn on a second light
    in a different location. The resulting phenomenon is called

    _____ movement.   stroboscopic

16. If the ground is moving and a figure is stationary in the visual field, the figure is seen as moving. This phenomenon of illusory movement is called _____ movement.   induced

17. The perception of movement in one of two stimuli depends on which is seen as a stationary _____ of reference.   frame

18. Perceived _____ seems to be a result of the brain's compensation for the retinal displacement caused by voluntary eye movements.   stability

PERCEPTUAL SELECTION: ATTENTION

19. The ways by which we perceive selectively are grouped under the label "_____."   attention

20. On the average, our eyes move four or five times per second. Each time they move they _____ at one particular region.   fixate

21. When stimuli are presented over earphones so that each ear receives a different message, this is called a _____ presentation.   dichotic

22. When a subject is asked to _____ a message, he is repeating it aloud, word for word, as it comes over one of his earphones.   shadow

23. The attentional _____ attenuates irrelevant messages as a whole, but may pass items from them that are important or familiar.   filter

INNATE FACTORS IN PERCEPTUAL ORGANIZATION

24. Infants appear to have an innate form preference for _____ _____.   human faces

25. When William Molyneux asked John Locke about how a man born blind would see the world if his vision were suddenly restored, he was asking about the effect of sensory _____.   deprivation

26. Cataract patients with restored vision can distinguish between figure and ground but have difficulty in perceiving _____ _____.   form equivalence

27. A nerve cell in a sensory system that is found to respond only to a narrow range of physical stimulation has been called a _____ _____. The "bug sensitive" cell in the frog is an example of such a cell.   feature detector

28. Some of the cells found by Hubel and Wiesel, called _____ cortical cells, react to stationary lines of a particular orientation.   simple

29. A kind of cell which reacts to stationary or moving lines of certain orientation over a wide range of locations on the retina is called a _____ cortical cell.   complex

30. If one looks at a waterfall for a while and then turns away to look at the riverbank, that bank and the trees upon it will

seem to float upward. This is an example of the _____ of visual movement.

aftereffect

LEARNED FACTORS IN PERCEPTUAL ORGANIZATION

31. One kind of perceptual learning that results when an organism has been exposed to a particular pattern of stimulation for a

long time is called perceptual _____. An example is the classic inverted lens experiment by Stratton.

adaptation

32. Fingerprint experts, wine connoisseurs, and various other experts have learned to respond to distinctive features of various stimuli that the rest of us simply fail to perceive. The

Gibsons call this phenomenon perceptual _____.

differentiation

33. Attributes of an object that distinguish it from others in its

class are called _____ _____.

distinctive features

34. An approach to pattern recognition based on an analysis of

visual features is called _____ _____.

feature analysis

35. The _____ _____ process of pattern recognition starts with small component parts (the features) and builds up to larger units (letters, words, phrases, etc.).

bottom-up

36. The _____ _____ process of pattern recognition begins with higher units, because it is often affected by higher-level knowledge and expectations.

top-down

37. _____ effects demonstrate that there is some top-down processing in the perceptual process.

Context

38. Perceptual processing is necessarily in both directions: from

_____ _____ and also from _____ _____.

top down, bottom up

39. An _____ figure poses a perceptual contradiction for a subject. It poses a perceptual problem which cannot be solved.

impossible

THE PERCEPTION OF REALITY

40. The perceptual system responds to real objects outside regardless of variations in their proximal images. This is best illus-

trated by the perceptual _____: lightness, size, and shape.

constancies

41. The apparent lightness of an object remains fairly constant despite rather drastic changes in the amount of illumination

that falls upon it. This is called _____ _____.

lightness constancy

42. A Boeing 707 at a distance of 1,000 feet will look larger than a single-engine two-seater at a distance of 50 feet despite the fact that the retinal image of the latter will be greater than

that of the former. This is called _____ _____. An

size constancy

analogous phenomenon occurs in the perception of _____.

shape

43. Since we compensate for distance when perceiving size, mis-

    judgment of distance can lead to perceptual _____ .   illusions

Self Test

1. Which of the following is not true of the proximal stimulus?
   a. it is two-dimensional in vision
   b. it can vary in size and shape
   c. it alone enables us to perceive the constant properties of objects
   d. it is the retinal image of the distal stimulus in vision

2. Unconscious inference:
   a. is a nativist argument
   b. operates independently of depth cues
   c. operates independently of retinal image
   d. depends on prior learning of a general rule

3. Segregating figure from ground (as in a reversible figure):
   a. is a high-level perceptual process that requires a good deal of preliminary analysis
   b. can only be done with reversible figures
   c. is accomplished by perceiving the contour separating the two regions as belonging to the ground
   d. is too elementary a perceptual process to be used effectively by artists
   e. none of the above

Reversible figure that can be perceived either as two faces in profile or as a white vase (Rubin, 1921).

4. For reversible figures such as the one in the left column, which of the following is false?
   a. the figure is generally seen in front of the ground
   b. a reversible figure-ground display is characterized by two adjoining regions alternately acting as figures
   c. a contour can be seen as simultaneously belonging to figure and ground
   d. none of the above

5. All of the following are "laws of perceptual organization" except:
   a. proximity
   b. similarity
   c. good continuation
   d. simplicity
   e. closure

6. The law of proximity states that:
   a. the closer an object is to an observer, the easier it is to identify it
   b. the closer two objects are to each other, the greater the chance that they will be grouped together perceptually
   c. given any two objects, one is always nearer (perceptually) to an arbitrary third object than the other
   d. none of the above

7. Closure is a special case of:
   a. proximity
   b. similarity
   c. good continuation
   d. perspective

8. The phenomenon of transposition refers to:
   a. figure-ground reversal
   b. the same percept resulting from different proximal stimuli
   c. the overlap of two figures, which causes the viewer to see them in depth
   d. the induced movement caused by the repositioning of a surrounding contour
   e. none of the above

9. According to the Gestalt point of view, we perceive _____ rather than individual retinal points per se.
   a. features of forms
   b. closure

c. relations among stimuli
d. all of the above

10. Binocular disparity is caused by:
    a. a slight difference in the size of the two eyes
    b. small imperfections in the lens and/or cornea
    c. the slightly different position of each eye
    d. the favoring of one eye over the other

11. Binocular disparity:
    a. is an effective cue to depth for long distances
    b. is due to the fact that our eyes receive virtually the same image
    c. is not by itself a sufficient cue to depth
    d. can be simulated by viewing specially designed 2-dimensional drawings
    e. is only effective for familiar objects

12. The figure below illustrates all of the following monocular cues to depth except:
    a. linear perspective
    b. relative size
    c. binocular disparity
    d. texture gradients
    e. interposition

13. The impression of a "visual cliff" is accounted for by which depth cue?
    a. linear perspective
    b. relative size
    c. texture gradients
    d. interposition

14. One of the most effective monocular depth cues is _____, which is absent in pictorial representations but present in real life.
    a. linear perspective
    b. relative size
    c. interposition
    d. motion parallax

15. Stroboscopic movement refers to:
    a. the perception of movement when two stimuli are presented in alternation at the proper temporal and spatial intervals
    b. the perception of movement of a target when in fact it is stationary but the background is moving
    c. the perception of self-movement when you are stationary but the scene that you are watching is moving
    d. all of the above
    e. none of the above

16. Induced movement differs from stroboscopic movement in that:
    a. in the former case it is the figure that moves, while in the latter case it is the ground that moves
    b. the former is a physical phenomenon, while the latter is a retinal phenomenon
    c. induced movement is based on relative displacement, while stroboscopic movement is based on absolute displacement
    d. none of the above

17. Which two of the following are examples of induced movement?
    a. the moon moving through the clouds
    b. perceiving movement of a stationary spot of light in darkness
    c. perceiving movement of a stationary spot of light when the rectangular frame around it moves
    d. perceiving that the moon moves when you move with respect to it
    e. perceiving movement in the successive frames in a movie

18. When several investigators temporarily paralyzed their eye muscles and then tried to move their eyes, they saw objects move in their visual field even though their eyes did not actually move (nor did the objects). This suggests that:
    a. paralyzing the eye muscles doesn't affect motion perception
    b. perceived stability is produced by compensating for motor movement
    c. perceived motion is produced by compensating for motor movement
    d. none of the above

19. Orienting movements like turning of the head and convergence and accommodation of the eyes are all external manifestations of:
    a. differentiation
    b. attention
    c. recalibration
    d. adaptation

20. Which of the following is untrue of dichotic presentations?
    a. the subject is asked to shadow the to-be-attended message
    b. he is able to recall the message that came by way of the unattended ear
    c. he does not notice if the speaker on the unattended ear shifts into another language
    d. he wears two earphones and receives different messages through each of them

21. The results of Gibson and Walk's visual cliff experiment (illustrated below) suggests that:
    a. infants cannot use motion parallax as a cue to depth
    b. infants' eye fixations tend to be directed to edges and vertices
    c. depth perception is largely innately given
    d. texture gradients are not useful cues to distance
    e. none of the above

22. Research on the effects of early visual deprivation in humans and other animals has demonstrated all of the following except:
    a. form perception and form discrimination are seriously impaired after prolonged deprivation
    b. size discrimination is not very seriously affected
    c. color discrimination is not very seriously affected
    d. depth perception is not affected by prolonged visual deprivation

23. Studies of humans who have recovered sight suggest that:
    a. such individuals can't "see" unless they can also touch
    b. all form perception is learned
    c. all form perception is innate
    d. there is a period of serious deficiency following recovery

24. After a long presentation of a red light, the retinal receptors do not respond very much to further presentation of the light. This is an example of:
    a. adaptation
    b. sensitization
    c. generalization
    d. none of the above

25. Selective visual adaptation experiments have demonstrated which of the following?
    a. there are cells in the visual system sensitive to directional movement
    b. whole patterns disappear when their images are stabilized on the retina
    c. detectors for complex figures exist in the visual cortex
    d. none of the above

26. Which of the following statements about perception is not true?
    a. the same proximal stimulus can lead to more than one percept
    b. self-produced movement plays a vital role in some perceptual learning
    c. a subject whose movements have accommodated to distorted visual input will respond normally as soon as the distorting goggles are removed
    d. subjects' upside-down view of the world appears normal after they have been wearing inverted prisms for a period of time
    e. the visual system is capable of adaptation to extreme distortion of the visual world

27. A subject wears goggles with wedge prisms that distort all vertical lines into curves to the left. The effect of the goggles is shown in the figure below. Panel A shows a figure seen without goggles; panel B shows the same figure seen head-on with goggles; panel C shows the contraction that results when looking at the left of the figure with goggles; panel D shows the expansion that results when looking at the right of the figure. The subject wears these goggles for a week, during which time all vertical lines like | are distorted to look like (. After a week, the subject removes the goggles, then he looks at a curve that objectively is this: (. How will it appear?

   a.)   c. (
   b. | d. ⊂

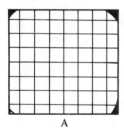
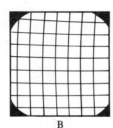

A   B

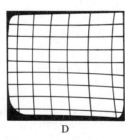

C   D

28. While wearing displacing goggles, subjects were asked to point to a target with their right hand. They were not able to see their left hand. Upon removal of the goggles, subjects displayed the usual visual aftereffect with their right hand but not with their left. This finding:
    a. makes the position that sight is dominant over touch untenable
    b. makes the position that touch is dominant over sight untenable
    c. says nothing about the relation between sight and touch
    d. violates the law of transposition

29. There are many studies dealing with sensory adaptation. Some involve chromatic adaptation; others concern inversions, displacement, or curvature. In all cases, though, when the adapting stimulus is removed:
    a. the system swings too far in the other direction
    b. the effects noted during adaptation remain
    c. the subject cannot tell whether he is seeing things "normally" or not
    d. misjudgments as in the "moon illusion" are common

30. The ability to learn to respond to distinctive features is known as:
    a. stimulus specificity
    b. generalization
    c. differentiation
    d. response specificity

31. Which of the following is not true of the effects of selective attention?
    a. some information from an unattended channel can trigger attention while the rest is lost
    b. information blocked by an attenuation mechanism nonetheless can affect the connotative meaning of what we attend to
    c. response bias effects may account for some selective attention phenomena
    d. response bias may account for the effect of better tachistoscopic recognition of frequent as opposed to infrequent words
    e. none of the above

32. Pattern recognition is a:
    a. top-down process
    b. horizontal process
    c. bottom-up process
    d. a and c
    e. a and b

33. A professor is giving a lecture on the state of the U.S. economy. His lecture is suddenly broken up by several coughs which interrupt but do not stop his speech stream. Although there are physical gaps in the utterance, the students hear and understand the presentation. This is an example of:
    a. feature analysis
    b. context effect
    c. bottom-up processing
    d. attention

34. The fact that a white object in the shade appears lighter than a gray object in the sunlight (even though the gray object has greater luminance) is called:
    a. relative luminance
    b. perceived intensity
    c. lightness constancy
    d. none of the above

35. It is likely that six-month-old infants exhibit some measure of:
    a. angle constancy
    b. depth constancy
    c. lightness constancy
    d. size constancy

36. The moon looks larger at the horizon than it does when up in the sky because:
    a. the horizon looks farther away than the overhead sky
    b. the sky looks farther away than the horizon
    c. the retinal image of the moon is different in each case
    d. none of the above

Answer Key for Self Test

1. c	p. 180	19. b	p. 191
2. d	p. 181	20. b	pp. 193–94
3. e	p. 182	21. c	p. 195
4. c	p. 182	22. d	pp. 196–97
5. d	pp. 183–85	23. d	pp. 196–97
6. b	p. 183	24. a	pp. 197–98
7. c	p. 185	25. a	p. 198
8. b	p. 185	26. c	p. 200
9. c	pp. 185–86	27. b	p. 200
10. c	p. 186	28. b	p. 200
11. d	pp. 186–87	29. a	p. 200
12. c	pp. 186–88	30. c	p. 201
13. c	p. 188	31. e	pp. 193–94
14. d	p. 189	32. d	pp. 202–203
15. a	p. 189	33. b	p. 203
16. c	pp. 189–90	34. c	p. 207
17. a,c	p. 190	35. d	p. 209
18. b	p. 191	36. a	p. 210

Investigating Psychological Phenomena

THE EFFECT OF MENTAL SET

Equipment: Stimuli are included
Subjects: One
Time per subject: Twenty minutes
Time for experimenter: Twenty minutes

The issue of how past experience influences perception (an example of top-down processing) is an important one in psychology and has generated quite a bit of research. This is a difficult issue to resolve because there are many ways in which past experience might influence perceptual processes. In this problem you are asked to consider a series of hypothetical experiments (modeled after a study by Epstein and Rock, 1960) and to provide alternative interpretations of the hypothetical results. As you move through the experiments, try to develop one hypothesis which will account for all of the results that are described. The stimuli for all the experiments are the ambiguous and unambiguous versions of Leeper's old woman—young woman figure shown on the next page.

Notice that the first picture (A) can be seen either as a young woman or as an old woman, that is, it is ambiguous. The second picture (Y) is quite similar to the first (A) except that some detail has been changed so that it has become a fairly unambiguous picture of a young woman. Likewise, the third picture (O) is a fairly unambiguous version of an old woman. The purpose of all the experiments is to determine how prior exposure to the unambiguous versions of the figure influences whether subjects call the ambiguous version an old woman or a young woman. Imagine that twenty subjects are run in each hypothetical experiment.

EXPERIMENT 1

Each subject is shown the following series of slides (at a rate of one slide every eight seconds) and asked to name each picture as "young" or "old" as it is presented: YYOOOOOOOOA (Y refers to a presentation of the unambiguous young woman, O refers to a presentation of the unambiguous old woman). All subjects name the Y and O versions of the figure correctly. On the critical trial, the ambiguous picture A, the results are as follows: Twenty subjects call it "old," no subjects call it "young." One interpretation of this result is that the more frequently presented unambiguous version determined the perception of the ambiguous picture. This is listed as hypothesis 1 on the answer sheet. What alternative explanations can you propose to explain the responses of subjects in this hypothetical experiment? Write them on the answer sheet. There are at least three other plausible possibilities.

Before you go on to experiments 2 through 4, check to see whether the hypotheses you have developed coincide with those given in the answers to the problem. If not, use the given hypotheses as the basis for your answers to the questions posed in experiments 2 through 4.

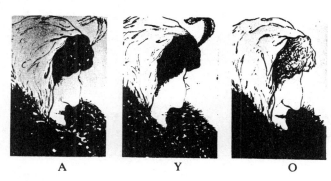

A   Y   O

EXPERIMENT 2

A new set of twenty subjects receives the series: YYYYYOOOOOA. Again the responses to all the Y and O stimuli are correct, and the responses to the A stimulus are as follows: Twenty subjects respond "old woman," none respond "young woman." Consider each of the four hypotheses raised to account for the results of experiment 1 and evaluate how each fares with the results of this experiment. Record your responses under experiment 2 on the answer sheet.

EXPERIMENT 3

Twenty subjects each receive the series: OOOOOOOYYYA. All respond correctly to the Y and O stimuli; the responses to A are: Twenty subjects call it "young woman," none call it "old

woman." Again evaluate the success of each of the four hypotheses at accounting for these results.*

EXPERIMENT 4

Twenty new subjects are shown the series: YYOYYOYYOA. All O's and all Y's are identified correctly; the data on the A presentations are: Eighteen subjects respond "old woman," two subjects respond "young woman." (A reliable difference.) Which of the four hypotheses can explain these results? Is one of the four hypotheses confirmed by the results of all four experiments?

*We continue to consider hypothesis 1 even though experiment 2 cannot be explained by it; scientists do not typically discard an hypothesis because of a single contradictory finding.

ANSWER SHEET

Experiment 1

Hypothesis 1 Frequency of presentation determines the response to the ambiguous figure.

Hypothesis 2 _____

_____

Hypothesis 3 _____

_____

Hypothesis 4 _____

_____

Experiment 2

Hypothesis 1 _____

_____

Hypothesis 2 _____

_____

Hypothesis 3 _____

_____

Hypothesis 4 _____

_____

Experiment 3

Hypothesis 1 _____

_____

Hypothesis 2 _____

_____

Hypothesis 3 _____

_____

Hypothesis 4 _____

_____

Experiment 4

Which of the four hypotheses can account for these results? _____

_____

_____

Which hypothesis can account for the results of all four experiments? _____

_____

_____

Answers to problem

EXPERIMENT 1:

Hypothesis 2: It is possible that the interpretation of the ambiguous picture was entirely influenced by the perception of the immediately preceding picture of the old woman. If so, this would be called a "recency effect," because the most recently presented picture would have had the strongest influence on perception of the ambiguous picture.

Hypothesis 3: An alternative possibility has to do with what the subject might be expecting to be presented on the last trial. He has just seen eight consecutive pictures of the old woman and so he might reasonably expect that the next picture will also be that of an old woman. Thus, if this were the case, the subject's cognitive expectations would be guiding his perceptions.

Hypothesis 4: A final possibility is that subjects in general have a bias to respond with the name "old woman." One might suppose that such a bias exists (for some reason) even independently of what the subject actually sees. That is, subjects are biased to call the ambiguous version an "old woman" regardless of what precedes it.

EXPERIMENT 2:

This experiment rules out hypothesis 1, the frequency hypothesis. Both unambiguous versions were presented equally frequently before the ambiguous version was presented. Thus, a subject's perception of the ambiguous version could not have been influenced by the more frequently presented unambiguous version. None of the alternative hypotheses is ruled out by these results: (a) The response to the ambiguous version was the same as that to the most recently presented unambiguous version. Thus, recency is a viable interpretation of these results. (b) Because the responses to the sixth through tenth stimuli were "old woman," the subjects may have built up an expectation that the eleventh stimulus would be an old woman as well. So cognitive expectations may well have guided their response to the ambiguous item. (c) The fact that most subjects identified the ambiguous picture as an old woman is consistent with the possibility that they have a bias to call it that regardless of their immediately prior perceptual experience.

EXPERIMENT 3:

Once again this experiment disconfirms the frequency hypothesis. This time subjects responded to the test picture with the name of the *least* frequently presented unambiguous picture. Also, this experiment rules out hypothesis 4, which states that subjects have a predisposing bias to call

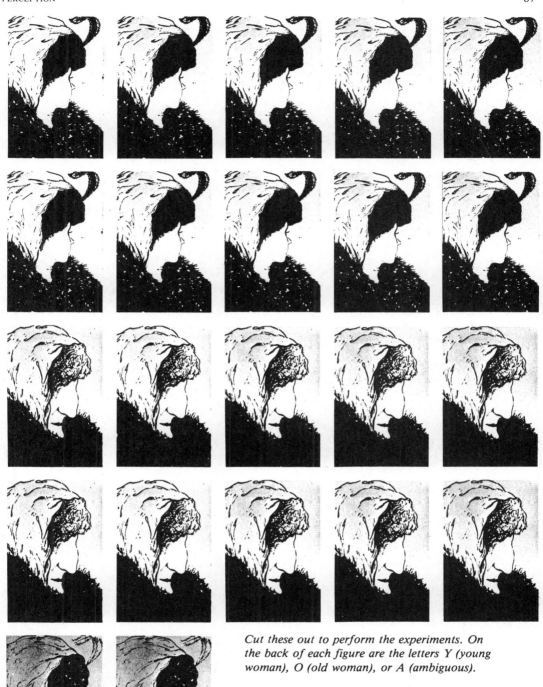

Cut these out to perform the experiments. On the back of each figure are the letters Y (young woman), O (old woman), or A (ambiguous).

Y   Y   Y   Y   Y

Y   Y   Y   Y   Y

O   O   O   O   O

O   O   O   O   O

A   A

the ambiguous version an old woman. But both the recency and the cognitive expectation hypotheses can account for the results.

EXPERIMENT 4:

The cognitive expectation hypothesis probably is ruled out. In responding to the unambiguous versions, subjects were following a regular pattern of two "young woman" responses followed by one "old woman" response. The last unambiguous picture was that of the old woman; thus, subjects should have been expecting a young woman next. Instead most responded "old woman," a result that can only be explained by noting that the most recently presented unambiguous picture was that of the old woman. Thus, the recency explanation is compatible with these results. Once again the frequency hypothesis is disconfirmed because the most frequently presented unambiguous picture was the young woman. The response bias explanation might be brought up to explain the results of this experiment except that it was ruled out by experiment 3. Thus, the only explanation which satisfactorily can explain the results of all four experiments is hypothesis 2, which claims that the picture which a subject sees most recently will affect his current perception.

This exercise demonstrates how it is sometimes possible to start with several potential explanations of a phenomenon and successfully rule out the incorrect ones with further experimentation. Initially there were four plausible interpretations of the results of hypothetical experiment 1. The results of hypothetical experiments 2 through 4, however, rule out all but one of the alternatives.

Even though the experiments described above are only hypothetical, they illustrate this process of narrowing down alternative interpretations. You may want to try out any of these experiments to determine the actual results. On page 87 you will find sets of pictures of both the unambiguous versions and the ambiguous version of the figure. Cut them out and return to the previous pages of this section. Perform the experiments as described there and record the results. Do your results correspond to the hypothetical data? Do the same hypotheses apply?

Reference

Epstein, W., and Rock, I. Perceptual set as an artifact of recency. *American Journal of Psychology*, 1960, *73*, 214–228.

CHAPTER 7

Memory

Learning Objectives

ACQUISITION, STORAGE, AND RETRIEVAL

1. You should know that there are three major processes that must be understood in studying memory: acquisition, storage, and retrieval.

Encoding

2. What is meant by encoding? Is there more than one possible way of encoding an item? Explain.

Recall and recognition

3. What is the difference between retrieval by recall and retrieval by recognition?

THE SENSORY REGISTERS

The icon

4. How did Sperling demonstrate the existence of the icon using a partial report procedure? What is the logic behind this procedure? What happens when the partial report cue is delayed?

5. What evidence argues against the view that the icon is an afterimage?

Icon and echo as unprocessed information

6. Be aware of the kind of information that the sensory registers are presumed to store. To what extent is information processed at this level?

SHORT-TERM MEMORY

Some characteristics of short-term memory

7. Is the capacity of short-term memory limited or unlimited? How do you know?

8. What is the memory span of normal adults, and what does this number represent?

The paths from short-term memory

9. Describe a way of measuring forgetting in short-term memory. Why is it important to prevent rehearsal?

10. What is the difference between decay and displacement theories of forgetting?

11. Because information can be retrieved from both long-term and short-term memory, one can't always tell which store retained it. How does the study of free recall help deal with this problem?

12. Describe how reaction time methodology allows one to study retrieval from short-term memory. What are the predictions of serial versus parallel search theories about retrieval reaction times? What does the evidence show?

THE ACQUISITION OF LONG-TERM MEMORIES

The associationist tradition

13. Describe the major claims of philosophers who believed that associations are the glue that binds memories.

14. Be cognizant of Ebbinghaus's major findings. Recount his assumptions and reasoning, and describe the technique he used to study memory.

15. What does transfer of training tell us about the role of associations in memory?

Long-term memory and organization

16. Describe some general arguments that suggest that one must go beyond the study of associations to understand memory.

17. Why is recoding of input information an important process in the transfer of information from short-term to long-term memory?
18. Chunks of items can be created in various ways. You should be aware of the roles of grammatical relationships and semantic relationships in this process.
19. Be aware that encoding of information within a thematic context will help in recall.
20. How are items best memorized in the absence of any explicit organization?
21. Compare intentional and incidental learning. Why does intentional learning typically result in better recall?

RETRIEVAL FROM LONG-TERM MEMORY

Retrieval cues
22. What is the role of retrieval cues in recall? How do they relate to the organized storage of long-term memories?
23. Explain the principle of encoding specificity.

Memory search
24. Describe one memory search strategy.
25. Describe the implications of the tip-of-the-tongue phenomenon for the process of searching long-term memory.

Retrieval and reconstruction
26. How is retrieval often reconstructive? Examine the evidence on the fallibility of eyewitness testimony to help answer this question.
27. Is hypnosis a reliable way of helping a witness remember an event? Why?
28. How is what is remembered often different from what is stored in memory?

STRATEGIES FOR REMEMBERING

Rehearsal
29. What is maintenance rehearsal, and how does it affect storage in long-term memory?
30. Name some methods of elaborative rehearsal and why this form of rehearsal makes retrieval easier for the subject.
31. What does retention and retrieval of material depend on?

Mnemonics
32. Describe some verbal and nonverbal mnemonics. Why is imagery a useful mnemonic? What kinds of imagery help?

Rehearsal and mnemonics as strategies
33. Name some of the strategies of memory, and explain why young children and retarded adults do not use these.

FORGETTING FROM LONG-TERM MEMORY

Decay
34. Recount the evidence both for and against a decay theory of memory.

Interference
35. You should know the experimental techniques that are used to study proactive and retroactive inhibition.

Change of retrieval cues
36. How might a theory based on changing retrieval cues explain everyday forgetting? Explain how such a theory could be applied to the forgetting of childhood memories.

VARIETIES OF LONG-TERM MEMORY

Generic memory
37. Be aware of the difference between episodic and generic memory.
38. Describe how studies of memory activation reveal important aspects of the organization of semantic memory.
39. Semantic memory is apparently searched hierarchically. How have sentence verification studies helped to establish this? What is the role of reaction time measurements in these studies? What are the problems with these studies?

Visual memory
40. How have self-judgments of imagery not been illuminating?
41. What are the characteristics of eidetic imagery? How frequent and useful is it?
42. Discuss studies using reaction time measures in image rotation and scanning as evidence for visual memory.

DISORDERED MEMORY

Anterograde amnesia
43. You should know what anterograde amnesia is, how it occurs, and what characteristics the patient may exhibit.

Retrograde amnesia
44. Define retrograde amnesia and the hypothesis that accounts for the loss of memories during retrograde amnesia.

Current issues in the interpretation of amnesia
45. What are two existing explanations for why anterograde amnesics can acquire certain long-term memories but not others? Include the definitions of procedural and declarative knowledge in your answer.

Programmed Exercises

ACQUISITION, STORAGE, RETRIEVAL

1. The first stage of memory is _____, in which information   acquisition
   is brought into the system.

2. The records of experience made on the nervous system are

   called memory _____.   traces

3. The second stage of memory is _____, during which infor-   storage

   mation is filed away. The final stage is _____, the point at   retrieval
   which one tries to remember.

4. There are two general techniques for testing whether a person
   has remembered something. The first involves asking the per-

   son to produce or name the item and is known as _____,   recall
   while the second only requires that the person know the item

   when he sees or hears it and is called _____.   recognition

THE SENSORY REGISTERS

5. The first memory system in which information from the out-

   side world is stored is the _____ _____.   sensory register

6. The sensory register for vision is called the _____.   icon

7. An experimental technique that permits one to investigate the
   capacity of the sensory registers by sampling information from

   them is Sperling's _____ _____ procedure.   partial report

8. The sensory register for the auditory modality is called the

   _____.   echo

SHORT-TERM MEMORY

9. _____ _____ memory holds information for a brief   Short-term

   interval. _____ _____ memory stores information for   Long-term
   longer periods of time.

10. The _____ _____ is the number of items an individual   memory span
    can recall after just one presentation. This quantity, 7 ± 2, is

    sometimes called the _____ _____.   magic number

11. The interval between acquisition and retrieval is the

    _____ _____.   retention interval

12. _____ is one way of either keeping an item in short-term   Rehearsal
    memory or allowing it to pass into long-term memory.

13. If it was found that items faded from short-term memory even
    though no new information entered, this would support a

    _____ theory of forgetting.   decay

14. If one found that forgetting in short-term memory only occurred when new material came into the system, we would

have evidence for a _____ theory of forgetting.   displacement

15. The method of _____ _____ allows a subject who is   free recall
presented with a list of unrelated items to report them in any
order desired.

16. Of a long list of presented items, a subject is most apt to

remember the first few (known as the _____ effect), and   primacy

the last few (known as the _____ effect).   recency

17. A _____ search process is one in which search proceeds   parallel
simultaneously through all items in short-term memory,

whereas a _____ search process is one in which search is   serial
sequential.

THE ACQUISITION OF LONG-TERM MEMORIES

18. Locke and Berkeley believed that words, images, and ideas are

linked in memory through the principle of _____.   association

19. Locke, Berkeley, and even Aristotle believed that the progres-

sion of ideas termed _____ _____ _____ illustrates   train of thought
the association principle.

20. _____ _____, a German psychologist, was a pioneer in   Hermann Ebbinghaus
the area of memory, using himself as both subject and experimenter.

21. Deb, jag, mep, and zig are all examples of _____ _____,   nonsense syllables
stimuli used by Ebbinghaus in his studies of memory.

22. One method for studying memory is _____ _____. In   serial anticipation
this procedure, a subject memorizes a list, then on a signal he
must recall the first item. The correct first item is then re-
vealed, which signals recall of the second item, and so forth.

23. In a task where a subject continues to study a list of items
even after achieving perfect recall performance, we say that

_____ is taking place.   overlearning

24. Overlearning tends to flatten the _____ curve.   forgetting

25. If a person first learns to drive a car and then has an easier
time than most people in learning to operate a motorcycle,

then we might believe that some positive _____ has occurred.   transfer

26. Tennis players often avoid playing squash or racquetball,
claiming that it interferes with their tennis game. In so doing,
these players are trying to avoid the effects of negative

_____.   transfer

27. An alternative approach to the associationist's theoretical

framework is based on the concept of memory _____.   organization

28. Patterns of recall errors for words in sentences indicate that

    subjects tend to _____ the words into higher-order units,   recode

    or _____, based on their grammatical structure.   chunks

29. Recall _____ demonstrates that subjects organize lists of   clustering
    items by category. Items that belong to the same category tend
    to be recalled together.

30. _____ organization demonstrates that even if a list of items   Subjective
    has no categorical structure, subjects will impose their own.

31. If attention to a list of items while engaging in some sort of
    "cover" task leads to accurate recall of many of the items in a

    surprise recall test, then _____ learning has taken place.   incidental

RETRIEVAL FROM LONG-TERM MEMORY

32. Category names and the stimulus terms of paired associates

    may both serve as _____ _____ for inaccessible material.   retrieval cues

33. The principle of _____ _____ states that retrieval suc-   encoding specificity
    cess is most likely if the context at the time of retrieval
    approximates that during original encoding.

34. Many investigators assume that retrieval is always preceded by

    an internal process called _____ _____.   memory search

35. The _____ phenomenon is an example of unsuccessful   tip-of-the-tongue
    retrieval in which the subject comes close to the searched-for
    item in his memory search but cannot quite find the right
    memory location.

36. As Bartlett demonstrated with subjects' recall of stories,

    retrieval is often a _____ event, since partial knowledge of   reconstructive
    an event is pieced together in recall.

37. The technique of _____ _____ used by Bartlett involves   serial reproduction
    having a subject recall a story, having a second subject store
    and recall that story, and so on.

STRATEGIES FOR REMEMBERING

38. The various devices designed to improve memory, for example

    the peg-word system, are called _____.   mnemonics

39. _____ _____ is a process that holds information in   Maintenance rehearsal

    short-term memory for a while. On the other hand, _____   elaborative

    _____ consists of the organization of information in short-   rehearsal
    term memory so that it can be transferred to long-term memory.

40. The method of _____ requires the learner to visualize each   loci
    of the items he wants to remember in a different spatial loca-
    tion.

41. Recent experiments demonstrate that mental images that are

    _____ produce the best increase in memory scores.   unified (interacting)

42. The _____ _____ is the time period between original   retention interval
    learning and testing in a memory experiment.

43. One example of an interference effect is _____ _____,   retroactive inhibition
    in which new learning hampers recall of old material. Another

    example is _____ _____, in which the interference is   proactive inhibition
    from old material on the recall of new items.

44. One possible reason that we can't recall childhood memories is

    the drastic change in _____ _____ between childhood   retrieval cues
    and adulthood.

VARIETIES OF LONG-TERM MEMORY

45. _____ memory is the memory for particular events of one's   Episodic
    own life. They are "tagged" by time or place.

46. The term used to denote the sum total of a person's knowledge

    is "_____ memory." One component of this is _____   generic, semantic
    memory, the memory of words and concepts.

47. The phenomenon of memory _____ shows that a semantic   activation
    trace can be primed by previously presented material that is
    similar to the trace. This facilitates retrieval of the trace.

48. Sentence verification studies have found that it takes longer to
    decide that a bird is an animal than to decide that a bird has

    wings. This evidence suggests that a _____ search process   hierarchical
    occurs when we search for an item in long-term memory.

49. Sentence verification reaction times seem to depend on the

    _____ of the item in question. For example, it takes longer   typicality
    to verify that "a whale is a mammal" than to verify that "a
    cow is a mammal."

50. The often-discussed phenomenon of "photographic memory"

    is also known as _____ _____.   eidetic imagery

51. Studies of _____ _____ and _____ _____ reveal   mental rotation, image scanning
    that in some ways mental images are like mental pictures.

52. A patient suffers a hippocampal lesion. Subsequent recall of
    events which occurred before his accident is intact, but the
    patient is not able to remember new events (post-trauma) for

    very long. This patient suffers from _____ amnesia.   anterograde

53. An alcoholic with symptoms of anterograde amnesia likely

    suffers from _____ _____.   Korsakoff's syndrome

54. It is frequently reported that events immediately preceding
    some trauma to the brain are forgotten. This provides some

    support for a _____ _____ view of memory, in which   trace consolidation
    information is presumed to be transferred from short-term to
    long-term memory over time.

55. A patient has suffered an accident involving trauma to the head. Following this, his ability to learn new things is unimpaired, but he seems to have forgotten some things which happened prior to surgery. This is an example of _____ _____.   retrograde amnesia

56. An amnesic's memory is relatively unaffected when the memory task involves _____ _____, but his memory is   procedural knowledge

drastically impaired when it involves _____ _____.   declarative knowledge

Self Test

1. In order for us to remember something, we must first engage in the process of:
   a. storage
   b. rehearsal
   c. acquisition
   d. recall

2. An enduring physical record of a memory is called a:
   a. memory trace
   b. chunk
   c. sensory register
   d. none of the above

3. Suppose you are given a choice between a multiple-choice test and a short-answer test for the final exam in this course. Suppose you want to maximize the chance of doing well. Based on what you know about recall and recognition, all other things being equal, which test should you choose?
   a. short answer
   b. multiple choice
   c. either, there is no difference
   d. it depends on the difficulty of the material

4. Complete the following analogy: Multiple-choice questions are to fill-in-the-blank questions as:
   a. recognition is to recall
   b. recall is to retention
   c. recognition is to retention
   d. learning is to memory

5. One difference between the sensory registers and short-term memory is that:
   a. the sensory registers cannot store information using an acoustic code
   b. the sensory registers' storage cannot be interfered with by newly entering information

   c. short-term memory is not subject to decay
   d. none of the above

6. Sperling demonstrated the existence of a type of memory called the _____ through his _____ procedure, which involves sampling recall of a display of items that subjects briefly see.
   a. trace consolidation, cued recall
   b. memory span, retention interval
   c. memory trace, free recall
   d. sensory register, partial report

7. Which of the following is an example of a sensory register memory?
   a. remembering the smell of pumpkin pie you ate last Thanksgiving
   b. remembering a tune you heard on the radio yesterday
   c. the clear recollection of the sound of a voice immediately after you hear it
   d. suddenly recalling something that you had been trying to remember for some time

8. The following are all characteristics of short-term memory except:
   a. limited capacity
   b. contents disappear without rehearsal
   c. primarily semantic representation
   d. rapid access

9. It has been found that people can hold about seven items in short-term memory. When more items are presented, complete recall is generally not possible. This demonstrates the _____ of short-term memory.
   a. retention interval
   b. memory trace
   c. partial report
   d. memory span

10. Suppose you are given driving directions by a gas station attendant and you repeat them over and over to yourself, "First left, second right, left at the first light, third right." Now suppose that your repetition of the directions is interrupted by an emergency driving maneuver. This would likely cause you to forget the directions, thereby demonstrating the importance of _____ in preserving short-term memory.
   a. storage capacity
   b. retrieval
   c. accessibility
   d. rehearsal

11. Suppose cryogenics (freezing patients and awakening them at some future time) were possible. If you were to discover that after being awakened, the patients had retained very accurate memories of what they had experienced immediately before freezing, this would be evidence for which hypothesis of forgetting in short-term memory?
   a. interference
   b. decay
   c. neither displacement nor decay
   d. either displacement or decay

12. At a party you are taken around the room by the host and are introduced to the other guests. Some time after the introductions are finished, one of these people comes up to talk to you. All other things being equal, you have the best chance of remembering her name if she was one of the _____ people you met. This phenomenon is called _____ .
   a. first, primacy
   b. middle, inhibition
   c. last, recency
   d. first or last, partial report

13. Now imagine the same situation (as in No. 12) except that the person comes up to you immediately after you have been very quickly introduced to everyone. Again, other things being equal, you would have the worst chance of remembering her name if she was one of the _____ people you met and the best chance if she was one of the _____ .
   a. first, last
   b. middle, last
   c. middle, first, or last
   d. last, first, or middle

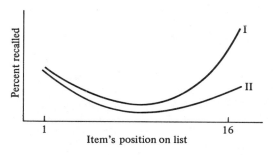

14. The figure above depicts recall curves for a list of 16 items. Two conditions were employed, I and II. What was the difference between the conditions?
   a. the interval between each item was longer for I than II
   b. the interval between each item was longer for II than I
   c. the interval between the last item and the recall test was longer for I than II
   d. the interval between the last item and the recall test was longer for II than I

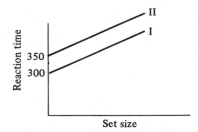

15. A memory search experiment is conducted under two conditions, I and II. The results are shown above. Reaction time is plotted as a function of memory set size. What do you think might have been the difference between the two conditions?
   a. parallel search in I; serial search in II
   b. serial search in I; parallel search in II
   c. size of memory set smaller in I than II
   d. response key easier to press in I than II

16. Suppose Ebbinghaus had extended his original work on memory by examining the relationship between serial anticipation and paired-associate learning tasks. In particular, suppose that he had measured serial recall for the list of letters B, L, R, C, M, S, F, T, E, then paired-associate recall for the list B-L, L-R, R-C, C-M, M-S, S-F, F-T, T-E.

You would expect:
a. negative transfer
b. positive transfer
c. no transfer
d. specific transfer

17. Without necessarily knowing it, professional actors often know a good deal of psychology. Even after they know their lines perfectly, they continue to rehearse. They know that _____ changes the _____
_____.
a. rehearsal, retrieval cues
b. overlearning, paired associations
c. recall, free recall
d. overlearning, forgetting curve

18. Which of the following tasks would you expect to transfer positively to learning how to ride a motorcycle?
a. swimming
b. riding a bicycle
c. horseback riding
d. none of the above

19. Which of the following best describes the major characteristics of long-term memory for verbal material?
a. unlimited capacity, primarily semantic coding, relatively permanent
b. limited capacity, primarily semantic coding, fades rapidly
c. unknown capacity, primarily acoustic coding, relatively permanent
d. unlimited capacity, primarily acoustic coding, fades rapidly

20. Suppose subjects are asked to memorize sentences such as "The old banker christened the new yacht." In recalling such a sentence, a subject would be likeliest to make an error on:
a. "banker," given that he correctly recalled "old"
b. "yacht," given that he correctly recalled "new"
c. "the," given that he correctly recalled "christened"
d. "christened," given that he correctly recalled "banker"

21. In a free recall experiment, given the list of items "car, pants, tulip, rose, train, shirt, lily, jacket, boat," subjects would be likely to recall which pair of items together?
a. rose, train
b. shirt, lily
c. car, train
d. car, jacket

22. Which of the following processes will not result in the effective storage of memory traces in long-term memory?
a. maintenance rehearsal
b. clustering
c. elaborative rehearsal
d. organization by phrases

23. Two groups of subjects are each given twenty-five index cards on each of which is printed the name of a U.S. president. Group 1 is told to alphabetize the cards. Group 2 is told to memorize the names. Both groups are then tested on free recall of the names, and it is discovered that group 2 does much better than group 1. This is an example of the superiority of _____ over _____.
a. recall, recognition
b. recognition, recall
c. overlearning, underlearning
d. intentional learning, incidental learning

24. You have been trying to remember the name of a street that a friend lives on. Despite all of your efforts you are unable to recall it. While in the kitchen looking for a snack (to console yourself) you reach for a can of nuts, and suddenly the street name comes to you—Walnut. This is an example of the role of _____ _____.
a. incidental learning
b. retrograde amnesia
c. partial report
d. retrieval cues

25. Retrieval cues are most effective if they:
a. coincide with the way in which a trace was originally encoded
b. are presented at the time of recall not at encoding
c. are quite concrete
d. elicit visual images

26. The tip-of-the-tongue phenomenon provides us with evidence concerning:
a. the hierarchical organization of long-term memory
b. accessibility in short-term memory
c. the search process in long-term memory
d. the use of retrieval cues in short-term memory

27. Having something "on the tip of the tongue" indicates a problem:
a. in the way the item was chunked
b. with reconstruction
c. with proactive inhibition
d. with retrieval

28. It is believed that retrieval is generally preceded by:
    a. chunking
    b. memory activation
    c. memory search
    d. recognition

29. Bartlett's experiments and evidence about the fallibility of eyewitness testimony highlight the importance of which of the following factors about recall?
    a. reconstruction
    b. proactive inhibition
    c. retrieval cues
    d. retroactive inhibition

30. Mnemonic devices (memorizing aids) use the principle of:
    a. consolidation of retrieval
    b. fading icons
    c. recoding
    d. retrieval of consolidation

31. The kind of rehearsal that establishes long-term memories is _____. The type of rehearsal that holds material in short-term memory temporarily is _____.
    a. mnemonics, chunking
    b. maintenance rehearsal, elaborative rehearsal
    c. elaborative rehearsal, maintenance rehearsal
    d. method of loci, method of pegs

32. The methods of loci and pegs are similar mnemonic devices in that:
    a. both relate distinctive features of the retrieval scheme to characteristics of the item
    b. both use visual imagery
    c. both make use of a paired-associate learning technique
    d. all of the above

33. Which of the following images would produce the greatest increase in recall performance for the pair of items horse-rock?
    a. a horse standing next to a rock
    b. a horse dragging a rock
    c. a horse and rock pictured separately
    d. all of the above would be equivalent

34. According to a decay theory of forgetting, if a subject learning a list of words was then subjected to one of the following procedures, he would forget the greatest number of words if:
    a. he slept for four versus two hours
    b. he learned other lists for four versus two hours

    c. he performed arithmetic problems for four versus two hours
    d. all of the above would be comparable

35. Consider the following experimental design:

    control group:
    learn A → rest → test A
    experimental group:
    learn A → learn B → test A

    This design would be used to test forgetting due to which factor?
    a. proactive inhibition
    b. retroactive inhibition
    c. decay
    d. generalization

36. A college sophomore participates in a nonsense syllable learning experiment. The first list takes him only four trials to learn. The second list takes five trials, and the third list takes eight trials. These results can be taken as a demonstration of:
    a. memory activation
    b. retroactive interference
    c. proactive interference
    d. retrograde forgetting

37. Studies of paired-associate learning and serial recall test for memory of which kind?
    a. generic memory
    b. semantic memory
    c. episodic memory
    d. short-term memory

38. Which sentence will take the longest time for subjects to verify?
    a. A collie has long hair.
    b. A collie can bark.
    c. A collie can bear puppies.
    d. A collie can breathe.

39. Which of the following sentences would take the least time to verify?
    a. A robin is a bird.
    b. A penguin is a bird.
    c. A chicken is a bird.
    d. all would be equivalent

40. Evidence for a mental rotation ability comes from studies of:
    a. reaction times in identifying objects
    b. image ratings
    c. errors in recognizing inverted characters
    d. none of the above

41. Studies of mental rotation and image scanning draw on an analogy between image analysis and:
    a. feature analysis
    b. concept analysis

c. picture analysis
d. semantic analysis

42. Three major symptoms characterize antero-grade amnesia. They are:
   a. accurate memory for pretrauma events, normal short-term memory, inaccurate memory for most posttrauma events
   b. inaccurate memory for pretrauma events, normal short-term memory, inaccurate memory for most posttrauma events
   c. accurate memory for pretrauma events, abnormal short-term memory, accurate memory for most posttrauma events
   d. inaccurate memory for pretrauma events, normal short-term memory, accurate memory for most posttrauma events

43. Korsakoff's syndrome is typically associated with:
   a. brain surgery
   b. alcoholism
   c. senility
   d. more than one of the above

44. Milner's subject H. M. (an anterograde amnesic) was tested for his memory span for unrelated nouns. What is your best guess about his span?
   a. 0
   b. 4
   c. 7
   d. 10

45. A theory of memory which says that memory needs time to be fixed into a permanent form is called:
   a. rehearsal
   b. spreading activation
   c. trace consolidation
   d. memory priming

46. You witness an automobile accident in which one of the drivers hits his head on the windshield. He appears uninjured, but when a policeman asks him what happened just prior to the accident, the man seems confused and is unable to answer. The policeman is about to haul the man off to jail (assuming that he must be drunk) when you step forward and (having studied your psychology text) say, "This man is suffering from _____ _____!"
   a. trace consolidation
   b. anterograde amnesia
   c. retrograde amnesia
   d. Korsakoff's syndrome

Answer Key for Self Test

1. c p. 222	24. d pp. 236–37
2. a p. 222	25. a pp. 237–38
3. b p. 222	26. c pp. 238–39
4. a p. 222	27. d pp. 238–39
5. d pp. 223, 225	28. c p. 238
6. d p. 223	29. a p. 240
7. c p. 223	30. c p. 242
8. c p. 225	31. c p. 243
9. d p. 225	32. d p. 245
10. d p. 226	33. b p. 246
11. d p. 226	34. d p. 247–48
12. a p. 227	35. b p. 248
13. b p. 227	36. c p. 248
14. d p. 227	37. c p. 250
15. d p. 228	38. d pp. 251–53
16. b pp. 230–31	39. a pp. 251–53
17. d p. 231	40. a p. 254
18. b p. 231	41. c pp. 254–55
19. a pp. 229–30, 233	42. a p. 256
20. d p. 233	43. b p. 256
21. c pp. 233–35	44. c p. 256
22. a p. 243	45. c p. 258
23. d pp. 235–36	46. c p. 258

Investigating Psychological Phenomena

THE EFFECT OF IMAGERY INSTRUCTIONS ON MEMORY

Equipment: None
Subjects: One
Time per subject: Fifteen minutes
Time for experimenter: Twenty minutes

As Professor Gleitman discusses, there are several mnemonic techniques that will improve memory performance. One of these is the use of images. By now there is a good deal of research that demonstrates the memorial effectiveness of asking subjects to create images of the objects or events that they are trying to commit to memory. In the present experiment you will have an opportunity to demonstrate the effectiveness of imagery instructions for yourself in an experiment that involves learning paired-associate lists.

The procedure is quite simple. Below you will find two lists of twenty noun pairs each that you can use as stimuli for the experiment. You will need just one subject to participate in the experiment. The procedure is as follows:

First, read the following instructions to the subject:

This is a memory experiment in which you will be required to memorize and recall two lists of words, each of which is composed of twenty pairs of fairly common nouns. First I will read aloud the twenty noun pairs from list 1 at the rate of one pair every seven seconds or so. While I am reading the pairs, just sit quietly and listen to them, trying as best you can to memorize the words in each pair. After I have presented all the pairs, I shall go through the list again, this time reading only the first noun in each pair. As I read each of these nouns, I would like you to recall the appropriate second noun that was paired with it when I originally presented the list. You will have seven seconds or so to recall the second noun for each pair and write it in the space provided on your answer sheet. Do you have any questions?

After you have read these instructions to the subject, give him or her the report sheet for this chapter in Appendix B. Then follow the testing procedure outlined in the instructions. After you have completed the procedure for list 1, read the following instructions to the subject:

Now I shall present you with another list of twenty noun pairs that I would like you to memorize. The procedure for this list will be identical to that for the first list except for one change: This time, when you are presented with each pair, try to form a mental image of the words in which there is some sort of interaction. For example, if you were presented with the pair "horse-rock," you might form an image of a horse that is harnessed to a large boulder and is dragging the boulder along the ground. Such images should help you memorize the words. Do you have any questions?

Now present list 2 exactly as list 1 was presented after you have given the subject another answer sheet for list 2.

To score the subject's performance, simply count up the number of items that were answered correctly on each list. If all went well, the subject should have scored better on list 2 (unless the subject was already forming mental images for the nouns in list 1).

Now at this point you may raise a question. Was the subject's performance on list 2 better because of the influence of the imagery instructions, or could it have been better for some other reason? For example, it may have already occurred to you that performance on list 2 may have been better than list 1 because list 2 was presented *after* list 1 and therefore the subject may simply have been better practiced at memorizing words. Before reading on, try to think of a way that you might have run this experiment that would have avoided this problem.

One way to have avoided a practice effect would have been to use two different subjects. The first subject would have received only list 1 with its instructions while the second would have received only list 2 with its imagery instructions. If performance on list 2 was still better than on list 1, you might feel more confident in attributing this difference to the effect of the instructions (assuming that your two subjects were fairly comparable in their overall memory ability). At least practice could not account for the difference.

But, you might object, there might *still* be an explanation for the difference between lists that has nothing to do with the effect of imagery instructions. Suppose, for instance, list 2 was composed of words that were more common or concrete than the words on list 1 (e.g., horse versus liberty). This alone might make list 2 more memorable. There are two ways that one might control for this possibility. The first is to choose words for the two lists that are equated for frequency of usage and concreteness (and, for that matter, whatever else you might think of that would affect the memorability of words). The second method is to balance experimentally which word lists are paired with which instructions. The following table shows one arrangement that should work in which you would have to run at least 4 subjects:

	neutral instructions	imagery instructions
word list 1	subject 1	subject 2
word list 2	subject 3	subject 4

If you were to run this experiment, then you could tell whether the word lists differ from one another in memorability and/or whether there is an effect of instructions. If word list 2 is more memorable than word list 1, then subjects 3 and 4 should perform better than 1 and 2. If imagery instructions produce better preformance than neutral instructions, then subjects 2 and 4 should perform better than 1 and 3. If list 2 is more memorable than list 1 *and* imagery instructions produce better performance than neutral instructions, then subject 4 should perform best of all.

If you want to check on the possible influence of practice in the experiment that you ran, and if you want to be sure that the word lists are comparable (they have actually been balanced for meaningfulness and commonness of the words), then you should try this last experiment. Whether you do try it or not, however, you should realize that one of the points of this exercise was to show that even a fairly simple experiment such as the one that you ran with the word lists is sometimes open to several interpretations. To find the right one requires careful experimentation.

Noun pairs for list 1
1. building-letter
2. grass-meat
3. animal-village
4. house-lip
5. sky-seat
6. dress-apple
7. fur-mountain
8. flag-coast
9. sugar-ship
10. mother-city
11. market-church
12. plant-baby
13. sea-iron
14. woods-engine
15. arm-boulder
16. woman-forest
17. table-blood
18. queen-college
19. bar-diamond
20. cotton-street

Noun pairs for list 2
1. sail-bowl
2. coffee-lake
3. girl-flood
4. corn-river
5. stone-bottle
6. paper-shore
7. dust-army
8. ocean-fire
9. clothing-board
10. door-king
11. butler-tree
12. gold-chair
13. flower-car
14. bird-skin
15. hall-child
16. garden-book
17. money-shoes
18. cat-camp
19. wife-storm
20. dollar-machine

CHAPTER 8

Thinking

Learning Objectives

THE ELEMENTS OF THOUGHT

1. How are motor movements in thought supposed to be different from motor movements in overt action? Is there any evidence that motor movements accompany thought? Describe the evidence suggesting that such movements are not necessary for thinking.
2. Understand the argument that thought is primarily guided by images. What is the evidence against this position?

Abstract thought
3. What does it mean for something to represent something else?
4. Be familiar with the terms "concept" and "proposition." You should be able to give examples of each. Also, you should be able to discuss how each of the features of thinking is abstract in character.

PROBLEM SOLVING

5. Hobbes and Locke considered thinking as a matter of chaining ideas. What are the arguments showing that it is more organized than this?

Hierarchical organization and chunking
6. How is thinking goal-directed? How is it hierarchical? How do these features bear on Locke's position?
7. What is the shape of the learning curve in the development of skill?

8. Be able to describe how chunking ability differentiates novices from experts. How is automatization relevant?
9. Describe the Stroop effect.
10. Does the performance of skilled acts depend on motor chaining? Why or why not?
11. Be familiar with some of the classic puzzle problems that have been used to study thinking.
12. Show how research on problem solving demonstrates that subjects use hierarchical plans. In line with this, what are the major differences between masters and beginners in problem solving.

Artificial intelligence: problem solving by computer
13. Why are computers valuable analogues to humans as problem solvers? How is the analogy weak?
14. Define the terms "algorithm" and "heuristic." Describe some useful heuristics in problem solving. Why are algorithms often inefficient but exact?
15. What is MYCIN and what can it do? What are MYCIN's limitations?
16. Why are different strategies required for well-defined versus ill-defined problems? What is the difference between these two kinds of problems, and how is this difference relevant to the comparison of humans and computers?

Obstacles to problem solving
17. Be aware of the effects of set, mechanization, and motivation on problem solving. How does set influence solution strategies? What is functional fixedness, and how does it hinder problem solving?

Restructuring

18. What is restructuring? How is it related to creative thinking?

19. How is incubation related to the effects of set? How is it related to creative thinking?

20. How is restructuring in problem solving similar to the process required to appreciate certain kinds of humor? What do humor and scientific insight share in common?

SPATIAL THINKING

Spatial problem solving and imagery

21. How do mental pictures help solve spatial problems?

22. Explain the difference between mental maps that are picturelike and those that are conceptual.

23. What makes our spatial knowledge not entirely picturelike? Give an example to substantiate this.

Is spatial knowledge visual?

24. What evidence leads to the conclusion that spatial knowledge is not necessarily visual? By what means do blind people obtain information about space?

REASONING AND DECISION MAKING

Deductive reasoning

25. What is a syllogism? What are the reasons that cause many subjects to do poorly on syllogism tasks?

Inductive reasoning

26. Be able to explain the difference between deductive and inductive reasoning.

27. What is the confirmation bias? Why are disconfirmations more helpful in proving hypotheses than confirmations?

Decision making

28. Why can the availability heuristic sometimes lead to grave errors in estimating likelihoods? Be able to state two examples in which the availability heuristic may affect estimations.

29. Describe the conjunction fallacy and the explanation for it.

Are people really irrational?

30. What factors make it more possible for us to use our capacity for logical thinking?

31. What analogy has been drawn between errors of thought and perceptual illusions? Of what use might errors of thought be to psychologists studying thinking?

A BACKWARD LOOK AT PERCEPTION, MEMORY, AND THINKING

32. How do the broad domains of cognition, perception, memory, and thinking overlap? What is the importance of this spillover?

Programmed Exercises

THE ELEMENTS OF THOUGHT

1. Watson and other behaviorists believe that thoughts include

   _____ _____.   muscle movements

2. Watson believed that motor reactions were not just a concomi-

   tant of the thought process but were _____ for thought.   necessary

3. According to Berkeley and other British empiricists, all thought

   is ultimately comprised of _____ _____, which enter   mental images
   and exit from consciousness.

4. Unlike pictures, _____ are abstract and symbolic.   words

5. The term "_____" is generally used to describe a class that   concept
   subsumes a number of individual instances.

6. A _____ concept doesn't apply to any one item in isolation;   relational
   it can only be defined with respect to two or more objects.

7. A _____ makes some assertion that relates a subject and a predicate in a way that can be true or false.

proposition

PROBLEM SOLVING

8. Hobbes, Locke, and their many descendants believed that the stream of activity that characterizes thinking is produced by a

   chain of _____ ideas, each triggered by the one before.

associated

9. The use of master plans to organize subsidiary actions suggests

   that thought is organized into _____.

hierarchies

10. The ability to organize many details into larger _____ is one of the crucial features of directed activity, including thinking.

chunks

11. Much of the difference between a master and an apprentice is in the degree to which subcomponents of an activity have been chunked hierarchically; to the master, the substeps have be-

    come _____.

automatic

12. The _____ and subsequent rise found in many learning curves for motor skills suggest that the learner gradually transforms this task.

plateau

13. The _____ effect is an example of how reading letter strings has become an automatized activity for adults. Reading incompatible color names interferes with naming colors in which the color words are printed.

Stroop

14. Locke's explanation for chunking involves _____: a first movement provides a kinesthetic stimulus for a second movement, which in turn is a stimulus for a third, etc.

chaining

15. Karl Duncker demonstrated that _____ _____ is a common feature of problem solving; his subjects first formulated a plan of attack and then generated specific solutions.

hierarchical organization

16. As Adrian de Groot demonstrated with chess, master problem

    solvers use _____ that contain more information than do those of beginners.

chunks

17. One way in which humans and computers are similar is that

    both are _____ _____ systems.

information-processing

18. The field of _____ _____ is concerned with programming computers to solve various intellectual problems.

artificial intelligence

19. A procedure in which all of the operations required to achieve

    the solution are specified step by step is called an _____.

algorithm

20. A _____ differs from an algorithm in that it is a rule of thumb rather than a fixed sequence of steps.

heuristic

21. One of Newell and Simon's chess programs includes a heuristic

    in which the computer strives toward _____ such as occupation of the center squares.

subgoals

22. _____ _____ are problem-solving programs which deal with problems in a limited domain of knowledge.

Expert systems

23. _____ is an example of a problem-solving program that   MYCIN
    helps doctors in the treatment of infectious diseases.

24. A newspaper proofreader is asked to check a piece of text for

    spelling errors. This is an example of a(n) _____ _____   well-defined
    problem.

25. A student is asked to write a "good" paper. This is an example

    of a(n) _____ _____ problem.   ill-defined

26. When a person becomes _____ on one approach to a task,   fixated
    it is hard for him to approach it any other way.

27. A person who attempts to solve a problem by thinking along a
    line of thought created by previous thinking is operating under

    a _____ _____.   mental set

28. The Luchins water jug problem, an example of mental set, is

    one of the classic demonstrations of _____ in problem   mechanization
    solving.

29. In general, the greater the _____ toward reaching a   motivation

    solution, the greater the _____ with which the problem is   set
    approached.

30. Thinking of objects in terms of their normal function is

    termed _____ _____ and can hinder problem solving.   functional fixedness

31. Solutions of difficult problems often involve a perceptual

    _____ of the problem in order to break a false perceptual   restructuring
    set.

32. The phenomenon whereby one arrives at an insightful solution
    to a problem after intense preparation followed by rest is

    called _____.   incubation

33. It has been suggested that both _____ and _____ involve   humor, insight
    a dramatic shift from one cognitive organization to another.

34. According to some authors, the simultaneous membership of

    an item in two radically different cognitive _____ is a   contexts
    crucial aspect of humor, scientific insight, and artistic creation.

SPATIAL THINKING

35. When we try to determine a shortcut between two locations,

    we are using _____ reasoning.   spatial

36. A _____ _____ is a picturelike image of a geographical   mental map
    area that is formed in the mind.

37. In addition to mental maps that are picturelike, there are those

    that are abstract and _____.   conceptual

38. We know that spatial knowledge is not necessarily visual

    because it has been found to exist in _____ persons.   blind

REASONING AND DECISION MAKING

39. A _____ contains two premises and a conclusion.   syllogism

40. The _____ _____ leads to a tendency to affirm a con-   atmosphere effect
    clusion that contains an "all" if both premises contain "all,"
    and to affirm one that contains a "some" if both premises
    contain "some."

41. The statement "All A are B and therefore all B are A" is an

    _____ inference.   invalid

42. In _____ reasoning we apply a general rule to a particular   deductive
    case.

43. In _____ reasoning we consider different cases and try to   inductive
    find the rule that covers them all.

44. The fact that people primarily seek evidence that will confirm

    their hypotheses suggests that there is a strong

    _____ _____.   confirmation bias

45. One _____ shows that a hypothesis is false, but countless   disconfirmation
    confirmations cannot prove that it is true.

46. When we estimate the frequency of certain events by consider-
    ing how many such events readily come to mind, we are using

    the _____ _____.   availability heuristic

47. _____ is the joint occurrence of two independent events.   Conjunction

48. A conjunction of two events is _____ probable than each   less
    event taken alone.

49. If someone takes a conjunction to be more likely than one (or
    both) of the two events regarded alone, he is committing the

    _____ _____.   conjunction fallacy

50. There is a good deal of evidence that throws a poor light on

    human _____.   rationality

51. We owe many of our great intellectual achievements to many

    past _____, who gave us not only bits of new knowledge,   generations
    but also ways of gaining further knowledge.

52. It is hoped that the study of errors of thought will help psy-

    chologists understand the general process of _____, in   thinking
    which we do relatively well.

A BACKWARD LOOK AT PERCEPTION, MEMORY, AND THINKING

53. There are no clear boundaries between the domains of

    _____, _____, and _____.   perception, memory, thinking

Self Test

1. Researchers have found that with the proper instructions they can detect small movements of the tongue and larynx during thought. Such movements are called _____ _____ and might be considered to be some support for the _____ position.
   a. speech tremors, empiricist
   b. implicit speech, empiricist
   c. motor empathy, behaviorist
   d. implicit speech, behaviorist

2. John B. Watson proposed that thinking:
   a. was a bodily activity
   b. was quantitatively, but not qualitatively, different from any other activity
   c. involves motor reactions
   d. all of the above

3. A strong disproof of Watson's belief that motor reactions are the constituents of thought involved:
   a. showing that deaf people think
   b. the use of curare
   c. the use of tasks which interfere with implicit speech (e.g., gargling, clamping of tongue, etc.)
   d. all of the above
   e. b and c, but not a

4. Imageless thought:
   a. does not exist
   b. is not found even in persons who are capable of vivid images
   c. has been described as wordless and imageless but having a sense of relationships
   d. none of the above

5. A concept:
   a. must have a finite number of instances
   b. must not refer to a relationship
   c. may designate qualities or dimensions
   d. all of the above

6. A proposition:
   a. can be simply a mental image
   b. has a truth value
   c. can be simply a sentence
   d. none of the above

7. All of the following are examples of directed thinking except:
   a. discovery of a geometric proof
   b. deciding on the next move in a chess game
   c. daydreaming about last night's meal
   d. trying to figure out why a car will not start

8. Learning curves involving such tasks as receiving Morse code have a characteristic plateau preceded and followed by rises. This is because:
   a. people tend to get bored with tasks like this, and so their performance falls off
   b. people begin to use mental imagery after a little practice
   c. with practice people can make more efficient use of chunks
   d. none of the above

9. The Stroop effect clearly shows that:
   a. certain mental activities become automatized
   b. colors are named faster than words
   c. words are named faster than colors
   d. Lashley was wrong in his description of behavior sequences

10. To explain chunking, many associationists claim that skilled acts are highly practiced stimulus-response strings. For such strings the first movement serves as a stimulus for the second, which does the same thing for the third, etc. This is known as:
    a. a heuristic
    b. an algorithm
    c. mental set
    d. none of the above

11. Typical solutions to Karl Duncker's X-ray problem:
    a. involved hierarchical thought patterns
    b. involved reformulating the problem to produce a plan of attack
    c. show that subjects entertain classes of solutions before converging on one
    d. all of the above

12. Research has shown that master chess players are better than novices in:
    a. solving algorithms
    b. chunking chess moves
    c. looking farther ahead to plan chess moves
    d. memorizing random patterns of chess pieces

13. In general, expert problem solvers seem to excel at using:
    a. hierarchical strategies
    b. subgoals
    c. heuristics
    d. all of the above

14. Humans and computers are similar in that:
    a. both are information-processing systems
    b. the activities of both can be described by flow diagrams
    c. both can use algorithms
    d. all of the above

15. A food recipe specifies what ingredients are to be added together, in what amounts, and in what order. Such a recipe would be:
    a. a heuristic
    b. an algorithm
    c. a subgoal
    d. a scheme

16. Which of the following would make most efficient use of heuristics?
    i. an initial diagnosis made by a physician
    ii. an architect designing a hotel
    iii. a search for a particular word in a dictionary
    iv. deciding where to hang a new picture
    a. i, ii, iii
    b. ii, iii, iv
    c. iii, iv
    d. i, ii, iv

17. Examples of the appropriate use of subgoals and heuristics might be:
    a. trying for a position in the center of a board in a game of chess
    b. going for a checkmate
    c. finding the general area of an automotive problem (i.e., electrical vs. mechanical)
    d. all of the above

18. Ill-defined problems differ from well-defined problems in that:
    a. ill-defined problems have more difficult and complex solutions
    b. well-defined problems always have solutions, while ill-defined problems are unsolvable
    c. it is hard to define what changes are needed to reach the goal stated in ill-defined problems
    d. all of the above

19. The analogy between computers and the human mind is weak because:
    a. computers are made of transistors
    b. the mind uses nerve signals, not electrical impulses
    c. humans can solve ill-defined problems
    d. none of the above

20. A person is asked to solve a series of math problems. The first five problems can only be solved one way, each the same. The sixth problem can also be solved using this method, but there is also a much simpler solution. The subject solves this problem in the way he solved the first five. This person's problem-solving ability has been hampered by:

    a. functional fixedness
    b. a lack of motivation
    c. mental set
    d. an improper heuristic

21. Several subjects are told that they will receive ten dollars if they are able to solve a problem in fifteen minutes. A second group is given no such promise. These groups demonstrate the inverse relationship between _____ and _____.
    a. motivation, set
    b. effort, success
    c. attitude, money
    d. none of the above

22. An inability to think of objects except in terms of their normal function can be a hindrance in problem solving and is known as:
    a. perceptual set
    b. restructuring
    c. functional fixedness
    d. none of the above

23. All of the following problems discussed in the text require perceptual restructuring for a solution except:
    a. the nine-dot problem
    b. the match puzzle
    c. the horse-and-rider problem
    d. unscrambling words (anagrams)

24. All of the following often contribute to insights except:
    a. a period of intense preparation
    b. a period of retreat
    c. a different environment
    d. functional fixedness

25. One likely reason that incubation helps in reaching a problem solution is that:
    a. it allows for perceptual restructuring
    b. it helps break mental set
    c. it gives time to set up subgoals
    d. none of the above

26. The concept of an incubation period (in the explanation of insight) is unsatisfactory because:
    a. it tells us nothing of the underlying processes
    b. the term "unconscious thought" is too vague
    c. it has been demonstrated to be false
    d. a and b but not c

27. Insight and humor are similar in that:
    a. both involve heuristics
    b. both can be based on cognitive restructuring

c. neither will work if the subject is mentally set

d. none of the above

28. One would most likely construct a mental map for all of the following activities except:
    a. getting from one end of the college campus to the other
    b. rearranging furniture in a living room
    c. taking a walk around the block
    d. finding a shortcut to work

29. Suppose subjects are required to provide estimates of certain distances. The estimation time of which distance would be the longest?
    a. 1/2 mile
    b. 1 mile
    c. 2 miles
    d. 3 miles

30. Spatial knowledge is sometimes affected by:
    a. rotation
    b. conceptual knowledge
    c. perceptual knowledge
    d. none of the above

31. All A are B
    Some B are C
    Therefore some A are C. This is a(n):
    a. invalid syllogism
    b. valid syllogism
    c. invalid algorithm
    d. valid algorithm

32. Which of the following statements is true?
    a. people often set out to see whether their hypotheses are false
    b. people rarely set out to see whether their hypotheses are false
    c. people do not seek evidence that will confirm their hypotheses
    d. none of the above

33. When a decision is affected by events that come readily to mind, this is a manifestation of:
    a. inductive reasoning
    b. deductive reasoning
    c. conjunction
    d. the availability heuristic

34. The probability of event A is .5. The probability of event B is .2. The conjunction of events A and B is:
    a. .7
    b. .3
    c. .10
    d. .25

35. All of the following are shortcomings of human rationality except:
    a. people cannot perform the operations of addition, subtraction, multiplication, and division adequately
    b. people make errors in deductive reasoning
    c. people make errors in inductive reasoning
    d. people are not concerned with demonstrating that their hypotheses are wrong

36. According to some leading investigators, errors of thought:
    a. are the rule and not the exception
    b. indicate to us that humans are exceptionally irrational
    c. are distortions of patterns of thought that often work for us
    d. all of the above

Answer Key for Self Test

1. d p. 263	19. d pp. 276–77
2. d p. 263	20. c p. 277
3. e p. 263	21. a pp. 278–79
4. c p. 265	22. c p. 279
5. c p. 265	23. d pp. 279–80
6. b pp. 265–66	24. d pp. 279–81
7. c pp. 267–68	25. b pp. 280–81
8. c pp. 268–69	26. d pp. 280–81
9. a p. 269	27. b pp. 281–82
10. d p. 270	28. c p. 283
11. d pp. 270–71	29. d p. 283
12. b p. 272	30. b pp. 283–84
13. d pp. 273–75	31. a p. 286
14. d p. 274	32. b p. 287
15. b p. 274	33. d p. 289
16. d pp. 274–75	34. c p. 290
17. d p. 275	35. a p. 291
18. c p. 276	36. c p. 292

Investigating Psychological Phenomena

THE STROOP EFFECT

Equipment: Included (see insert)
Subjects: One
Time per subject: Thirty minutes
Time for experiment: Forty minutes

It is frequently observed that as people are given more experience at the task of reading, the skill becomes more and more automatic in character. One symptom of this increasing automatization is that it is difficult to prevent a skilled reader from reading material that he is exposed to. This appears to be a general characteristic of skills that become automated. Given the proper conditions for the occurrence of such a skill, it is difficult to inhibit it.

Since automatization is a prominent characteristic of skilled activities ranging from reading to motor behavior to problem-solving routines, it is useful to investigate it to determine its characteristics. One task that has been studied extensively in this regard is the Stroop task (turn to the text for a full description of the task). The following three experiments are designed to demonstrate the basic Stroop effect and to extend it somewhat so that you can develop some intuitions about why it occurs.

EXPERIMENT 1

First, before performing Stroop's actual demonstration you should conduct a simpler version of it that will provide some baseline data on the effectiveness of our ability to ignore irrelevant information (see Chapter 6, "Perception," for a full discussion of this ability). In this experiment subjects are required to name colors. In the control condition of the experiment the colors are simply displayed in patches. In the experimental condition the colors are presented by having randomly ordered letter strings, each string of a different color. The question is whether having the letters present interferes with a subject's ability to name the colors. In principle, if the subject is capable of selectively attending to color, having the letters present should not interfere with his color-naming performance. Thus, naming the colors of the letter strings should be as easy as naming the colors of the color patches. On the other hand, the extent to which the subject cannot ignore the letter information is the extent to which his performance in color naming will decline.

Your measure of ease of color naming will be the amount of time it takes a subject to name a string of fifteen colors. To obtain reliable data you should have the subject name the colors in five lists of color patches and in five lists of letter strings, alternating between the two kinds of lists (see the number below each list).* The procedure is as follows: Cut out the ten lists of stimuli for ex-

periment 1. On each trial have the appropriate list in front of the subject turned over so that he cannot see the stimuli (see book insert for these lists). Then read the following instructions:

When I say "go," turn over the list in front of you and name the colors in the list from top to bottom. There will be fifteen colors total. Name these colors as fast but as accurately as possible. After you have named the last color, say "stop!" We will do this with ten different lists. Five have the colors printed in patches of ink, the other five have the colors printed in strings of randomly arranged letters. You should *ignore* how the colors are presented and simply name them. Any questions?

You should keep time from when you say "go" until when the subject says "stop." Make sure to present the ten lists in the order indicated by the number under the list. Record the time elapsed for each list and the number of errors for each list in the spaces provided on the report sheet on page 113.

Average the times for each type of list and total the errors. Does it appear that there is a difference between the average naming time or the total number of errors comparing the two types of lists? How would you interpret the data?

EXPERIMENT 2

In this experiment you are going to duplicate Stroop's demonstration. In the previous experiment you probably found either no effect or a very small effect of list type. The question we now ask is: Are there any conditions under which the subject cannot selectively attend well? In this experiment we have constructed such a condition by having the letters in the experimental condition spell color words themselves. Subjects are still required to name the color of the word, not what it spells, but now the name of what it spells is itself going to be a color name. If selective attention is not very effective, these names should interfere with the subject's response and slow him down relative to a control condition that has neutral (noncolor) words printed in color.

Follow the same procedure as before, but read the following new set of instructions:

*Notice that the two types of lists are matched for the length of the stimulus. That is, the color patches of lists 1, 3, 5, 7, and 9 are matched in length to the letter strings of length 2, 4, 6, 8, and 10. Why is this an important control? How have the lists of experiments 2 and 3 been matched? Why?

In this experiment you are going to perform the same task as in the previous experiment. This time, however, the ink colors will be printed in the form of words. For half the lists, the words will be randomly chosen. For the other half, they will be color words. In both lists, however, you are to ignore the meaning of the words themselves and simply name the colors in which they are printed from the top to the bottom of each list. Remember that you should be as fast and as accurate as possible. Don't turn over each list until I say "go," and when you have finished be sure to say "stop!"

When you record the data, keep track of both the time to read the list and the number of errors made. Average the time and errors for each type of list. Is the difference in average time and total errors between list types greater than the difference found in experiment 1? How would you interpret this?

EXPERIMENT 3

Now we will try a somewhat more subtle version of the Stroop experiment to get a better idea of the extent to which the subject can selectively attend. In the experimental condition, the words printed in color represent nouns whose referents themselves have a characteristic color (this color is never the same as the color in which the word is written). If the word suggests the characteristic color of its referent to the subject, this color might interfere with naming the color in which the word is printed (Majeres, 1974).

Follow the same procedure as in experiments 1 and 2, but read the following instructions to the subject:

In this experiment you are going to perform the same task as in the previous experiments; that is, you will be naming colors. This time the ink colors will be printed in the form of words that themselves are not colors. For example, one of the lists might contain the word "stove" printed in green ink. Disregard the word that is present and simply name the ink color of each word in the list. Remember that you should not turn over the list until I say "go," you should name the colors as quickly as possible, and you should say "stop" when you are done.

Conduct this experiment as you did the others. Is there a difference in performance between the lists? Is it larger or smaller than in experiment 2? What does this suggest about selective attention? What does it suggest about the automaticity of the reading process? *(If your instructor collects the data, fill out the report sheet in Appendix B.)*

References

Stroop, J. R. Studies of interference in serial verbal reactions. *Journal of Experimental Psychology*, 1935, *18*, 643-62.

Majeres, R. L. The combined effects of stimulus and response conditions on the delay in identifying the print color of words. *Journal of Experimental Psychology*, 1974, *102*, 868-74.

Report Sheet

Experiment 1

Color patch list

List 1 _____ sec. _____ errors

List 3 _____ sec. _____ errors

List 5 _____ sec. _____ errors

List 7 _____ sec. _____ errors

List 9 _____ sec. _____ errors

Average = _____ sec.

Total errors = _____

Letter string list

List 2 _____ sec. _____ errors

List 4 _____ sec. _____ errors

List 6 _____ sec. _____ errors

List 8 _____ sec. _____ errors

List 10 _____ sec. _____ errors

Average = _____ sec.

Total errors = _____

Experiment 2

Neutral words

List 1 _____ sec. _____ errors

List 3 _____ sec. _____ errors

List 5 _____ sec. _____ errors

List 7 _____ sec. _____ errors

List 9 _____ sec. _____ errors

Average = _____ sec.

Total errors = _____

Color words

List 2 _____ sec. _____ errors

List 4 _____ sec. _____ errors

List 6 _____ sec. _____ errors

List 8 _____ sec. _____ errors

List 10 _____ sec. _____ errors

Average = _____ sec.

Total errors = _____

Experiment 3

Neutral words

List 1 _____ sec. _____ errors

List 3 _____ sec. _____ errors

List 5 _____ sec. _____ errors

List 7 _____ sec. _____ errors

List 9 _____ sec. _____ errors

Average = _____ sec.

Total errors = _____

Color referent words

List 2 _____ sec. _____ errors

List 4 _____ sec. _____ errors

List 6 _____ sec. _____ errors

List 8 _____ sec. _____ errors

List 10 _____ sec. _____ errors

Average = _____ sec.

Total errors = _____

CHAPTER 9

Language

Learning Objectives

MAJOR PROPERTIES OF LANGUAGE

Language use is creative
1. Describe some everyday facts that undermine the view that language is a habit.

Language is structured
2. Explain the difference between the structural principles and the prescriptive rules of a language.
3. What is the misconception about nonstandard English, and how does nonstandard English differ from standard English? How is it similar to standard English?

THE STRUCTURE OF LANGUAGE

Phonemes
4. What is a phoneme? Give examples. Are the same phonemes used in different languages?
5. Are phonemes combined haphazardly? Give examples.

Morphemes and words
6. What is a morpheme? Give examples. How are morphemes combined?
7. Be prepared to argue why meaning is not the same as reference.
8. Does meaning derive from mental images? Why or why not?
9. What are semantic features? How is meaning decomposable into such features?
10. What is the weakness of feature analysis?

11. How does the concept of "family resemblance" overcome the problems of definitional theory?
12. According to the prototype theory, how are word meanings stored in memory? How does this theory differ from one based on mental images?
13. How can one reconcile definitional and prototype theories?
14. What is the meaning of lexical access? How does word frequency affect the results of a lexical access task?
15. Is semantic relatedness a basis for storing and filing words in the mental lexicon? Explain.
16. What evidence does the tip-of-the-tongue phenomenon give to substantiate the principle of sound similarity in lexical organization?
17. Explain the role of grammar in the organization of words in the mental lexicon. Distinguish between open-class and closed-class morphemes.

Sentences
18. How is phrase structure related to meaning?
19. Describe the reason for supposing that humans have knowledge of both surface and underlying phrase structures. What is the difference between these two structures?
20. How do linguists represent surface phrase structure?
21. In what sense is surface phrase structure "natural"?
22. Describe how proposition and attitude combine to form underlying structure.
23. What evidence suggests that people tend to remember underlying structure rather than surface structure?

24. Describe paraphrases in terms of underlying structure.
25. Understand how ambiguities can be explained with reference to underlying structure. What structural properties might give rise to ambiguity?
26. How can listeners reconstruct the logical meaning of sentences from the underlying structure?

THE ORGANIZATION AND USE OF LANGUAGE

Comprehension
27. What problem faces the listener in calculating the underlying structure of a sentence?
28. Describe how SAM analyzes a sentence, and indicate the first strategy that he uses.
29. What is the time difference in the comprehension of active and passive sentences? What accounts for this time difference?
30. Consider the following sentence: "The princess kissed the frog and the king knighted the frog." Be able to list the steps that SAM takes in order to understand the two propositions contained in this sentence.
31. Consider the following sentence: "The horse raced past the barn fell." Why does SAM have a difficult time analyzing this sentence?

Speech production
32. What evidence is there to show that speech is planned?

33. Speech errors involve what type of morphemes? Give examples of speech errors that are transpositions.
34. What are the characteristics of aphasia?
35. What are the characteristics of patients suffering from Broca's aphasia? What are the effects of Broca's aphasia on speech?
36. How do lesions in Wernicke's area of the brain affect the speech of a patient?
37. What do the processes of speaking and comprehending have in common?

LANGUAGE AS AN INTERPERSONAL HUMAN ENDEAVOR

38. How does social context play a crucial role in language production and comprehension?
39. Discuss the ways in which principles of conversation enhance communication.

LANGUAGE AS A HUMAN CAPACITY

Language in chimpanzees
40. Compare vocabulary learning in chimpanzees and humans. Which method works best to teach chimpanzees vocabulary?
41. Describe the evidence that suggests the use of primitive propositions by chimpanzees.
42. What evidence has suggested early syntax acquisition in chimpanzees? Be able to evaluate the quality of this evidence.

Programmed Exercises

SOME PROPERTIES OF LANGUAGE

1. There are about _____ human languages now in use on earth.

   5,500

2. Although animal and human languages are similar in that both have sounds and words (or something like words), animal languages do not have _____.

   sentences

3. We are able to make up novel sentences at will. This tells us that language is _____.

   creative

4. An estimate of the number of English sentences that are twenty words or fewer is _____.

   10^{30}

5. A rule such as "it is not correct to say 'ain't'" is a _____ rule.

   prescriptive

6. In English, the _____ dialect is elevated for professional, literary, and other formal purposes.

   standard

7. Nonstandard black dialects of American English are often

   considered _____ .   substandard

8. Every human community uses one or more _____ that   languages
   include an abstract set of structural principles.

THE STRUCTURE OF LANGUAGE

9. We can think of language as existing at a number of levels,
   from sounds to ideas. The structure of language, then, is

   _____ .   hierarchical

10. The spoken words "bed" and "dead" differ only in the "b"
    and "d" sounds at the beginning. This is a difference in one

    _____ .   phoneme

11. English uses about _____ speech sounds.   forty

12. Some of the facts about how phonemes combine in words are

    accidental choices. Others are _____ choices.   systematic

13. Morphemes are the smallest language units that carry _____ .   meaning

14. "Strange," "er," and "s" are all _____ .   morphemes

15. An old (and insufficient) view of word and phrase meaning is
    that meaning is whatever a word or phrase points to in the

    real world. This view equates meaning and _____ .   reference

16. Another view states that meaning is a kind of internal picture
    of whatever it refers to. This theory says that meanings are

    _____ _____ .   mental images

17. Another theory says that the meaning of a word is synony-

    mous with a list of characteristics, or _____ . This theory   features

    of meaning is called the _____ theory.   definitional

18. The _____ theory of meaning is similar to the feature   prototype
    theory, except that no one feature is sufficient or necessary.
    Instead, a whole group of features may be present. This theory
    accounts nicely for the fact that certain words are better exam-
    ples of their respective categories than other words.

19. Words are related through groups of features shared unequally

    among word meanings. This concept is termed _____   family

    _____ structures.   resemblance

20. _____ access means recognizing and understanding a word.   Lexical

21. The more _____ a word is in a language, the more quickly   frequent
    it is accessed for speech and understanding.

22. Words that are related in _____ are more likely to be filed   meaning
    and organized together in the mental lexicon.

23. The tip-of-the-tongue phenomenon is evidence that words are

    filed in the mental lexicon according to _____ similarity.   sound

24. The fact that nouns, verbs, and adjectives are stored in different ways gives evidence that _____ category is another property that determines how words are filed in the mental lexicon.   grammatical

25. The system by which we combine words into meaningful sentences are collectively known as _____.   syntax

26. An organized grouping of words is known as a _____, the unit from which sentences are composed.   phrase

27. Two sentences that are different in their ordering of phrases differ in _____ phrase structure.   surface

28. Two sentences that appear different, but are nearly identical in meaning, share a common _____ phrase structure.   underlying

29. In the sentence "The boy saw the ice-cream truck," the phrase "the boy" is called the _____ phrase.   noun

30. A _____ _____ is a useful way of partitioning a sentence to show its hierarchical structure.   tree diagram

31. The basic thought that a sentence expresses is called its _____.   proposition

32. The subtle difference in meaning of sentences like "The boy played with the ball" and "The ball was played with by the boy" is due to differences in _____.   attitude

33. Three examples of attitudes that may be expressed by a sentence are _____, _____, and _____.   focus, assertion, negation

34. People often forget the _____ structure of sentences in a story, but they usually remember the _____ structure.   surface / underlying

35. Two sentences whose meanings are essentially equivalent are called _____ of one another.   paraphrases

36. An ambiguous sentence is ambiguous because it is decomposable into more than one _____ representation.   underlying

THE ORGANIZATION AND USE OF LANGUAGE

37. SAM is the name given to the _____ _____ _____.   Sentence Analyzing Machinery

38. SAM's first assumption is that he will encounter a simple complete sentence. This consists of a _____ phrase, a _____, and another _____ phrase.   noun / verb, noun

39. The phrases in No. 38 represent the _____, the _____, and the _____.   doer, action / done-to

40. Studies show that it will take longer to understand a _____ sentence than an active sentence.   passive

41. The sentence "The princess kissed the frog and the king

    knighted the frog" contains two _____.   propositions

42. A _____ has occurred when parts of morphemes are inter-   transposition
    changed.

43. Transpositions only occur when the morphemes belong to the

    _____ _____ (content words), whose function is lexical.   open class

44. The function of the _____ _____ morphemes is to pro-   closed-class
    vide the syntactic structure of the sentence.

45. Closed-class morphemes are never _____.   transposed

46. A person afflicted with _____ can move his mouth and   aphasia
    tongue, can see and hear, but is impaired in his ability to
    speak and/or comprehend speech.

47. Patients suffering from _____ _____ speak only with   Broca's aphasia
    great effort. They can use many open-class words, but omit
    almost all closed-class items.

48. The following is an example of a sentence uttered by a patient

    with _____ _____: "And then they went and did it with   Wernicke's aphasia
    them and they did it and got the supermarket and that all over
    there."

LANGUAGE AS AN INTERPERSONAL HUMAN ENDEAVOR

49. The wording of a sentence often depends on what we believe
    about the listener's knowledge, attitudes, beliefs, etc. In this

    sense, language is _____, that is, it is intended for com-   interpersonal
    munication.

50. Conversation goes beyond the actual words that are spoken.
    Intelligent communication requires that its participants make

    complicated _____ about the meaning and intent of the   inferences
    conversation.

51. Those things which govern how we say things to people are

    called _____ principles.   conversational

LANGUAGE AS A HUMAN CAPACITY

52. The first language in children is _____. This is followed by   babbling
    one-word sentences, two-word sentences, and sentences of
    more complex forms.

53. Various investigators have reasoned that the failure to teach
    oral language to the chimpanzee Viki was due to her inability

    to _____.   articulate

54. After having been taught ASL for four years, Washoe had

    learned _____ signs. Some of these were acquired by   130

    _____, others by having her hands physically molded into   imitation
    a desired position.

55. The relation between doer, action, and done-to is known as

_____ meaning. propositional

56. Premack's studies of the concept of _____ in chimpanzees causation
showed that they were quite successful in performing a task in
which they were required to identify an object that could produce a change of state in another object.

57. Even if chimpanzees were shown to have some sense of

_____, this would not be sufficient to claim that they have sequence
knowledge of syntax.

58. Chimpanzees cannot be said to be "linguistic beasts" because

they lack the _____ that makes language communication organization
possible.

Self Test

1. A new group of people is discovered who
possesses a language which has never been
studied before. After a good deal of work,
linguists are able to translate anything said
in this language into English. This is further
evidence that all language:
   a. is unrelated
   b. is similar in what can be expressed
   c. uses the same sounds
   d. uses the same words

2. All of the following describe language use
except:
   a. it is creative
   b. it has a rule-governed structure
   c. it is a habit
   d. our propensity for it is innate

3. The fact that there is an infinite number of
sentences which can be uttered upon seeing
a rabbit is an argument against the behaviorist position and demonstrates the _____
of language.
   a. uncertainty
   b. variability
   c. creativity
   d. rigidity

4. The fact that the words "boys," "kiss,"
and "girls" can be arranged in different orders to give different meanings (i.e., Boys
kiss girls, Girls kiss boys) demonstrates another universal characteristic of language.
Language is:
   a. rule-governed
   b. unpredictable
   c. implicit
   d. prototypical

5. The general organizing principles which
structure a language are called:
   a. features
   b. morphemes
   c. syntax
   d. prescriptive rules of grammar

6. The dialect used for the intercommunica-
tions of many social, geographical, and eth-
nic groupings in a culture is referred to as
the:
   a. regional dialect
   b. substantiated dialect
   c. standard dialect
   d. nonstandard dialect

7. The fact that both standard English and
Black English have very precise rules about
the use of the copula suggests that:
   a. neither standard English nor Black
English is logical
   b. both are poor vehicles for expressing
meaning
   c. neither dialect is superior to the other
   d. each group respects the speech of the
other group

8. When we say that language is hierarchical,
we mean that:
   a. different language uses demonstrate
social class differences
   b. language structure exists at many levels
   c. language has developed from other cognitive functions
   d. modern languages are descended from
other languages

9. Which of the following represents the actual
hierarchy of language structures?
   a. phrase, word, phoneme, morpheme
   b. word, morpheme, phrase, phoneme

c. phoneme, morpheme, word, phrase
d. morpheme, phoneme, word, phrase

10. The perceptual units of speech are:
    a. phonemes
    b. morphemes
    c. syllables
    d. words

11. One reason that foreign languages sound strange is that:
    a. the same phonemes are pronounced differently
    b. other languages are spoken more rapidly than English
    c. there are fewer "gaps" in foreign languages than in English
    d. some of the phonemes are different from those of English

12. New words are being coined every day. Some sound combinations are not used, though. This is due to _____ rules.
    a. syntactic
    b. semantic
    c. pragmatic
    d. none of the above

13. A morpheme is a:
    a. word
    b. single sound
    c. perceptual unit
    d. unit of meaning

14. The area of knowledge dealing solely with meaning is called:
    a. linguistics
    b. semantics
    c. phonetics
    d. none of the above

15. A view of meaning as simply referring to objects in the world is not sufficient, since:
    a. the same object can be referred to in more than one way
    b. it's hard to describe the reference of words like "truth"
    c. both of the above
    d. none of the above

16. The fact that a sentence is grammatical does not mean that it is acceptable. Thus a sentence like "This is the sixth week of February" might raise some eyebrows. Not only is language grammatical, it is also:
    a. invariant
    b. referential
    c. deterministic
    d. nativistic

17. The definitional theory attempts to define the _____ attributes that define a given concept.
    a. necessary
    b. sufficient
    c. both of the above
    d. none of the above

18. One problem with the definitional theory is that:
    a. some attributes are used to describe more than one concept
    b. some concepts involve more than one attribute
    c. some concepts have no attributes
    d. some members of a category seem to be better examples of that category than other members

19. The major characteristic of a prototype theory of meaning is that:
    a. no feature is individually necessary
    b. no feature is individually sufficient
    c. a whole set of features describes word meaning
    d. all of the above

20. A robin will be judged to be an exemplary member of the bird family because:
    a. it has wings
    b. it has feathers
    c. the robin is close to the presumed prototype of a bird
    d. a robin is more like a bird than an ostrich

21. All of the following are ways in which words are organized in the mental lexicon except:
    a. word frequency
    b. configuration
    c. word meaning
    d. sound similarity

22. Which of the following words would probably be stored with the word "surgeon" in the mental lexicon?
    a. doctor
    b. blood
    c. antiseptic
    d. anesthetic

23. A subject was asked to add one word to the following list of words: house, barrel, steak. Which word would he be most likely to generate?
    a. up
    b. anxiously

c. bird
d. friendly

24. Which of the following is not a closed-class word?
    a. and
    b. the
    c. of
    d. she

25. Which of the following is not an open-class word?
    a. therefore
    b. intercept
    c. beautiful
    d. battery

26. That part of language which organizes words into sentences is called:
    a. semantics
    b. syntax
    c. phonetics
    d. morphology

27. Instead of producing sentences, we might invent a new word for each idea we want to convey. The problem with this is that:
    a. all the words have already been used
    b. some letter combinations cannot occur
    c. we could never remember such a huge number of words
    d. none of the above

28. The two types of phrase structures are:
    a. syntactic, semantic
    b. underlying, syntactic
    c. surface, syntactic
    d. surface, underlying

29. The phrase structure that describes the sequence of phrases in a sentence as it is spoken is called the _____ structure.
    a. morphological
    b. semantic
    c. surface
    d. underlying

30. Partitioning of sentences suggests that phrase structure rules:
    a. do not exist psychologically
    b. are psychologically natural
    c. exist but are usually ignored
    d. require more attention than other grammars

31. In which of the following pairs of sentences are the two underlying structures similar?
    a. "The girl kissed the boy." "The boy kissed the girl."
    b. "The girl kissed the boy." "The girl was kissed by the boy."
    c. "The girl kissed the boy." "The boy was kissed by the girl."
    d. all of the above

32. The two sentences "The boy hit the ball" and "The ball hit the boy" differ in:
    a. underlying structure
    b. surface structure
    c. both
    d. neither

33. Which of the following nonsense strings would be easiest to memorize, given what you know about syntax?
    a. All zills mig dilly in boder delf.
    b. The Dizz witz bis in wib gof.
    c. The pretz vint bri in drom bis.
    d. A prit gred dif in pil viff.

34. Which sentence below has a different proposition from the others?
    a. "The girl kissed the boy."
    b. "The boy was kissed by the girl."
    c. "The girl did not kiss the boy."
    d. all of the above include the same proposition

35. Sentences a, b, and c above (question 34) differ in:
    a. attitude
    b. proposition
    c. proposition and attitude
    d. neither proposition nor attitude

36. Subjects were read a story which contains the sentence "Skinner disagreed with the psycholinguists' view of language." In a subsequent session the sentences below were presented to the subjects, who had to determine whether that exact sentence was actually presented. Which sentence is most likely to be mistakenly recognized?
    a. The psycholinguists disagreed with Skinner about the nature of language.
    b. Skinner did not disagree with the psycholinguists' view of language.
    c. The psycholinguists did not agree with Skinner's view of language.
    d. It was the psycholinguists' view of language which Skinner disagreed with.

37. The two sentences "All students like psychology" and "Psychology is liked by all students" represent:
    a. paraphrases

b. different propositions

c. the same attitude

d. different underlying structures

38. The sentence "Flying airplanes can be dangerous" is ambiguous because:
    a. there are two possible surface structures
    b. there are two possible underlying structures
    c. there are two possible surface and two possible underlying structures
    d. there is no explanation for the ambiguity of this particular sentence

39. Consider the following sentences, all produced in the same situation: "It's under the table." "It's under the large table." "The ball is under the table." What differentiates these sentences is:
    a. the intelligence of the speaker
    b. the knowledge that the speaker believes the listener has
    c. the knowledge that the listener believes the speaker has
    d. all of the above

40. Some support for the hypothesis that listeners use the "first noun phrase did it" strategy is that subjects comprehend _____ sentences faster than they do _____ ones.
    a. active, passive
    b. passive, active
    c. ambiguous, simple
    d. simple, paraphrased

41. Which of the following sentences will take the longest time to understand?
    a. The boy hit the ball.
    b. The boy did not hit the ball.
    c. The ball was hit by the boy.
    d. all of the above will take the same time to understand

42. Evidence that a speaker formulates a mental plan that directs his sentence expression is:
    a. that only regular, never irregular, verbs are used
    b. that an adjective can be placed only once in a sentence
    c. the use of pronouns to replace nouns that come later in the sentence
    d. the use of adverbs to modify verbs that come earlier in the sentence

43. When "queer old dean" is spoken for "dear old queen," a _____ has occurred.
    a. transformation
    b. transposition

c. transmutation

d. transference

44. The parts of a sentence that are interchanged are:
    a. closed-class morphemes
    b. adjectives
    c. phonemes
    d. none of the above

45. The loss or disturbance of language function is known as:
    a. aphasia
    b. anorexia
    c. asphyxia
    d. aphaeresis

46. The symptom(s) most likely to be demonstrated by an aphasic is (are):
    a. inability to talk in an understandable way
    b. inability to comprehend
    c. a and b
    d. neither a nor b

47. The speech disorder characterized by fluent and rapid speech and a deficient open-class vocabulary is:
    a. Broca's aphasia
    b. expressive aphasia
    c. Wernicke's aphasia
    d. none of the above

48. Language in chimpanzees:
    a. seems to involve propositions
    b. uses a hierarchical structure
    c. approaches the complexity of human language
    d. progresses at about the same rate as for children

Answer Key for Self Test

1. b p. 296	13. d p. 301
2. c pp. 296–99	14. b p. 302
3. c p. 297	15. c p. 302
4. a p. 298	16. b p. 302
5. d p. 298	17. c pp. 303–304
6. c p. 298	18. d p. 304
7. c p. 299	19. d p. 305
8. b p. 299	20. c pp. 304–306
9. c p. 299	21. b pp. 307–308
10. a p. 300	22. a pp. 307–308
11. d p. 300	23. c p. 308
12. d p. 301	24. d p. 308

Investigating Psychological Phenomena

MEASURING LEXICAL RETRIEVAL TIME

Equipment: Stimuli are included; watch with second hand
Subjects: Two
Time per subject: Fifteen minutes
Time per experimenter: Forty-five minutes

As described in the text, there have been developed several techniques for measuring aspects of the representation of word meaning. One of these tasks involves lexical access—that is, recognizing and understanding a word. In the present exercise, you can demonstrate two of the phenomena that are important results from the lexical access task. One is that frequent words are recognized faster than are infrequent words, and the other is that recognizing a word is facilitated by having just had to recognize another word that is related in meaning.

The experiment requires subjects to scan through four lists of forty-eight strings of letters. Next to each one, they are to mark either a "+" or a "−" depending on whether the string of letters forms a word or not. Subjects are required to complete the task as quickly and as accurately as possible, trying to avoid making any errors if they can. The lists differ according to two variables. One is the frequency with which the average word on a list appears in print in the English language. The other is whether words in the lists are related to one another or not. These two variables are combined so that there is a list in which words are of high frequency, with the words related (list 1); a list in which the words are of lower frequency, but

related (list 2); a list with unrelated words of high frequency (list 3); and a list of lower-frequency words that are unrelated (list 4). Each subject will be given each of the four lists in a different order to counterbalance for a possible effect of practice that might improve performance. The orders are as follows:

Subject 1: List 1 → List 4 → List 2 → List 3
Subject 2: List 3 → List 2 → List 4 → List 1

Use the following instructions to your subjects:
"I am going to present you with four lists of strings of letters. Some of the strings on each list form words, and others don't. Your task is to decide which of the strings is a word, and which is not. For example, if you saw the string of letters A-P-P-L-E, the answer would obviously be that this spells a word. If you saw the string P-L-A-M-E, however, this wouldn't spell a word. For each string that you see, you will have to decide whether a word is spelled or not. None of the words that you see will be bizarre or so rare that you wouldn't recognize it, so you should be nearly one hundred percent accurate on the task, and I want you to try to get all the strings right. Within this constraint, however, I want you to make each decision as quickly as possible since I will be timing you.

"The strings are printed in four lists of forty-eight strings each. I will ask you to close your eyes for each list as I place it in front of you. When I say 'Go,' you should open your eyes, start at the top of the list, and decide for each string whether it spells a word or not. If it does, put a '+' sign on the line to the left of the string; if it doesn't, put a '−' sign. When you are done with a list, shout 'Stop.' I will time you from the time I say 'Go' until you yell 'Stop.' Remember to be as accurate as possible, yet as fast as possible. Any questions?"

Cut out the lists below for each subject, and time the duration of each list as subjects go through it. As indicated in the text, there should be two effects evident in the data. First, lists with high-frequency words (lists 1 and 3) should result in faster times than lists with low-frequency words (lists 2 and 4). Second, lists with related words (lists 1 and 2) should be faster than lists with unrelated words (lists 3 and 4). Did you verify these predictions? If so, what does this tell you about retrieval of information from memory and about word meaning? How could you modify the experiment to explore the time course of activation of meaning in memory? (Hint: Think about the time interval between the presentation of words that are related.)

Stimulus Lists

REPORT SHEET

Subject 1	Subject 2
List 1 _____	List 1 _____
List 2 _____	List 2 _____
List 3 _____	List 3 _____
List 4 _____	List 4 _____

Subject 1

LIST 1	LIST 2	LIST 3	LIST 4
CLOSE	DRIST	HERE	HIKE
OPEN	HAMMER	DAKE	MOTH
SIMEL	FOTCH	JINE	NART
SNOCK	NAIL	RIGHT	FLESS
WHITE	TANGO	WORK	CRUNK
BLACK	DANCE	LUTIM	BUTLER
DAY	HUPLE	MOICH	GERM
GACK	HOG	BECAUSE	SOCCER
TREEK	PIG	HAVE	CUB
NIGHT	MECT	FROM	MORM
DOWN	STARVED	THEY	RIRTH
VING	HUNGRY	TRUCKEL	PAIL
UP	BEAVER	WANK	TAIN
EVEN	SITCH	WITHOUT	SLY
BLANTY	DABER	ALL	FRAUD
DEEK	DAM	LABE	ANT
ODD	PYTHON	GREEL	SPEAR
HIM	SNAKE	GET	TOLBON
HER	CHARB	PEOPLE	DOUBROT
SAPER	DIAMOND	CRIV	YACHT
RAST	BURDIT	FOR	SPIDER
OVER	STONE	COUNTRY	BIFTY
UNDER	BELLY	BREEN	BADGE
LESS	ANK	BUT	JUITER
MORE	STOMACH	YOU	PET
PIND	ROUGH	REAT	SHINE
DOX	SEVEL	GLUNT	SNADE
ALWAYS	SMOOTH	FRAIP	CARROT
NEVER	BLOTTER	HOUSE	RAT
BULE	INK	FAR	TRUNK
ONE	ROTBER	CHURCH	CORK
HACTOM	WALM	WITH	SPLAMPEN
DIND	URLACK	GELDLE	FLEA
TWO	TROUT	BERVE	CRUMB
SMALL	KIRE	MAN	VOON
FLOBE	FISH	DUMET	COBER
SPOTHER	CANARY	GOOD	RANET
LARGE	NECERT	PEATOL	APE
NOKE	BIRD	CITY	TACK
SECOND	COAL	SEE	SOOF
TIME	MINER	NORDER	DOCK
LATTLE	MUTICE	MADE	HORN
PART	HAINT	COURSE	RANEY
WHOLE	PARROW	VERY	NUCK
HORK	CAPSULE	RULLEGE	JELLY
LURST	PILL	SUPET	SOMTLE
BOY	GLECK	LONG	FRINER
GIRL	DRIST	OLD	MAPLE

Subject 2

LIST 1	LIST 2	LIST 3	LIST 4
_____ CLOSE	_____ DRIST	_____ HERE	_____ HIKE
_____ OPEN	_____ HAMMER	_____ DAKE	_____ MOTH
_____ SIMEL	_____ FOTCH	_____ JINE	_____ NART
_____ SNOCK	_____ NAIL	_____ RIGHT	_____ FLESS
_____ WHITE	_____ TANGO	_____ WORK	_____ CRUNK
_____ BLACK	_____ DANCE	_____ LUTIM	_____ BUTLER
_____ DAY	_____ HUPLE	_____ MOICH	_____ GERM
_____ GACK	_____ HOG	_____ BECAUSE	_____ SOCCER
_____ TREEK	_____ PIG	_____ HAVE	_____ CUB
_____ NIGHT	_____ MECT	_____ FROM	_____ MORM
_____ DOWN	_____ STARVED	_____ THEY	_____ RIRTH
_____ VING	_____ HUNGRY	_____ TRUCKEL	_____ PAIL
_____ UP	_____ BEAVER	_____ WANK	_____ TAIN
_____ EVEN	_____ SITCH	_____ WITHOUT	_____ SLY
_____ BLANTY	_____ DABER	_____ ALL	_____ FRAUD
_____ DEEK	_____ DAM	_____ LABE	_____ ANT
_____ ODD	_____ PYTHON	_____ GREEL	_____ SPEAR
_____ HIM	_____ SNAKE	_____ GET	_____ TOLBON
_____ HER	_____ CHARB	_____ PEOPLE	_____ DOUBROT
_____ SAPER	_____ DIAMOND	_____ CRIV	_____ YACHT
_____ RAST	_____ BURDIT	_____ FOR	_____ SPIDER
_____ OVER	_____ STONE	_____ COUNTRY	_____ BIFTY
_____ UNDER	_____ BELLY	_____ BREEN	_____ BADGE
_____ LESS	_____ ANK	_____ BUT	_____ JUITER
_____ MORE	_____ STOMACH	_____ YOU	_____ PET
_____ PIND	_____ ROUGH	_____ REAT	_____ SHINE
_____ DOX	_____ SEVEL	_____ GLUNT	_____ SNADE
_____ ALWAYS	_____ SMOOTH	_____ FRAIP	_____ CARROT
_____ NEVER	_____ BLOTTER	_____ HOUSE	_____ RAT
_____ BULE	_____ INK	_____ FAR	_____ TRUNK
_____ ONE	_____ ROTBER	_____ CHURCH	_____ CORK
_____ HACTOM	_____ WALM	_____ WITH	_____ SPLAMPEN
_____ DIND	_____ URLACK	_____ GELDLE	_____ FLEA
_____ TWO	_____ TROUT	_____ BERVE	_____ CRUMB
_____ SMALL	_____ KIRE	_____ MAN	_____ VOON
_____ FLOBE	_____ FISH	_____ DUMET	_____ COBER
_____ SPOTHER	_____ CANARY	_____ GOOD	_____ RANET
_____ LARGE	_____ NECERT	_____ PEATOL	_____ APE
_____ NOKE	_____ BIRD	_____ CITY	_____ TACK
_____ SECOND	_____ COAL	_____ SEE	_____ SOOF
_____ TIME	_____ MINER	_____ NORDER	_____ DOCK
_____ LATTLE	_____ MUTICE	_____ MADE	_____ HORN
_____ PART	_____ HAINT	_____ COURSE	_____ RANEY
_____ WHOLE	_____ PARROW	_____ VERY	_____ NUCK
_____ HORK	_____ CAPSULE	_____ RULLEGE	_____ JELLY
_____ LURST	_____ PILL	_____ SUPET	_____ SOMTLE
_____ BOY	_____ GLECK	_____ LONG	_____ FRINER
_____ GIRL	_____ DRIST	_____ OLD	_____ MAPLE

CHAPTER 10

The Biological Basis of Social Behavior

Learning Objectives

THE SOCIAL NATURE OF HUMANS AND ANIMALS

1. Explain Hobbes's conception of human nature and contrast it with that of sociobiology.

Natural selection and evolution: Charles Darwin
2. Outline the basic principles of Darwin's theory of evolution.
3. Are humans an inherently social species? Does Darwin's theory of evolution answer this question?

Instinctive social patterns and ethology
4. Describe the basic principles of ethology, including the concepts of display, fixed-action pattern, and releaser.

THE BIOLOGICAL SOURCES OF AGGRESSION

Conflict between species: Predation and defense
5. Is aggression a component of predatory attack? Explain.
6. Is it fair to describe much of aggressive behavior between different species as defensive? Explain.

Conflicts between like and like
7. Discuss the relation between testosterone and aggression.
8. Discuss the nature and function of territory.
9. Explain mechanisms for limiting aggression in humans and in animals.
10. Are humans territorial? Explain.

THE BIOLOGICAL BASIS OF LOVE: THE MALE-FEMALE BOND

Sexual behavior in animals
11. What is the selective advantage of sexual reproduction?
12. Describe the nature and function of courtship rituals.
13. Explain why the female is more selective in mate selection than the male.
14. Explain the role of sex hormones in sexual behavior in animals and humans.

Human sexuality
15. List some special and unique characteristics of the human pair bond.
16. Contrast the sexual and reproductive hypotheses as explanations of the strength of the human pair bond.

THE BIOLOGICAL BASIS OF LOVE: THE PARENT-CHILD BOND

The infant's attachment to the mother
17. To what extent is the child's love for the mother explained by the fact that the mother fulfills the child's basic biological needs?

The mother's attachment to the infant
18. What is the function of maternal attachment?
19. What characteristics of the infant are important in establishing maternal attachment?

SELF-SACRIFICE AND ALTRUISM

Altruism in animals
20. Explain how self-sacrifice ("altruism") is consistent with evolutionary theory.

21. Distinguish among enlightened self-interest, kin selection, and reciprocal altruism as accounts for altruistic behavior.

    Altruism in humans
22. Discuss sociobiological accounts of altruism in humans, and the criticism of this approach.

COMMUNICATING MOTIVES

Expressive movements: animal display
23. Describe the role of displays in communication, and comment on their evolution.
24. What is the relation between displays and intention movements?

The expression of emotions in humans
25. Review the evidence for human facial expressions as products of both biology and culture.

The difference between display and language
26. Why aren't displays adequate for human communication?
27. What are the fundamental differences between human and animal communication?

ETHOLOGY AND HUMAN NATURE

28. Indicate the extent to which human social behavior can be explained in biological terms.

Programmed Exercises

THE SOCIAL NATURE OF HUMANS AND ANIMALS

1. The view that man is an inherently solitary creature, who invents society as a means of taming his brutish nature, is

   associated with the British philosopher _____ _____. Thomas Hobbes

2. According to Darwin, evolution proceeds because variants of a species with superior characteristics are more likely to survive.

   This process is called _____ _____. natural selection

3. Those characteristics which confer survival and reproductive

   advantage are considered to have high _____ _____. adaptive value

4. The branch of biology that studies animal behavior, particularly under natural conditions and within an evolutionary

   framework, is called _____. ethology

5. Stereotyped, species-specific movements are called

   _____ _____ _____. fixed-action patterns

6. When a female stickleback enters a nest, the male prods her rhythmically at the base of her tail. This action causes the female to deposit her eggs, a species-specific response. We can

   term such prodding a _____ _____. releasing stimulus

7. Since this prodding stimulus is a product of the male's behavior, it can also be called a _____. display

THE BIOLOGICAL SOURCES OF AGGRESSION

8. An attack by a lion on a zebra seems qualitatively different from a fight or threat sequence between two members of the

   same species. We call the former _____ and the latter predation

   _____. aggression

9. The generally higher level of aggression seen in males of most species has been attributed to higher levels of the male

   hormone _____ .   testosterone

10. Animals often defend a particular area against other members of their species. This area probably serves to guarantee them

    essential _____ and is called a _____ .   resources, territory

11. One mechanism for limiting aggression involves a display that essentially indicates "surrender." Such a display is called an

    _____ _____ .   appeasement signal

12. In a _____ _____ , a group of animals of the same   dominance hierarchy
    species develops a stable social order based on the establish-
    ment of ranks as a result of mutual aggressive encounters.

13. A person walks up to a stranger, approaching her until their bodies are just inches apart. This can be considered a violation

    of _____ _____ .   personal space

THE BIOLOGICAL BASIS OF LOVE: THE MALE-FEMALE BOND

14. The tendency to affiliate with others of one's own kind is

    called _____ .   bonding

15. This is accomplished in some animals, such as monkeys, by activities including caring for the fur of another member of

    the species. This activity is called _____ .   grooming

16. In sexual reproduction, the _____ and _____ unite to   sperm, ovum

    produce the fertilized egg, or _____ .   zygote

17. The rooster's comb, the stag's antlers, and possibly the en-
    larged breast of the human female are all instances of struc-

    tural _____ .   displays

18. The relatively complex behavior patterns that constitute sexual

    displays in many animals are called _____ _____ .   courtship rituals

19. Elaborate courtship patterns ensure that mating is restricted to members of the displayer's own species, thus guaranteeing

    reproductive _____ .   isolation

20. In most species the _____ (male or female) has the major   female
    role in "deciding" whether or not to mate.

21. Except for primates, mammals mate only when the female is

    in "heat" or _____ .   estrus

22. The most important hormones involved in the mammalian

    female reproductive cycle are _____ and _____ .   estrogen, progesterone

23. Implantation of male hormones, or _____ , into the hypo-   androgens
    thalamus can cause a castrated male animal to show male
    sexual behavior.

24. While the biological aspects of the human female reproductive

cycle are controlled by hormones, human _____ _____   sexual activity (or
is relatively independent of these.   sexual behavior)

25. Some have proposed that the prevalence of human sexual activity outside of fertile periods suggests that sexual relationships

may play a role in maintaining the human _____ _____.   pair bond

THE BIOLOGICAL BASIS OF LOVE: THE PARENT-CHILD BOND

26. The human infant's cry or the chirp of a newly hatched bird

are examples of _____ calls.   distress

27. The _____ is the human infant's built-in means of com-   smile
municating with adults and maintaining their attention while
indicating a generally positive state.

SELF-SACRIFICE AND ALTRUISM

28. "Self-sacrifice" by a parent animal can be understood within
an evolutionary framework, since it may ultimately serve to

increase the number of the parent's _____ in the population. genes

29. When this (question 28) is accomplished by sparing the lives of

relatives, it is called _____ _____.   kin selection

30. "Unselfish" acts may also be adaptive because the recipients
of these acts may later return the favor. This is called

_____ _____.   reciprocal altruism

31. Edmund Wilson's view, that altruism in humans is based in

our genes, is part of the general position of _____.   sociobiology

COMMUNICATING MOTIVES

32. The message of a display can be inferred by noting the

_____ between the occurrence of the display and the   correlation (relation)
animal's behavior just before and after the occurrence.

33. Threat postures often include preparatory movements that
normally procede attack. Such actions are called

_____ _____.   intention movements

34.

The figures illustrate mating behavior in two fly species, and
they illustrate the origin of a courtship ritual by use of the

_____ _____.   comparative method

35. Human _____ _____ are displays that probably in-   facial expressions
    dicate emotional states.

36. Although there are some variations across cultures, there

    seem to be a number of _____ human facial expressions.   universal

37. Human language differs in many ways from animal displays.
    One critical difference is that while animals only express
    specific displays in appropriate contexts, human language

    constitutes a _____ system necessary for communicating   productive
    diverse combinations of information.

ETHOLOGY AND HUMAN NATURE

38. Contrary to the position taken by Hobbes, it now seems clear

    that the human organism is, in its biological nature, a _____   social
    creature.

Self Test

1. The Darwinian principle of natural selection
   implies that:
   a. social behavior cannot be subject to
      evolution because it is not inherited
   b. in the struggle to survive and reproduce,
      human beings are self-centered and
      solitary creatures restrained only by the
      constraints imposed by society
   c. social or altruistic behavior may evolve
      only of it serves to increase the frequen-
      cies of the genes of the animal showing
      this behavior
   d. coupled with the principles of ethology
      and genetics, social and altruistic behav-
      ior will evolve as long as there is appro-
      priate display or communication

2. Ethologists are particularly concerned with
   the study of:
   a. species-specific behavior
   b. behavior in natural settings
   c. social behavior
   d. all of the above
   e. none of the above

3. Releasing stimulus : fixed-action pattern ::
   a. species-specific : general
   b. cause : effect
   c. learned : innate
   d. predation : aggression
   e. house : door

4. This picture of three-spined sticklebacks
   illustrates:

   a. aggressive behavior
   b. territory
   c. releasers and fixed-action patterns
   d. the hormonal control of sexual behavior
   e. the role of learning in animal behavior

5. An observer notes that animal A, a male of
   a particular species, is, at a particular time,
   more aggressive than animal B. In an effort
   to increase the aggressiveness of animal B,
   the observer could:
   a. introduce a dominant animal of the
      same species into B's environment
   b. inject B with any sex hormone in an ap-
      propriate dose

c. place B in its own territory and arrange for another male to approach the territory border

d. place B in the territory of another male

e. limit B's resources and deprive B of the releasers it would normally encounter

6. Aggressive encounters between members of the same species are often concerned with the establishment of:
   a. mobbing
   b. predation
   c. appropriate defense mechanisms
   d. territories

7. The adaptive value of territories is that they:
   a. increase the aggressiveness of the territory holder
   b. preserve resources for the territory holder
   c. prevent threat displays
   d. decrease personal space and allow for greater reproduction

8. The damage caused by aggressive encounters within a species is controlled by all but one of the following. Which of the alternatives is not a means of controlling aggression?
   a. appeasement signals
   b. dominance hierarchies
   c. displays
   d. establishment of territories
   e. imprinting

9. This picture illustrates one stage of:

   a. predation
   b. defense
   c. feeding
   d. courtship
   e. contact comfort

10. Courtship rituals serve all but one of the following purposes. Which of the items below is *not* a function of courtship rituals:
    a. to synchronize the sexual activities of male and female
    b. to attract members of the opposite sex
    c. to increase the size of a territory
    d. to identify the sex and sexual readiness of the partners

11. To the extent that the male of a species spends time and energy in the care of the young, we would expect that:
    a. he would be more selective about mating partners
    b. he would have lower levels of testosterone than expected
    c. he would show more structural sexual displays
    d. he would be less likely to have a territory

12. During estrus, the female (nonprimate) mammal is:
    a. secreting estrogen
    b. most receptive to sexual approach of males
    c. fertile
    d. all of the above
    e. none of the above

13. In some species where the female has a clearly defined estrus cycle, the male is always ready for sexual activity. This would make sense if it were the case that in these species:
    a. all females come into estrus at the same time
    b. estrus is dependent on the season
    c. estrus occurs throughout the year and females are not synchronized in their cycles
    d. a and b
    e. hormonal factors are especially important in determining the receptivity of the female

14. Which of the following features of human sexual behavior is shared most completely with other mammals?
    a. the hormone independence of female receptivity
    b. the existence of sexual displays
    c. the importance of learning in the sexual response
    d. the persistence of sexual behavior following castration

15. A probable adaptive value of hormone independence of sexual receptivity in the human female is:
    a. increasing the time period when the female is fertile
    b. aiding the establishment of a strong pair bond
    c. reducing the importance of territories
    d. allowing the female to participate in the hunt

16. The great strength of the human pair bond may be explained as:
    a. an adaption to the necessity for a long period of intense infant care
    b. related to the importance of hormones in controlling sexual behavior
    c. related to the constant receptivity of the human female
    d. all of the above
    e. a and c

17. Features of the human infant, such as the upturned nose and chubby cheeks, are:
    a. the stimuli through which we learn to recognize specific children
    b. the vehicles for the establishment of basic trust
    c. releasers of parental behavior
    d. instances of distress displays

18. Consider a case in which an animal risks death from a predator by distracting it from the children of the animal's sister. Which of the possibilities listed below are possible accounts of this "altruistic" behavior?
    a. kin selection
    b. reciprocal altruism
    c. all of the above
    d. none of the above

19. Consider a different case, in which an animal A risks death from a predator by distracting the predator from another adult, B, of its species. And suppose that B is not related to A, and furthermore, that B is not a member of A's group, and is only transiently in A's presence. This apparently altruistic act would be most easily accounted for as:
    a. kin selection
    b. reciprocal altruism
    c. all of the above
    d. none of the above

20. On a sociobiological (evolutionary and genetic) account, which of the following

"altruistic" human acts would be most difficult to explain?
    a. a man sacrificing his life to save four of his sister's children
    b. a woman sacrificing her life to save four of her sister's children
    c. a grandmother sacrificing her life to save one grandchild
    d. a grandchild sacrificing his life to save one grandparent
    e. a or c

21. Expressive movements by animal A may inform other members of its species about:
    a. its current motivation
    b. a motivational conflict that it is in
    c. how likely it is that it will behave in one way or another
    d. a and b
    e. all of the above

22. The dog's snarl, as a threat display, can be interpreted as:
    a. an example of the comparative method
    b. an alarm call
    c. kin selection
    d. an intention movement
    e. learned

23. Intention movement : display :: airplane :
    a. automobile
    b. rocket ship
    c. wing
    d. engine

24. Some claim that at least some human facial displays are innately linked to certain emotional states. Which of the following invalidate such a view?
    a. across many cultures, people seem to associate the same facial expressions with the same situations (emotions)
    b. blind children show some of the basic facial expressions in appropriate situations
    c. deaf children show some of the appropriate facial expressions in some situations
    d. on some occasions, some people can mask the facial expression they would normally make under the circumstances
    e. none of the above

25. Human language differs from animal displays in that:
    a. it can express emotional states
    b. it has a long evolutionary history

c. it is a form of communication

d. it can produce statements about the world as well as about internal states or tendencies

e. it has more than ten different "displays" that convey different meanings

26. Hobbes and the sociobiologists would agree that:

a. there is something that might be called basic (biological) human nature

b. humans are inherently social

c. any apparently unselfish act of humans is a result of culture and works against basic human nature

d. humans are basically aggressive

Answer Key for Self Test

1. c p. 336	14. b p. 351
2. d p. 337	15. b p. 352
3. b p. 338	16. e pp. 352–53
4. c p. 338	17. c p. 355
5. c p. 340	18. c pp. 356–57
6. d p. 340	19. d p. 357
7. b p. 340	20. d pp. 356–57
8. e pp. 341–44	21. e pp. 358–59
9. d p. 347	22. d p. 360
10. c pp. 347–49	23. b p. 360
11. a pp. 348–49	24. e p. 362
12. d p. 349	25. d p. 364
13. c p. 349	26. a p. 364

Investigating Psychological Phenomena

PERSONAL SPACE: BEHAVIOR IN ELEVATORS

Equipment: A bank of a least two public elevators
Number of subjects: None
Time per subject: None
Time for experimenter: Thirty minutes to one hour

Whatever one's view of the precise way in which the basic phenomena of territoriality in animals are experienced in humans, it is clear that humans prefer to avoid close contact with strangers. Strangers interact at respectable distances, and one typically feels uncomfortable when a stranger approaches to within much less

than a meter. Observations of this sort lead to the notion of personal space, a "territory" around the body. The distant spacing of students seated at libraries or riders on public transportation speaks to the same issue.

In this study we will attempt to gather direct evidence for the idea of personal space. To do so, we must find a common situation in which strangers find themselves in close confinement. Elevators seem particularly suited for this study.

Our study will based on observations of where people stand in elevators. Given that an elevator already requires that all riders stand in close proximity, a personal space approach would certainly predict that *strangers* would maximize the distance among them. In order to test this idea, we will have to make some decisions about where, when, and how to make observations. (Although it would seem easy to just go and observe people in elevators, to do so without some thought, planning, and preliminary casual observation, would almost surely result in unreliable and not very meaningful data.)

What are the predictions? We must realize that elevators are typically asymmetrical: there is a door on one wall, and there is usually a button panel on one or both sides of the door. When people enter, they normally go to the panel to see if their floor has been pressed. Since it is likely that each person who gets on will go to the panel, it would be natural to maximize the distance from the panel in anticipation of the arrival of the next person. A personal space approach would also predict that strangers would not look at each other, but rather would tend to look straight ahead (toward the door) or up or down. On the basis of personal space, we would make the following predictions with respect to the positions in the schematic elevator diagrammed on the next page.

1. In elevators with only one rider, the rider would usually stand along the back wall. In anticipation of a second rider, the first rider would be expected to stand in one back corner, thus leaving the other back corner for the second rider (and keeping both away from the button panels, which an additional rider would approach on entering). In terms of the schematic elevator layout on the next page, a single person should be located either in square 7 or square 9.

2. The second rider would be inclined to maximize distance from both the first rider and a potential third rider, who would be expected to approach the button panel(s) on entering the elevator. Therefore, in the schematic elevator

layout below, two people should occupy squares 7 and 9. (Note: squares 7 and 6, 4 and 9, and 4 and 6 would also constitute reasonable distributions, but would not be as optimal as 7 and 9.)

1	2	3
4	5	6
7	8	9

Schematic elevator, divided into a 3 × 3 unit array. The door is at 2.

Conditions of Observation: The observer cannot be on the elevator, as he would then be influencing the results. Therefore, observations must be made when an elevator arrives or departs and the door is open. Since people are likely to be leaving or entering, quick observation will be necessary at a stable moment: Just as the doors open or just as they close. (If you are lucky enough to be near an office or other building with video security monitors for the elevators in the lobby, you can use the monitors to record the positions of people between floors.)

Personal space rules would not necessarily hold among friends, and certainly not between lovers. Therefore, a fair test of personal space should eliminate any data including people who know each other well. To do this as best as possible, we will adopt two policies:

1. We will eliminate any observation (that is, the data collected from any particular elevator at a particular time) if any two people in the elevator are talking to one another or showing personal involvement in any way (e.g., holding hands).

2. We will try to make observations at places and at times when the number of people knowing each other well would be minimal. Ideal locations would be elevators in department stores or office buildings. Time would also be an important factor. We should avoid taking observations around the noon hour. (Why? Because it is very common to go out for lunch with friends, so the level of friend pairs or groups in elevators might be particularly high. This holds as well for people returning from lunch.)

Finally, precise conditions of measurement must be determined. Only record stable patterns:

No one should be moving. Your critical time for observation is the moment before the doors close (it is harder to use the moment they open, because it is likely that a passenger intending to exit has moved toward the door as the elevator comes to his or her floor). If, at the time of departure, the elevator contains one or two people who have settled into position and if they do not appear to be friends (by the criteria above) then record their location on the data sheet. Assign each person to whichever of the nine squares best locates him or her.

To minimize data collection time, try to find a bank of elevators (at least two), and try to go at a time of moderate use, so you won't have to deal with the infrequent or empty elevators. But don't use the lunch period, as discussed above. Normally the first floor is the natural place to make observations. But if you have a great deal of trouble with subjects moving in the elevator, you could go to another floor and push the call buttons, so that the elevator will stop on your floor. (The second floor would be best for these purposes. Why?)

Make sufficient observations so that you can get fifteen cases of elevators with one rider and fifteen of elevators with two riders. Indicate on the two data sheets the plan of the elevator, its location, and the time of day. Record one-person elevators on one data sheet and two-person elevators on the other.

When you have fifteen observations of each type, enter your data in the boxes in the table below. Do your data support the personal space theory? In order to help you make this evaluation, we have given you an indication of what would be statistically significant findings.

For the one-person elevator, there are nine possible positions. The theory predicts that one of two (positions 7 or 9) will be occupied. If people positioned themselves randomly in the elevator, we would expect them to be at 7 or 9 2/9 of the time, or for fifteen cases, $2/9 \times 15 = 3.3$ times (see table). By statistical calculations, we have determined that if there was actually an equal chance of someone's standing in any square, the chances of finding nine or more subjects out of fifteen in squares 7 or 9 is less than one in 100. This seems highly unlikely, so we would reject the idea that people stand randomly in the elevator and claim that the results supported the personal space hypothesis. These calculations are worked out in the table.

For the case of two people in the elevator, we

have made similar calculations. It turns out that there are thirty-six different pairs of spaces that could be occupied in our 9-square elevator. The 7-9 combination is just one of them, and hence, if people were standing in random positions, there would only be one case in thirty-six where the 7-9 position was occupied. Therefore, the expected numer of 7-9 locations in fifteen trials would be 15 × 1/36 = 0.4. A value of three or more people in this pair of locations would come about by chance less than one time in 100.

We can use one other measure with the two-person elevators. Personal space theory predicts, in general, that these people will stand far apart. We can translate this into the prediction that two people will not stand in boxes that are touching (even on the diagonal). Pairs 7-9, 4-6, 1-9 and others would meet this criterion. Altogether, of the thirty-six pairs of locations, twenty are touching (contiguous). Thus, we would expect that (since

there are sixteen nontouching pairs), in 16/36 × 15 cases, we would expect people in nontouching pairs, assuming that people distributed themselves randomly. A score of twelve or more pairs in nontouching squares would come about less than one time in 100 by chance and would be evidence for the personal space hypothesis. (See calculations in table below.)

For comparison purposes, we have made measurements like those we asked you to make in this study. We took advantage of a special situation that allows unusually easy data collection. The data we present comes from elevators in an office building in New York City. In this building, there is a video security camera in the ceiling of each elevator. Therefore, we could watch the bank of video monitors, and record the location of people. Furthermore, we could make the measurements between floors, so that there was no movement to or from the door.

(If your instructor collects the data, fill out the report sheet in Appendix B.)

Analysis of Results

Elevator type	Location prediction	# in predicted place/15	Expected random #	# significant*
1 person	7 or 9	☐/15	3.3	9
2 person	7 and 9	☐/15	0.4	3
New York data				
1 person	7 or 9	28/57	12.7	20
2 person	7 and 9	15/32	0.9	5
		# in noncontiguous squares	Expected random #	# significant*
2 person	16 noncontiguous pairs out of 36 total pairs	☐/15	6.7	12
New York data				
2 person	16 noncontiguous pairs out of 36 total pairs	31/32	14.2	21

*# significant means that one would expect this or a larger number of cases by chance no more than one time in one hundred.

Indicate panel location and other unusual features on diagram below.

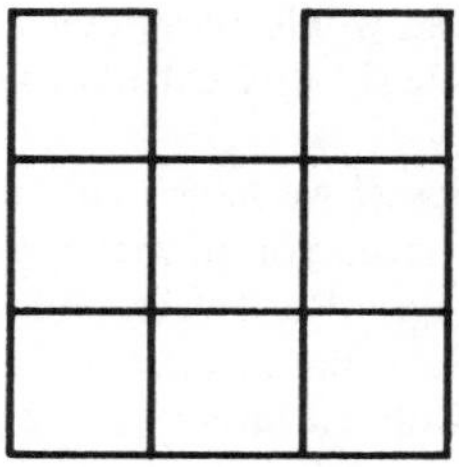

Name _____   Location _____

_____ Persons in Elevator   Time _____

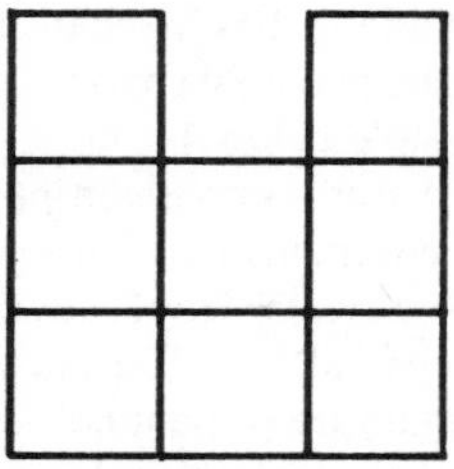

1

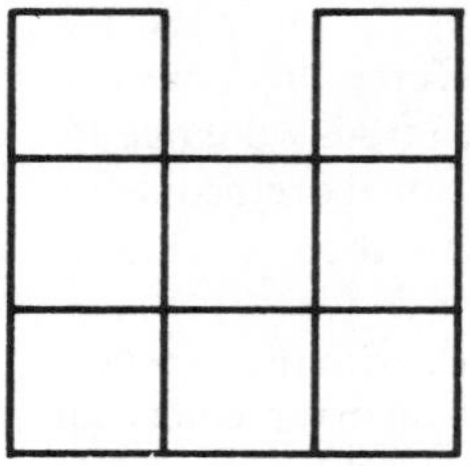

2

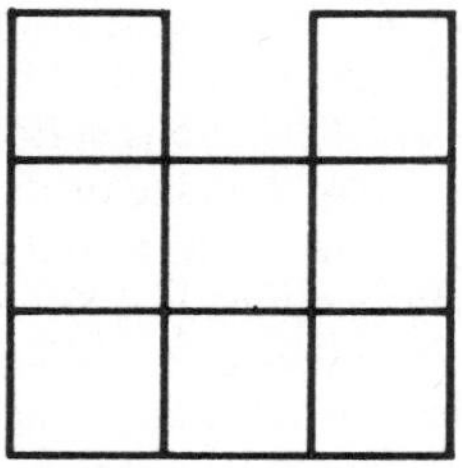

3

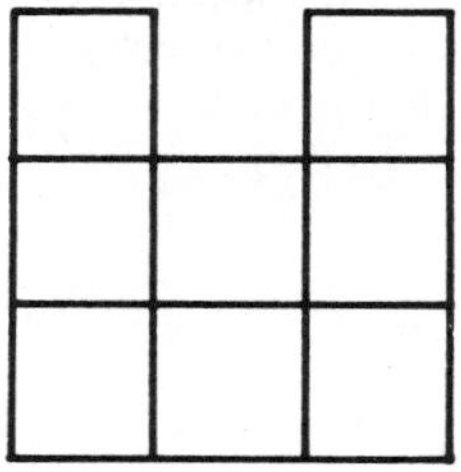

4

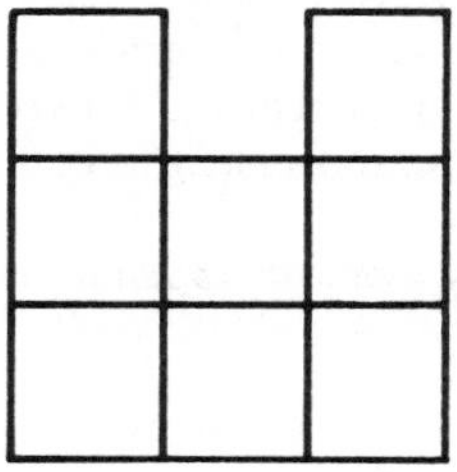

5

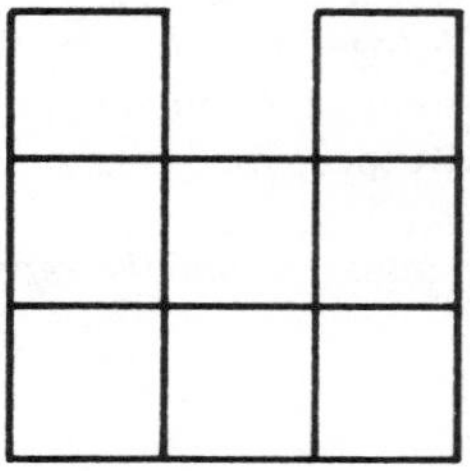

6

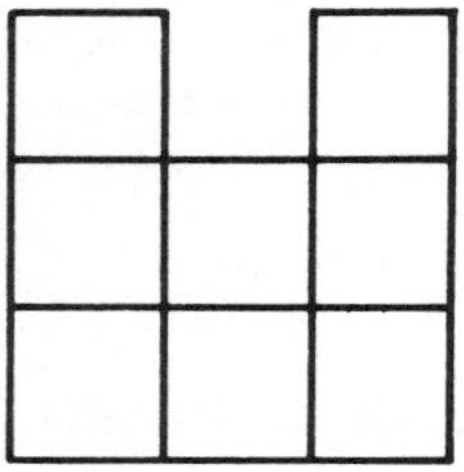

7

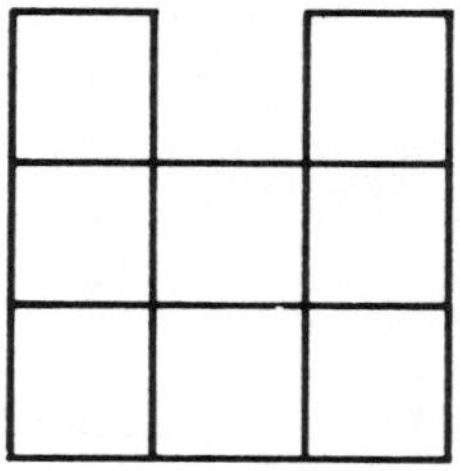

8

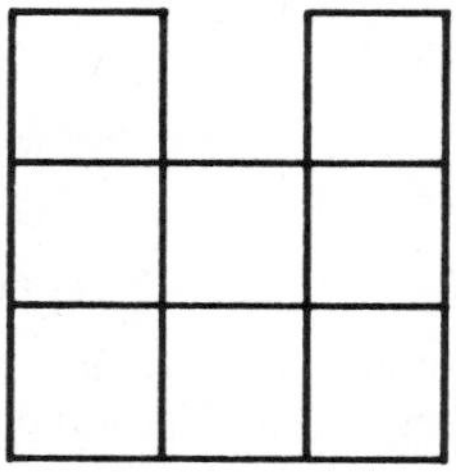

9

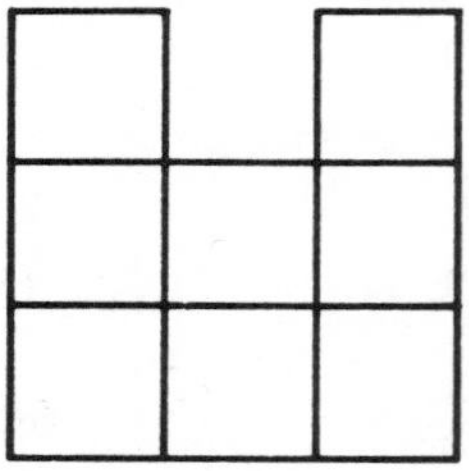

10

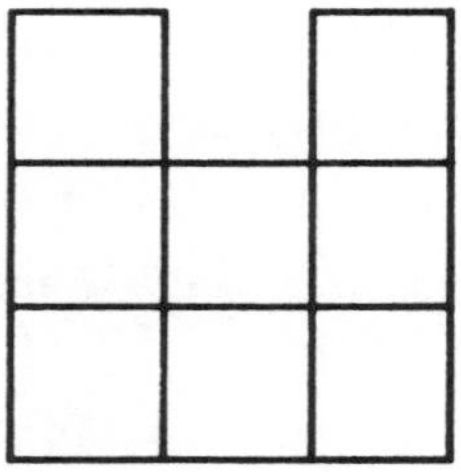

11

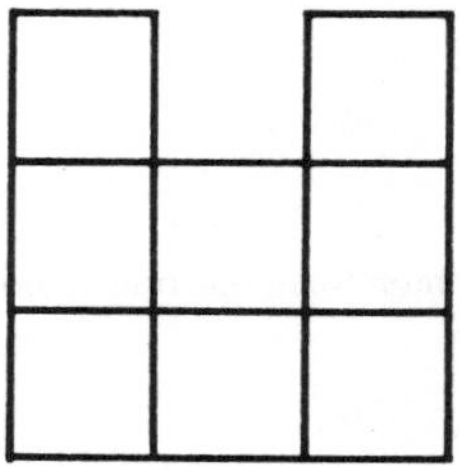

12

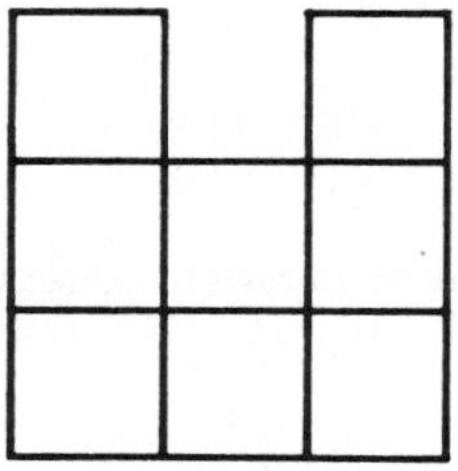

13

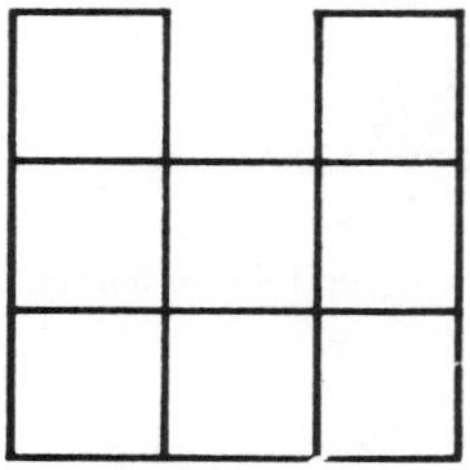

14

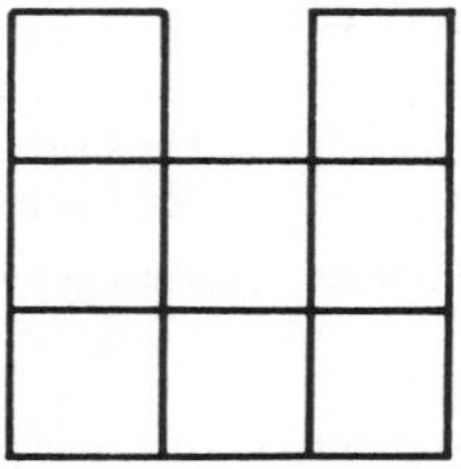

15

Indicate panel location
and other unusual features
on diagram below.

Name _____ Location _____

_____ Persons in Elevator   Time _____

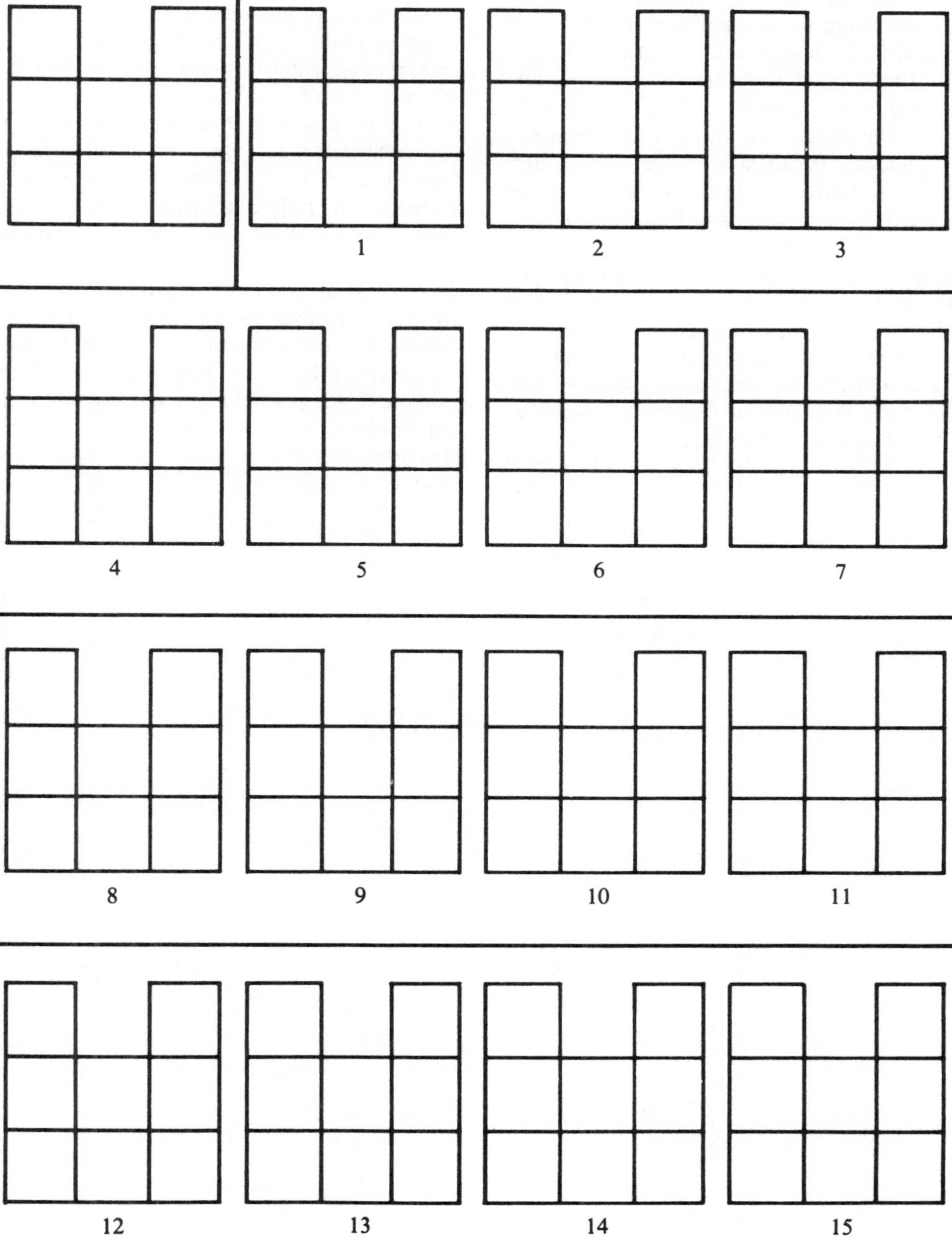

1   2   3

4   5   6   7

8   9   10   11

12   13   14   15

FURTHER STUDIES:

1. You can extend these observations. In elevators with a button panel on one side of the door, you can make the further predictions that: 1. the first person will stand in the back corner opposite to the panel; 2. in three-person elevators, the third person should stand in the front corner that does not have the button panel.

2. You can extend this study to elevators with three persons. In elevators with two button panels, it is hard to make precise predictions about where people will stand (see item 1 above, for predictions in single-panel elevators). However, personal space theory would predict that people would stand as far apart as possible, so that they should not stand in contiguous squares. There are eighty-four possible arrangements of three people, assigned to three of the nine squares. Only nine of these eight-four arrangements involve no person in a square contiguous to another (e.g., 1, 3, 9; 6, 1, 7; 1, 3, 8). Run another fifteen elevators, this time with three persons. How many have no one in a square contiguous with any other? We would predict, based on random location of people, $9/84 \times 15 = 1.6$ cases of people in noncontiguous squares. A significant result (less than one time in 100, by chance) would be six or more cases out of fifteen with no one in contiguous squares.

3. You can make observations like the elevator observations in any place where strangers are in an enclosed area. Library tables or seats on vehicles of public transportation are natural places to see if distances between strangers are maximized.

4. What do you think would happen if the rules of personal space were purposely violated? How would the desire for privacy and isolation from strangers affect the behavior of the person violated? Also, would you think that the sex of the subjects, in cases when there are two or more persons per elevator, would be influential in any way?

CHAPTER 11

Social Psychology

Learning Objectives

1. Indicate the ways in which human social behavior is qualitatively different from that of animals.

BELIEF AND SOCIAL REALITY

The interpersonal nature of belief
2. Describe Asch's experiment on the social basis of physical "reality," and state its implications. What are the limits of social pressure?

Social comparison
3. What is social comparison, and how does it function in ambiguous situations?

Cognitive consistency and beliefs
4. What is meant by cognitive consistency?
5. Explain cognitive dissonance and give an example.

ATTITUDES

6. Distinguish attitudes and beliefs.

Attitudes and behavior
7. Indicate some factors that could explain discrepancies between attitudes and behavior.

Attitude change
8. What accounts for the effectiveness of persuasive communications?
9. Explain how aspects of cognitive consistency, particularly bringing one's own behavior into line with one's attitudes, causes attitude change. Include retrospective justification of effort and forced compliance in the discussion.

10. Describe how protecting the self-picture can account for many instances of attitude change, and distinguish this motivation from cognitive consistency.

Attitude stability
11. What are the factors that account for the stability of most attitudes?

PERCEIVING OTHERS

Forming impressions
12. How is visual perception analogous to social perception?
13. Describe Asch's experiment on impression formation.
14. What is a "central trait" and in what sense are people perceived as more than the sum of their attributes?
15. What factors influence impression formation? Refer to mental sets and primacy effects.

Attribution
16. Summarize the approach of attribution theory to the interpretation of social behavior.
17. Evaluate the roles of situational and dispositional factors in judgments about other people.
18. Why are people more inclined to make situational attributions about their own behavior, as opposed to the behavior of others (the actor-observer difference)?

Perceiving others while being seen
19. Discuss the problem of social interaction in social perception. What is impression management? What are keys?

Attraction

20. Why is proximity a major determinant of attraction?
21. Review the evidence for similarity and physical attractiveness in attraction.
22. Why is physical attraction so important in mutual liking of potential mates? Include a discussion of the halo effect, and the effect on one's personality of being physically attractive.
23. Describe the matching hypothesis.
24. Evaluate the roles of biological and cultural factors as determinants of sexual attractiveness.

PERCEIVING ONESELF

The self-concept

25. Describe the factors that contribute to the developing perception of the self. Distinguish bodily and social self.

Self-perception and attribution

26. What is self-perception theory? What is the evidence for the influence of one's own behavior on one's attitudes?

EMOTION: PERCEIVING ONE'S OWN INNER STATE

The James-Lange theory

27. Describe the James-Lange theory of emotion and the major objections to it.

The cognitive theory of emotion

28. Describe the cognitive theory of emotion put forth by Schachter and Singer. Contrast this theory with the James-Lange theory. What is the role of physiological state in each theory?

A compromise approach

29. How can the idea of physiologically (or facially) distinct basic emotions be combined with cognitive factors to produce the full range of emotional experience?

Emotion and the theater

30. Discuss the experience of emotion in the theater, and the idea of "as if" emotions.

BLIND OBEDIENCE

Obedience and personality structure

31. What characterizes the authoritarian personality? How does the trait relate to prejudice against minorities?

Obedience and the situation

32. Describe Milgram's basic study on obedience.
33. Discuss the importance of seeing oneself as another's agent. Relate this to the Nazi massacre of the Jews or other atrocities.
34. Discuss how dehumanization, psychological distance, and gradual escalation influence blind obedience.
35. Contrast personality with situational factors as causes of blind obedience.

CROWD BEHAVIOR

The panicky crowd

36. Evaluate the statement that "people become 'primitive' or irrational in crowds."
37. Describe the circumstances under which panic is likely to spread in a crowd.
38. What is the prisoner's dilemma? Provide examples of payoff matrices as illustrations.

The hostile crowd

39. Discuss the motivation for hostile behavior in crowds, using lynching as an example.
40. Explain the role of diffusion of responsibility, deindividuation, and pluralistic ignorance in hostile crowd behavior.

The apathetic crowd

41. Indicate how uncertainty of the situation and diffusion of responsibility can explain apathetic behavior in crowds in the face of some apparent offense.

Programmed Exercises

BELIEF AND SOCIAL REALITY

1. In Asch's experiment on judging line length, subjects become disturbed because the behavior of the confederates challenges their shared sense of _physical reality_   physical reality

2. A subject in Asch's experiment is much less likely to yield to group "pressure" if at least _one_ other subject(s) _agree_ one, agree(s) with him/her.

3. When people have to make difficult judgments, they often seek the opinion of others, demonstrating the need for

   social comparison   social comparison

4. These "others" tend to share common assumptions and views with the person, and constitute a _reference_ group.   reference

5. The perception by a person of inconsistency in beliefs, feelings, or behavior sets up an unpleasant internal state called

   _____ _____.   cognitive dissonance

6. Cognitive consistency refers to the fact that people try to

   _____ contradictions among their attitudes and beliefs.   resolve

ATTITUDES

7. An _____ is a rather stable, evaluative mental position held   attitude
   toward some idea or object or person.

8. Unlike beliefs, attitudes are _____.   evaluative (or emotionally
                                                            tinged)

9. Situational pressures are one factor that explain why attitudes

   measured by _____ _____ often do not predict _____.   self-report, behavior

10. Messages that openly try to convince us of something, called

    _____ communications, are more effective if they come   persuasive

    from a _____ source.   credible

11. According to dissonance theory, a goal will be valued all the

    higher, the _____ it was to reach.   harder

12. Attitudes toward a goal often become more positive after a person makes sacrifices to attain the goal. This is called retro-

    spective _____ of _____.   justification, effort

13. If people behave inconsistently with their beliefs under

    _____ _____, they are unlikely to change their beliefs   forced compliance
    or attitudes.

14. An alternative to cognitive consistency as an explanation of attitude change involves more emotional or evaluative factors,

    and is described as protecting the _____ _____.   self-picture

PERCEIVING OTHERS

15. In both object and person perception, the observer extracts

    certain _____ from the flow of events.   consistencies (invariances)

16. According to Asch, both form perception and person percep-

    tion result from combinations of attributes into _____   organized
    wholes.

17. Asch's experiments on impressions of others showed that certain attributes had an organizing effect on the integration of other attributes. Such "organizing" attributes were called

    _____ _____.   central traits

18. Impressions of others can be seen as patterns, based on the relations among elements. One basis for this process is a set of organized expectations about the way in which different be-

   haviors of people hang together, called a _____. Another   schema

   idea is that our perception of others is based on a _____, a   prototype
   mental concept of the typical way that a person would act.

19. The special importance of the first information we receive about a person in forming an impression of him is called the

   _____ _____. This effect is an example of the general   primacy effect
   tendency to incorporate new information into existing patterns

   of organization, called _____ _____.   mental set

20. _____ _____ deals with the study of how people infer   Attribution theory
   the causes of other people's behavior.

21. Studies of attribution show that in judging others people tend

   to rely too much on internal causation, or _____ factors,   dispositional

   as opposed to _____ factors in explaining behavior.   situational

22. People are more likely to attribute their own (as opposed to others') behavior to situational factors. This is called the

   _____ _____ _____.   actor-observer difference

23. Goffman holds that much human behavior is "putting up a front," that is, behaving in accordance with the expectations

   for some role. This is called _____ _____.   impression management

24. According to Goffman, a _____ is a signal that indicates   key
   the sense in which some act or utterance should be taken.

25. Two people who have spent a fair amount of time in physical

   _____ to one another are more likely than not to become   proximity
   friends.

26. In addition to proximity, two major factors that cause one to   similarity,
   like another are _____ and _____ _____.   physical attractiveness

27. The strong tendency for people to marry other people very

   similar to themselves is called _____.   homogamy

28. The personal characteristic that most influences initial liking

   for a person in American culture is _____ _____.   physical attractiveness

29. The tendency to believe that people who have one positive characteristic (e.g., physical attractiveness) will have other

   positive characteristics as well is called the _____ _____.   halo effect

30. Although there may be some universal characteristics that lead to sexual attraction, to a large extent the criteria of sexual

   attractiveness vary in different _____.   cultures

PERCEIVING ONESELF

31. The infant or child's experience of the effects of touching herself or the relation between intending something and doing it contribute to the development of her concept of a

    _____ _____ .   bodily self

32. Bem and some other cognitive social psychologists believe that conceptions of the self are built up from attribution processes of the same type used in forming conceptions of other people.

    This position is called _____ _____ _____ .   self-perception theory

33. According to this theory, _____ determines attitudes, rather   behavior
    than the other way around.

34. The "foot-in-the-door" technique is an example of how

    _____ can lead to attitude change.   behavior

EMOTION: PERCEIVING ONE'S OWN INNER STATE

35. According to the _____ _____ theory, the subjective   James-Lange
    experience of emotion results from our awareness of bodily
    changes in the presence of certain stimuli.

36. According to Schachter and Singer's cognitive theory of emo-

    tion, emotion depends on the interpretation of _____   autonomic arousal

    _____ by a subject, in light of the total situation.

37. Studies of physiological or facial response patterns in different

    emotional situations suggest that there are about _____   any number from six to ten
    basic emotions.

38. A compromise theory of emotion suggests that the basic, bio-
    logically defined, emotions described in question 37 are shaped

    into more differentiated and varied emotions through _____   cognitive (or interpretive)
    processes.

39. The esthetic flavor and emotional responses produced in a

    theater audience depend on the creation of an _____ _____   as if
    emotion. This, in turn, depends on a delicate balance between

    belief and disbelief, and between too little _____ and too   arousal
    much.

BLIND OBEDIENCE

40. People who emphasize the importance of power, dominance,

    and obedience have been described as having an _____   authoritarian
    personality.

41. According to some investigators, people who score high on

    minority prejudice and authoritarianism often have _____   harsh (punitive, stern,
    fathers. In psychoanalytic terms, as children they repressed   all-powerful)
    their hostility toward their father and developed a

    _____ _____ in which obedience and submission to all   reaction formation
    authority became exalted virtues.

42. In Milgram's first experiments on obedience, approximately

    _____ percent of subjects shocked the learner up to the   65 (50–75 percent would be
    maximum amount.   acceptable)

43. Milgram's experiments suggest that it is not necessary to have

    an _____ personality to exhibit blind obedience.   authoritarian

44. An important factor that causes people to perform acts that
    they might otherwise consider abhorrent is the feeling that

    they are another person's _____.   agent

45. The obedient person who causes pain to another person may

    treat that person as an object. This is called _____.   dehumanization

46. The cognitive reorientation required in producing obedience is

    best accomplished by a _____ _____ in obedience re-   gradual increase
    quirements.

CROWD BEHAVIOR

47. The prisoner's dilemma presents an individual with a choice in
    a situation with mixed risks and benefits, described in a

    _____ _____.   payoff matrix

48. The prisoner's dilemma analysis is an attempt to explain the

    apparently _____ behavior of a crowd in terms of the   irrational

    _____ behavior of individuals.   rational

49. _____, a weakened sense of personal identity, disinhibits   Deindividuation
    impulsive actions that are normally under restraint.

50. The large size and apparent unanimity of the mob causes some
    of its members to perform acts that they would not normally

    perform, because of a _____ of responsibility.   diffusion

51. Although the mob may be far from homogeneous, the ap-

    parent unanimity leads to _____ _____ of the crowd   pluralistic ignorance
    members.

52. The larger the group watching an apparent medical emergency,

    the less likely there will be any _____ intervention.   bystander

53. Feelings of anonymity in the violent crowd may precipitate

    antisocial acts of _____. However, in a crowd of onlookers   commission
    observing a violent encounter, the resultant behaviors are more

    likely to be antisocial acts of _____.   omission

Self Test

1. In Asch's experiment on the effect of social   a. many subjects yielded to social pressure,
   pressure on judgments of noticeably differ-   but their perceptions of line length did
   ent line lengths, he found that: not necessarily change

b. the actual perceptions of line length were changed in the subject

c. the perceptions of line length were changed in the confederates

d. the shared sense of physical reality can affect perception

e. disagreement with most, but not all subjects usually causes a subject to yield

2. Indicate which of the following statements about social comparison is false:

a. in making social decisions, people tend to consult with others who share similar views

b. social comparison is more likely to occur when someone is faced with a difficult decision

c. social comparison occurs more frequently when someone is trying to solve a non-social problem, like judging line length

d. social comparison is more likely to occur in a situation in which there is some ambiguity

3. Fred supports the cause of the A's, in their war against the B's. He then sees on television that the A's are killing innocent children. He decides that the A's must be being forced to do this by the B's, and that the A's have no choice. This type of thinking in Fred is an example of:

a. social comparison

b. stimulus-response association

c. resolution of cognitive dissonance

d. reference to comparison groups to change attitudes

e. all of the above

4. Sandy holds that French food is good and Canadian food is bad. These views represent:

a. attitudes

b. beliefs

c. cognitive consistency

d. cognitive dissonance

5. Attitudes are usually measured by:

a. questionnaire

b. observation of behavior

c. experimental studies

d. physiological measures

e. a and c

6. Attitudes do not always predict behavior. This could be because:

a. attitudes, as measured, are often very general, and behavior deals with specific situations

b. attitudes are evaluative and behavior is not

c. specific aspects of situations may prevent attitudes from being expressed

d. behavior is not affected by cognitive consistency or cognitive dissonance

e. a and c

7. According to cognitive dissonance theory, which of the following would be the best way to cause someone to change an attitude?

a. pay them a lot to make believe they hold the new attitude

b. force them to behave as if they support the new attitude for at least a few weeks

c. tell them that they will be prejudiced if they continue with their current attitude

d. show them that their current attitude is inconsistent with their actual behavior

e. urge them to consult with an appropriate social comparison group

8. This graph illustrates the relation between:

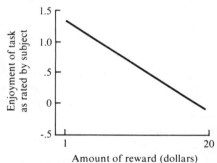

a. attitudes and beliefs

b. cognitive dissonance and forced compliance

c. cognitive dissonance and cognitive consistency

d. social comparison and ambiguity

9. After working as a volunteer for a political candidate for a month, Jonathan finds that his support for the candidate has increased, even though he has never met her. This is an instance of:

a. forced compliance

b. retrospective justification of effort

c. persuasive communications

d. a and b

e. all of the above

10. Which of the following techniques is *not* considered an effective way to produce a positive change in attitude toward a message?

a. use of a credible and trustworthy source
b. use of a message that is regarded favorably by a social comparison group
c. openly forcing a person to behave in a way that supports the message
d. linking the message to past behavior by the person that supports the message

11. Which of the following is involved both in maintaining stable attitudes and in attitude change?
    a. attitude questionnaires
    b. forced compliance
    c. cognitive consistency
    d. striking and unexpected events
    e. changing reference groups

12. Perception of objects and people have in common the fact that:
    a. both rely almost exclusively on vision
    b. both involve the construction of stable or invariant characteristics
    c. both are fixed in their nature by first impressions
    d. both involve the resolution of cognitive dissonance between the object (or person) and its perception

13. After a few encounters, Susan decided that Gary was stupid. She maintained this impression even after she discovered that he got the highest grade on a physical chemistry examination, and assumed that he cheated. Susan's behavior is an example of:
    a. resolution of cognitive dissonance
    b. mental set
    c. the primacy effect
    d. all of the above
    e. none of the above

14. People have a tendency to believe that actors in the theater are really like the roles that they play. This is an example of:
    a. the resolution of cognitive dissonance
    b. the dominance of dispositional over situational factors in attribution
    c. the primacy effect in impressions
    d. the distinction between the bodily self and the social self
    e. the interaction of social and biological factors in the determination of behavior

15. The actor-observer difference describes the fact that people are *less* likely to make _____ attributions about themselves than others.

a. dispositional
b. correct
c. cognitively consistent
d. situational
e. c and d

16. Explanations of the actor-observer difference include the fact that:
    a. people know themselves better than they know others
    b. people cannot literally see themselves in social situations
    c. attribution theory only applies to judging other people
    d. a and b
    e. all of the above

17. Having become bored with the guests at a dinner party, Kermit excuses himself by saying that he has to get up very early the next morning (which is not true) to take a trip out of town. According to Goffman's analysis, this performance can be explained as:
    a. an example of Kermit's theatrical sense
    b. a key
    c. an attempt to leave without seeming rude and without insulting the guests
    d. an attempt to alter the social perception of the audience by providing them with an ambiguous social stimulus

18. Proximity is an important factor in attraction. There is evidence that this relation results from the fact that:
    a. one must ordinarily meet someone in order to be attracted to him/her
    b. familiarity promotes attraction, but familiarity is increased by proximity
    c. similarity normally presupposes proximity
    d. all of the above

19. Mildred and Herb have been dating for years. Both are physically unattractive, and one acquaintance wonders what they see in each other. Which of the following factors could contribute to their mutual attractiveness?
    a. proximity
    b. similarity
    c. matching
    d. a and c
    e. all of the above

20. In a first impressions study, four groups of subjects each hear a different list of adjectives describing a person. The lists are as follows:

Group 1: trustworthy, sensitive, subtle, detached, stingy, envious

Group 2: same as group 1, but in the opposite order

Group 3: same as group 1, but with physically attractive added as the first adjective (making this a seven-adjective list)

Group 4: same as group 1, but with physically attractive added at the end of the list

Subjects are then asked to rate how charming the person is. We would expect the subjects in which group to give the highest charm rating?

a. 1
b. 2
c. 3
d. 4
e. 3 and 4 equally

21. The prediction in question 20 is based on:
a. similarity
b. the primacy effect
c. the halo effect
d. the matching hypothesis
e. b and c

22. The recognition of one's own body, one's continuity over time, and one's identity as a social creature, all contribute to the development of:
a. cognitive consistency
b. obedience
c. the self
d. behavioral attitudes

23. According to self-perception theory:
a. one's own behavior can influence one's attitudes
b. cognitive dissonance is a self-fulfilling prophecy
c. social roles determine behavior
d. the bodily self-concept must depend on the cognitions of others
e. attitudes are formed more or less independent of behavior

24. Which of the following illustrates how one's feelings or beliefs may be the result of one's actions?
a. the "foot-in-the-door" technique
b. impression management
c. the primacy effect
d. the need for comparison groups
e. none of the above

25. Bert, after a great deal of effort, convinces Sarah to go to a movie with him. Although Sarah finds Bert's company to be exactly what she expected, she ends up liking him more than she had anticipated. This could be explained in terms of:
a. the James-Lange theory of emotion
b. the principle of displacement
c. either self-perception theory or cognitive dissonance
d. the notion of emotion as an attribution process
e. Bert's captivating, but subtle, personality

26. Both self-perception theory and the James-Lange theory of emotion make the similar claim that:
a. the bodily self must interact with the social self to produce emotion
b. behavioral or bodily events cause mental changes
c. subjective phenomena cannot be studied
d. attribution plays no role in emotion

27. After running for a quarter mile, a person shows increased heart rate and various other signs of arousal but may not feel any strong emotion. This fact is particularly damaging to which of the following theories?
a. the cognitive theory of emotion
b. the James-Lange theory
c. Cannon's idea that subjective emotion leads to physiological responses
d. a and b
e. all of the above

28. An experiment has shown that subjects alter their ratings of the attractiveness of nude photos in response to feedback about the increase or decrease of their heart rate. This result can be taken to support:
a. the cognitive theory (Schachter-Singer) of emotion
b. the James-Lange theory
c. Cannon's theory (subjective emotion leads to the physiological responses, but the latter do not cause the former)
d. a and b
e. all of the above

29. Consider the reasonable finding (probably true, but not yet demonstrated) that the most satisfactory emotional experience in a theater audience is most likely to occur in people sitting a moderate distance from the stage. According to the "as if" interpretation in the text, this would be because at this distance there is an ideal balance between:

a. autonomic and somatic arousal
b. distance and closeness
c. belief and disbelief
d. as and if
e. attribution and physiological response

30. An explanation of blind obedience that emphasizes the authoritarian personality of the person in question relies on:
   a. situational factors
   b. dispositional factors
   c. cognitive dissonance
   d. cognitive consistency
   e. attribution of emotional experience

31. Both Milgram's obedience experiment and Asch's line judgment studies show the importance of _____ in determining behavior.
   a. attribution
   b. cognitive dissonance
   c. compliance
   d. dispositional factors
   e. none of the above

32. Which of the following would tend to *prevent* obedience in a situation of the type that Milgram studies?
   a. making a person feel like the agent of another
   b. dehumanizing the person being punished
   c. describing the experiment as a scientific enterprise
   d. decreasing the psychological distance between the subject and the person being punished
   e. none of the above

33. Brown suggests that panic is more likely in situations where:
   a. a serious danger is perceived
   b. the escape routes appear to be inadequate
   c. the people involved have well-defined roles
   d. a and b
   e. all of the above

34. The prisoner's dilemma analysis explains:
   a. the use of payoff matrices
   b. how obedience is based on a past history of stern parental treatment
   c. how maladaptive crowd behavior can result from rational behavior of individuals
   d. the importance of roles in controlling the crowd panic reaction
   e. b and c

35. Hostile behavior of mobs is encouraged by:
   a. diffusion of responsibility

b. bystander apathy
c. the prisoner's dilemma
d. cognitive reinterpretations

36. The behavior of hostile crowds is motivated. In the case of lynching, an important motive was:
   a. forestalling a socioeconomic threat
   b. diffusion of responsibility
   c. extermination of the lower class
   d. countering bystander apathy
   e. all of the above

37. Bystander apathy and mob violence are both more likely to occur in situations where there is:
   a. high motivation and aggressiveness
   b. diffusion of responsibility
   c. a blurring of roles
   d. cognitive dissonance

Answer Key for Self Test

1. a p. 367	20. c pp. 379, 385
2. c p. 369	21. e pp. 379, 385
3. c p. 371	22. c p. 388
4. a p. 372	23. a p. 389
5. a p. 372	24. a p. 389
6. e pp. 372–73	25. c pp. 389–90
7. d p. 375	26. b pp. 389, 391
8. b p. 375	27. b pp. 391–92
9. b p. 374	28. d pp. 391–95
10. c pp. 374–76	29. c p. 396
11. c p. 376	30. b p. 397
12. b p. 377	31. c pp. 368, 400
13. d p. 379	32. d p. 401
14. b p. 380	33. d p. 404
15. a p. 380	34. c pp. 404–406
16. d p. 381	35. a p. 408
17. c p. 382	36. a p. 407
18. d pp. 383–85	37. b p. 408
19. e pp. 383–85	

Investigating Psychological Phenomena

PERSON PERCEPTION: THE EFFECT OF CONTEXT OR SET ON FIRST IMPRESSIONS
Equipment: Paper and pencil, a stopwatch or a watch that indicates seconds
Subjects: At least eight
Time per subject: Five minutes
Time for experimenter: Forty minutes

Social perception bears many analogies to more traditional areas of perception (see page 377 in the text). In both cases, information is taken in selectively and put together into some organized percept. This aspect of person perception was illustrated in the text with special reference to the classic studies of Solomon Asch. Asch's work argued for an organizational basis for impression formation. This approach is in keeping with the position of Gestalt psychology. In Asch's view, impressions were not formed by "summing" different items of information about a particular person. One particular aspect of the active process of impression formation is the effect of set. One is constantly forming impressions of people: New information on any person is integrated with an already existing impression: the new information will be interpreted to be as consistent as possible with the existing impression. Under the circumstances, one would expect that the first information one gets about a person would be especially important, since it might color what comes in later. Therefore, an organizational view would predict that the *order* of items of information about a person would affect the resulting impression, whereas a simple *summation* hypothesis would predict that order would not matter.

Asch tested his hypothesis in a very simple manner: He gave college students a list of six adjectives that ostensibly described someone and recorded the impressions that they subsequently formed of this imaginary person. By manipulating the types of adjectives used and the order of their presentation, Asch attempted to produce systematic changes in the elicited impression formations. We will repeat his experiment on word order in precisely the same way that it was performed by Asch.

Try to get at least eight (student) subjects. It might be useful for you to team up with a few friends from the course and run up to twenty subjects, so that your results might be more meaningful. Subjects must be divided into two groups. You can run as many subjects as you want at the same time, so long as they are all from the same group. Since this experiment will compare the results of subjects from one group with the results from another group, it is important that the two groups be similar in general characteristics. For example, keep the percentage of females the same in both groups, and try not to run a group of friends together, since they may share many similar characteristics. If you run one subject at a time, simply assign the first subject to group A, the second to group B, and so on. This should give you a random and "unbiased" sample.

The list for group A	The list for group B
intelligent	envious
industrious	stubborn
impulsive	critical
critical	impulsive
stubborn	industrious
envious	intelligent

Note that the adjectives in group B are in the reverse order of group A. This arrangement is designed to enhance any effect of order, by putting adjectives that would lead to quite different impressions on opposite ends of the adjective list.

Subjects should be seated comfortably, and should have in front of them a blank piece of paper and a pencil. Make sure to put the group letter (A or B) on the paper and on the checklist. The experimenter reads the following instructions:

I shall read you a number of characteristics that belong to a particular person. Please listen to them carefully and try to form an impression of the kind of person described. You will later be asked to give a brief characterization of the person in just a few sentences. I will read the list slowly and will repeat it once.

Read the list of six adjectives out loud in a steady voice, with an interval of five seconds between terms. Then say:

I will now read the list again.

(Repeat the reading of the list)

Now please write a brief characterization of this person.

(Subject writes)

Finally, tell the subjects while handing them the checklist (see pages 155 and 157):

Here is a list of pairs of adjectives. For each pair, please circle the adjective that better characterizes the person we have been describing.

After the subject has completed this task, he or she is finished.

NOTES ON PROCEDURE

In setting up any experiment, many decisions must be made. Here, these include selecting the adjectives for the list, and for the checklist, deciding on the number of adjectives in the list, and so on. In most cases there are specific reasons for making these decisions. In this experiment, for example, ask yourself:

1. Why does the experimenter read the list instead of allowing the subject to read the list?

2. Why is the subject asked to write an impression before seeing the checklist rather than after filling out the check list?

RESULTS

You should end up with eight or more written sketches and eight or more marked checklists. About half should be in each group. There is no simple way to score the written impressions. Read them over and try to summarize the impressions written by the two groups (the procedure used by Asch). You could also give the written impressions to another person and ask that person to sort them into piles, about equal in size. One pile would be for the more desirable impressions (persons) and the other for the less desirable ones. See if the impressions based on the adjective list with more desirable traits first are usually classified as more desirable. (It would be a good idea to fold back the part of the impressions paper with the group letter on it before reading and analyzing the character summaries.)

It is easier to analyze the data from the check lists. Simply record the percent of subjects who selected the more favorable adjective of each pair, for each group. This is the procedure used by Asch. His results, based on twenty-four student subjects in group A and thirty-four in group B, are presented in the table on the next page. Record your data in the columns next to his data. Compare your results with his. If we take a difference of 20 percentage points as worthy of note, he reported big differences, in favor of group A, on happy, humorous, sociable, popular, good-looking, and restrained.

(You can increase the significance of your data by combining it with data from a few friends in the class, so that you would have 20 or more subjects in each group.)

Based on your results, what is the conclusion about the validity of the organizaton (set, Gestalt) versus simple summation explanations of impression formation?

Try to explain why some particular adjectives show clear effects and others do not. Obviously, in real life people form impressions from interactions with other people or by hearing about them from other people. To what extent do you think that Asch's procedure gives an indication of how people actually form impressions? The hallmark of a good experiment is that it simplifies a situation but still preserves its essential features. Is that true of this experiment?

FURTHER STUDY

You can use Asch's technique to address other questions. You can change specific adjectives on the list. You can use brief statements about a person's *behavior* (e.g., John consistently drives over the speed limit; John is always on time, etc.), rather than general characteristics. You can see which types of adjectives cause a subject to guess that a person is male or female. There are many possibilities, should this problem interest you. Some of the possibilities that you will come up with may never have been investigated.

Reference

Asch, S. E. Forming impressions of personality. *Journal of Abnormal and Social Psychology,* 1946, *41*, 258–90.

	Percent of subjects checking favorable adjective at left			
	Asch's Data		Your Data	
Adjective Pair	group A (24 students)	group B (34 students)	group A (__ students)	group B (__ students)
generous	24	10		
wise	18	17		
happy	32	5		
good-natured	18	0		
humorous	52	21		
sociable	56	27		
popular	35	14		
reliable	84	91		
good-looking	74	35		
serious	97	100		
restrained	64	9		
honest	80	79		

CHECKLISTS

There are eight checklists on the next two pages.
Cut one out for each subject. (Asch used eighteen
adjective pairs. We use twelve of these pairs.)

Circle the most relevant adjective:

generous—ungenerous

shrewd—wise

unhappy—happy

irritable—good-natured

humorous—humorless

sociable—unsociable

popular—unpopular

unreliable—reliable

good-looking—unattractive

frivolous—serious

restrained—talkative

dishonest—honest

Group _____

Circle the most relevant adjective:

generous—ungenerous

shrewd—wise

unhappy—happy

irritable—good-natured

humorous—humorless

sociable—unsociable

popular—unpopular

unreliable—reliable

good-looking—unattractive

frivolous—serious

restrained—talkative

dishonest—honest

Group _____

--- *Cut here* ---

Circle the most relevant adjective:

generous—ungenerous

shrewd—wise

unhappy—happy

irritable—good-natured

humorous—humorless

sociable—unsociable

popular—unpopular

unreliable—reliable

good-looking—unattractive

frivolous—serious

restrained—talkative

dishonest—honest

Group _____

Circle the most relevant adjective:

generous—ungenerous

shrewd—wise

unhappy—happy

irritable—good-natured

humorous—humorless

sociable—unsociable

popular—unpopular

unreliable—reliable

good-looking—unattractive

frivolous—serious

restrained—talkative

dishonest—honest

Group _____

Circle the most relevant adjective:

generous—ungenerous

shrewd—wise

unhappy—happy

irritable—good-natured

humorous—humorless

sociable—unsociable

popular—unpopular

unreliable—reliable

good-looking—unattractive

frivolous—serious

restrained—talkative

dishonest—honest

Group _____

Circle the most relevant adjective:

generous—ungenerous

shrewd—wise

unhappy—happy

irritable—good-natured

humorous—humorless

sociable—unsociable

popular—unpopular

unreliable—reliable

good-looking—unattractive

frivolous—serious

restrained—talkative

dishonest—honest

Group _____

-- *Cut here* --

Circle the most relevant adjective:

generous—ungenerous

shrewd—wise

unhappy—happy

irritable—good-natured

humorous—humorless

sociable—unsociable

popular—unpopular

unreliable—reliable

good-looking—unattractive

frivolous—serious

restrained—talkative

dishonest—honest

Group _____

Circle the most relevant adjective:

generous—ungenerous

shrewd—wise

unhappy—happy

irritable—good-natured

humorous—humorless

sociable—unsociable

popular—unpopular

unreliable—reliable

good-looking—unattractive

frivolous—serious

restrained—talkative

dishonest—honest

Group _____

The Individual and Society: The Contributions of Sigmund Freud

Learning Objectives

THE ORIGINS OF PSYCHOANALYTIC THOUGHT

1. Understand Freud's contribution to the controversy between the romantic movement and those whose faith lay in reason.
2. How did Freud view the process of taming the savage, selfish human nature? How is this process related to unconscious conflicts?

Hysteria and hypnosis
3. Describe the symptoms of hysteria. Why is this illness termed a psychogenic disorder?
4. Understand the relationship between hysteria and hypnosis and the central role of suggestibility.
5. How did Freud propose to treat hysteria?

Resistance and repression
6. What is the method of free association? What is the significance of resistance?
7. Understand the central role played by repression in Freud's theory. What happens to repressed material, and how is it expressed by the conscious self?

UNCONSCIOUS CONFLICT

The antagonists of inner conflict
8. Understand the nature of unconscious conflict and its effect on behavior.
9. What are the three divisions of personality according to Freud? How do these develop, and how do they interact to give rise to conflict and resolution?

The nature of unconscious conflict
10. Be cognizant of the major role of anxiety as a motivating force in keeping unacceptable urges repressed.
11. How does repression affect the realm of thought in addition to that of behavior?
12. What is displacement?
13. Describe additional defense mechanisms invoked to keep conflicts hidden.

Unconscious conflict in normal life
14. What is the psychopathology of everyday life, and how does it reflect underlying motives and conflicts?
15. Freud's theory of dreams focused on the content of dreams. Understand the motive of wish fulfillment and its symbolic expression, the difference between the latent and the manifest dream, and the contribution of day residues in relation to this theory.

Origins of unconscious conflict
16. What are Freud's stages of psychosexual development, and what conflicts arise during each?
17. What is a reaction formation? Give three examples of a reaction formation.
18. In Freud's view, the Oedipus complex is the most important aspect of psychosexual development. Discuss this theory with respect to both sexes.
19. What is the delayed effect of the resolution of the Oedipus conflict as expressed in adolescence?
20. What are the difficulties in Freud's view of the psychosexual development of girls?

A REEXAMINATION OF FREUDIAN THEORY

Testing Freud's theories

21. Recount some of the empirical and conceptual difficulties in testing Freud's theories.

The evidence for repression and defense

22. Summarize the issues and arguments against and in favor of Freud's reliance on repression and defense mechanisms in dealing with unconscious conflicts. Refer to memory lapses and word association tests in terms of "motivated forgetting," and to perceptual defense motivated by anxiety.

23. Not all individuals resort to repression when presented with anxiety-inducing materials. Elaborate on this statement.

Problems of Freud's dream theory

24. What evidence is there for Freud's theory that dreams reflect the conscious and unconscious preoccupations of the dreamer in condensed and symbolic form?

25. What evidence militates against Freud's emphasis on wish fulfillment in the interpretation of dreams?

26. Freud believed that the manifest dream was a disguised and censored version of the latent dream that deals with unacceptable urges. What is an alternative view?

Biology or culture?

27. Freud's theories are often attacked under the rubric of the nativist/empiricist debate. Explain Freud's view and the argument of the neo-Freudians.

28. What is the contribution of cultural anthropology in evaluating Freud's theories?

Critiques of Freud's theories of development

29. Freud believed that severe toilet training could lead to a childhood reaction formation producing obstinacy and stinginess in the adult. These characteristics have been found to occur together quite often, but is there any evidence that they result from parental toilet-training practices?

30. How universal is the Oedipus complex?

31. As a child grows up, how is his personality shaped, and who or what does the shaping?

PSYCHOANALYTIC INTERPRETATION OF CULTURE, MYTHS, AND LITERATURE

32. Describe Freud's view of early civilization and the origin of the incest taboo as a social contract. What are alternative explanations for the universality of this taboo?

33. Understand Freud's emphasis on the family as the medium of societal transmission of rules and prohibitions.

FREUD'S CONTRIBUTIONS IN RETROSPECT

34. What are Freud's major contributions to our understanding of human nature and to the field of psychology?

Programmed Exercises

THE ORIGINS OF PSYCHOANALYTIC THOUGHT

1. To understand human social nature, we must ask how people

   transmit their _____ from one generation to the next.   culture

2. Freud has been compared to Hobbes, since both men believed

   that man is basically _____. But Freud differs from Hobbes   savage (or selfish)

   in that he believes that the taming force of society is _____   internalized
   in each of us.

3. According to Freud's view, forbidden impulses are never completely controlled, despite repressive measures by the individual. This division of the individual (one part fighting another) gives

   rise to _____ conflicts.   unconscious

4. In the early 1900s a patient exhibiting partial blindness, glove anesthesia, and memory gaps would likely have been diagnosed as suffering from _____ .

hysteria

5. If organic damage is ruled out in the above case (number 4), then the origin of the symptoms must be _____ .

psychogenic

6. Due to the similarities of the characteristics of hysteria and _____ , it was believed at one time that the two might be related.

hypnosis

7. Because of the similarities mentioned above (question 6), it was hypothesized that hysterical symptoms could be eliminated by _____ .

suggestion

8. A subject asked to forget everything that happened while under hypnosis will generally demonstrate _____ _____ upon awakening, but will nonetheless respond to _____ sugges-tions.

posthypnotic amnesia
posthypnotic

9. Freud and Breuer came to the conclusion that the symptoms of hysteria could not be just suggested away; the underlying _____ that such symptoms block must be recovered. The resulting _____ will then have therapeutic effects.

memories
catharsis

10. Although Freud began by using hypnosis, he later abandoned this approach, since not all of his patients were hypnotizable and since the same crucial memories could be obtained in the waking state through the method of _____ _____ .

free association

11. A patient is told to say anything that enters his mind, yet struggles at times to change the subject or forgets what he was going to say. This subject is demonstrating _____ to the recovery of _____ memories.

resistance
repressed

12. According to Freud, repression is a _____ against the intolerable pain that would be caused by unacceptable thoughts and wishes.

defense

13. Repressed wishes are usually related to _____ _____ , the direct expression of which is forbidden by society.

biological urges

14. Freud investigated unconscious conflicts: their origin, effects, and removal. He termed his exploration and interpretation of these phenomena _____ .

psychoanalysis

UNCONSCIOUS CONFLICT

15. The two major aspects of Freud's theory concern the _____ of unconscious conflicts and the _____ of these conflicts.

mechanisms
origins

16. The three distinct systems of the human personality, according to Freud, are the _____ , the _____ , and the _____ .

id, ego, superego

17. The most primitive portion of personality is the _____.   id

    It operates according to the _____ principle, with the single   pleasure
    goal being immediate satisfaction.

18. As the id-dominated infant encounters the frustration of the

    real world, he develops a(n) _____, which attempts to   ego

    satisfy the urges of the id according to a _____ principle.   reality

19. The young child refrains from doing wrong only through fear
    of being caught. As the rules and admonitions of the parents

    are _____, however, the _____ develops and suppresses   internalized, superego
    forbidden behavior even in the absence of negative conse-
    quences.

20. _____ is the crucial factor in the mechanism underlying   Anxiety
    repression. Internal thoughts and feelings that evoke this state
    must be escaped and are thus suppressed.

21. When fear of retaliation blocks the expression of anger, a
    person may vent his feelings on another recipient, resulting in

    _____ _____.   displaced aggression

22. When a repressed thought or wish manifests itself as a diamet-
    rically opposite wish or thought, it is a result of

    _____ _____.   reaction formation

23. _____ is another defense mechanism in which a repressed   Rationalization
    thought is reinterpreted in more acceptable terms.

24. Cognitive reorganization also plays a role in _____, in   projection
    which forbidden urges are attributed to others rather than to
    the self.

25. _____ _____ represents an extreme form of projection,   Paranoid schizophrenia
    in which the patient's feelings of rage are exacerbated by his
    perception of hatred in other people, constituting a vicious
    cycle of hostility.

26. Through his study of dreams, Freud came to the conclusion

    that dreams are an attempt at _____ _____. Desires   wish fulfillment
    suppressed by considerations of reality and by the superego
    emerge and are gratified in dreams.

27. The _____ dream is the disguised expression of the   manifest

    _____ dream, which represents hidden and forbidden wishes.   latent

28. The manifest dream employs _____ and incorporates   symbolism

    _____ _____ in its attempt at wish fulfillment.   day residues

ORIGINS OF UNCONSCIOUS CONFLICT

29. Freud's theory of _____ development postulates biologically   psychosexual
    determined stages of emotional and sexual development.

30. Freud maintained that the young child seeks pleasure. This
    pleasure is often obtained by touching body parts which are
    particularly sensitive, such as the mouth, anus, and genitals.

    These areas are known as _____ _____.   erogenous zones

31. Seeking pleasure through the mouth is characteristic of the

    _____ stage, which yields to the _____ stage as toilet   oral, anal

    training begins. The _____ stage focuses on the stimulation   phallic
    of the genitals, while interest in the satisfaction of others as

    well as one's own satisfaction characterizes the _____ stage.   genital

32. The family drama from which grows the child's internalized
    morality and identification with the same-sex parent is called

    the _____ _____.   Oedipus complex

33. The _____ urges of the boy at ages three and four are   phallic

    directed toward the _____ as the source of previous gratifi-   mother
    cation during the oral stage.

34. The young boy's _____ of the father leads to _____ and   jealousy, hostility

    a fear of retaliation which is termed _____ _____.   castration fear

35. As the young boy's anxiety about retaliation increases, the boy

    _____ with the father in the hope that this will eventually   identifies
    secure him an erotic partnership like the father's.

36. The renunciation of genital pleasures endures from about five

    to twelve years of age and is termed the _____ _____.   latency period

37. Jealousy between brothers and sisters is called _____ _____   sibling rivalry
    and also contributes to psychosexual development.

38. The weakest aspect of Freud's theory of psychosexual devel-
    opment concerns the young girl's progression of sexual
    interests. Specifically, why does the little girl desire the father
    instead of the mother? Freud attributed this transference of

    attachment to _____ _____, as the girl believes she has   penis envy

    been _____.   castrated

A REEXAMINATION OF FREUDIAN THEORY

39. The fact that clinical psychologists cannot be totally objective
    about a patient's behavior patterns and problems is one of the

    difficulties of _____ theory.   psychoanalytic

40. Repression, or _____ _____, has been studied through   motivated forgetting

    analysis of _____ lapses.   memory

41. A word association test described in the text employing emo-
    tionally charged words measured anxiety according to the

    patterns of _____ _____ and of _____ _____   heart rate, galvanic skin

    _____.   response

42. When the recognition of briefly presented syllables which have
    previously been paired with shock is impaired, we attribute the

    effect to _____ _____.   perceptual defense

43. In the study described in question 42, the authors concluded that anxiety-provoking stimuli are recognized subconsciously.

    This _____ triggers anxiety which blocks conscious recogni-   subception
    tion.

44. An alternate explanation for the phenomenon described in

    question 42 is that anxiety is conditioned to the _____ of   components
    anxiety-producing stimuli; thus, recognition never proceeds
    past an early stage.

45. Individuals who fail to recall or recognize anxiety-arousing

    materials are termed _____. Those who are unable to over-   repressors

    look or forget such material are known as _____.   sensitizers

46. _____ are likely to complain of minor bodily ills, thus   Repressors
    exhibiting one of the characteristics of the personality pattern

    of _____.   hysterics

47. Freud's belief that dreams reflect current emotional preoccu-

    pations is supported by the dreams of _____ patients.   preoperative

48. The same urge may sometimes be disguised and sometimes be
    expressed openly in a dream. Freud's assertion that the

    manifest dream represents a _____ disguise cannot handle   defensive
    this facet, but C. S. Hall's proposal that the dream functions

    to _____ an underlying idea can.   express

49. Freud believed that the progression of emotional development

    is rooted in _____, and is thus universal.   biology

50. Some psychoanalytic practitioners acknowledge the importance
    of social factors in development. These psychologists are

    termed _____ _____.   neo-Freudians

51. Freud maintained that neurotic conflict centers on the repres-

    sion of _____ impulses. Others, such as Erich Fromm,   erotic

    emphasize the area of _____ relationships.   interpersonal

52. Evidence from _____ anthropology supports an antibiolog-   cultural
    ical bias in the analysis of personality development.

53. Studies of other cultures have indicated that the hostility of
    the young boy toward the father in our culture is a product,

    not of sexual _____, but rather of the father's role as a   jealousy

    _____.   disciplinarian

54. The method of _____ _____ _____ looks for corre-   cross-cultural comparison
    lations between various cultural and/or psychological factors
    over a large number of different societies.

**PSYCHOANALYTIC INTERPRETATION OF
CULTURE, MYTHS, AND LITERATURE**

55. Freud's theory of the nature and development of human personality was meant to encompass all human beings. He viewed
the Oedipus complex as an important factor in the origin of

society, resulting in the almost universal _____ _____.   incest taboo

56. A prohibition against inbreeding is selectively advantageous

from _____, _____, and _____ viewpoints.   genetic, economic, social

FREUD'S CONTRIBUTIONS IN RETROSPECT

57. Despite the criticisms of Freud's theoretical proposals, his

conception of _____ conflict and the sheer scope of his   internal (or unconscious)
ideas rank him as one of the giants of psychology.

Self Test

1. Which of the following adjectives would not
be used by Freud to describe basic human
nature?
a. sexually motivated
b. selfish
c. pleasure-seeking
d. conflict-free

2. At first the child's behavior is based on a
fear of direct social consequences. Later he
will avoid certain behaviors even when there
is no chance of punishment. Freud would
say that the control put on the child by
society is then _____.
a. eliminated
b. internalized
c. externalized
d. repressed

3. Freud made a major contribution to the
understanding of human nature when he
suggested that the apparent irrationality of
much human behavior was a symptom of

_____ _____.
a. basic insanity
b. severe hysteria
c. unconscious conflicts
d. wish fulfillment

4. Which of the following are symptoms of
hysteria?
i. partial or total blindness ✓
ii. paralysis ✓
iii. feelings of helplessness
iv. uncontrollable tremblings ✓
v. uncontrollable urges

a. i, iii, v
b. i, ii, iv, v
c. ii, iii, iv
d. i, ii, iv

5. Jean Charcot discovered that hysteria is

_____.
a. inherited
b. psychogenic
c. the result of physical trauma (injury to
the brain)
d. incurable

6. It was suggested at one time that hysteria
and _____ were related, due to the similarity of effects produced in the two conditions.
a. drug addiction
b. true (physiological) paralysis
c. hypnosis
d. none of the above

7. Due to the similarities mentioned in question 6, it was hypothesized that the two conditions were related through _____.
a. suggestion
b. neurosis
c. organic damage
d. amnesia

8. The explosive release of emotions which ac-
companies the remembrance of certain long-
forgotten memories is called _____.
a. resistance
b. memory release
c. transference
d. catharsis

9. A patient is asked merely to say whatever comes to his mind during a therapy session. The term applied to this psychoanalytic technique is:
   a. transference
   b. free association
   c. resistance formation
   d. wish fulfillment

10. All of the following statements (made by a patient during free association) are examples of resistance except:
    a. "I really can't think of anything right now."
    b. "I just forgot what I was about to say."
    c. "I'm thinking of something which has nothing to do with my problem."
    d. "I just remembered a terrible experience from my childhood."
    e. "What I'm thinking about now is too unimportant to tell you."

11. According to Freud, repressed thoughts:
    a. are always connected to a wish or thought that a person is unable to face without intense anxiety
    b. are always linked to basic biological urges
    c. often date back to early life
    d. all of the above
    e. none of the above

12. Freud was interested in unconscious conflicts. This interest included which of the following?
    a. the origin of these conflicts
    b. their present effects
    c. treatment
    d. all of the above
    e. a and c

13. Which of Freud's subsystems would be responsible for a desire to eat or drink?
    a. ego
    b. superego
    c. id
    d. a combination of ego and superego

14. If a child wants a drink, we often find that he asks for something rather than just taking it. Which subsystem is responsible for this?
    a. ego
    b. superego
    c. id
    d. a combination of ego and superego

15. The reality principle controls:
    a. the ego
    b. the superego
    c. the id
    d. all of the subsystems to one degree or another

16. When a child begins to think of himself as if he were the parent, the _____ has begun to develop:
    a. ego
    b. superego
    c. id
    d. impossible to tell from this description

17. Conflicts develop because the _____ and _____ often issue conflicting commands to the _____.
    a. id, ego, superego
    b. id, superego, ego
    c. ego, superego, id
    d. all three systems issue commands to every other system

18. On what is the mechanism underlying repression based?
    a. irrationality
    b. biological urges
    c. anxiety
    d. fear

19. Why are thoughts and memories repressed as well as actions?
    a. thinking about an act is similar to performing it
    b. young children cannot properly distinguish between thought and action, nor do they realize that thoughts are private
    c. both of the above are possible explanations
    d. none of the above are possible explanations

20. A child is punished for something he did. He then hits his brother. This is an example of:
    a. repression
    b. transference
    c. hysteria
    d. displaced aggression

21. Three defense mechanisms which come into play once a forbidden impulse cannot be kept down any longer are:
    a. tranference, projection, reaction formation

b. repression, transference, reaction formation
c. reaction formation, projection, rationalization
d. displaced aggression, repression, rationalization

22. A child has deeply hidden feelings of hostility toward a younger sibling. However, the child treats his sibling with apparent love. This is an example of the defense mechanism known as:
    a. projection
    b. reaction formation
    c. rationalization
    d. transference

23. After failing to be offered a good job, an applicant decides that he wouldn't have liked the job anyway. This person is displaying a defense mechanism called:
    a. rationalization
    b. projection
    c. reaction formation
    d. paranoia

24. When a person attributes his own thoughts and feelings to someone else, we call this:
    a. rationalization
    b. projection
    c. reaction formation
    d. repression

25. A person feels that other people are conspiring against him. He attributes his feelings of hate to others and then reacts to this perceived hate with more hate. This vicious cycle is known as:
    a. rationalization
    b. reaction formation
    c. delusions of omnipotence
    d. none of the above

26. Freud believed that the basis of every dream was:
    a. projection
    b. schizophrenia
    c. wish fulfillment
    d. day residues

27. Freud distinguished between two parts of the dream, which he termed:
    a. conscious and unconscious
    b. latent and manifest
    c. normal and deviant
    d. wish fulfillment and disguise

28. Dreams, metaphor, and poetry all involve:
    a. displaced activity
    b. repression
    c. suppression
    d. symbolism

29. Parts of the body which are particularly sensitive to touch are called:
    a. arousal zones
    b. pleasure zones
    c. sensitivity zones
    d. erogenous zones

30. Which of the following presents the correct stages of psychosexual development in the right order?
    a. oral, anal, erogenous, phallic, genital
    b. oral, anal, phallic, genital
    c. anal, oral, erogenous, phallic
    d. oral, anal, phallic, erogenous

31. A child who displays a behavior diametrically opposed to his frustrated true desires is demonstrating:
    a. reaction formation
    b. displacement
    c. projection
    d. none of the above

32. All of the following are components of Freud's family triangle except:
    a. love
    b. inadequacy
    c. fear
    d. jealousy

33. The drama of the Oedipus complex unfolds according to the following progression of events:
    a. identification, love, fear, hate, renunciation
    b. love, fear, hate, renunciation, identification
    c. hate, fear, renunciation, identification, love
    d. love, hate, fear, renunciation, identification

34. The motivation for the young boy's identification with his father is:
    a. perception of sexual similarities
    b. castration anxiety
    c. the father's acts of retaliation
    d. vicarious enjoyment of the mother through the father

35. The stage following resolution of the Oedipus complex comprises:
    a. the latency period
    b. increased masturbation
    c. puberty
    d. all of the above

36. Perceptual defense is caused by:
    a. the subception of anxiety-triggering items blocking conscious recognition
    b. increased autonomic arousal distracting attention from the visual mode

c. individual components of the stimuli associated with anxiety, preventing recognition

d. no one really knows; the above alternatives include only hypotheses

37. The distinction between repressors and sensitizers is based on:
   a. the representation of the characteristics of hysterics in their respective personalities
   b. their ability to shut the door on their anxieties by overlooking or forgetting what disturbs them
   c. the degree to which they complain about bodily ills
   d. their everyday psychopathology

38. In a recent study, a test was made of Freud's view of the dream as an attempt at gratification. Most very thirsty subjects reported:
   a. dreams in which they drank
   b. dreams in which they did not drink
   c. no dreams whatsoever
   d. dreams in which the act of drinking was represented symbolically

39. Which of the following statements is not in accordance with C. S. Hall's view about dreams?
   a. the dream symbol expresses, rather than disguises, an underlying idea
   b. the dream is a concrete form of mental shorthand that embodies a feeling or emotion
   c. the dream is an abstract form of mental longhand that elaborates on a feeling or emotion
   d. the function of the dream is analogous to that of a cartoonist's picture

40. Neo-Freudians believe that Freud erred in:
   a. emphasizing sexual motivations
   b. his view of dreams as wish fulfillment
   c. his perception of oral and anal characteristics
   d. his assertion that the key to emotional development is in biology

41. Cross-cultural comparisons of male initiation rites, maternal dependency, and sleeping arrangements have shown that:
   a. there is a relationship between Oedipal rivalry and the conditions of early childhood
   b. male puberty rites are not related to the psychological separation of the boy and his mother
   c. some initiation rites entail sharing the mother's bed for a year in partial enactment of the Oedipus conflict

d. the severity of the rite of passage symbolically represents the castration of the boy in retaliation for his attachment to the mother, thus resolving his conflict

42. There is little evidence for all of the following assertions of psychoanalytic theory except:
   a. the existence of unconscious conflict
   b. the general theory of psychosexual development
   c. the importance of biology in emotional development
   d. personality is essentially fixed by the age of five or six

43. According to Freud, the incest taboo developed as:
   a. the genetic problems of inbreeding selected against incest
   b. a form of sexual social contract
   c. a defense against Oedipal desires
   d. a result of the temptation caused by proximity of siblings

44. Advantages of the incest taboo included all of the following except:
   a. increased genetic fitness
   b. extension of emotional ties
   c. decreased moral turpitude
   d. larger tribes

Answer Key for Self Test

1. d pp. 412–14	23. a p. 421
2. b pp. 413–14	24. b p. 421
3. c p. 417	25. d p. 421
4. d p. 414	26. c p. 422
5. b p. 414	27. b p. 423
6. c p. 415	28. d pp. 423–24
7. a p. 415	29. d p. 424
8. d p. 415	30. b p. 424
9. b p. 416	31. a pp. 420, 425
10. d p. 416	32. b p. 425
11. d p. 416	33. d pp. 425–27
12. d p. 417	34. b p. 426
13. c p. 418	35. a p. 427
14. d pp. 418–19	36. d pp. 431–32
15. a p. 418	37. b p. 432
16. b pp. 418–19	38. b p. 433
17. b p. 419	39. c pp. 433–34
18. c p. 419	40. d p. 434
19. c p. 420	41. a p. 436
20. d p. 420	42. a pp. 440–41
21. c pp. 420–21	43. b p. 437
22. b pp. 420–21	44. c pp. 437–38

Investigating Psychological Phenomena

ANALYSIS OF DREAM CONTENT

Equipment: None
Number of subjects: One or more
Time per subject: Thirty minutes
Time for experimenter: Thirty minutes

The study and analysis of dream content has been of considerable concern to psychologists at least since the publication of Freud's classic work on dreams in 1900. A variety of hypotheses have been proposed to account for the content of dreams and for the way in which our past experiences and expectations about the future are frequently incorporated into our dreamwork.

Given the sparse evidence concerning dream content, there is still a good deal of controversy concerning the facts. One phenomenon of particular interest that is still controversial is whether present motivational states or expectations about the future (e.g., wish fulfillment) influence our dream content.

The present experiment further tests the hypothesis that dream content is influenced by present motivational state. The test is similar to the experiment of William Dement and Edward Wolpert cited in the Gleitman text, in which these investigators induced thirst in their subjects, then analyzed the subjects' dreams to determine whether there was evidence in the dream content for increased thirst.

You will be the subject in the present experiment. Starting on the next page, you will find eight pairs of dream reports. These are the reports of actual dreams from eight students enrolled in an introductory psychology course. One of the reports in each pair is the report of a dream from early in the term in which these students were enrolled in introductory psychology. The other report in each pair represents a dream that occurred on the night preceding a major midterm examination in the psychology course. The question we ask in this experiment is whether the specific issues involved in this examination or general anxiety about the examination was reflected in the dreams of these eight subjects. In other words, we are testing for evidence of "day residues" in the subject's dream content.

In order to address this question, you should read each dream and try to decide which dream in each pair was the one that occurred *prior* to the examination. Be careful to consider the possibility, as Freud theorized, that conflicts or concerns may be either manifest or latent in dream content. That is, there may be direct or transformed reference to the event in question. For each dream pair, mark your answer sheet A or B according to which member of the pair you think was the dream that preceded the examination. In each case, think about the reasons for your choice and assess your confidence in your decision. After listing your choices, check them with the answers given.

DREAM PAIRS

1A Someone was singing a rousing song about a coat. An audience of women, mostly of the type interviewed in commercials, was sitting on the floor of a large room. They were asked to describe how they had put together their outfits. Most were wearing the sweater-and-skirt sort of thing, but one woman in a peculiar-looking caftan told how she had bought the trim first and had then searched for something to use it on. The trim didn't look very good on the caftan.

1B A record store. The stuff that had been pasted up all over the walls (posters, clippings, etc.) had yellowed, creating an antique atmosphere. Some balloons. The store was giving away something for free—furniture I think. There was some argument. Something about a snake who liked a trollop. A young and quarrelsome married couple from a film I'd seen more or less reenacted their roles. I was in a strange room in a hotel or dormitory. There was, to my surprise, a small wrought-iron balcony. Night. From the balcony I could see the lights and reflections of the city gleaming white and yellow all around me. The lights began to go out, all at once—the restaurants and bars were closing. I was seeing into a little restaurant or ice cream parlor, very white and empty. Three people wearily got up and left as the place closed up for the night.

2A I was knocking at the door of my best friend's house. (Earlier in the dream I had seen her working on campus and spoken to her. [She lives in San Antonio, Texas.]) I covered the peephole to the front door, as is my custom, when she became very excited and yelled for her parents. She seemed to be very frightened. This is when the dream ended and I woke up.

2 B Someone I didn't recognize was walking down Locust Walk wearing shoes exactly like some of mine, except for the color. Mine are red and blue. Hers were green and blue.

3 A I dreamed I was sitting at a table with several people eating brownies with whipped cream and soap suds, fighting with one of my friends.

3 B I dreamed that my kitten looked like a guinea pig. (I went home for the weekend and she had changed.) She wasn't tiger striped, she was only solid black and rust colored. Her ears were not pointed, they were small and flat. She had no tail and her legs were short.

4 A I was going to go swimming. I sat on a bench on the side of the street waiting for a taxi or bus. With me were a girl and a German teacher. The man had a beach umbrella. He grew tired of waiting and left. I went to a different beach to look for the father from a foreign family I spent a year with.

4 B I was with a boyfriend while he was making sandwiches for a party. Beaded strings were in the crevice between the wall and the ceiling. Another girl was there making coffee with a weird machine. Outside I played catch with a friend. First we used a ball, then an orange, and lastly a key. We almost lost the key in the snow. I was skiing with another girl and she kept complimenting Yamaha skis. I tried to park the car in front of my house but there were no spaces. Two guys who I didn't particularly like from high school were in one of the cars drinking. They were not my type. When they asked me to go drinking I declined. Finally I went to a party. A minister I know said grace. A guest commented that a girl's jewelry didn't match her clothes, yet it really did. A lot of people were talking and eating.

5 A The dream opened with me having just had a baby, but for some reason the kid (a boy) was about the size of a year-old baby—maybe a couple of months younger. I didn't recall getting pregnant or delivering the kid. Somehow I knew that the kid (baby) had my boyfriend's nickname. I got extreme pleasure from hugging the baby and knowing he was mine, although I didn't know who the father was. Suddenly I realized that I was in high school

and my mother would never let me keep the baby. So I had to give him up for adoption. I was very sad at handing him over to a stranger and the thought that I would never see him grow up was upsetting. This was a pleasurable dream until the last scene.

5 B I went back to visit my prep school and I bumped into my favorite teacher there. She was terribly aged and frail, having had some sort of drastic operation. I kissed her hello on the cheek and she was very cold, as though I had misbehaved recently at school or something. I don't remember the rest of the dream clearly except that the teacher kept turning into my mother and back into the teacher, and evidently I had done something awful but no one would tell me what. It was a very anxious and unpleasant dream.

6 A I was riding on a trolley coming home from high school. The driver asked me for my fare and I found out I didn't have any money. I ran to the back to try to get out. Then I woke up.

6 B I dreamt I had a sexual affair with my psychology professor. He told me I was one of his best friends.

7 A Dreamt about color vision. Repeatedly remembered seeing one page in the reading.

7 B Dreamt that I woke up late for chemistry lab and that experiment failed.

8 A I rode on a short train ride and on the return trip I met a very good friend who is coming to visit me for the weekend. However, the train departure is delayed so I sit down to lunch with my family and another three friends (I don't know where they came from). My family wants me to tell them about school, but I am more interested in seeing one of my friends— procuring tea bags and knives for my apartment (which I need). Another incident—I pass a stand with two older ladies selling home-made doughnuts (and cake) but I don't buy any, even though I see a girl sinking her teeth into one. Also, while I am walking toward the train station, the sidewalk is being paved (by males and females).

8 B I have been waiting three weeks to see my boyfriend. Finally the weekend arrives and he comes to visit me. But, of course, we can't be alone since my best friend also drops in on me. Then I find out my grandmother has

passed away (however, she is still among us when we all sit down to a mourning feast). When we finally get a chance to be alone again, my boyfriend and I are walking down a street. A car honks its horn and it turns out to be his old girlfriend asking for a ride home. During this same dream I remember buying a new bicycle and a pair of army boots.

Answer Sheet

Dream pair	Dream preceding examination (A or B)	Reason for choice
1.	_____	_____
2.	_____	_____
3.	_____	_____
4.	_____	_____
5.	_____	_____
6.	_____	_____
7.	_____	_____
8.	_____	_____

ANSWERS

1. B   2. A   3. A   4. B   5. B   6. B   7. A   8. B

QUESTIONS TO THINK ABOUT

1. Were you accurate? What does this suggest about the content of dreams and about how well they blend with life events?

2. Were there certain pairs where the choice seemed more obvious than for other pairs? Were you more accurate on these?

3. How might you improve on the experiment?

CHAPTER 13

General Issues in Development

Learning Objectives

CHANGING CONCEPTIONS OF CHILDHOOD

1. What social forces, in the last few centuries, have led to the emergence of the idea of childhood (after age six) as a special stage of life?

THE CONCEPT OF DEVELOPMENT AS PROGRESSIVE CHANGE

Development in the embryo
2. Describe recapitulation theory, evidence for it, and its influence on the emergence of child psychology.
3. What is differentiation, and how does it account for similarities in the embryos of different species?

Differentiation and behavior
4. In what ways does differentiation describe the course of development of behavior in humans and other animals?

SOME CHARACTERISTICS OF DEVELOPMENT

Development as growth
5. Review the major events in physical growth of humans from conception to adulthood.
6. How does humans' physical growth (especially of the nervous system) compare with that of other animals?
7. Review the basic sensory and response capacities of the human infant.

Development as orderly progression
8. Describe the sequence of early development of locomotion and language in humans, and indicate how the order of many accomplishments is fixed.

THE INTERACTION OF HEREDITY AND ENVIRONMENT

9. Indicate why it is necessary to invoke both heredity (nature) and environment (nurture) to account for behavior.

Heredity
10. Define chromosomes. Indicate how sex is determined by chromosomes, and describe how the process of meiosis increases variability in offspring.
11. Define genes. Distinguish between dominant and recessive genes, giving an example.
12. Distinguish between genotype and phenotype.
13. Explain polygenic inheritance, and distinguish it from inheritance based on a single pair of genes.
14. Describe the cause and genetic basis of phenylketonuria, and know how it illustrates the fact that inborn characteristics may be changeable.
15. Describe how research on twins can provide evidence for a genetic determination of specific behaviors.

Environments at different points of development
16. Review gene-environment interactions in the embryo, including the role of both the cellular and hormonal environments in development.

17. Indicate how the significant aspects of the postbirth environment change with age, and define and describe critical periods.

The organism helps to shape its own environment

18. Describe how the organism shapes its environment, and the resulting continuing interaction between genetic and environmental factors. Use the development of typical male and female behaviors as an example, and think of another example as well.

Environment and maturation

19. Define maturation. What is the evidence for maturation of some basic abilities, such as walking?

20. Distinguish between general and specific environmental effects in development, and discuss the effects of sensory deprivation and enrichment in animals and humans.

21. Summarize the ways in which environment and genes interact in development.

Programmed Exercises

CHANGING CONCEPTIONS OF CHILDHOOD

1. Prior to the eighteenth century, there was no concept of childhood after age five or six; rather, children were treated as

    _____ _____.

    little adults

THE CONCEPT OF DEVELOPMENT AS PROGRESSIVE CHANGE

2. According to _____ theory, each individual, in its own history, goes through the evolutionary history of the species of which it is a member.

    recapitulation

3. The process of _____ involves a progressive change from the more general to the more particular, from the simpler to the more complex.

    differentiation

4. Differentiation predicts and accounts for the fact that development occurs in an _____ progression.

    orderly

SOME CHARACTERISTICS OF DEVELOPMENT

5. Physical growth continues until approximately the end of the _____ decade of life.

    second

6. The part of the human body that grows at a disproportionately high rate before birth is the _____.

    head (brain)

7. Because of extensive growth of the brain after birth, humans have a longer period of _____ than most other species.

    dependency

8. The _____ reflex is elicited in an infant by a touch to the cheek, which makes the infant turn its head toward the stimulating object.

    rooting

9. In general, the infant's sensory capacities are _____ advanced at birth than its _____ capacities.

    more

    response (motor)

10. The human baby begins to walk alone at an age of about _____ months.

    15 (12 to 18)

11. The first words typically occur at about _____ months.   10 (8 to 12)

12. Although some children develop faster than others, the major

    motor and language accomplishments occur in a _____   fixed (orderly)
    sequence.

THE INTERACTION OF HEREDITY AND ENVIRONMENT

13. The genetic material of humans is arranged in twenty-three

    pairs of structures called _____ .   chromosomes

14. In reproduction, the sperm and egg cells each contain _____ half
    the number of chromosomes as other cells. The process of cell
    division through which this reduction in chromosome number

    is carried out is called _____ .   meiosis

15. The process of meiosis produces greater _____ in offspring. variability

16. In contrast to a female, who has two X chromosomes, a male

    has a(n) _____ and a(n) _____ chromosome in each   X, Y
    body cell.

17. The unit of hereditary transmission is the _____ .   gene

18. A gene that exerts its effect regardless of the identity of the

    other member of its pair is called _____ . A gene that will dominant
    express itself only if the other member of its pair is compatible

    is called _____ .   recessive

19. The observed characteristics of an organism are called its

    _____ , while the underlying genetic blueprint is called its phenotype

    _____ .   genotype

20. Traits that are controlled by genes but show many different

    values are determined by _____ inheritance.   polygenic

21. A form of mental retardation that is caused by a single reces-

    sive gene is _____ .   phenylketonuria

22. Under most circumstances, a trait has some genetic determina-

    tion if it is more similar among _____ than _____ twins. identical, fraternal

23. In mammalian embryos, the genitals will develop as _____   female

    unless the body is exposed to _____ sex hormone, called   male

    _____ .   androgen

24. Consider a person with a male (XY) genetic makeup, but
    whose tissues are not sensitive to male hormone. Such a per-
    son will develop female genitals. Unlike a typical male, such a

    person shows a disparity between _____ and _____ .   phenotype,
                                                                     genotype (either order)

25. During _____ periods in development, certain important   critical
    events will have an impact that they would not have (or would
    have to a much lesser extent) at earlier or later times.

26. In sexual development, the _____ are determined by the   gonads
    genes, and control the secretion of sex hormones. These hor-

    mones determine the form of the _____ _____, which   external genitals

    in turn determine the _____ in which the parents raise the   environment
    child.

27. The inevitable unfolding of behavior patterns that is geneti-
    cally programmed into the species and is independent of spe-

    cific environmental conditions is called _____.   maturation

28. Behaviors that mature are usually not subject to the influence

    of _____ experience, but are affected by _____ experience. specific, general

29. Animals reared in darkness show later deficits in their visual

    system. This rearing procedure is called _____ _____.   sensory deprivation
    Some claim that deprivation of a variety of experiences in

    some _____ children also leads to a variety of deficits in   institutionalized
    behavior.

30. In contrast to the sensory deprivation work, there are some

    reports that sensory _____ can exert positive effects on   enrichment
    development.

Self Test

1. Social forces that led to the emergence of a
   conception of childhood (after age five to
   six) as a special period in life include:
   a. scattering of the extended family
   b. a less rigid class system
   c. the rise of apprenticeships
   d. the recognition that some behavior is
      inherited
   e. a and b

2. The fact that, at early stages, embryos of
   many very different species look very much
   alike, and have a much simpler structure
   than adults, can be taken as evidence for:
   a. recapitulation theory
   b. differentiation
   c. the inheritance of behavior
   d. all of the above
   e. a and b

3. The fact that some of the structures seen in
   the embryos referred to in question 2 are
   never seen in adults of any possible ances-
   tors argues against:
   a. recapitulation theory
   b. differentiation
   c. the inheritance of behavior
   d. all of the above
   e. a and b

4.

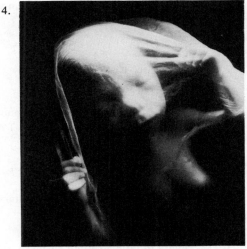

The figure corresponds to a human being of
about what age (beginning with conception
as zero)?
   a. one month
   b. four months
   c. eight months
   d. birth (nine months)
   e. one year (postconception)

5. All but one of the following are distinctive features of human development, in comparison with most other mammals. Which is not a distinctively human feature?
   a. long period of dependency on the parent
   b. being born at a very immature stage
   c. presence of reflexes at birth
   d. continuation of growth until about twenty years of age
   e. b and c

6. Major features of motor, language, and other types of development often occur in a fixed order in children who develop at different rates. A major reason for this is that:
   a. development must occur in stages
   b. some capacities depend on the existence of other capacities
   c. sense organs mature before response capacities
   d. language depends on locomotion ability
   e. the infant begins with reflexes like grasping before it can learn

7. Assume an animal with six pairs of chromosomes. After meiosis, how many chromosomes would be expected in each sperm and egg cell?
   a. three
   b. six
   c. nine
   d. twelve
   e. twenty-four

8. Offspring often do not resemble one another or their parents on all characteristics. This variability is promoted by:
   a. meiosis
   b. the existence of dominant and recessive genes
   c. the occurrence of polygenic inheritance
   d. all of the above
   e. none of the above

9. The ability to taste a certain chemical called PTC is genetically determined, and controlled by a single pair of genes. All children of nontasters are nontasters, but some of the children with two taster parents are also nontasters. This suggests that the gene that codes for tasting is:
   a. polygenic
   b. on at least two chromosomes
   c. dominant
   d. recessive
   e. rare

10. Phenotype and genotype are not always in close correspondence because:
    a. some genes are recessive
    b. some inheritance is polygenic
    c. only females have two X chromosomes
    d. a and c
    e. all of the above

11. Phenylketonuria would be expected to be:
    a. more common in females
    b. always present in one identical twin if present in the other
    c. always present in one fraternal twin if present in the other
    d. b and c
    e. none of the above

12. Consider two adults. One has no genes for phenylketonuria, and the other has one gene for phenylketonuria and one normal gene. Since both of these adults are of normal intelligence, we can say that:
    a. they have similar phenotypes and different genotypes
    b. neither can have a phenylketonuric child, no matter whom the other parent is
    c. they have the same genotype
    d. a and b
    e. none of the above

13. A genetic female who is exposed to androgen as a fetus and develops male genitals and a person with phenylketonuria that is treated from birth and develops no symptoms both illustrate:
    a. that behavior is inherited
    b. that recessive traits can occur in both sex and intelligence
    c. that inborn, genetically determined traits can be changed by environmental factors
    d. that environmental factors, under some circumstances, have no influence on behavior
    e. that behavior is related to sex chromosomes

14. Studies of transplanted embryonic tissues indicate:
    a. important roles for both environment and genes
    b. a dominant role for genes in development
    c. a dominant role for the environment in development
    d. that up to a certain point, a tissue may be able to develop in many ways, but later (after a critical period) it may be less changeable
    e. a and d

15. The fact that at different ages organisms perceive their environment differently, and the existence of critical periods, argue for the view that:
    a. it is not possible to describe the meaningful environment for an animal by just listing all the physical and social events that are occurring
    b. initially behavior is controlled by genes, and later by environment
    c. it is not possible to evaluate the role of environment in determining behavior
    d. b and c
    e. all of the above

16. It is probably true that, on the average, by the time they are adolescents, taller people are better basketball players. Insofar as this is because, being taller (a trait under a strong degree of genetic control), they are given more opportunities and encouragement to play basketball, this is an example of:
    a. critical periods
    b. maturation
    c. the organism shaping its environment
    d. b and c
    e. all of the above

17. A behavior appears at adolescence. Evidence for the position that this is a case of maturation would be that the behavior:
    a. depends on specific experience
    b. does not depend on general experience
    c. appears very frequently in adopted children
    d. is present at birth
    e. none of the above

18. Which of the following argues for an important role for environmental factors in a particular ability?
    a. the development of the ability follows a time course that suggests maturation
    b. ability scores are much more similar in identical as opposed to fraternal twins

    c. the ability is present in children institutionalized since infancy
    d. ability scores are very similar in biologically unrelated adopted children living in the same home
    e. none of the above

19. There are some reports that young children who suffer *severe* deprivation of experience because their parents deny them access to the world (e.g., they are raised in a dark room or closet) show many deficits in behavior in later childhood. We cannot certainly attribute these deficits to *sensory* deprivation, because these children:
    a. may have had specific negative experiences, as well
    b. might have been abnormal before the parental mistreatment
    c. are not compared with a control group (e.g., siblings who are not severely deprived)
    d. all of the above
    e. none of the above

20. Phenotype : genotype::
    a. building : building plan
    b. maturation : motor development
    c. fetus : embryo
    d. recapitulation : differentiation
    e. hamburger : roll

Answer Key for Self Test

1. e pp. 443–44	11. b p. 457
2. e pp. 446–47	12. a pp. 456–57
3. a pp. 446–47	13. c pp. 458–60
4. b p. 449	14. e p. 459
5. c pp. 450–52	15. a pp. 460–61
6. b pp. 452–54	16. c p. 462
7. b p. 455	17. e p. 463
8. d pp. 455–57	18. d pp. 457–58
9. c p. 456	19. d pp. 464–65
10. a p. 456	20. a p. 456

CHAPTER 14

Cognitive Development: Thought

Learning Objectives

PIAGET'S THEORY OF COGNITIVE DEVELOPMENT

1. What are the major philosophical positions on development? How does Piaget's theory relate to these? What is the major characteristic of Piaget's theory?

Sensory-motor intelligence

2. Describe the hallmarks of this stage. How does the child see himself and objects around him? What distinctions develop during this period?

3. Why is object permanence seen as an end to this stage of development?

4. Describe how imitation develops during this period and how it depends on internal schemas. What does Piaget mean by the term "representation"? What are some examples of representations?

5. What is the difference between Piaget's conception of early cognitive development and Freud's view of early ego development?

The preoperational period

6. How is the name of this period derived?

7. Be familiar with various tests of conservation. How does the child's conservation ability develop during this period? Why do children fail to conserve at the beginning of this period? What operations are crucial for conservation?

8. Describe a test that demonstrates egocentrism.

Concrete and formal operations

9. What is the difference between these stages? How does Piaget study formal operations? Give examples of thinking patterns that would qualify for this stage.

PERCEPTION AND MOTOR ACTION IN INFANCY

The Gibsonian approach to perception

10. Explain how the Gibsonian approach to perception differs from that of Piaget.

Links between eye and ear

11. What evidence indicates that there may be a correspondence between sight and sound in young infants? How does this differ from Piaget's ideas about the interconnection of the senses?

Links between eye and hand

12. What is the research that suggests that there is coherence between sight and directed movement in newborns and young infants?

The perception of objects

13. What is occlusion? How does it affect adult object perception?

14. What is the habituation procedure, and how is it used to study perception?

THE PRESCHOOLER AND THE STAGE CONCEPT

The meaning of mental stage

15. What are the characteristics of a developmental "stage" as Piaget uses the term?

The question of discreteness

16. How has a recent finding suggested that Piaget overestimated the extent of egocentrism during the preoperational period?

17. Describe recent research on conservation of number. What does this reveal about Piaget's theory? What does it suggest about children's conceptions of number?

18. Preschool children are apparently capable of conservation in simple, constrained situations. What does this imply about their general in-

tellectual maturity? Have they necessarily mastered the skills of the preoperational period?

THE CAUSES OF COGNITIVE GROWTH

The nativist approach: maturation
19. Be aware of the role of cross-cultural data in evaluating the maturational hypothesis.

The empiricist approach: specific learning
20. Be able to discuss the basic issue distinguishing the positions of specific learning and maturation. What is Piaget's position? What is the relevant evidence?
21. How does a specific learning position explain the fairly fixed orders of development that characterize various stages?

Piaget's approach: assimilation and accommodation
22. Describe how Piaget sees assimilation and accommodation as explanations of cognitive growth.

The information-processing approach: chunking and strategies
23. What are adults better at remembering than young children? How do the neo-Piagetians answer this question?
24. Describe some strategies for remembering that adults use. How do young children approach a memory task, and how does their approach change as they mature?
25. What is meant by the term "metacognition"? How is metacognition manifested in memory, perception, language, thinking, and problem solving? At what approximate age does metacognition manifest itself?
26. How does cognitive development occur from an information-processing point of view? Compare this with Piaget's theory and indicate similarities.

Programmed Exercises

PIAGET'S THEORY OF COGNITIVE DEVELOPMENT

1. Jean Piaget and other developmental psychologists usually

   look for _____ differences between children and adults; they do not see children as adults in miniature.   qualitative

2. Piaget regards cognitive development as a dynamic process in

   which the child progresses through several _____.   stages

3. A child has begun to learn that he lives in a stable world which can be distinguished from his sensory impression. This

   child is most likely in the _____ _____ stage.   sensory-motor

4. Children develop the notion of _____ _____ near the   object permanence
   end of the sensory-motor stage as they become aware that objects exist independently of their sensory experience and motor manipulations.

5. Perhaps the most significant accomplishment of children in

   the sensory-motor stage is their ability to _____ objects or   represent
   events in their absence, rather than merely reacting to their presence.

6. Recurrent action patterns (such as sucking, swallowing, and head and eye movement) are the first mental elements, or

   _____. It is in terms of these that the infant organizes the   schemas
   world.

7. Although we regard _____ as a mental activity that is fairly   imitation
   primitive, it is a sign that a child has grasped the relation
   between his own movements and those produced by another.

8. A pseudo-imitation is an extension of a _____ _____ in   circular reaction
   which an infant repeats a pattern of behavior over and over.

9. Representations may be internalized actions, images, or words;

   in all cases they function as _____, which stand for what-   symbols
   ever they may signify.

10. _____ imitation is a case in which a child imitates an action   Deferred
    that occurred in the past, such as a playmate's temper tantrum
    observed a day before.

11. According to Piaget, all intellectual processes are ultimately

    descended from _____ _____.   motor activity (action)

12. According to Piaget, a conceptual system of thought can only
    be constructed by means of higher-order schemas. These

    _____ allow the internal manipulation of ideas according to   operations
    a stable set of rules and emerge at age seven or so; the period

    from two to seven is therefore termed _____.   preoperational

13. Piaget states that the ability to form _____ precedes lin-   representations
    guistic expression and is a prerequisite for it.

14. A characteristic of children in the preoperational stage is their

    inability to _____ quantity, as shown by their lack of   conserve
    knowledge about relative quantities of liquids in two glasses.

15. One of the crucial concepts which children must grasp if they

    are to conserve is that manipulations upon objects are _____.   reversible

16. A preoperational child is incapable of attending to all of the

    relevant _____ of an object simultaneously.   dimensions

17. Piaget believes that a child can learn to chunk dimensions

    together when he learns to focus upon the _____ from one   transformations
    experience to another rather than upon the individual experi-
    ences themselves.

18. A preoperational child believes his point of view is the only

    one. Such a belief is known as _____.   egocentrism

19. A child can determine whether a given number is odd or even
    and can also add one to any number. The child finds that 3 +
    1 is even, and 5 + 1 is even, but doesn't understand that any
    odd number added to one results in an even number. This

    child would be categorized as being in the _____ _____   concrete operations
    stage.

20. A child in the concrete operations stage has operations which

    are applicable to _____ events but which do not work too   concrete

    well when applied to _____ concepts.   abstract

21. The ability to entertain hypothetical possibilities and deal with potential relationships is characteristic only of the stage of

_____ _____.   formal operations

PERCEPTION AND MOTOR ACTION IN INFANCY

22. According to Eleanor and James Gibson, objects and events in

the environment give rise to patterns of _____ _____   high-order

_____ that provide information about the objects and   stimulation
events to the individual.

23. Recent findings concern the way infants link sight, sound, and

touch. These indicate that some _____ relations may be   intersensory
present in young infants.

24. The fact that an infant can perceive an object that is partially blocked by another object gives evidence that infants are capable of reacting appropriately to the perceptual effect of

_____.   occlusion

25. The procedure in which a perceptual display is kept in view

until an infant becomes bored is called _____.   habituation

THE PRESCHOOLER AND THE STAGE CONCEPT

26. Piaget asserts that cognitive development goes through several

distinct _____, each one having its own consistent and dis-   stages
crete characteristics.

27. Recent results with a task in which young children were re-quired to show their mothers a picture demonstrate that these

children are not as _____ as Piaget has claimed.   egocentric

28. Recent, more sensitive tests of _____ conservation, using a   number
"surprise" technique, demonstrate that spatial rearrangement

of objects is not a cause for surprise, but a change in _____   number
[same word as above] is.

29. Examination of early concepts of number suggest that children

do have a consistent way of _____ even though their num-   counting
ber tags may not match those of the adult.

30. Most developmental psychologists would say that Piaget's cognitive milestones are not a succession of mental stages, similar to those found in embryological development, but

rather a _____ of mental steps.   sequence

THE CAUSES OF COGNITIVE GROWTH

31. Nativists would state that mental development depends on

_____, a pre-programmed growth process based on changes   maturation
in underlying neural structures.

32. While children of different cultures may reach each Piagetian

    stage at different _____, they pass through these stages in   ages

    the same _____.   order

33. The alternative to the maturation-centered approach is one

    that emphasizes the acquisition of specific _____ through   patterns
    exposure to the environment.

34. Piaget believes that at the same time that the environment is

    _____ to the child's schemas, the schemas _____ to the   assimilated, accommodate
    environment.

35. A more current approach to cognitive development asserts that

    it results from a change in _____ _____.   information processing

36. According to this approach, mental growth is partly based on

    the acquisition of better and larger _____ of information   chunks

    and of various _____ for thinking and remembering.   strategies

37. As children get older, _____ repetition is substituted by   rote

    various forms of active _____, in which the items to be   rehearsal
    remembered are grouped and organized.

38. The fact that adults can reflect on the cognitive operations
    whereby they gain knowledge shows that they are capable of

    _____.   metacognition

39. The cognitive attainments characteristic of concrete operations

    are analogous to the higher-order _____ of a master of   chunks
    some skill (e.g., chess).

Self Test

1. A nativist:
   a. thinks of the child's mind as similar to
      an adult's, only with fewer associations
   b. thinks of a child's mind as qualitatively
      different from an adult's
   c. conceptualizes the growth of a child's
      mind as progression through a series of
      natural stages
   d. views basic cognitive categories as given
      a priori at birth

2. A child has learned that whether a toy box
   is open or closed, there are toys inside. It
   could be said that the child has attained the
   concept of:
   a. object permanence
   b. representations
   c. directed action
   d. solipsism

3. When a child becomes aware that objects
   exist independent of his own sensory experi-

ence, he would most likely have just completed which Piagetian stage?
   a. sensory-motor
   b. preoperational
   c. concrete operations
   d. formal operations

4. Recurring action patterns such as sucking
   and swallowing are:
   a. simple reflexes which have little develop-
      mental interest
   b. the first mental elements with which the
      infant organizes his world
   c. examples of intentional acts
   d. none of the above

5. The concept of ___C___ _____, where
   one behavior sequence serves as a stimulus
   for a second (identical sequence), is similar
   to the associationist concept of _____.
   a. deferred imitation, representation
   b. perceptual restructuring, schemas
   c. circular reactions, chaining
   d. none of the above

6. The main difference between imitation and pseudo-imitation in the child is that:
   a. the amount of pseudo-imitation increases with age
   b. imitation is an extension of a circular reaction
   c. pseudo-imitation involves a repeated cycling of the child's own behavior
   d. none of the above

7. A toy is hidden under a box in the presence of a child. The child is prevented from reaching the box for a few seconds. When he is released he immediately lifts the box off the toy. The earliest stage that this child could be in is _____.
   a. sensory-motor
   b. preoperational
   c. concrete operations
   d. formal operations

8. Demonstrations of the child's understanding that symbols (i.e., internalized actions, images, or words) may stand for objects but are not equivalent to them include all of the following *except*:
   a. object permanence
   b. deferred imitation
   c. make-believe play
   d. motor overflow

9. The concept unknown to a child who doesn't conserve quantity is:
   a. reversibility
   b. accuracy
   c. size
   d. weight

10. Children who don't conserve are:
    a. unable to attend to all of the relevant dimensions of a stimulus
    b. usually in the concrete operations stage
    c. usually in the formal operation stage
    d. none of the above

11. The social counterpart of an inability to attend to more than one dimension in a conservation task is:
    a. aggressive behavior
    b. having only one friend during a particular time interval
    c. egocentrism
    d. none of the above

12. The major difference between a child in the concrete operations stage and one in the formal operations stage is:
    a. the former is incapable of following the rules.

    b. The former cannot deal with numbers
    c. the former cannot deal with abstract concepts
    d. all of the above

13. Piaget's assertion is that perception:
    a. is achieved because of the innate capacity of the organism
    b. is not present in an organism until the age of two
    c. is built out of piecemeal impressions provided by the different senses
    d. has little to do with experience and learning

14. James and Eleanor Gibson maintain that higher-order patterns of stimulation:
    a. are learned gradually by the organism
    b. provide the organism with information about objects and events
    c. are a built-in endowment of an organism
    d. b and c

15. Which of the following intersensory correspondences has been shown in young infants?
    a. sight—hearing
    b. sight—taste
    c. smell—touch
    d. smell—sight

16. What are two characteristics of a developmental stage as Piaget uses the term?
    a. consistent, continuous
    b. continuous, discrete
    c. consistent, concrete
    d. consistent, discrete

17. The fact that cognitive achievements like conservation have precursors that appear possibly years before the concrete operational stage leads investigators to question the _____ of Piaget's developmental stages.
    a. concreteness
    b. discreteness
    c. consistency
    d. validity

18. The fact that children often count in unusual ways (e.g., one, two, four, twelve) consistently suggests:
    a. that they can't conserve numbers
    b. that they understand the one-to-one counting principle
    c. that they don't understand what counting means
    d. none of the above

19. According to the theory of maturation:
    a. behavior change is associated with neurological changes
    b. environmental changes have great impact on the development of the child
    c. learning takes place independently of age
    d. all of the above

20. According to the theory of specific learning:
    a. learning is the acquisition of specific patterns
    b. most things could be learned at any time
    c. the speed with which a child learns depends on his age
    d. a and b but not c

21. Which of the following statements about Piaget is true?
    a. he asserts that development involves a constant interchange between the child and the environment
    b. he asserts that specific learning causes the progression from one stage to another
    c. he asserts that the age at which each stage begins is consistent across cultures
    d. he says that the child's schemas assimilate to the environment, as well as the environment being accommodated to the schema

22. An approach to cognitive development asserts that mental growth is based partly on the acquisition of better and larger chunks of information. This approach explains cognitive development as a change in:
    a. maturation
    b. information processing
    c. specific learning
    d. assimilation

23. Which of the following is not an example of metacognition?
    a. being realistic about how many numbers you can recall at one time
    b. recognizing the difference between reality and illusion
    c. using strategies for reaching solutions
    d. reading and following directions for a recipe

Answer Key for Self Test

1. d p. 468
2. a p. 469
3. a pp. 469–70
4. b p. 470
5. c p. 470
6. c pp. 470–71
7. b pp. 471–72
8. d pp. 469, 471
9. a p. 473
10. a p. 474
11. c p. 475
12. c pp. 475–76
13. c p. 476
14. d p. 477
15. a pp. 477–78
16. d p. 482
17. b pp. 484–85
18. b p. 484
19. a p. 486
20. d pp. 487–88
21. a p. 488
22. b p. 488
23. d pp. 491–92

Investigating Psychological Phenomena

CONSERVATION OF NUMBER

Equipment: Thirty-three red poker chips and thirty-four blue ones
Number of subjects: One, age four or five (preoperational stage, according to Piaget)
Time per subject: Fifteen minutes
Time for experimenter: Thirty minutes

In Chapter 14, Professor Gleitman discusses the development of conservation ability as children move into what Piaget calls the stage of concrete operations. The characteristic of this ability is that children come to use a set of mental rules, or operations, to govern their thought about objects in the world. For example, they learn that a certain volume of water is unchanged by the characteristics of the container that happens to contain it. Thus, pouring a certain amount of water from a low and wide container into one that is tall and thin does not change its volume even though the water achieves a greater height in the tall container.

There is also research, described later in the chapter, suggesting that Piaget may have underestimated the ability of children to conserve. Apparently, when faced with somewhat less demanding tasks, which nevertheless are formal tests of conservation ability, young children who should be in a preoperational stage show some signs of conservation. This has been shown most impressively with the conservation of number. Recall that the problem that preoperational children face in conserving number is that they confuse numerosity with the physical length of the series which contains the items whose number must be judged. For example, they frequently judge that a row of items contains more items if it is simply longer than another row of items.

The present exercise allows you to take an empirical look at this issue. As suggested in the text, one of the variables that may influence whether children show evidence of conservation or not is the number of items that are included in a test. Common sense suggests that the more objects in a set whose number must be judged, the more difficult will be the judgment. We shall test this hypothesis in the context of a number conservation test in which the number of objects whose number must be judged will vary. In both conditions of the experiment, your subject will be asked to judge which of two rows contains more objects. In one condition, the number of objects in each row will be less than in the other condition.

In order to conduct this experiment most efficiently, and with the greatest chance of keeping the attention of your subject, prearrange the stimulus arrays before you begin. The figure on the next page shows you the five stimulus arrangements for each of the two numerosity conditions. Each letter in the figure represents a chip of the appropriate color (B = blue, R = red). On the left are the arrangements for the lower numerosity condition. The first arrangement is the control condition in which each row contains the same number of chips, and in which the two rows are of equal length. In the second figure, the two rows contain the same number, but the lengths of the rows differ. In the third figure, the lengths are equal, but one row contains more chips than the other. The fourth arrangement pits the two variables against one another: the row that is longest also contains fewer chips than the shorter row. On the right are comparable arrangements for the condition in which more chips are used. The four arrangements are in the same order as the ones on the left of the figure.

Make each of the eight arrangements on a separate piece of cardboard, and place them out of sight. Then seat your subject comfortably and ex-

plain to him/her that you are going to play a game in which the child has to say which row of chips has more chips. Take out arrangement 1 first and ask the child, "Which row has more, the one with red or the one with blue, or are they the same?" If the child answers that they are not the same, then lengthen or shorten one of the rows so that the child agrees that they are equal. Be sure that the red and blue chips line up above one another, so there is a one-to-one correspondence.

Now move on to arrangement 2. Continue with the same line of questioning, asking which row contains more, the red one or the blue one. After getting an answer, which you should record on the protocol form that is given below, ask your subject to explain his/her response. That is, ask why he/she judged one of the rows as having more (or less, or equal, depending upon his/her answer) chips, and record the substance of this answer on the protocol form. Continue with arrangements three and four, after which you should move on to arrangements five through eight. In each case, record the data in the spaces provided on the answer sheet. For each arrangement decide whether your subject was paying attention to the number or the length of the series in making his/her judgment. Which condition shows better number conservation overall?

The critical comparison that is of interest in this experiment is whether your subject shows evidence of competence in number conservation with fewer chips, but falters with a greater number of chips. If this is so, how does it fit in which the discussion in the text about the development of conservation? What does it imply about a stage theory of development?

Some other questions that might be raised by this exercise are the following: Would your results have been any different if the two conditions had been run in the opposite order, from the more to the less difficult? Is there something inherent in the questioning of the subject that may bias him/her to attend to length rather than number? Why might number conservation be better with fewer chips in the stimuli? What kinds of operations did your subject seem to be using as the basis for his/her judgments? What kinds of tests could be constructed to discover whether other conservation skills might also develop earlier than previously thought?

STIMULI FOR NUMBER CONSERVATION EXPERIMENT

Small Numbers	*Large Numbers*

1. B B B
    R R R

2.   B B B
      R   R   R

3. B   B
    R R R

4. B   B
      R   R   R

5. B B B B B B
    R R R R R R

6.   B B B B B
       R R R R R

7. B B B B B
    R R R R R R

8. B   B   B   B   B
      R R R R R

ANSWER SHEET FOR NUMBER CONSERVATION EXPERIMENT

1. More blue _____
   More red _____
   Both equal _____

   Explanation:

5. More blue _____
   More red _____
   Both equal _____

   Explanation:

2. More blue _____
   More red _____
   Both equal _____

   Explanation:

6. More blue _____
   More red _____
   Both equal _____

   Explanation:

3. More blue _____
   More red _____
   Both equal _____

   Explanation:

7. More blue _____
   More red _____
   Both equal _____

   Explanation:

4. More blue _____
   More red _____
   Both equal _____

   Explanation:

8. More blue _____
   More red _____
   Both equal _____

   Explanation:

CHAPTER 15

Cognitive Development: Language

Learning Objectives

THE PROBLEM OF LANGUAGE LEARNING

1. What are some of the problems of the language learner? What factors play an important part in language learning? How do children of different countries and backgrounds compare with each other in learning a language at a young age?

IS LANGUAGE LEARNING THE ACQUISITION OF A SKILL?

Language learning and imitation
2. Why is imitation insufficient to account for either sentence or word acquisition?

Language learning and correction
3. Characterize the kinds of speech corrections that children often receive. What is the implication for language learning?

THE NORMAL COURSE OF LANGUAGE LEARNING

The social origins of speech production
4. Characterize the verbal behavior of the prelinguistic child.

Discovering the forms of language
5. Initially, infants are capable of responding to all sound distinctions made in any language. What change occurs in the later stages of language learning?
6. What is Motherese and what are its characteristics? What specific uses does Motherese have in language learning?

The one-word speaker
7. What kind of words do children learn first?

8. Relate theories of children's word meaning to comparable theories of adults' word meaning.
9. What are two common problems for the language learner who is trying to comprehend the meaning of a word?
10. Can propositions be conveyed by the child's single words?

The two-word (telegraphic) speaker
11. How are words ordered in two-word speech?
12. What is the underlying propositional structure of this speech?

Later stages of language learning
13. Describe the phenomenon of overgeneralization. What does it indicate?
14. Understand the different ways in which young learners discover and understand the meanings of new words.

LANGUAGE LEARNING AND LANGUAGE CHANGE

15. Describe the pressures of language learning that cause language change.
16. Understand what other factors cause language change.

LANGUAGE LEARNING IN CHANGED ENVIRONMENTS

Wild children and isolated children
17. What arguments for the nature-nurture controversy can be made from data about wild children and isolated children?

Language without sound
18. Describe the characteristics of American Sign Language (ASL). Why is this an important example of language from a theoretical point of view?

Language without a model
19. Describe the language-learner studies with deaf children of hearing parents. What do the results imply?

LANGUAGE LEARNING AND CRITICAL PERIODS

20. Summarize the evidence that points out the importance of critical periods in language learning.

THE NECESSARY CONDITIONS FOR LANGUAGE LEARNING

21. What predisposition do children likely have that permits efficient language learning?

THE GROWTH OF THE MIND

22. How do modern developmental psychologists view cognitive development?

Programmed Exercises

IS LANGUAGE LEARNING THE ACQUISITION OF A SKILL?

1. Language learning by _____ is not a sufficient explanation, since children often speak novel sentences.

imitation

2. _____ cannot account for language learning, since it is impossible for the child to know what parts of a sentence are being praised.

Reinforcement

3. _____ cannot account for language learning, since grammatical errors are seldom successfully changed by parents.

Correction

THE NORMAL COURSE OF LANGUAGE LEARNING

4. The childish behavior of making sounds which sound like real words but have no meaning is called _____.

babbling

5. Speech production is preceded by _____ interactions such as looks, gestures, and caresses.

social (interpersonal)

6. Although infants can respond to all sound distinctions made in any language, they learn to _____ the distinctions that don't matter in their language.

ignore

7. A specific speech style that is adopted by adults when talking to infants is called _____.

Motherese

8. The _____ _____ words and suffixes are totally missing from one-word speech.

closed-class

9. Two-word speech is known as _____ speech.

telegraphic

10. Even though children utter only two-word sequences at one stage in their acquisition of language, there is reason to believe that they have _____ parts to their propositional ideas.

three

11. After a child learns that the past tense of the verbs "play" and "walk" are "played" and "walked," "runned" may be given as the past tense of "run" although "ran" was previously used. This phenomenon is known as _____.

overgeneralization

12. When a child says "Mommy eated me" to mean "Mommy fed me," he is inventing a _____ verb.

causative

LANGUAGE LEARNING AND LANGUAGE CHANGE

13. The continual change of languages is partially accounted for

    by the _____ of children in learning them.   errors

14. _____ verbs tend to follow the regular rule for making the   Uncommon

    past tense, while _____ verbs tend to be irregular in this   common
    respect.

15. An important factor in language change is language _____,   mixture
    the influence of foreign speakers, whose own native languages
    impose themselves on the new language.

16. Another factor in language change has to do with _____,   rhetoric
    the desire for variation and alternative forms in poetry and
    oratory.

LANGUAGE LEARNING IN CHANGED ENVIRONMENTS

17. Cases of wild children raised by animals were initially regarded

    as crucial cases for the _____ _____controversy about   nature-nurture
    language development.

18. Evidence that language can develop without sound comes

    from studies of _____ children.   deaf

19. A widely used manual communication system among the deaf
                                                                    American Sign Language
    is _____ _____ _____.   (ASL)

20. Children in normal circumstances first learn the _____ of a   basics
    language (open-class words, simple sentences), and then the

    _____ (closed-class words, complex sentences).   elaborations

21. In comparing adults with children, it is clear that _____   children
    pick up a second language more easily and more quickly than

    _____ do.   adults

22. A biological _____ enables children to learn language basics,   predisposition
    whether they invent the basics themselves (if there is no
    language model) or follow the model that they are exposed to.

LANGUAGE LEARNING AND CRITICAL PERIODS

23. When language capacities are lost or diminished because of
    damage to a cerebral hemisphere (usually the left), this state

    is termed _____.   aphasia

24. One hypothesis of language learning postulates an ideal time
    to learn languages, after which the learning process is signifi-
    cantly more difficult. This time is known as the

    _____ _____.   critical period

25. Isabelle was deprived of language until age six. Genie was deprived of language until age fourteen. Isabelle eventually gained a good working knowledge of English, while Genie

    never did. This suggests that _____ may delimit the end of the ideal language-learning time in humans.   puberty

26. The hypothesis discussed in questions 24 and 25 is supported

    by studies of recovery from _____ and of second-language learning.   aphasia

Self Test

1. Which of the following can be used to explain first-language learning?
   a. imitation
   b. reinforcement
   c. correction
   d. none of the above

2. A major difference between deaf and hearing infants is that:
   a. while both babble, deaf children eventually stop vocalizing
   b. deaf children babble for a longer period of time than do hearing children
   c. deaf children only babble in the presence of an adult
   d. deaf children do not babble

3. All of the following are forms of preverbal communication except:
   a. crawling
   b. babbling
   c. gesturing
   d. touching

4. Which of the following statements is true about sound discrimination in early language learning?
   a. initially infants respond only to the sounds of their own language
   b. initially infants respond to all sounds in all languages
   c. initially infants cannot respond to sound distinctions at all
   d. initially infants respond only to the most common sound distinctions of their own language

5. Which of the following is not a characteristic of Motherese?
   a. exaggerated intonations
   b. high pitch
   c. infrequent pauses
   d. slow rate of talking

6. Which of the following words is most likely to be among a child's first words?
   a. push
   b. wall
   c. the
   d. pain

7. Which of the following approaches has been used to describe early word meanings in children?
   a. function
   b. features
   c. prototypes
   d. all of the above

8. Two-word speech is known as _____ speech.
   a. functor
   b. telegraphic
   c. syntactic
   d. propositional

9. Evidence that two-word speakers conceive of entire propositions (even though they cannot produce them) includes all of the following except:
   a. children respond more often to complete sentences from adults than to two-word speech
   b. when a negative is added, one of the other words is dropped
   c. two-word speakers will often produce complete three-word sentences with the full proposition
   d. once three-word speech begins, the final component of the proposition appears

10. The use of a word form like "sitted" by a child is known as:
    a. telegraphic
    b. undergeneralization
    c. overgeneralization
    d. syntactics

11. Which of the following verbs are children least likely to use properly in the past tense?
    a. like
    b. sing
    c. paint
    d. skip

12. Which of the following is a "basic level" word?
    a. beagle
    b. animal
    c. poodle
    d. dog

13. All of the following factors influence language change except:
    a. rhetoric
    b. language learning by children
    c. language mixture
    d. grammarians who alter certain irregular words

14. Evidence from wild children supports a(n) _____ view of language.
    a. nativist or environmentalist
    b. environmentalist
    c. nativist
    d. imitative

15. Language development does not depend on hearing language, as evidenced by:
    a. wild children
    b. deaf signers of American Sign Language (ASL)
    c. isolated children
    d. retarded children

16. Deaf children whose parents did not teach them sign language demonstrated language development similar to that of normal language in that:
    a. the children went through one-word speech, two-word speech, etc.
    b. they began by pointing to "action objects," and only later "talking" about things like "walls"
    c. they eventually put signs together to form sentences
    d. all of the above

17. The following individuals were deprived of exposure to language since birth. Which one has the best chance of learning to speak?
    a. an eight-year-old girl
    b. a fourteen-year-old boy
    c. a twenty-year-old man
    d. a thirty-year-old woman

18. The loss of language function is known as:
    a. aphasia
    b. anorexia
    c. asphyxia
    d. aphaeresis

19. First-language learning, second-language learning, and recovery from aphasia may depend on:
    a. intelligence
    b. the particular language involved
    c. generalization
    d. the critical period

Answer Key for Self Test

1. d pp. 495–97	11. b p. 505
2. a p. 497	12. d p. 507
3. a pp. 497–98	13. d pp. 507–10
4. b p. 498	14. a pp. 510–11
5. c p. 499	15. b p. 514
6. a p. 501	16. d pp. 512–13
7. d p. 502	17. a pp. 515–16
8. b p. 503	18. a pp. 517–18
9. c pp. 504–505	19. d pp. 515–18
10. c p. 505	

Investigating Psychological Phenomena

IMPLICIT LEARNING

Equipment: A stopwatch or a watch that indicates seconds, index cards
Subjects: One
Time per subject: Thirty minutes
Time for experimenter: Forty minutes

One of the most impressive aspects of language is its acquisition: children learn an enormous amount about their language without ever being explicitly taught. Consider syntax, for instance. Not until children have already learned a substantial number of syntactic rules do parents correct syntactic constructions that their children use. Somehow the growing child manages to induce the syntactic rules of language from the variety of utterances that he or she happens to encounter.

This ability to induce complex rules from examples is an ability that we use all the time, but its use without intention, or even awareness, and with complex linguistic construction is what makes it impressive as a characteristic of language acquisition. Having just learned about language acquisition, you can now begin to appreciate how complex the language-learning process must be, especially since it is largely mediated by implicit induction.

You can demonstrate this implicit induction process using the following experiment modeled after one by Arthur Reber (1967). There are two phases to the experiment. In the first phase, your subject will memorize a series of strings of letters after being told only that he is a subject in a memory experiment. In the second phase, the subject will be told that the letter strings from the first phase were constructed using a rule. Then the subject will be shown twenty-four new strings that he has never seen before and asked to judge which of twelve of these were constructed from the same rule used in phase 1. If the subject correctly categorized more of these twenty-four strings than we would expect by chance alone (twelve by chance, since there are only two responses the subject can make), then we can conclude that the subject has learned something about the rule even though he wasn't trying to in phase 1.

PHASE 1

Instruct your subject as follows:

"This experiment concerns memory for unmeaningful material. You will be presented with twenty strings of letters that you must memorize and recall. These strings of letters will be presented in groups of four which you can study for fifteen seconds. Then the groups will be taken away and you will be required to recall all four strings (in any order). Following this you will be presented with the same strings again for another fifteen-second study period. This will be followed by another recall attempt. In all, each of the five groups of strings will be presented five times each for study and recall."

The stimulus materials for this first phase are at the end of this section. Write each of the five lists of strings on index cards and present them to the subject individually. Provide the subject with twenty slips of paper on each of which he can write the recall for one quadruplet of strings. Be sure to remove each recall attempt before showing the next repetition of a set of strings or before going on to a new set of strings.

PHASE 2

Instructions:

"The strings of letters were constructed according to a rule. The rule dictated the orders in which letters were allowed to follow one another. In the second phase you will be shown twenty-four new strings of letters, and you must decide for each one whether it was or was not constructed according to the same rule for the letter strings in phase 1. When you decide, you should place your answer in the appropriate place on the answer sheet."

Score the subject's answers after he has completed phase 2, using the answer key provided. Did he do better than chance? Ask him whether he has any guesses about what the rule is. You will probably be surprised to discover how little the subject appears to be aware of the rule even though he can use it (in some sense) to make judgments about individual instances.

A diagrammatic representation of the rule is shown below. It works as follows: If you begin at "start" and trace through the diagram along any path in the direction of the arrows, you can get to "end." By noting the order of the letters that you pass along the way, you can construct a string. Notice that because of loops, some strings may be quite long but still permissible according to the rule.

Think about some of the following issues: In what way does this experiment mimic language learning? In what way is language learning different? As a model of language learning, why was it important not to tell subjects about the rule until the end of phase 1? What do the results suggest about language learning?

References

Reber, A. S., Implicit learning of artificial grammars, *Journal of Verbal Learning and Verbal Behavior*, 1967, *6*, 855–63.

PHASE 1: STIMULUS LISTS

(Write these on index cards or pieces of paper for presentation to the subject.)

List 1	List 2	List 3	List 4	List 5
VVTRXRR	VVRXRR	VTRRR	VVTRXR	XMVTRX
XMVTTRX	XXRR	XMVRXRR	VTRR	XMTRRRR
XMVRXR	VVRMVRX	VVTTRMT	VVRMTRR	XMVRX
VVTRX	XMVRMT	VVRMTR	XMVTRMT	XXRRR

PHASE 2: LIST OF ALTERNATIVES FOR RECOGNITION TEST.

(Write these on index cards as well.)

1. RXTTVMXR		13. VVTTRX
2. XMTR		14. VVRX
3. MXXR		15. VVRRRTX
4. XMVRXRRR		16. MT
5. VVRXR		17. VVTRMVRX
6. VTTX		18. VM
7. MVTTTXVR		19. XXR
8. XX		20. XMT
9. VRT		21. RXTMV
10. VVTTTRX		22. XXM
11. TTV		23. TTRXXM
12. VT		24. VTR

RECOGNITION TEST REPORT SHEET

(You can find this report sheet in Appendix B; cut it out and give it to the subject.)

ANSWERS

1. no	9. no	17. yes
2. yes	10. yes	18. no
3. no	11. no	19. yes
4. yes	12. yes	20. yes
5. yes	13. yes	21. no
6. no	14. yes	22. no
7. no	15. no	23. no
8. yes	16. no	24. yes

RULE FOR LETTER-STRING CONSTRUCTION

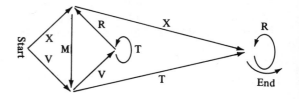

CHAPTER 16

Social Development

Learning Objectives

Patterns of child rearing

17. Describe the autocratic, permissive, and authoritative-reciprocal patterns of child rearing. What are the characteristic behaviors of children raised under each of these approaches?

The child's effect on the parents

18. Explain the interaction between the child's temperament and the parent's pattern of child rearing, and indicate how this interaction complicates the task of relating patterns of child rearing to the child's personality.

THE DEVELOPMENT OF MORALITY

Not doing wrong

19. What does it mean to internalize moral values? What is the role of punishment in internalization, and what is the principle of minimal sufficiency?

Doing good

20. How does empathy function in supporting altruistic behavior?

Moral reasoning

21. Describe Kohlberg's stages of moral reasoning, and discuss their relation to moral conduct.

THE DEVELOPMENT OF SEX ROLES

22. Distinguish among gender roles, sexual orientation, and gender identity.

Gender roles

23. What is sex typing and what are gender role stereotypes?

Constitutional factors and sex differences

24. Evaluate the role of nature (biological-genetic) factors in establishing gender roles, with respect to gender differences in aggression and pattern of intellectual abilities.

Social factors and sex differences

25. Discuss how small constitutional differences can be amplified by social forces. Describe fear of failure. Indicate how learned helplessness and the different ways that teachers bestow rewards and punishments on children affect their fear of failure.

26. Discuss sex reassignment and the possibility of a critical period for gender identity determination. What is the effect of early exposure to sex hormones on gender identity and gender role?

Theories of sex typing

27. Compare and contrast three theories of sex typing: psychoanalytic, social learning, and cognitive-developmental. What is the critical mechanism of sex typing for each theory?

Sexual orientation

28. Discuss the classification of homosexuality as a mental illness versus an alternative life-style.

29. Discuss some possible causes of homosexuality or, more generally, sexual orientation.

DEVELOPMENT AFTER CHILDHOOD

30. Describe Erik Erikson's conception of human growth. What are his "eight ages of man"? To what extent do they hold across cultures?

Adolescence

31. Discuss the particular problems of adolescence as a transition to adulthood in the United States and in other cultures. Is adolescence always turbulent?

Adulthood

32. Describe the mid-life transition. Indicate how changes in American society have markedly changed the experience of old age.

Programmed Exercises

SOME GENERAL CHARACTERISTICS OF SOCIAL DEVELOPMENT

1. The only person who has offered a general, broad, and yet

   detailed theory of social development is _____.   Freud

ATTACHMENT

2. According to Freud, love for the mother derives from the fact

   that she is associated with the _____ of hunger, thirst, and   alleviation (reduction,
   pain.   decrease)

3. Harlow's experiments with terry-cloth mothers suggest that, in monkeys, the nutrient provided by the mother is less important

   for attachment than the _____ _____ that she provides.   contact comfort

4. According to _____ theory of attachment, fear of the unknown forms the basis for attachment.   Bowlby's

5. The built-in fear referred to above is initially unspecific, and

   corresponds to what psychiatrists call _____ _____ anxiety.   free-floating

6. The formation of strong attachments by the young of a species to objects (typically the parent) encountered early in life is

   called _____.   imprinting

7. This type of attachment (imprinting) tends to occur during a

   special time, early in life, called the _____ _____.   critical period

8. According to Bowlby, proximity to an attachment figure provides _____ and _____, and separation from it leads to   comfort, security

   _____.   distress

9. Fear of strangers and specific recognition of the mother occur at about the same time, cross-culturally. This time is from

   _____ to _____ months of age.   six, eight

10. In Ainsworth's "Strange Situation" measurements, a child who explores freely when the mother is present, shows some distress at her leaving, and greets her return with enthusiasm is

    called _____ _____.   securely attached

11. In this situation, disappearance of the father produces some

    _____, but _____ than that shown when the mother disappears.   distress, less

12. Motherless monkeys and humans reared in some _____ show marked deficits in social performance.   institutions

13. Maternal deprivation has severe effects in both monkeys and

    humans, but not if it occurs for no more than a few _____.   months

14. Freud claimed that early experience (in the first six years or so

    of life) was _____ for appropriate adult social adjustments, and that the effects of abnormal early experience were   critical

    _____.   irreversible

15. Studies using younger monkey therapists with motherless monkeys and studies on children put in nurturant environments after being in institutions indicate that many of the

    effects of maternal deprivation are _____.   reversible

CHILDHOOD SOCIALIZATION

16. _____ is the process by which the child acquires the patterns of thought and behavior that are characteristic of the society in which she is born.   Socialization

17. In the process of socialization in America, working-class

    people stress _____ while middle-class people stress   obedience

    _____.   self-control

18. Both Freudian and reinforcement theories explain socialization
                                                                                 pain (punishment),
    in terms of the opposite influences of _____ and _____.   pleasure (reward)

19. Researchers who believe that the basic Pavlovian and instru-
    mental learning processes must be supplemented to explain

    socialization are called _____ _____ theorists.   social learning

20. Such theorists (see previous question) add to the basic learning
                                                                                 observational learning
    processes the mechanism of _____ _____.   (modeling)

21. Performance of an observed act depends, in part, upon the

    characteristics of the _____.   model

22. The _____ approach to socialization emphasizes the role of   cognitive
    understanding or competence in the socialization process.

23. According to cognitive theories, imitation is motivated by a

    desire for _____.   competence

24. The child-rearing style in which the parent controls the child
    strictly, and does not explain the justification for the govern-

    ing rules to the child, is called the _____ pattern. The op-   autocratic

    posite extreme is called the _____ pattern. An intermediate   permissive
    approach, in which the parents exercise power, but also recog-

    nize the child's point of view, is called the _____ _____   authoritative-reciprocal
    pattern.

25. Of these patterns (see question 24), the one that leads to the

    best-adjusted children is the _____ _____ pattern.   authoritative-reciprocal

26. Some differences in the pattern of child rearing may result

    from differences in _____ in children, some of which are   temperament
    present at birth.

THE DEVELOPMENT OF MORALITY

27. We say a moral value is _____ when an individual avoids   internalized
    transgressions because he feels that they are wrong, and not
    because he is afraid of being punished.

28. According to the principle of _____ _____, internaliza-   minimal sufficiency
    tion occurs best under mild social pressure.

29. A direct emotional response to another person's emotions is

    called _____.   empathy

30. Kohlberg has interviewed both adults and children in an at-

    tempt to describe the development of _____ _____.   moral reasoning

31. Kohlberg describes this development, in accordance with the

    theories of Piaget, in a series of successive _____.   stages

32. According to Kohlberg, moral reasoning develops along a course in which right and wrong are defined by, first:

_____ _____ _____; second: _____; and third:

_____ _____ _____.

1. fear of punishment and/or desire for gain, 2. convention 3. internalized (or abstract) moral principles

33. A criticism of Kohlberg's cognitive approach to moral be-

havior is that although it may be able to _____ moral

rules, they may not actually guide _____.

describe

behavior

THE DEVELOPMENT OF SEX ROLES

34. A definition of maleness or femaleness would have to consider three different "domains" or aspects. One is our inner sense

of being male or female, called _____ _____.

gender identity

35. A second aspect (see above) is a group of behavior patterns that our culture deems appropriate for each sex, called

_____ _____.

gender roles

36. A third aspect (see above) is our choice of sexual partner,

called _____ _____.

sexual orientation

37. The expectation that someone "labeled" as a male will be more aggressive and more interested in things than people is

an example of _____ _____.

sex-typing

38.

This figure illustrates the phenomenon of gender role _____.

stereotypes

39. Characteristics of the female gender role stereotype in American society include (list 3) _____ _____ _____.

submissiveness, interest in people, emotionality, fear of success, talkativeness, gentleness

40. There seems to be a constitutional basis for some sex differences: for example, in the area of motivation, males tend to be more _____ than females.

aggressive

41. There may also be constitutional basis for male superiority in _____ ability.

spatial

42. In many cases, culture or social factors act to _____ existing small constitutional sex differences.

exaggerate (or amplify or increase)

43. In schools in the United States, boys are reprimanded more often than girls for their _____, while girls are more often criticized for their _____ performance.

conduct

intellectual

44. A child that has reproductive organs that are difficult to classify as male or female is called a _____.

hermaphrodite

45. People who are genetically male but raised as female from infancy show normal female gender _____, but a tendency to a masculine gender _____.

identity

role

46. A female who sees herself as female and is sexually attracted to males but is aggressive and athletic could be said to have some characteristics of the male _____ _____.

gender role

47. Most sex reassignment studies indicate that if the reassignment is made within the first _____ years of life, the child will grow up with a normal gender _____, appropriate to his or her sex of rearing. However, recent studies from the Dominican Republic suggest that successful sex reassignment can occur at _____.

three (or four)

identity

puberty

48. According to Freud, the basic mechanism of sex typing is _____.

identification

49. According to the social learning view, little girls show typical female interests because they are _____ for doing so.

rewarded (reinforced)

50. Cognitive developmental theorists point out that a three-year-old who believes that a girl can become a boy if given a haircut fails to show _____ _____. Failure to achieve this at an early age is probably a consequence of the fact that children less than five or six years of age are still in the Piagetian stage of _____ _____.

gender constancy

preoperational thought

51. According to cognitive developmental theory, and in contrast to social learning theory, identification with a same-sex model _____ (precedes or follows) the acquisition of gender identity.

follows

52. According to social learning theorists, the first aspect of sex

    differences that is established is _____ _____.   gender role

53. The majority of men and women are _____ in that they   heterosexual
    seek sexual partners of the opposite sex.

54. The incidence of male homosexuality in the United States is

    about _____ percent of all adult males (as of 1948).   4

55. According to the American Psychiatric Association, homosex-

    uality is not considered a _____.   disease (psychiatric disorder)

56. As a group, homosexuals are not different from other mem-

    bers of their biological sex in terms of _____ _____ and   gender identity

    _____ _____.   gender role

57. At this time, there is not clear evidence for a biological basis
    for homosexuality, in terms of either different levels of
                                                                             sex hormones (androgens)
    _____ _____ or _____ predispositions.   genetic

DEVELOPMENT AFTER CHILDHOOD

58. Erikson's "Eight Ages of Man" span the entire life cycle,

    each stage accompanied by a critical _____.   conflict (or crisis)

59. The stage of transition from childhood to adulthood is called

    _____. At this stage, the major conflict is described as an   adolescence

    _____ _____.   identity crisis

60. In some cultures, the transition to adulthood is marked clearly,
    with a ceremony or more extended set of activities called

    _____ _____.   initiation rites

61. In the _____ _____, people of middle age reappraise   mid-life transition
    what they have done with their lives, and may reevaluate their
    marriage and career.

62. In Erikson's scheme, although there are some important bio-

    logical markers in growth past childhood, such as _____,   puberty (or menopause)
    the quality and duration of each stage is substantially influ-

    enced by _____.   culture

Self Test

1. Freud and Piaget have in common an
   emphasis on:
   a. the interaction of the child with the
      mother
   b. sexual development
   c. analysis of development into stages
   d. securing data from direct observation
   e. the animal origins of human behavior

2. Harlow's results, showing a preference for a
   "terry-cloth mother" over a wire mother
   that provides food, by infant monkeys,
   argues:
   a. in favor of Freud's view of attachment
   b. in favor of Bowlby's view of attachment
   c. that nutrition has no effect in producing
      attachment between infant and mother
   d. a and b
   e. all of the above

3. Which of the following statements about imprinting is false?
   a. imprinting depends on the fact that the parents will be the most salient objects around the offspring in the first part of life
   b. imprinting is based on experience
   c. animals may lose the capacity to imprint after a certain age
   d. one would not expect to find imprinting in a "parasitic" species that is typically raised by adults of another species
   e. none of the above

4. Bowlby's theory of attachment:
   a. may include imprinting to a familiar object
   b. assumes that infants fear unfamiliar objects
   c. assumes infants have a tendency to be attached to objects with certain characteristics
   d. all of the above
   e. none of the above

5. Proximity : comfort :: separation :
   a. imprinting
   b. critical periods
   c. providing nutrients
   d. distress
   e. satisfaction

6. Infants show less distress at their father's than their mother's departure, in Ainsworth's Strange Situation. Which of the following would be most likely to increase the infants' distress response to the father's disappearance?
   a. dress the father as a woman
   b. dress the father as a strange man
   c. find a father who had had much more contact with his child
   d. find a child who had been severely punished by his mother
   e. give the child a free-floating anxiety toy

7. The effects of maternal deprivation on subsequent behavior of monkeys and humans are:
   a. severe, and almost the same
   b. severe for humans, mild for monkeys
   c. severe for monkeys, mild for humans
   d. minimal
   e. irreversible

8. A conclusion that can be drawn from monkey and human maternal deprivation studies is that:
   a. adequate nutrition is not sufficient to produce normal social behavior

   b. behavior to peers is unaffected by maternal deprivation
   c. imprinting does not have anything to do with later sexual or maternal behavior
   d. the effects of maternal deprivation are very different in humans and monkeys
   e. maternal deprivation effects are especially severe if the deprivation occurs in the first few months of life

9. Monkeys deprived of mothers in about the first six months of life:
   a. show a temporary depression in social behavior
   b. are abnormal in social behavior, but will usually be successful parents
   c. are permanently deficient in all domains of social behavior
   d. show severe deficits in social behavior that are completely irreversible
   e. show severe deficits in social behavior that can be at least partly cured by carefully designed "therapy"

10. Institutionalized human children and motherless monkeys show social abnormalities characterized by:
    a. a "critical period" beginning at the time of birth and ending at about three months
    b. social withdrawal
    c. long-term effects that are irreversible
    d. a and b
    e. all of the above

11. Freud claimed that early experience had 1) a critical and 2) an irreversible effect on social development. Results from research up to this time suggest that:
    a. these two principles are basically correct
    b. early experiences have important effects, but many are reversible
    c. these two principles are totally incorrect
    d. early experiences have some significant effects, and these effects are irreversible
    e. none of the above

12. Both the Freudian approach and social learning or reinforcement theory agree that _____ is a major factor in socialization.
    a. imitation
    b. modeling
    c. the child's understanding of the importance of older people
    d. gender identity
    e. none of the above

13. According to social learning theory, a critical aspect of socialization is:
    a. observational learning from models

b. making models

c. Pavlovian conditioning

d. imprinting

e. none of the above

14. Little Bertram watches a seedy character steal a tip from a restaurant table and get away with it. Is Bertram likely to imitate this behavior? According to social learning theorists:

a. yes, because the stealing was reinforced

b. no, because the seedy character is a poor model

c. yes and no; the act is reinforced, but the actor is a poor model

d. yes and no; the act is not violent, but the consequences are not performed or modeled

e. none of the above

15. Wendy sees her big sister smoking a cigarette. A few hours later she sneaks over to a pack of cigarettes, takes one out, holds it with two fingers, and puts it into her mouth, looking as debonair as possible. Then she lights it up, and inhales her first breath, coughing and gagging. But she continues to smoke the whole cigarette. This performance presents problems for Freudian-reinforcement views of socialization because:

a. there is observational learning without immediate performance

b. there seems to be negative reinforcement (gagging) for smoking

c. there seem to be no basic biological reinforcements for her smoking

d. it is not clear why she would want to imitate her sister

e. all of the above

16. According to cognitive-developmental theory, the motivation for imitation is _____, while according to social learning theory, the motivation for imitation is _____.

a. to increase competence, to gain reinforcements

b. to understand the model, to model

c. to gain reinforcements, to gain social reinforcements

d. to increase competence, to decrease competence

e. to model competence, to model reinforcement

17. Ironically, children raised in the opposite autocratic and permissive styles share some common behavioral characteristics. Both types of children tend to:

a. be socially responsible

b. be more attached to their father

c. lack independence

d. be high in originality

e. a and c

18. Imagine that a study reports that most cranky five-year-olds had parents who closed the door to their infants' bedrooms at night, so the baby wouldn't wake them. What might be possible explanations of this result?

a. isolating infants causes them to be cranky later in life

b. cranky infants are more likely to be isolated by their parents

c. parents who isolate their children in this way also do other things in child rearing that cause crankiness

d. crankiness is inherited; cranky parents are more likely to be irritated by a crying child, and so are more likely to isolate it

e. all of the above

19. Authoritative-reciprocal rearing style : optimal adjustment :: mild social pressure : _____.

a. doing good

b. not doing wrong

c. maximum internalization

d. permissive rearing style

e. autocratic rearing style

20. In order to show altruistic or unselfish helping behavior, a child (or adult) must:

a. experience empathic distress

b. be at a high stage of moral reasoning

c. know how to be helpful in the particular situation

d. a and b

e. a and c

21. Consider the following three objections to making three reservations on different airlines at the same time for one person: A. It is against the unwritten rules of the airlines. B. It interferes with the access of others with no tangible gain to the party in question. C. It can be detected, and penalties can be assessed. According to Kohlberg, how would these three reasons be arranged in terms of the development of moral reasoning; indicate the earliest stage first.

a. A, B, C

b. B, C, A

c. C, B, A

d. B, A, C

e. C, A, B

22. Seymour speaks eloquently on the issue of equal rights for all races and religions but is actually quite racially prejudiced when he hires workers at his business. This illustrates:

a. the effects of reinforcement

b. the influence of the Freudian unconscious

c. the distinction between moral reasoning and moral conduct

d. the conflict between the social learning view and more traditional reinforcement explanations of moral behavior

e. egocentrism

23. A person says that one shouldn't double park because it is against the law. This explanation is an example of:

a. preconventional morality

b. conventional morality

c. postconventional morality

d. empathy

e. none of the above

24. Which of the following is illustrative of gender role:

a. thinking of oneself as a female

b. attraction to the opposite sex

c. submissiveness and emotionality in a female

d. homosexual tendencies

e. none of the above

25. The finding that, in American culture, females express emotion more readily than do males, should be interpreted to mean:

a. that females are constitutionally more inclined to express emotions

b. that our society teaches females to be more expressive

c. that the average female is more emotionally expressive than the average male, but that there is a great deal of overlap

d. sex typing is not a sufficient explanation of sex differences, and one must also consider gender identity

26. There is some evidence for a specific gene that is partly responsible for sex differences in:

a. aggression

b. spatial ability

c. emotionality

d. verbal ability

e. none of the above

27. The idea that there is a constitutional factor contributing to sex differences in aggression or spatial orientation is (or would be) supported by all but which of the following:

a. in early humans, the stronger male was responsible for almost all hunting and fighting

b. these differences are seen in many cultures

c. some of these differences are also seen in animals

d. early sex "changes" can erase some of these differences

28. Fear of failure in school is higher in girls than in boys, even though girls get better grades than boys in elementary school. This paradox has been related to the fact that:

a. teachers criticize girls relatively more than boys for their intellectual performance

b. teachers show more empathy for boys

c. boys are constitutionally better in reading and mathematics

d. a and c

e. all of the above

29. Studies of early sex reassignment indicate that:

a. gender identity and role are completely shifted to the new sex

b. sexual orientation is usually not changed

c. gender identity shifts successfully, but there are some effects of the original gender role

d. all three aspects of sex (role, gender, and orientation) show significant resistance to change

30. The presence of hormones of the opposite "sex" in young children can influence their:

a. gender identity

b. gender role

c. sexual orientation

d. all of the above

e. none of the above

31. According to the psychoanalytic view, the basic mechanism of sex typing is:

a. imitation

b. conditioning

c. repression

d. identification

32. Kohlberg's cognitive developmental view criticizes both the Freudian concept of identification and the social learning notion of imitation in the first few years of life on all but which of the following grounds:

a. little children don't show gender constancy

b. little children don't have a basis for recognizing which of their parents is of their sex

c. gender role precedes gender identity

d. young children may not understand that males have a penis and females don't

33. The psychoanalytic notion that the young boy identifies with his father in order to avoid punishment for his erotic feelings toward his mother assumes:

a. a necessary linkage among gender role and identity and sexual orientation

b. that the boy understands his fundamental sexual similarity to his father

c. that erotic factors form the basis for sex typing

d. all of the above

e. none of the above

34. According to Kohlberg's cognitive view of sex typing, gender identity depends critically on:

a. identification

b. constitutional factors

c. achievement of gender constancy

d. preoperational thought

35. For which theory (or theories) of sex typing is the fact that the little boy has a penis of special importance?

a. psychoanalytic

b. social learning

c. cognitive social

d. a and b

e. all of the above

36. Homosexuality, by itself, is now not considered a psychiatric disorder. Only one of the following would constitute an argument *for* considering it a disorder. Which one?

a. about 4 percent of the male U.S. population are exclusively homosexual at some time in their life

b. many homosexuals do not publicly admit their homosexuality

c. many characteristics frequently seen in homosexuals are common in any persecuted minority

d. homosexuals seeking psychiatric help have been judged to be more disturbed than others

e. it is hard to change a homosexual into a heterosexual

37. The psychoanalytic view suggests that male homosexuality may result when the child resolves fears aroused during the Oedipal conflict by identifying with the mother instead of the father. This theory would have difficulty explaining:

a. the fact that many homosexuals do not consult psychiatrists

b. the absence of sex hormone differences between male homosexuals and heterosexuals

c. the reported high frequency of hostile and detached fathers of homosexual males who seek psychiatric help

d. the fact that, typically, male homosexuals have traditional male gender identity and roles

e. all of the above

38. The data from sex reassignment and the fact that in most cases, homosexuals report homosexual tendencies early in life both argue for:

a. the psychoanalytic approach

b. attachment to the mother at the time of the Oedipal crisis

c. a genetic basis for important aspects of sexual orientation or gender identity

d. none of the above

39. A clear and substantial difference has been documented between male homosexuals and heterosexuals with respect to:

a. gender role

b. gender identity

c. testosterone (androgen) levels

d. passivity

e. none of the above

40. The transition from adolescence to adulthood:

a. occurs at about the same age in all cultures

b. is always a turbulent period

c. usually occurs at the onset of sexual maturity

d. all of the above

e. none of the above

41. Initiation rites, retirement parties, and marriages have in common that they:

a. explicitly mark important life transitions

b. occur in virtually all cultures

c. are explicitly predicted by Erikson's scheme

d. match Freud's views of major life events

e. make for gradual transitions from one stage to another

42. In some societies, children gradually assume adult responsibilities, and in some societies,

old family members live in the home, taking care of grandchildren (or great-grandchildren) and giving advice. These traditions:

a. emphasize transitions from one stage of life to another
b. ease transition from one stage of life to another
c. emphasize the importance of biological factors in life history
d. prove the correctness of Erikson's stages
e. none of the above

Answer Key for Self Test

1. c p. 522	22. c pp. 546–47
2. b pp. 524–25	23. b p. 546
3. e pp. 525–26	24. c p. 548
4. d p. 525	25. c p. 549
5. d p. 527	26. b p. 551
6. c pp. 528–29	27. d p. 551
7. a pp. 530–31	28. a pp. 552–53
8. a pp. 530–31	29. c pp. 553–55
9. e p. 532	30. b pp. 554–55
10. b p. 531	31. d p. 556
11. b pp. 533–34	32. c p. 557
12. e pp. 535–37	33. d p. 556
13. a p. 536	34. c p. 557
14. c p. 537	35. a p. 556
15. e pp. 535–37	36. d pp. 559–60
16. a pp. 536–38	37. d pp. 559, 561
17. c p. 540	38. d pp. 560–61
18. e p. 541	39. e p. 560
19. c pp. 540, 543	40. c pp. 563–65
20. e pp. 544–45	41. a p. 564
21. e p. 546	42. b pp. 564, 568

Investigating Psychological Phenomena

SEX DIFFERENCES

Equipment: None
Number of subjects: Twelve
Time per subject: Five minutes
Time for experimenter: Sixty minutes

Sex differences can be analyzed into three different categories:

1. Gender identity—thinking of oneself as male or female.

2. Sexual orientation—sex of desired sexual partners, leading to the heterosexual-homosexual distinction.

3. Gender role—behavior patterns or attitudes associated with one or the other sex.

The relative role of experience (nurture) and genes (nature) has been debated for each of these aspects of sex. But before such studies can be done definitively, we must be clear on the nature of the differences to be explained. This is more or less clear for gender identity and sexual orientation. But the major behavioral and attitudinal differences between the sexes are not that obvious and surely differ across cultures.

This study is an attempt to define some reliable sex differences among American college students. We have developed seventeen questions that promise to reveal sex differences (we will use as a criterion of a question that discriminates between the sexes a response pattern in which there is at least a 25 percentage point difference between males and females).

First: Answer the questionnaire. *Do not read on until you finish it.*

Questionnaire on Sex Differences

> Sex: Male   Female
> (Circle one)

1. Would you be willing to kill a cockroach by slapping it with your hands?
   a) yes   b) no
2. What is Queen Anne's lace?
   a) flower   b) embroidery
   c) perfume   d) doily
   e) spice
3. How many times in the last twenty-four hours have you used the word "shit"?
   a) less than 5 times   b) 5 or more times
4. Can you sew well enough to make clothes?
   a) yes   b) no
5. Do you believe in sexual intercourse only after a spiritual love exists between you and your partner?
   a) yes   b) no
6. Do you walk around freely in the nude in a locker room?
   a) yes   b) no
7. How often do you cry?
   a) very often   b) often
   c) only with good   d) very infrequently
      reason
   e) never
8. At times I feel like smashing things.
   a) true   b) false

9. Do you know your chest measurement?
   a) yes   b) no
10. Can you change a tire easily?
    a) yes   b) no
11. I spend no more than one hour during an average school day playing the radio or listening to records.
    a) true   b) false
12. Would you prefer to be the dominant one in a relationship?
    a) yes   b) no
13. Do you think that you are overweight?
    a) yes   b) no
14. When you get depressed, does washing your hair make you feel better?
    a) yes   b) no
15. Do you sleep in the nude?
    a) yes   b) no
16. Which parent are you closest to?
    a) mother   b) father
17. I try to keep my room as neat as possible.
    a) true   b) false

These questions have been made up by faculty and students in introductory psychology courses. Each question has been "tested" with at least 100 undergraduate students in psychology courses. Therefore, we know how well these questions discriminate between college age males and females (at least in 1971–1973, when the questions were tested). Of the seventeen questions, we know from past testing that five do *not* discriminate males from females. Try and guess, in advance, which questions would not discriminate. Then check your guesses against the data presented on the final page of this study. *Guess before you read on.*

List questions that would not discriminate:

———————————

Note the type of successful questions in this questionnaire. Some relate to traditional male-female differences. Thus, males are more aggressive (item 12 on dominance, but note no difference on item 8—smashing things). Similarly males are less squeamish (item 1, cockroach) and more restrained emotionally (item 7, crying).

Other questions refer to knowledge or abilities that tend to go with gender in our society. This would include information about flowers (item 2, Queen Anne's lace), sewing ability (item 4), ability to change a tire (item 10), and knowledge of body measurements (item 9).

There are in addition some "miscellaneous" questions that tap into reliable differences (item 5, attitudes to intercourse; item 6, attitude to walking around nude in a locker room; item 13, perception of fatness in self; item 14, washing of hair as a response to depression; and item 17, neatness).

Second, collaborate with at least one or two other students in the class, so that you can collect enough data. Give the twelve copies of this questionnaire, located on pp. 209–14, to twelve undergraduates, six males and six females. (Try to get them to fill out the questionnaire when you give it to them; otherwise, you will find that you don't get a very high return rate.) Aim for a minimum of five completed questionnaires for each sex. Combine your results with the results of as many classmates as you can: It would be desirable to end up with at least fifteen students of each sex.

Third, tabulate your results (see p. 207) in the following way. For the "yes" or "no" questions (e.g., item 1), add up the number of subjects who answered "yes." Then calculate what percentage answered "yes." For the "true" or "false" questions (e.g., item 8), record those who answer "true." For other items (e.g., item 2), add up the number of subjects whose answers are the same as those indicated in parentheses under "Item" (e.g., item 1—flower).

Fourth, we have devised a "femaleness" score, by indicating the more common female response to each of the questions that discriminates sex. Compute such a score for each of your subjects by counting one point for each of the following answers:

1. no	9. yes
2. flower	10. no
4. yes	12. no
5. yes	13. yes
6. no	14. yes
7. very often, often, or with good reason	17. yes

Indicate here the total number of subjects of each sex from whom you have collected data:

Male _____   Female _____

		Your data (combined with classmate's data)			U. of Pa. Students**	
		Male		Female		Male	Female
Item	#	%	#	%	%	%
1. Killing cockroach	_____	_____	_____	_____	37	* 7
2. Queen Anne's lace (correct answer: flower)	_____	_____	_____		50	*82
3. Using word "shit" (less than 5 times)	_____	_____	_____	_____	49	50
4. Sew clothes	_____	_____	_____	_____	4	*59
5. Intercourse only after spiritual love	_____	_____	_____	_____	30	*75
6. Nude in locker room	_____	_____	_____	_____	72	*31
7. Crying frequency (very often, often, or only with good reason)	_____	_____	_____	_____	22	*78
8. Feel like smashing things	_____	_____	_____	_____	75	70
9. Chest measurement	_____	_____	_____	_____	28	*78
10. Change tire	_____	_____	_____	_____	76	*13
11. Playing radio	_____	_____	_____	_____	41	42
12. Prefer dominance in relationship	_____	_____	_____	_____	72	*10
13. Overweight	_____	_____	_____	_____	17	*60
14. Washing hair when depressed	_____	_____	_____	_____	19	*53
15. Sleep in nude	_____	_____	_____	_____	39	44
16. Closest parent (mother)	_____	_____	_____	_____	61	72
17. Keep room neat	_____	_____	_____	_____	51	*77

*A male-female difference of least 25 percentage points
**Responses to items in the sex difference questionnaire by undergraduate introductory psychology students at the University of Pennsylvania (1971–1973). Responses are based on from 70 to 270 males and from 88 to 292 females, depending on the item.

SCORES OF MALES AND FEMALES ON "FEMALENESS" SCORE

Plot the number of males and females with each score. Use solid lines for the males and broken lines for the females. The graph at the left contains data gathered from fifteen undergraduate males and seventeen undergraduate females in 1980. Plot your data on the blank graph on the right. How well does this score separate biological females from biological males? What percent of females score less than the highest male? How would you go about making a better behavioral discriminator of the sexes? (Note: We have avoided asking questions that might trivially distinguish males from females, such as: Do you wash the hair on your chest? or do you ever wear dresses?)

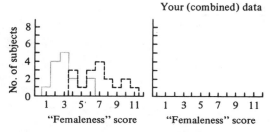

Your (combined) data

You may note some major differences between your data and the data we reported in 1971–1973. In fact, we tried the questionnaire on fifteen male and seventeen female undergraduate students in 1980 (the subjects used in the femaleness ratings), and found some differences from our 1971–1973 study. The biggest effects were that male-female differences disappeared for Queen Anne's lace (question 2), overweight (question 13: Over half of the men as well as women thought they were overweight), and washing hair when depressed (question 14: Practically no one in our recent sample answered yes to this).

There are basically three ways to explain discrepancies (our recent data or your data) from the original large sample of 1971–1973.

1. A general change in society over the last decade. It would seem fair to say that female gender roles have become more like male gender roles in this period. Does your data show this trend for any items? (Note that this would mean that female scores could move closer to male scores, and *not* that male scores would move closer to female scores. Of course, it is also possible to argue that the roles are becoming less distinct, but not necessarily moving toward the traditional male role.)

2. A difference in the populations sampled. Students from different parts of the country or from institutions with different styles or emphases might differ markedly in gender roles. Do you think your student sample would be likely to be very different from University of Pennsylvania students? In what ways? Is this reflected in differences on any scores? (Note, the differences might not just appear as male-female differences, but as generally higher or lower levels of response. For example, one might expect a generally higher positive response on sewing or changing a tire in people from rural backgrounds.)

3. Sampling error. Some observed differences may simply result from the fact that all samples from the same population don't have precisely the same scores (see Statistical Appendix to the textbook). With a small sample such as you have collected (as opposed to the large sample that we originally used), a wider variation from sample to sample would be expected. We would ordinarily use statistical methods to indicate how confident we would be that a difference between samples was not due to chance.

FURTHER ACTIVITIES

You might wish to try out some other questions that would relate gender identity to gender role. You could get a suggestion as to whether your questions were good discriminators with samples as low as twenty.

You can also try to use behavior rather than verbal responses to questionnaires. Can you think of obvious differences in such activities as: manner of walking or eating, facial expressions, behavior in front of mirrors, motorcycle riding, etc. Test your hypotheses by direct observation.

(If your instructor collects the data, fill out the report sheet in Appendix B.)

Questionnaire on Sex Differences

Sex: Male   Female
(Circle one)

1. Would you be willing to kill a cockroach by slapping it with your hands?
   a) yes   b) no
2. What is Queen Anne's lace?
   a) flower   b) embroidery
   c) perfume   d) doily
   e) spice
3. How many times in the last twenty-four hours have you used the word "shit"?
   a) less than 5 times   b) 5 or more times
4. Can you sew well enough to make clothes?
   a) yes   b) no
5. Do you believe in sexual intercourse only after a spiritual love exists between you and your partner?
   a) yes   b) no
6. Do you walk around freely in the nude in a locker room?
   a) yes   b) no
7. How often do you cry?
   a) very often   b) often
   c) only with good d) very infrequently
      reason
   e) never
8. At times I feel like smashing things.
   a) true   b) false
9. Do you know your chest measurement?
   a) yes   b) no
10. Can you change a tire easily?
    a) yes   b) no
11. I spend no more than one hour during an average school day playing the radio or listening to records.
    a) true   b) false
12. Would you prefer to be the dominant one in a relationship?
    a) yes   b) no
13. Do you think that you are overweight?
    a) yes   b) no
14. When you get depressed, does washing your hair make you feel better?
    a) yes   b) no
15. Do you sleep in the nude?
    a) yes   b) no
16. Which parent are you closest to?
    a) mother   b) father
17. I try to keep my room as neat as possible.
    a) true   b) false

Questionnaire on Sex Differences

Sex: Male   Female
(Circle one)

1. Would you be willing to kill a cockroach by slapping it with your hands?
   a) yes   b) no
2. What is Queen Anne's lace?
   a) flower   b) embroidery
   c) perfume   d) doily
   e) spice
3. How many times in the last twenty-four hours have you used the word "shit"?
   a) less than 5 times   b) 5 or more times
4. Can you sew well enough to make clothes?
   a) yes   b) no
5. Do you believe in sexual intercourse only after a spiritual love exists between you and your partner?
   a) yes   b) no
6. Do you walk around freely in the nude in a locker room?
   a) yes   b) no
7. How often do you cry?
   a) very often   b) often
   c) only with good d) very infrequently
      reason
   e) never
8. At times I feel like smashing things.
   a) true   b) false
9. Do you know your chest measurement?
   a) yes   b) no
10. Can you change a tire easily?
    a) yes   b) no
11. I spend no more than one hour during an average school day playing the radio or listening to records.
    a) true   b) false
12. Would you prefer to be the dominant one in a relationship?
    a) yes   b) no
13. Do you think that you are overweight?
    a) yes   b) no
14. When you get depressed, does washing your hair make you feel better?
    a) yes   b) no
15. Do you sleep in the nude?
    a) yes   b) no
16. Which parent are you closest to?
    a) mother   b) father
17. I try to keep my room as neat as possible.
    a) true   b) false

Questionnaire on Sex Differences

Sex: Male   Female
(Circle one)

1. Would you be willing to kill a cockroach by slapping it with your hands?
   a) yes   b) no
2. What is Queen Anne's lace?
   a) flower   b) embroidery
   c) perfume   d) doily
   e) spice
3. How many times in the last twenty-four hours have you used the word "shit"?
   a) less than 5 times   b) 5 or more times
4. Can you sew well enough to make clothes?
   a) yes   b) no
5. Do you believe in sexual intercourse only after a spiritual love exists between you and your partner?
   a) yes   b) no
6. Do you walk around freely in the nude in a locker room?
   a) yes   b) no
7. How often do you cry?
   a) very often   b) often
   c) only with good   d) very infrequently
      reason
   e) never
8. At times I feel like smashing things.
   a) true   b) false
9. Do you know your chest measurement?
   a) yes   b) no
10. Can you change a tire easily?
    a) yes   b) no
11. I spend no more than one hour during an average school day playing the radio or listening to records.
    a) true   b) false
12. Would you prefer to be the dominant one in a relationship?
    a) yes   b) no
13. Do you think that you are overweight?
    a) yes   b) no
14. When you get depressed, does washing your hair make you feel better?
    a) yes   b) no
15. Do you sleep in the nude?
    a) yes   b) no
16. Which parent are you closest to?
    a) mother   b) father
17. I try to keep my room as neat as possible.
    a) true   b) false

Questionnaire on Sex Differences

Sex: Male   Female
(Circle one)

1. Would you be willing to kill a cockroach by slapping it with your hands?
   a) yes   b) no
2. What is Queen Anne's lace?
   a) flower   b) embroidery
   c) perfume   d) doily
   e) spice
3. How many times in the last twenty-four hours have you used the word "shit"?
   a) less than 5 times   b) 5 or more times
4. Can you sew well enough to make clothes?
   a) yes   b) no
5. Do you believe in sexual intercourse only after a spiritual love exists between you and your partner?
   a) yes   b) no
6. Do you walk around freely in the nude in a locker room?
   a) yes   b) no
7. How often do you cry?
   a) very often   b) often
   c) only with good   d) very infrequently
      reason
   e) never
8. At times I feel like smashing things.
   a) true   b) false
9. Do you know your chest measurement?
   a) yes   b) no
10. Can you change a tire easily?
    a) yes   b) no
11. I spend no more than one hour during an average school day playing the radio or listening to records.
    a) true   b) false
12. Would you prefer to be the dominant one in a relationship?
    a) yes   b) no
13. Do you think that you are overweight?
    a) yes   b) no
14. When you get depressed, does washing your hair make you feel better?
    a) yes   b) no
15. Do you sleep in the nude?
    a) yes   b) no
16. Which parent are you closest to?
    a) mother   b) father
17. I try to keep my room as neat as possible.
    a) true   b) false

Questionnaire on Sex Differences

Sex: Male   Female
   (Circle one)

1. Would you be willing to kill a cockroach by slapping it with your hands?
   a) yes   b) no
2. What is Queen Anne's lace?
   a) flower   b) embroidery
   c) perfume   d) doily
   e) spice
3. How many times in the last twenty-four hours have you used the word "shit"?
   a) less than 5 times   b) 5 or more times
4. Can you sew well enough to make clothes?
   a) yes   b) no
5. Do you believe in sexual intercourse only after a spiritual love exists between you and your partner?
   a) yes   b) no
6. Do you walk around freely in the nude in a locker room?
   a) yes   b) no
7. How often do you cry?
   a) very often   b) often
   c) only with good   d) very infrequently
      reason
   e) never
8. At times I feel like smashing things.
   a) true   b) false
9. Do you know your chest measurement?
   a) yes   b) no
10. Can you change a tire easily?
   a) yes   b) no
11. I spend no more than one hour during an average school day playing the radio or listening to records.
   a) true   b) false
12. Would you prefer to be the dominant one in a relationship?
   a) yes   b) no
13. Do you think that you are overweight?
   a) yes   b) no
14. When you get depressed, does washing your hair make you feel better?
   a) yes   b) no
15. Do you sleep in the nude?
   a) yes   b) no
16. Which parent are you closest to?
   a) mother   b) father
17. I try to keep my room as neat as possible.
   a) true   b) false

Questionnaire on Sex Differences

Sex: Male   Female
   (Circle one)

1. Would you be willing to kill a cockroach by slapping it with your hands?
   a) yes   b) no
2. What is Queen Anne's lace?
   a) flower   b) embroidery
   c) perfume   d) doily
   e) spice
3. How many times in the last twenty-four hours have you used the word "shit"?
   a) less than 5 times   b) 5 or more times
4. Can you sew well enough to make clothes?
   a) yes   b) no
5. Do you believe in sexual intercourse only after a spiritual love exists between you and your partner?
   a) yes   b) no
6. Do you walk around freely in the nude in a locker room?
   a) yes   b) no
7. How often do you cry?
   a) very often   b) often
   c) only with good   d) very infrequently
      reason
   e) never
8. At times I feel like smashing things.
   a) true   b) false
9. Do you know your chest measurement?
   a) yes   b) no
10. Can you change a tire easily?
   a) yes   b) no
11. I spend no more than one hour during an average school day playing the radio or listening to records.
   a) true   b) false
12. Would you prefer to be the dominant one in a relationship?
   a) yes   b) no
13. Do you think that you are overweight?
   a) yes   b) no
14. When you get depressed, does washing your hair make you feel better?
   a) yes   b) no
15. Do you sleep in the nude?
   a) yes   b) no
16. Which parent are you closest to?
   a) mother   b) father
17. I try to keep my room as neat as possible.
   a) true   b) false

Questionnaire on Sex Differences

Sex: Male   Female
(Circle one)

1. Would you be willing to kill a cockroach by slapping it with your hands?
   a) yes   b) no
2. What is Queen Anne's lace?
   a) flower   b) embroidery
   c) perfume   d) doily
   e) spice
3. How many times in the last twenty-four hours have you used the word "shit"?
   a) less than 5 times   b) 5 or more times
4. Can you sew well enough to make clothes?
   a) yes   b) no
5. Do you believe in sexual intercourse only after a spiritual love exists between you and your partner?
   a) yes   b) no
6. Do you walk around freely in the nude in a locker room?
   a) yes   b) no
7. How often do you cry?
   a) very often   b) often
   c) only with good   d) very infrequently
      reason
   e) never
8. At times I feel like smashing things.
   a) true   b) false
9. Do you know your chest measurement?
   a) yes   b) no
10. Can you change a tire easily?
    a) yes   b) no
11. I spend no more than one hour during an average school day playing the radio or listening to records.
    a) true   b) false
12. Would you prefer to be the dominant one in a relationship?
    a) yes   b) no
13. Do you think that you are overweight?
    a) yes   b) no
14. When you get depressed, does washing your hair make you feel better?
    a) yes   b) no
15. Do you sleep in the nude?
    a) yes   b) no
16. Which parent are you closest to?
    a) mother   b) father
17. I try to keep my room as neat as possible.
    a) true   b) false

Questionnaire on Sex Differences

Sex: Male   Female
(Circle one)

1. Would you be willing to kill a cockroach by slapping it with your hands?
   a) yes   b) no
2. What is Queen Anne's lace?
   a) flower   b) embroidery
   c) perfume   d) doily
   e) spice
3. How many times in the last twenty-four hours have you used the word "shit"?
   a) less than 5 times   b) 5 or more times
4. Can you sew well enough to make clothes?
   a) yes   b) no
5. Do you believe in sexual intercourse only after a spiritual love exists between you and your partner?
   a) yes   b) no
6. Do you walk around freely in the nude in a locker room?
   a) yes   b) no
7. How often do you cry?
   a) very often   b) often
   c) only with good   d) very infrequently
      reason
   e) never
8. At times I feel like smashing things.
   a) true   b) false
9. Do you know your chest measurement?
   a) yes   b) no
10. Can you change a tire easily?
    a) yes   b) no
11. I spend no more than one hour during an average school day playing the radio or listening to records.
    a) true   b) false
12. Would you prefer to be the dominant one in a relationship?
    a) yes   b) no
13. Do you think that you are overweight?
    a) yes   b) no
14. When you get depressed, does washing your hair make you feel better?
    a) yes   b) no
15. Do you sleep in the nude?
    a) yes   b) no
16. Which parent are you closest to?
    a) mother   b) father
17. I try to keep my room as neat as possible.
    a) true   b) false

Questionnaire on Sex Differences

Sex: Male   Female
(Circle one)

1. Would you be willing to kill a cockroach by slapping it with your hands?
   a) yes   b) no
2. What is Queen Anne's lace?
   a) flower   b) embroidery
   c) perfume   d) doily
   e) spice
3. How many times in the last twenty-four hours have you used the word "shit"?
   a) less than 5 times   b) 5 or more times
4. Can you sew well enough to make clothes?
   a) yes   b) no
5. Do you believe in sexual intercourse only after a spiritual love exists between you and your partner?
   a) yes   b) no
6. Do you walk around freely in the nude in a locker room?
   a) yes   b) no
7. How often do you cry?
   a) very often   b) often
   c) only with good   d) very infrequently
      reason
   e) never
8. At times I feel like smashing things.
   a) true   b) false
9. Do you know your chest measurement?
   a) yes   b) no
10. Can you change a tire easily?
    a) yes   b) no
11. I spend no more than one hour during an average school day playing the radio or listening to records.
    a) true   b) false
12. Would you prefer to be the dominant one in a relationship?
    a) yes   b) no
13. Do you think that you are overweight?
    a) yes   b) no
14. When you get depressed, does washing your hair make you feel better?
    a) yes   b) no
15. Do you sleep in the nude?
    a) yes   b) no
16. Which parent are you closest to?
    a) mother   b) father
17. I try to keep my room as neat as possible.
    a) true   b) false

Questionnaire on Sex Differences

Sex: Male   Female
(Circle one)

1. Would you be willing to kill a cockroach by slapping it with your hands?
   a) yes   b) no
2. What is Queen Anne's lace?
   a) flower   b) embroidery
   c) perfume   d) doily
   e) spice
3. How many times in the last twenty-four hours have you used the word "shit"?
   a) less than 5 times   b) 5 or more times
4. Can you sew well enough to make clothes?
   a) yes   b) no
5. Do you believe in sexual intercourse only after a spiritual love exists between you and your partner?
   a) yes   b) no
6. Do you walk around freely in the nude in a locker room?
   a) yes   b) no
7. How often do you cry?
   a) very often   b) often
   c) only with good   d) very infrequently
      reason
   e) never
8. At times I feel like smashing things.
   a) true   b) false
9. Do you know your chest measurement?
   a) yes   b) no
10. Can you change a tire easily?
    a) yes   b) no
11. I spend no more than one hour during an average school day playing the radio or listening to records.
    a) true   b) false
12. Would you prefer to be the dominant one in a relationship?
    a) yes   b) no
13. Do you think that you are overweight?
    a) yes   b) no
14. When you get depressed, does washing your hair make you feel better?
    a) yes   b) no
15. Do you sleep in the nude?
    a) yes   b) no
16. Which parent are you closest to?
    a) mother   b) father
17. I try to keep my room as neat as possible.
    a) true   b) false

Questionnaire on Sex Differences

> Sex: Male   Female
> (Circle one)

1. Would you be willing to kill a cockroach by slapping it with your hands?
   a) yes   b) no
2. What is Queen Anne's lace?
   a) flower   b) embroidery
   c) perfume   d) doily
   e) spice
3. How many times in the last twenty-four hours have you used the word "shit"?
   a) less than 5 times   b) 5 or more times
4. Can you sew well enough to make clothes?
   a) yes   b) no
5. Do you believe in sexual intercourse only after a spiritual love exists between you and your partner?
   a) yes   b) no
6. Do you walk around freely in the nude in a locker room?
   a) yes   b) no
7. How often do you cry?
   a) very often   b) often
   c) only with good   d) very infrequently
      reason
   e) never
8. At times I feel like smashing things.
   a) true   b) false
9. Do you know your chest measurement?
   a) yes   b) no
10. Can you change a tire easily?
    a) yes   b) no
11. I spend no more than one hour during an average school day playing the radio or listening to records.
    a) true   b) false
12. Would you prefer to be the dominant one in a relationship?
    a) yes   b) no
13. Do you think that you are overweight?
    a) yes   b) no
14. When you get depressed, does washing your hair make you feel better?
    a) yes   b) no
15. Do you sleep in the nude?
    a) yes   b) no
16. Which parent are you closest to?
    a) mother   b) father
17. I try to keep my room as neat as possible.
    a) true   b) false

Questionnaire on Sex Differences

> Sex: Male   Female
> (Circle one)

1. Would you be willing to kill a cockroach by slapping it with your hands?
   a) yes   b) no
2. What is Queen Anne's lace?
   a) flower   b) embroidery
   c) perfume   d) doily
   e) spice
3. How many times in the last twenty-four hours have you used the word "shit"?
   a) less than 5 times   b) 5 or more times
4. Can you sew well enough to make clothes?
   a) yes   b) no
5. Do you believe in sexual intercourse only after a spiritual love exists between you and your partner?
   a) yes   b) no
6. Do you walk around freely in the nude in a locker room?
   a) yes   b) no
7. How often do you cry?
   a) very often   b) often
   c) only with good   d) very infrequently
      reason
   e) never
8. At times I feel like smashing things.
   a) true   b) false
9. Do you know your chest measurement?
   a) yes   b) no
10. Can you change a tire easily?
    a) yes   b) no
11. I spend no more than one hour during an average school day playing the radio or listening to records.
    a) true   b) false
12. Would you prefer to be the dominant one in a relationship?
    a) yes   b) no
13. Do you think that you are overweight?
    a) yes   b) no
14. When you get depressed, does washing your hair make you feel better?
    a) yes   b) no
15. Do you sleep in the nude?
    a) yes   b) no
16. Which parent are you closest to?
    a) mother   b) father
17. I try to keep my room as neat as possible.
    a) true   b) false

CHAPTER 17

Intelligence: Its Nature and Measurement

Learning Objectives

1. Explain the relation between the rise of mental testing and the structure of society.

MENTAL TESTS

2. Distinguish between achievement and aptitude tests.
3. Indicate some of the limitations of mental tests.

The study of variation
4. Define mean, variance, standard deviation, and normal curve.
5. Explain the meaning of correlation.

Evaluating mental tests
6. Explain the concept of reliability and different measures of reliability.
7. Explain predictive and construct validity and the procedure of standardization.

Using tests for selection
8. Indicate the factors that contribute to the setting of an appropriate cutoff score.

INTELLIGENCE TESTING

9. Indicate the difficulties in defining intelligence.

Measuring intelligence
10. Outline the major events in the history of intelligence testing.
11. Define and explain the rationale behind intelligence quotients (as calculated by Binet) and deviation IQs.

12. Describe the different types of intelligence tests: contrast the Wechsler and Binet tests.

An area of application: mental deficiency
13. Discuss the definition of mental retardation and the relation between retardation and productive functioning in society.
14. Contrast unifactor and multifactor theories of mental deficiency.

THE NATURE OF INTELLIGENCE

The psychometric approach
15. Describe the evidence for "g," and differentiate general factor and group factor theories.
16. Outline the major changes in intellectual ability in adulthood, including mention of fluid and crystallized intelligence.

The information-processing approach
17. Indicate the logic and evidence behind the suggestion that simple cognitive processes, such as name access time, may be components of intelligence.
18. What are the limitations on explanations of intelligence in terms of simple cognitive processes, and how does involvement of complex cognitive processes solve some of these problems?
19. Explain how analogical reasoning has been analyzed into components.
20. Discuss the role of strategies and strategies for using strategies in intelligence. Compare retardates, children, and normal adults on this dimension. Can retardates learn strategies?

The lack of a process theory
21. Explain and evaluate the statement "We may be able to measure intelligence, but we don't really know what it is."

HEREDITY, ENVIRONMENT, AND IQ

22. Review the history of positions on genetic factors in intelligence differences related to racial groups or social class.

Genetics and intelligence

23. Review basic terms in genetics (phenotype, genotype, dominant, recessive).
24. Explain why studies of the similarity in intelligence of members of the same family cannot be used to distinguish between genetic and environmental factors.
25. Explain how twin and adoption studies can be used to make this same distinction. Summarize the results of these studies and indicate problems in interpreting them.
26. Summarize the evidence for and against genetic and environmental explanations of differences in intelligence (IQ) in American whites, from twin and adoption studies and from situations where major environmental differences were studied.
27. Explain the idea of heritability and why it

only makes sense to use it to explain differences across individuals.

Group differences

28. Explain how heritability within groups can differ markedly from heritability of the same trait between groups.
29. Evaluate each of the following explanations of the reported difference between average IQ scores of American whites and blacks:
    1. the difference doesn't exist
    2. unfairness of the tests and test situations for blacks
    3. differences in environments between the groups
    4. genetic differences between the groups
30. Discuss the pros and cons of the value of determining the role of genetic factors in explaining interracial differences in terms of both scientific and sociopolitical issues.
31. What would be the consequences of a clear finding that some of the black-white IQ difference was attributable to genetic factors?

Programmed Exercises

MENTAL TESTS

1. Tests of _____ measure what an individual can do now, his present knowledge and competence in a particular area.

   achievement

2. Tests of _____ predict what an individual will be able to do later.

   aptitude

3. The frequency with which individual cases are distributed over different intervals of some measure is called a

   _____ _____.

   frequency distribution

4. The most common measure of central tendency is the _____.

   mean

5. The most common measure of variability is the

   _____ _____.

   standard deviation

6. Many physical and mental attributes show symmetrical bell-shaped frequency distributions, which are described as

   _____ _____.

   normal curves

7. Each point in the figure here represents the weight and IQ of

   one person. This display is called a _____ _____.

   scatter plot (diagram)

8. The _____ _____ is a statistic that describes the relations between two sets of measures. — correlation coefficient

9. If a test shows consistency in repeated measurements in similar circumstances, it is said to be _____. — reliable

10. This is measured as the _____ of the scores on two versions of the same basic test. — correlation

11. The higher the correlation between the score on a driving test and the number of accidents per year, the greater the _____ _____ of this test. — predictive validity

12. A test based on a theoretical scheme that accounts for the attribute being measured is said to have _____ _____. — construct validity

13. The magnitude of validity coefficients depends on the _____ _____ _____ within the group in which they are determined. — range of ability

14. In order to obtain norms against which to evaluate a test score, the test is administered to a large number of people, called the _____ _____. — standardization sample

15. In using a test for selection, setting a high cut-off point will minimize the number of _____ _____. — false accepts

16. The determination of a cutoff score is based on the costs and benefits that the tester assigns to each of the four possible outcomes, as represented in the _____ _____. — payoff matrix

INTELLIGENCE TESTING

17. According to Binet's system, a six-year-old who passed all the items at the nine-year-old level and none at the ten-year level would have a _____ _____ of nine years. — mental age

18. A person who gets the mean score for people of his age would have a deviation IQ of _____. — 100

19. A person with an IQ of 100 would have a _____ _____ of 50. — percentile rank

20. The Wechsler Adult Intelligence Scale was in part a response
to the emphasis on language in the Binet-Simon IQ tests. The

    Wechsler test has two parts, labeled _____ and _____.   performance, verbal

21. The majority of people classified as mentally retarded can

    function _____ in relatively simple life situations.   adequately

22. According to some, there are two forms of mental retardation.

    _____ forms usually involve mild retardation and represent   Multifactor

    the lower portion of the distribution of intelligence. _____   Unifactor
    forms correspond to more severe retardation and may result
    from a major pathology.

THE NATURE OF INTELLIGENCE

23. In the _____ approach, the results of intelligence tests are   psychometric
    studied and analyzed in an attempt to discover the structure of
    intelligence.

24. The fact that scores from a variety of different intelligence

    tests, specific and general, are positively _____, led Spear-   correlated

    man to introduce the factor of _____ _____.   general intelligence (g)

25. The technique used to try to extract the structure of intelli-

    gence from correlation matrices is called _____ _____.   factor analysis

26. The fact that some specific parts of intelligence tests correlate
    very highly with only some other parts, and that there are
    clusters of tests which highly correlate with one another, is

    evidence for the _____ _____ theories.   group factor

27. Spearman also recognized that certain very specific abilities
    were involved in the performance of any particular test, and

    named these abilities _____.   s

28. It seems to be the case that as one goes to older age, ability to

    deal with new problems or to respond rapidly, called _____   fluid
    intelligence, tends to deteriorate, while the repertoire of basic

    cognitive skills, knowledge, and strategy, called _____   crystallized
    intelligence, remains intact.

29. Measurements of changes in intelligence in later life are ideally
    done by testing the same person at different ages in what is

    called a _____ study.   longitudinal

30. Some have argued that basic abilities, such as the time it takes

    to access a _____ in memory, are _____ _____   name (word), simple cognitive

    _____ of intelligence.   correlates

31. A problem such as "car is to garage as person is to a house"

    is an example of _____ _____. Some believe that such   analogical reasoning

    tasks can be analyzed into _____ _____.   cognitive components

32. Humans improve their performance by using flexible _____   strategies
    to solve problems, learn, or remember.

33. The idea that strategies are fundamental to intelligence is supported by the fact that retardates do poorly in memory tasks

that require _____. Although they can be trained to use   rehearsal

this strategy, retardates do not seem to _____ it to other   generalize (transfer)
types of problems.

34. A higher-order cognitive process that may be a fundamental

dimension of human intelligence is _____ for using _____.   strategies, strategies

HEREDITY, ENVIRONMENT, AND IQ

35. The observed characteristics of an organism are called its

_____. But the underlying genetic blueprint is called the   phenotype

_____.   genotype

36. Assume that color of rat skin is determined by the genes at one locus. If a brown and a white rat mate and all the offspring are brown, we can guess that the gene for brown is

_____ and that these brown offspring have a different   dominant

_____ from their brown parent.   genotype

37. The fact that members of the same family have positively correlated intelligence and often share special abilities can be used

as evidence for both _____ and _____ factors.   hereditary (genetic), environmental

38. The pattern of a higher correlation of IQ scores in _____   identical

twin pairs than in _____ twin pairs, argues for a role for   fraternal
heredity in intelligence.

39. Two basic methods for estimating the role of inherited factors

in intelligence or other traits are _____ and _____ studies.   twin, adoption

40. The negative effects of poor environments on IQ are illustrated by data showing that the longer a child is in a deprived en-

vironment, the lower his IQ. This appears as a _____ cor-   negative
relation between IQ and age.

41. _____ is a concept that describes the percent of the varia-   Heritability
tion in a population that can be attributed to genetic factors.
It does not apply to individuals.

42. Some have argued that at least part of the American black-white difference in average IQ scores can be attributed to the fact that the test was designed for the white middle class, that

is to say, that the tests are not _____ fair.   culture

43. One cannot infer that, if a trait has high heritability within two populations, then population differences will also be ex-

plainable as largely due to _____.   heredity

44. A number of studies indicate that when differences in the environments of blacks and whites during childhood are markedly reduced or equated, the black-white IQ difference is

markedly _____.   reduced (diminished)

Self Test

1. Mental testing is primarily an American product, dating from the beginning of this century. America was a natural place for mental testing because:
   a. Americans embraced Freudian theory
   b. the American idea that all men are created equal required mental tests to show up their subtle differences
   c. of the high social and occupational mobility in America
   d. reinforcement was a popular concept in America
   e. Binet and Simon were Americans

2. One group of five people gets the following scores on a mathematics test: 85, 85, 90, 95, 95. Another group gets these five scores: 80, 80, 90, 100, 100. Which of the following statements about these groups is true?
   a. both have the same means and different standard deviations
   b. both have the same means and the same standard deviations
   c. both have different means and the same standard deviation
   d. both have different means and standard deviations
   e. it is impossible to say which group has a greater standard deviation

3. The diagram below represents the hypothetical scores of individual subjects on an IQ test and on a history achievement test. The correlation displayed would be closest to:
   a. +1.00
   b. + .50
   c. +0.00
   d. − .50
   e. −1.00

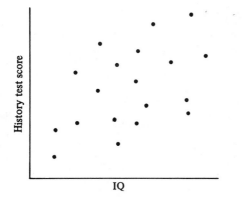

IQ

4. For which of the following pairs of variables would one expect to see a negative correlation?
   a. age and vocabulary
   b. height and visual acuity
   c. brain size and intelligence
   d. long-distance running ability and weight (among adults)
   e. social security number and intelligence (among adults)

5. A hypothetical air force needs a test to help select people for training as pilots. There is no adequate theory of the acquisition of flying skills, but air force investigators discover that the speed with which one can tap with the third finger correlates +.80 with survival in flying school. On the basis of this observation, one could say that the test had:
   a. high reliability
   b. high predictive validity
   c. high construct validity
   d. good standardization
   e. a limited range of ability

6. Further study with the finger-tapping test showed that though the correlation with survival in flying school was high, the correlation with the excellence of the pilot ten years later was only +.20. Since only about 10 percent of the graduates of flying school were actually flying ten years later and these were the best of the graduates, one might explain the drop in correlation as:
   a. loss of reliability
   b. the effect of limited range of ability
   c. the absence of norms
   d. the lack of construct validity of the test
   e. bad luck

7. An appropriate standardization sample for a test of artistic talent in elementary school children would be:
   a. elementary school children
   b. elementary school children fifty years ago
   c. older children who have selected art as a career
   d. elementary school children with artistic talent
   e. representative adults from the same country

8. A successful astronaut must have many special characteristics. Given the cost of training, it is important to minimize the number

of dropouts. Under the circumstances, it makes sense to establish a high cutoff on a test for astronautical ability, since this would:
a. maximize false rejects
b. increase the reliability
c. minimize false accepts
d. maximize false accepts
e. minimize false rejects

9. Intelligence testers face special problems because:
a. intelligence changes with age
b. intelligence tests are not reliable
c. all questions require prior knowledge, so that past experience determines the test score
d. there is no clear basis for determining construct or predictive validity

10. The deviation IQ is a better measure than the older intelligence quotient (mental age/chronological age), because:
a. it is newer
b. the deviation IQ is more reliable and is based on better tests
c. a person's deviation IQ will stay about the same, from age fifteen to fifty, for example
d. the deviation IQ increases with age, as does intelligence
e. it is based on the idea of 100 being average

11. Harry is eighteen and has a deviation IQ of 110. Carol is ten and has the same deviation IQ. In comparing them, we can say that:
a. both have the same percentile rank in their age group
b. both have the same mental age
c. a and b
d. none of the above

12. The SATs are a type of intelligence test. The scores are calculated as deviation IQs, with 500 as the mean score of those who have taken the test over the past few years. The mean deviation IQ of people with SAT scores of 500 is well over 100. This can be explained as a result of:
a. different types of questions on the two tests
b. high reliance on verbal ability in most IQ tests

c. superior intelligence in the standardization population for the SATs
d. a higher cut-off for false rejects in the SATs, which elevates the scores
e. a higher intake of cheese and other high protein foods in high school seniors

13. A student takes the same test of reaction time at 10:00 A.M. on two consecutive days. She gets very different scores on these two days. If this was true of many other test takers, it would suggest that this test is not:
a. valid
b. standardized
c. reliable
d. all of the above

14. In classifying people as mentally retarded on the basis of IQ test results, it would be especially important to:
a. place them in the correct retardation (mild, moderate, etc.) category
b. use a verbal test
c. minimize false accepts
d. use the mental age/chronological age ratio
e. use a unifactor intelligence test

15. Child A scores 15 on an IQ test, and child B scores 60. On the basis of this information, the most reasonable guess would be that:
a. A has a unifactor form of retardation
b. B has a multifactor form of retardation
c. A is more likely to have a well-defined genetic or chromosomal defect
d. all of the above
e. none of the above

16. A psychometrician examines a verbal and a spatial intelligence test, and finds that the scores on these two tests correlate +.38. From this he might conclude that:
a. performance on both tests is partly determined by "g" but mostly by specific factors
b. these tests measure very different things, and there is no "g" component here
c. both of these tests are excellent measures of "g"
d. these results constitute proof of the group factor theories

17. Considering the following matrix of correlations for four subtests of a large intelligence test (the data are made up):

	S	M	C	V
Spatial ability		.88	.38	.46
Mechanical ability			.31	.40
Creativity				.42
Verbal ability				

A group factor theorist might infer from this pattern that:
   a. there are four basic intelligence factors suggested by these results
   b. there are three basic intelligence factors suggested by these results
   c. there are two basic intelligence factors suggested by these results
   d. the data strongly support general factor, as opposed to group factor theory

18. Solve the following: "g" is to group factor as group factor is to:
   a. correlation matrix
   b. IQ
   c. Spearman
   d. s
   e. factor analysis

19. Gordon is really pretty ignorant, but he has a way of seeing relationships among ideas and figures and quickly comes up with new ways of doing things. He could be described as:
   a. high in "g"
   b. high in fluid, low in crystallized intelligence
   c. evidence for unifactor theories of intelligence
   d. someone who would do well on vocabulary tests
   e. someone who would do poorly on Raven's progressive matrices

20. Studies indicate that certain types of "intelligence" decline with age in adulthood and others do not. A type that improves or at least holds its own through most of adulthood is:
   a. "g"
   b. fluid intelligence
   c. crystallized intelligence
   d. group factors

21. Some believe that one can understand intelligence and predict IQs by analyzing intelligence into simple cognitive components, such as:
   a. strategies of problem solving
   b. logical abilities
   c. retrieval time of items from memory
   d. ability to look up or down
   e. none of the above

22. Complex intelligence-related tasks, like analogical reasoning, can be broken down into components such as identifying the common attribute of the first members of each pair in an analogy. This general route to the understanding of intelligence is called:
   a. the simple cognitive component approach
   b. the information-processing approach
   c. the psychometric approach
   d. the analogical approach
   e. none of the above

23. In contrast to retardates, normal children or adults:
   a. are able to learn strategies
   b. use strategies more
   c. generalize learned strategies more
   d. b and c
   e. all of the above

24. Cindy has to memorize the names of all of the American vice-presidents, and the dates that they held office. She considers doing it in alphabetical order, but then decides it would be better to try to remember them in chronological order. She is demonstrating:
   a. a primacy effect
   b. a recency effect
   c. a psychometric approach
   d. simple cognitive components
   e. strategies for using strategies

25. The observation that people on the political left tend to think of intelligence as more under environmental control, while those on the right tend to think of it as more under genetic control, suggests that:
   a. one must distinguish between within- and between-group differences
   b. the study of genetic and environmental influences on intelligence is inherently political
   c. sociopolitical factors influence judgments about the role of heredity in intelligence

d. there is no way to study scientifically the issue of the role of heredity and environment in intelligence

26. The fact that in the period between the two World Wars IQ scores of eastern European immigrant groups improved, the longer they were in the United States:
    a. justified a policy of excluding eastern Europeans from immigrating to the United States
    b. raises questions about U.S. immigration policy in the period between the wars
    c. demonstrates that intelligence is primarily under genetic control
    d. demonstrates that intelligence is primarily under environmental control

27. Jane and Phyllis have brown eyes. All of Jane's relatives have brown eyes. Phyllis's father has brown eyes, but her mother has blue eyes (brown eye color is dominant). From this information, we can guess that Jane and Phyllis have:
    a. the same genotype and phenotype
    b. the same genotype and different phenotypes
    c. different genotypes and the same phenotype
    d. different genotypes and phenotypes

28. Suppose the unlikely occurrence that a severely mentally retarded person married someone of normal intelligence, and that they had many children together. Suppose, further, that half of these children were severely retarded. This would suggest:
    a. that this was a single recessive gene effect
    b. that this type of retardation was due to recessive genes, and that the data support the multifactor theory of mental retardation
    c. that this retardation is probably due to a single dominant gene, confirming the unifactor theory for this case
    d. none of the above

29. The clustering of specific talents (e.g., music in the Bach family) or high intelligence in particular families, *across generations*, argues for:
    a. significant role for genetics in these abilities
    b. a significant role for environment in these abilities
    c. a and b
    d. a and/or b

30. If, counter to the results actually found, it was reported that fraternal and identical twins had the same high correlation in intelligence and that this was *higher* than the correlation between other siblings (e.g., brothers and sisters of different ages), one would be most justified in concluding that:
    a. the higher correlation in twins was due to environmental factors
    b. the higher correlation in twins was due to genetic factors
    c. fraternal twins are more closely related, genetically, than are other siblings
    d. a and c
    e. none of the above

31. Environmentalists explain the significant correlation between the IQ of adopted children and their biological parents in terms of *selective placement* of these children in adopted homes. This argument, however, is strongly weakened by:
    a. the studies on identical twins
    b. the fact that the IQ of adopted children correlates more highly with biological than adoptive parents
    c. the fact that there is a positive correlation between the IQ of adopted children and their adoptive parents
    d. b and c
    e. none of the above

32. All but one of these findings supports the idea of a hereditary component in intelligence differences. Which finding does not support such a view?
    a. higher IQ correlation in identical than fraternal twins
    b. higher IQ correlation between adoptive children and their biological parents than between these same children and their adoptive parents
    c. higher IQ correlation between siblings than between half siblings (sharing only one parent)
    d. equal correlations in IQ between fraternal twins and between other siblings
    e. positive correlation of adoptive child's IQ with the IQ of the adoptive parents

33. On the whole, the IQs of biological parents giving children up for adoption are below those of adopting parents (since the latter are screened by agencies). The observation that, whatever the correlation between IQ of adopted child and biological parent, the actual IQ of such adopted children tends to be

considerably higher than that of the biological parents, is evidence for:
a. hereditary effects
b. environmental effects
c. a and b
d. a heritability value

34. If intelligence (IQ scores) in a particular group showed a heritability of 1.0, this would mean that:
a. existing environments had no effects on intelligence
b. while existing environments have no effects on intelligence, presently nonexistent environments might have significant effects
c. genetic factors account for most of the variation in IQ in this particular group
d. genetic factors account for all of the variation in IQ in this particular group
e. none of the above

35. Which of the following traits would you expect to show the *lowest* heritability?
a. eye color
b. height
c. length of hair
d. visual acuity

36. Many have argued that IQ tests and the circumstances under which they are given favor whites over blacks. All but one of the following reported findings argue against this view: that is, all but one indicate that the tests are reasonably culture fair. Select the one reported finding that does not argue in favor of the culture fairness of tests or test situations:
a. the black-white IQ difference remains about the same when the black version of the test is translated into black English
b. the black-white difference is about the same for verbal tests and for the abstract Raven's progressive matrices
c. the black-white difference remains about the same whether the tester is black or white
d. the black-white difference remains about the same for tests of verbal and tests of spatial intelligence
e. the black-white difference decreases in the children in families that have children of both races through adoption

37. Assume two breeds of cattle: In both, size differences within the breed are completely determined by genes (heritability: 1.0). Assume further that one breed is found in New Zealand and the other in central Africa and that the New Zealand breed averages about 10 percent bigger than the African breed. What inferences can be make about the origin of this difference between breeds?
a. it is certainly due to heredity
b. it is certainly due to environment
c. the heritability of the population difference would be at least .50
d. the heritability of the population difference would be at least .10
e. no certain inference can be drawn about breed differences from this information

38. A fair summary of studies on environmental matching or change, as applied to the black-white IQ difference, would be:
a. there is generally a decreased black-white IQ difference when attempts are made to equalize environments in the comparison groups, and an improvement in black IQs when the environment is improved
b. appropriate manipulation of environments, to provide blacks with the full advantages of the white environment, leads to elimination of the black-white IQ difference
c. there is very little effect of environmental change or equalization on black IQ or black-white differences
d. none of the above

39. What would be educationally and scientifically *appropriate* sociopolitical responses to a *hypothetical* proof that a fair proportion of the difference in IQ scores between American blacks and whites could be assigned to hereditary factors?
a. curtailment of early enrichment programs
b. establishment of racial quotas
c. inclusion of race as an important factor in determining the ability of applicants for jobs involving intelligence
d. cessation of affirmative action programs
e. none of the above

Answer Key for Self Test

1. c p. 571–72
2. a p. 573
3. b pp. 574–75
4. d p. 575
5. b p. 577
6. b p. 577
7. a p. 578
8. c p. 579
9. d p. 582
10. c p. 583
11. a p. 584
12. c p. 586
13. c p. 576
14. c p. 587
15. d pp. 587–88
16. a pp. 590, 591
17. b p. 591
18. d pp. 590–91
19. b p. 593
20. c p. 593
21. c p. 594
22. b p. 596
23. d pp. 596–97
24. e p. 597
25. c pp. 598–99
26. b pp. 598–99
27. c pp. 599–600
28. c pp. 588, 600
29. d pp. 600–603
30. a pp. 601–602
31. b pp. 602–603
32. e pp. 601–603
33. b p. 602
34. d pp. 603–604
35. c pp. 603–604
36. e p. 605
37. e pp. 606–607
38. a p. 607
39. e pp. 608–609

Investigating Psychological Phenomena

"INTELLIGENCE TESTS"

Equipment: None
Number of subjects: One (yourself)
Time per subject: (Thirty minutes)
Time for experimenter: Thirty minutes

This is an experiment that will help you to understand the construction of intelligence. The procedure that you will go through will be like the procedure that might be used in the development of an intelligence test. The main concern is that you understand how a distribution of test scores is generated, and how an individual score is interpreted with respect to that distribution.

For this purpose, rather than making up a so-called intelligence test, we have chosen to try out a measure of a characteristic that is rarely tested: One's knowledge of foods and cooking. In this case, one begins with some idea of the ability or knowledge base that one is trying to assess. Questions or tasks are constructed that seem to measure these abilities. Then, pilot tests, like those we will give you, are distributed to a representative sample of the population for which the tests are intended. In your case, your class might serve as a sample of college undergraduates. Of course, students differ in different schools and in different regions, so this would not be anything like the random sample we would actually need were this a real test.

The results of the test are examined. Typically, most of the questions which all subjects get right or all get wrong are discarded, because such questions do not help to measure *differences* among people in the abilities under study. Then, some sort of retest studies are done, to make sure the test is reliable, and a validity study is done, to assure that the test measures what it is supposed to measure.

We will only deal with one phase of test construction here. We have made up a test that has never been used by psychologists before. (It is certainly not clear why a food knowledge test would be of interest to anyone in the real world.) We ask each of you to take the test. It is brief. The food knowledge test is in the format of a written test, with unlimited time. It is, of course, "closed book." Fill it out in a quiet place. Then score your answers, using the list of correct answers at the end of this section.

FOOD KNOWLEDGE TEST

Sex _____

Listed below are five countries:

Italy (southern Italy)
China
India
Mexico
Germany

Each of the following food items (1–14) is particularly characteristic of the cuisines of one of the five countries listed above. Write the name of the appropriate cuisine (country) beside the food item.

1. potatoes ____G____
2. corn ____M____
3. sesame oil ____I____
4. olive oil ____It____
5. soy sauce ____C____
6. cumin (two possible answers) ____C____
7. oregano ____M____

8. curry ____I____
9. chili pepper (two possible answers) ____M____
10. liverwurst ____G____
11. turmeric ____I____
12. yogurt ____G____
13. bean curd ____C____
14. ghee ____C____

Write in the name of the country associated with each of the following items:

15. sushi _____
16. lasagna _____
17. taco _____
18. paella _____
19. moussaka _____
20. goulash _____
21. sukiyaki _____

22. mousse _____
23. sate (pron: sä꞉tāy) _____
24. biryani _____
25. mole (pron: mŏ꞉lāy) _____
26. trifle _____
27. kim chee _____
28. champagne _____

29. What is the primary ingredient used in raising (leavening) bread? ___yeast___.
30. What is yogurt made from? ___milk___
31. What are raisins made from? ___grapes___
32. What is meringue made of? ___egg fw___
33. What animal does bacon come from? ___pig___
34. What are prunes made from? ___plums___
35. What type of fish is lox made from? ___salmon___
36. What vegetable are pickles usually made from? ___cucumber___
37. What fruit is wine usually made from? ___grapes___
38. What is sauerkraut made from? ___cabbage___
39. What are chitterlings made from? ___peas___
40. What does caviar come from? ___fish___
41. What is marzipan made from? ___almond paste___
42. What is the primary ingredient in guacamole? ___guac.___

Indicated below are five common cooking methods:

baking
sautéing or pan frying
braising
boiling
broiling

For each dish or food below, indicate by writing in the correct term from those listed above the primary cooking method used.

43. chicken soup _boil_

44. bread _bak_

45. scrambled eggs _pan_

46. pot roast _broil_

47. shish-kebab _broil_

48. spaghetti _boil_

49. soufflé _bak_

50. hash-brown potatoes _pan_

51. collard greens _boil_ .

TEST RESULTS AND "IQ" CALCULATIONS

The food knowledge test was taken by 153 University of Pennsylvania undergraduates in the introductory psychology course and twenty-one students in a University of Michigan class in learning and memory. The results were:

Mean score: 35.9 for 174 subjects
Standard deviation: 5.03
Range of scores: 22 (lowest) to 47 (highest)

Females do slightly better than males on this test (mean female score: 36.8; mean male score: 35.1).

CALCULATION OF A "CULINARY IQ"

As we will discuss below, much more work would have to be done with this test before it could actually be used in a meaningful way. For the sake of illustrating the scaling of psychological tests, we will use the data generated by undergraduates taking this test to develop a "deviation" scale like that used in IQ tests. You can then calculate your "culinary IQ."

The basic principle behind scaling of tests is the deviation score. Like a percentile score, it expresses where a particular score stands with respect to all of the other scores. The distribution of scores for tests usually falls into what is called a normal distribution. An ideal normal distribution is drawn below. Normal distributions are typically described by their mean value and their standard deviation, a measure of the spread or variability of the curve (see the statistical appendix to the text). In a normal distribution, 68 percent of all observations fall within one standard deviation of the mean, and 96 percent of all observations fall within two standard deviations of the mean (see figure below). Test scores are measured in units of deviation from the mean. For all IQ type tests, 100 is set as the mean value and 15 points as the standard deviation. Thus, an IQ of 115 corresponds to the score one standard deviation above the mean (85 to one standard deviation below); 130 corresponds to a score of two standard deviations above the mean (70 to two below), and so on. (An IQ of 105 would then be one third of a standard deviation above the mean). In percentile terms, an IQ of 130 would be at the 98th percentile, and an IQ of 85 would be at the 16th percentile (see figure).

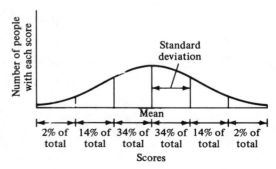

Normal distribution

Applying these ideas to our test, the mean score (35.9) on the food test would be assigned a scaled score of 100. Subtracting one standard deviation

(5.03) from this score, we get approximately 31, a score that would be assigned a scaled score of 85 (one standard deviation below the mean corresponds to 15 scaled points). We have performed the appropriate arithmetic for the food test, and provided the raw score (your actual score) and scaled score (converted to deviation units) equivalents in the table below. Because the standard deviation for the food knowledge scores is almost exactly 5, each additional point on the test is worth one-fifth of a standard deviation, or 3 "IQ" points.

FOOD TEST

Raw score (your actual score)	Scaled score ("IQ")
18	46
19	49
20	52
21	55
22	58
23	61
24	64
25	67
26	70
27	73
28	76
29	79
30	82
31	85
32	88
33	91
34	94
35	97
36	100
37	103
38	106
39	109
40	112
41	115
42	118
43	121
44	124
45	127
46	130
47	133
48	136
49	139
50	142
51	145

The next step in developing a test would be to improve the first version. For example, in the food knowledge test, there are a number of useless items: These are items that do not contribute to the measurement of differences in people. For three items (number 16—lasagna, 37—wine, and 44—bread), all 174 subjects got the right answer. Because of this, these items would normally be discarded. Three additional items were missed by less than 2% of the subjects and might also be discarded. There were no questions that were missed by all subjects. The "hardest" question was about the country of origin of sate (number 23—Indonesia), and 8.6% of subjects were correct on this item.

We would also eliminate any questions that turned out to be ambiguous. In this test, for example, some of the "What is X made from?" questions need clarification. Thus, for number 39—chitterlings (chitlings), some people answered "pig," and others said "intestine." We scored both as correct, but should have been more specific in the question. Similarly, for number 30—what is yogurt made from?—we intended that milk be the correct answer. But bacteria cultures are also components of yogurt. We should have asked, "What is the primary ingredient in yogurt?" See if you can find some other ambiguous questions. Finally, we would examine the correlation of correctness on each question with the total score on the test. Are there any items which don't seem to be measuring the same sort of thing as the rest of the test? (See the experiment on personality testing in the next chapter.) Such items might or might not be included but would at least be reexamined. Along these same lines, one might look at any questions which the top performers on the test all missed. Often such items are badly worded, or perhaps even in error. For the food test, there was no single item missed by all of the six top scorers.

Having streamlined the test, we would then use some type of test-retest procedure to determine their reliability. (Will the same person score about the same on two different occasions?) The reliability measures would be complicated, since one would expect improvement on the second time through.

We would then perform some sort of validity test. Is the test measuring what it is supposed to measure? If the food knowledge test is supposed to predict likely candidates for success in a cooking school, does it actually do so?

Finally, having satisfied ourselves that we had a reliable and valid test, we would then administer the test to a large sample of people (hundreds to thousands of people) randomly selected from the population of people for whom the test was designed (e.g., high school seniors, all adults, etc).

Ask yourself whether you believe the food test is meaningful. How would *you* validate it? What might it be used for? What would it correlate with?

FURTHER ACTIVITIES

Sketch out what you think would be an appropriate test for use in predicting success in a particular profession: e.g., fighter pilot, baseball player, or architect. Then ask yourself how you would validate the test.

Answer Sheet

Score one point for each correct answer
(Listed next to each answer are the percentages correct out of 174 students.)

1. potatoes—Germany (83.9%)
2. corn—Mexico (78.7%)
3. sesame oil—China (28.2%)
4. olive oil—Italy (93.7%)
5. soy sauce—China (97.7%)
6. cumin—India or Mexico (78.2%)
7. oregano—Italy (90.2%)
8. curry—India (73.0%)
9. chili—India or Mexico (90.2%)
10. liverwurst—Germany (97.7%)
11. turmeric—India (48.3%)
12. yogurt—India (44.8%)
13. bean curd—China (44.8%)
14. ghee—Japan (60.3%)
15. sushi—Japan (55.7%)
16. lasagna—Italy (100%)
17. taco—Mexico (98.8%)
18. paella—Spain (40.2%)
19. moussaka—Greece (43.7%)
20. goulash—Hungary (73.6%)
21. sukiyaki—Japan (76.4%)
22. mousse—France (74.7%)
23. sate—Indonesia (8.6%)
24. biryani—India (37.4%)
25. mole—Mexico (14.9%)
26. trifle—England (47.7%)
27. kim chee—Korea (13.2%)
28. champagne—France (80.4%)
29. bread—yeast (97.1%)
30. yogurt—milk (88.5%)
31. raisins—grapes (96.0%)
32. meringue—egg white (74.1%)
33. bacon—pig (99.9%)
34. prunes—plums (77.0%)
35. lox—salmon (66.7%)
36. pickle—cucumber (97.7%)
37. wine—grapes (100%)
38. sauerkraut—cabbage (89.1%)
39. chitterlings—pig or intestine or gut (29.3%)
40. caviar—fish eggs (91.4%)
41. marzipan—almond or sugar (31.0%)
42. guacamole—avocado (48.3%)
43. chicken soup—boil (96%)
44. bread—bake (100%)
45. scrambled eggs—pan fry (98.3%)
46. pot roast—braise (46.6%)
47. shish kebab—broil (57.5%)
48. spaghetti—boil (97.7%)
49. souffle—bake (83.3%)
50. hash-brown potatoes—pan fry-saute (96.6%)
51. collard greens—boil (55.7%)

CHAPTER 18

Personality Assessment

Learning Objectives

1. What constitutes a personality trait?
2. Be cognizant of the key assumption of trait theory and of the goal of personality tests.

METHODS OF ASSESSMENT

Structured personality tests
3. Understand the construction and the use of the Minnesota Multiphasic Personality Inventory (MMPI). What is the importance of score profiles and validity scales?
4. Why isn't the MMPI a commonly used test for normal people? What is one of the tests that is used instead?
5. Be familiar with the different types of test validity and how various personality tests measure up.
6. Why don't the uniformly small correlations between the psychopathic deviance scale of the MMPI and various behavioral patterns invalidate the Pd scale?

Unstructured personality tests
7. What is the rationale for projective techniques? Describe some of these procedures.
8. What scoring categories are used in the interpretation of Rorschach inkblots, and what general rules are employed?
9. Be familiar with the differences in interpretation between the Rorschach and the Thematic Apperception Test (TAT) in regard to perceived content.

10. Why is TAT interpretation impressionistic and global?
11. Summarize the issues and arguments in assessing the validity of the TAT and the Rorschach.
12. Of what value are projective tests in the clinical setting? Do they have any incremental validity?

TRAITS VERSUS SITUATIONS

The difficulties with trait theory
13. What is the importance of cross-situational consistency, or inconsistency, in the argument against trait theory?
14. How is the trait theory/situationism debate another manifestation of the nativist/empiricist controversy?

In defense of traits
15. Describe how superficially different expressions of a personality trait contribute to apparent behavioral inconsistency. What are the implications for trait theory?
16. Understand the importance of the interaction between a personality and situation in personality assessment. What is the drawback to this approach?

Person constancy
17. The idea of "person constancy" strikes a happy medium between the concepts of solid stability and complete plasticity of the individual personality. According to what dimensions of such constancies should persons be categorized together?

THE SEARCH FOR A TAXONOMY

18. What is meant by a taxonomy of personality traits?

Classification by factor analysis

19. How is factor analysis used to try to discover the basic dimensions of personality?
20. What is Cattell's approach in developing a taxonomy of personality traits? What modifications of Cattell's analysis have been suggested and why?
21. Discuss Eysenck's taxonomy of neuroticism and extraversion-introversion. What personality differences are encompassed by this scheme?
22. How does the dependence of factor analysis on the data set itself detract from the value of this procedure in establishing a taxonomy of personality traits?
23. How does Eysenck attempt to validate his extraversion-introversion scale?

Classification through biology

24. What is the hypothesized relationship between temperament and physique?
25. Recount Sheldon's theory of somatotypes. What are the components of body type and their allegedly related trait clusters?
26. What was the flaw in Sheldon's study of the relationship between physique and temperament?
27. Some studies of juvenile delinquency and body type support Sheldon's theory. Discuss the relevant evidence and also be aware of promising modifications of Sheldon's theory.
28. What are the different theories of causality in explaining the relationship between physique and temperament?
29. Discuss the evidence that certain personality traits may have a genetic component. What is the proposed relationship between heritability and central nature of a trait in personality? What traits are most heritable?

Is a classification system possible?

30. Compare and contrast the various approaches to the development of a taxonomy of personality differences.

Programmed Exercises

1. The way that people differ in their desires, attitudes, and behaviors reflects their _____ _____.

personality differences

2. Implicit in the use of personality tests is the assumption that personality patterns are essentially _____ over time.

consistent

3. _____ tests were developed to enable us to predict people's future behavior.

Personality

METHODS OF ASSESSMENT

4. The first personality test was administered to army recruits and was meant to identify _____ _____ soldiers.

emotionally disturbed

5. The MMPI is termed _____ because it assesses a number of personality _____ simultaneously.

multiphasic

traits

6. The MMPI is scored by comparing the scores on each of the ten major scales to those of the relevant _____ _____.

criterion group

7. The authors of the MMPI emphasize the _____ power of a question in distinguishing between the criterion group and normal subjects.

discriminatory

8. In interpreting scores on the MMPI, it is necessary to examine score _____, which present the scores on all the scales in graphic form.

    profiles

9. In order to detect whether or not subjects are lying on test items or are trying to fake mental illness, the MMPI uses two _____ _____ made up of items no one can honestly deny and of items so bizarre that few would endorse them.

    validity scales

10. It is difficult to interpret MMPI scores for _____ subjects since the criterion groups used to define the scales were composed of _____ patients.

    normal

    psychiatric

11. One test which was developed using normal subjects as the criterion group is the _____ _____ _____.

    California Personality Inventory

12. The degree to which a test can predict real-world events is called its _____ _____.

    predictive validity

13. Devising and testing hypotheses about the relation between an underlying trait and various behavioral effects comprises _____ _____.

    construct validation

14. High scores on the psychopathic deviance scale of the MMPI reflect _____, while low scorers are generally considered _____ _____.

    aggressiveness

    good-natured

15. The use of _____ _____ was, in part, a protest against the _____ _____ nature of paper-and-pencil techniques.

    projective techniques

    highly structured

16. One of the concerns of the originators of projective techniques was that a subject could _____ to _____ when taking a test like the MMPI.

    lie, himself

17. The idea behind projective techniques is that in _____ unstructured materials, a subject will reveal deeper facets of his _____.

    structuring

    personality

18. The three categories used in scoring Rorschach inkblots are _____, which concerns the portion of the blot used; _____, which notes the attributes of the stimulus that the subject responds to; and _____, which refers to what the subject sees.

    location

    determinants

    content

19. In interpretations of Rorschach inkblots, use of the entire blot is said to reflect _____ thinking, while attention to details suggests _____.

    integrative or conceptual

    compulsiveness (or rigidity)

20. Rorschach responses indicating human movement are interpreted as indicating _____, and those dominated by color suggest _____.

    imagination

    emotionality (or impulsivity)

21. Traditionally, _____ has been less important than the other categories in the interpretation of Rorschach inkblots.

    content

22. The _____ _____ _____, in which subjects tell stories about pictures, places a major emphasis on content.

Thematic Apperception Test (TAT)

23. Contrary to traditional beliefs, Rorschach _____ has been shown to correlate more highly with external criteria than do

content

_____ assessments based on verbatim protocols.

global

24. In addition to predictive validity, it is desirable for a test to

have _____ validity, so that the test provides knowledge not found by other means.

incremental

TRAITS VERSUS SITUATIONS

25. Some psychologists have argued that the reason that many tests, both introspective and projective, are not good predictors of future behavior is that most people exhibit a lack of

_____ _____ consistency.

cross-situational

26. _____ maintains that human behavior is largely determined by the situation a person is in, rather than by the actual, internal traits of the person.

Situationism

27. Contrary to situationistic claims, some _____ studies have

longitudinal

shown a fair amount of personal _____ of personality.

consistency

28. Another argument against situationism is that perceived

behavior inconsistency may be more _____ than _____

apparent, real

since the expression of a constant trait may _____ over time.

vary

29. When a person's reactions cannot be predicted adequately solely

by situation or by _____ _____, the critical factor may

individual differences

be their _____.

interaction

30. The intuitive belief that most people remain unchanged over

time is known as _____ _____ and is similar to size and shape constancy in perception.

person constancy

THE SEARCH FOR A TAXONOMY

31. The major task in determining the proper traits with which to

classify personality is the development of a _____ of personality difference.

taxonomy

32. Despite its limitations _____ _____ has proved a useful statistical tool in describing personality.

factor analysis

33. Cattell's taxonomy of personality is based on _____, using

language

factor analysis to discover how _____ _____ are interrelated.

trait words

34. Trait words are seldom purely _____ but generally incor-

descriptive

porate _____ judgments of the trait at hand. It is important to control for this latter aspect in personality test procedures.

evaluative

35. A _____ _____ of personality views several lower-level   hierarchical model
    traits (e.g., tidyness) as manifestations of a higher-order factor
    (e.g., conscientiousness).

36. According to Eysenck, both _____ and _____ are un-   introverts, neurotics
    sociable and withdrawn, but the former's unsociability is not
    tainted by fear of social activities.

37. According to Eysenck, introversion corresponds to a high level

    of _____; thus, persons of this type are actually more   arousal
    awake than others.

38. Sheldon's theory of somatotypes relates the following body

    types and personality traits: _____ with _____,   endomorphy, viscerotonia

    _____ with _____, and _____ with _____.   mesomorphy, somatotonia
                                                                          ectomorphy, cerebrotonia

39. Use of only skeletal height and width in determining body

    type excludes _____ body type. This seems justified since   endomorphic

    the _____ of this component over time is negligible.   constancy

40. Attributes like _____ and _____ _____ seem remark-   sociability, activity level
    ably stable from childhood to adolescence, in support of a

    theory of a _____ contribution to personality.   genetic

41. Identical twins show more similarity of personality than do

    fraternal twins, indicating some _____ of personality traits,   heritability
    but the proportion of variance thus accounted for is still low

    and appears _____ for most traits.   similar

Self Test

1. Personality differences include:
   a. intelligence, ability, and insight
   b. desires, feelings, and modes of expressing
      these needs and feelings
   c. none of the above
   d. both a and b

2. Trait theory:
   a. is consonant with the beliefs of Aristo-
      phones
   b. assumes consistency of personality
      patterns
   c. establishes personality prototypes such as
      the garrulous person, the flatterer, etc.
   d. a and b

3. The first personality and intelligence tests
   were similar in that both were _____ but
   differed in that the former was _____
   and the latter was _____.

   a. diagnostic, unstructured, structured
   b. unstructured, descriptive, normative
   c. diagnostic, poorly validated, well
      validated
   d. structured, descriptive, diagnostic

4. An appropriate criterion group for a diagnostic test of paranoid schizophrenics would
   be:
   a. normal individuals
   b. paranoid schizophrenics
   c. a mixture of a and b
   d. no criterion group is needed when the
      test is used as a diagnostic tool

5. The California Psychological Inventory
   (CPI) uses _____ criterion groups.
   a. no
   b. pathological
   c. normal
   d. random

6. When a test can foretell some real-world event, it is said to have:
   a. face validity
   b. incremental validity
   c. predictive validity
   d. unproven validity

7. Which of the following illustrates construct validation?
   a. correlating the Nielsen rankings of television shows with the amount of fan mail the stars receive and with the number of articles written about the show
   b. the correct choice of presidential candidates by the Gallup polls
   c. the confirmation of a proposed genetic theory through population studies
   d. the repeated modification and testing of a new car design to ensure safety and good performance

8. Projective techniques differ from tests such as the MMPI and CPI in that the former are more:
   a. structured
   b. quantitative
   c. variable
   d. all of the above
   e. none of the above

9. In structuring unstructured materials, it is expected that a subject:
   a. will reveal his capacity for conceptual organization
   b. will be relieved of objective test anxiety and will thus perform most effectively and honestly
   c. will project his deepest feelings and conflicts upon the ambiguous stimulus
   d. will be distracted from the psychologist's analysis of the subject's voice tone, body language, and gestures in responding

10. Two examples of projective tests are:
    a. the MMPI and the Thematic Apperception Test (TAT)
    b. the Rorschach and the TAT
    c. the Rorschach and the CPI
    d. all of the above

11. The three categories used in interpreting the Rorschach are:
    a. location, negativism, color
    b. location, content, determinants
    c. content, impulsiveness, use of white space
    d. impulsiveness, happiness, truth value

12. All of the following are used in systematic scoring procedures for the TAT *except*:
    a. the number of times a given motive recurs
    b. the ratio of positive to negative outcomes
    c. the suggestion of latent or overt homosexuality
    d. the characteristics of "mother" and "father" figures as threatening or supportive

13. Which of the following is *not* an established piece of evidence against the validity of the Rorschach inkblot test?
    a. the failure of highly intelligent people to use the entire inkblot more than others do
    b. the lack of relation between Rorschach indices and psychiatric diagnosis
    c. the failure of artists to demonstrate a preponderance of human movement in their perceptions
    d. the fact that individual Rorschach indices show little relation to external validity criteria

14. While the TAT has not fared well as a diagnostic tool, it has shown some promise as an indicator of:
    a. intelligence
    b. motives
    c. hidden fears
    d. imagination

15. Walter Mischel has found that children are _____ in their behavior in different circumstances. He saw this as evidence _____ the validity of personality traits.
    a. consistent, for
    b. inconsistent, for
    c. consistent, against
    d. inconsistent, against

16. The concept of situationism is most opposite to the assumptions underlying:
    a. the MMPI and CPI
    b. the Rorschach and TAT
    c. all of the above
    d. none of the above

17. Situationists:
    a. deny the existence of individual difference
    b. believe that social roles play a large role in the situations people get into
    c. claim that situations themselves are the best predictors of people's reactions
    d. believe that past situational experiences determine personality traits

18. A taxonomy is a:
   a. classification system
   b. rating scale used in psychiatric diagnosis
   c. a type of mental disorder
   d. a class of stable personality traits

19. Eysenck has formed a hypothesis that all personalities can be classified on the basis of a rating on two independent scales. They are _____ and _____ .
   a. paranoid, schizophrenic
   b. shy-outgoing, anxiety
   c. neuroticism, extraversion-introversion
   d. psychopathic deviance, extraversion-introversion

20. Introverts differ from extraverts in all of the following ways *except*:
   a. they are solitary
   b. they are aloof
   c. they are slow to change
   d. they have a lower pain threshold
   e. none of the above

21. Which of the following constitute problems for Eysenck's theory of personality based on neuroticism and introversion-extraversion?
   a. the dependence of factor analysis on the existing data set
   b. the possible nonindependence of these two dimensions
   c. the observation that introverted people tend to be more easily aroused than are extraverts
   d. a and b

22. William Sheldon proposed three classifications of body types. They are:
   a. viscerotonia, somatotonia, cerebrotonia
   b. tall, fat, strong
   c. endomorphic, mesomorphic, ectomorphic
   d. none of the above

23. According to Sheldon, the proper pairings of body type to personality traits are:
   a. mesomorphy-viscerotonia, endomorphy-cerebrotonia, ectomorphy-somatotonia
   b. mesomorphy-cerebrotonia, endomorphy-somatotonia, ectomorphy-viscerotonia
   c. mesomorphy-somatotonia, endomorphy-viscerotonia, ectomorphy-cerebrotonia

24. When Sheldon's theory (relating somatotypes to personality traits) was tested, a huge correlation was found between the two measures. The findings were criticized because:

a. it was determined that the experimenter knew nothing about personality traits
b. only ten men were tested, not enough to make the results significant
c. Sheldon himself did the ratings on both measures
d. all of the above

25. In the final analysis, it seems that:
   a. Sheldon's hypothesis has been disproven
   b. ectothermy is least reliable in predicting personality traits
   c. there probably is some relation between body type and personality traits
   d. American eating habits have obscured any existing relationship between body type and personality

26. An explanation for a relation between somatotype and personality may be that:
   a. certain physiques foster some behavioral patterns·over others
   b. stereotypes create such relationships
   c. both of the above
   d. there is no explanation since previous positive findings have been shown to be artifactual

27. In _____ with Mischel, some authors have claimed that there is a higher level of consistency in people's behavior than previously believed. They hypothesize that reactions that appear _____ in gross analysis are really different manifestations of _____ underlying sources.
   a. agreement, dissimilar, different
   b. agreement, dissimilar, the same
   c. disagreement, similar, different
   d. disagreement, dissimilar, the same

28. Studies by Endler and Hunt have looked at person-situation interactions. Their results suggest that the practicality of assigning traits like fear to people:
   a. is useless
   b. has been experimentally validated
   c. should be qualified to be more specific to individual circumstances
   d. is minimal since internal fluctuations in trait strength cause behavior to vary from situation to situation

29. Person constancy involves the notion that:
   a. all people behave in essentially the same way for a particular situation

b. people are not consistent but we perceive them as being that way

c. we tend to see a person in only one situation, so we only think of him in that situation

d. all of the above

e. none of the above

30. The use of language in search of a taxonomy has led researchers to suggest all of the following theories except:

a. the number of synonyms an adjective has is an indicator of the relative importance

of the trait described by the adjective

b. the number of languages that an adjective appears in is an indicator of the universality of the trait described by that adjective

c. analysis of the descriptive and evaluative meanings of words may provide a useful key in developing a taxonomy

d. adjectives which are most frequently misspelled are the ones that are least desirable in that society

Answer Key for Self Test

1. b p. 611	16. c pp. 622–23
2. b p. 612	17. c p. 623
3. c p. 612	18. a p. 628
4. b pp. 612–13	19. d p. 622
5. c p. 614	20. e pp. 630–31
6. c p. 615	21. d pp. 631–32
7. a p. 615	22. c p. 632
8. e p. 616	23. c p. 633
9. c p. 616	24. c p. 633
10. b p. 617	25. c p. 634
11. b p. 618	26. c p. 634
12. c pp. 618–19	27. d p. 624
13. a p. 620	28. c p. 626
14. b p. 620	29. e p. 627
15. d pp. 621–22	30. d p. 635

Investigating Psychological Phenomena

CONSTRUCTING A PERSONALITY INVENTORY

Equipment: None
Number of subjects: One (yourself)
Time per subject: Forty-five minutes
Time for experiment: Forty-five minutes

Constructing a test to assess a personality trait is an involved process. It requires the creation of test items and the validation of these items through administration of the test to large groups of subjects. While it would be impossible to illustrate all the steps in this process through a short

exercise such as this, it is possible to provide an idea about some of the issues that are involved. That is the purpose of this demonstration.

A first draft of a test for a particular personality trait has been created.* Before reading on, you should take this test. Listed below are twenty-one questions for you to answer. Try to put yourself in each of the following situations and on the answer sheet mark the choice that would best describe your reactions. Limit your replies to the choices given and answer every question.

*We thank Lisa Lange, John Prevost, Barb Merriam, Laurie Tunstall, and Julie Nuse for their permission to use the shyness inventory that was prepared as part of a course project supervised by Dr. Charles Morris. We also thank Dr. Morris for kindly supplying the correlational data.

Draft Personality Inventory

	strongly disagree	slightly disagree	slightly agree	strongly agree

1. I am in a crowded bar sitting with some friends. A good-looking individual comes up to me and asks me to dance. I like to dance but I notice that the dance floor is empty and answer no. — 1   2   3   4

2. I get an important exam back and I disagree with the grading on one of the problems. But I accept my grade, avoiding a confrontation with the professor. — 1   2   3   4

3. I enjoy attending seminars and discussion groups as opposed to large lectures. — 1   2   3   4

4. I'm in a restaurant and receive some bad food. Instead of saying something, I stay quiet but leave a small tip. — 1   2   3   4

5. My family is moving to another state and I will be attending a new school. I look forward to meeting new people and making new friends. — 1   2   3   4

6. I find it easy to liven up a dull occasion. — 1   2   3   4

7. I am required to form groups in a class and interact on a subject. The groups are formed but I tend to listen more than offer information. — 1   2   3   4

8. If I were in the waiting room of a doctor's office and a stranger sat down next to me, introduced himself, and started asking me questions, I would feel nervous and uncomfortable. — 1   2   3   4

9. I can usually enjoy myself at a party even if I know almost no one there. — 1   2   3   4

10. A teacher asks questions to which I know the answers, but I never raise my hand for fear that the answers might not be what the teacher is looking for. — 1   2   3   4

11. I become uncomfortable and at a loss for words, usually blushing, when I am given a compliment. — 1   2   3   4

12. I often find myself taking charge in group situations. — 1   2   3   4

13. I prefer being with people and going to parties rather than spending my spare time alone pursuing personal interests or hobbies. — 1   2   3   4

14. If someone was smoking a cigarette in a nonsmoking section and the smoke was bothering me, I wouldn't hesitate to ask the person to put out the cigarette. — 1   2   3   4

15. I often look back at a situation and think of things I should have done or said. — 1   2   3   4

16. I feel proud to be called on to give a toast at a social gathering. — 1   2   3   4

17. I would go out of my way to make a stranger feel comfortable in a group in which the people are unfamiliar to him. — 1   2   3   4

18. When I've been waiting in line for service for a long time and someone cuts in front of me, I feel angry but don't say anything about it. — 1   2   3   4

19. I prefer not to answer the door when I know it's a salesman because I have a hard time getting him to leave once he's inside the door. — 1   2   3   4

20. When I've struck up a conversation with the person sitting next to me, a long plane flight seems more enjoyable.   1   2   3   4

21. I consider myself to be a shy person.   1   2   3   4

Now that you have answered the questionnaire, you are probably aware that it is intended to assess shyness. The questions themselves were constructed as candidates that might have something to do with predicting how shy people are. How can one tell if the questionnaire accomplishes its purpose or which questions are the best predictors of shyness?

One possibility is to examine the face validity of each of the questions. Since you have just completed the questions yourself and since you are now aware that its purpose is to test for shyness, you can do this yourself. Examine each question and decide for yourself whether you think that it would be a good predictor of shyness. That is, does the question ask subjects about a reaction that should depend on how shy the subjects are? Try to pick out the four questions that you think would best predict shyness, and the four that would be least relevant. Note, by the way, that the questions are constructed so that for some (items 1, 2, 4, 7, 8, 10, 11, 15, 18, 19, and 21) a high score (e.g., 4) would indicate more shyness, while for the rest, a low score (e.g., 1) would indicate more shyness. This is only done to provide variety; your assessment of each question should be independent of this point.

Questions that would best predict shyness	Questions that would least predict shyness
1. _____	1. _____
2. _____	2. _____
3. _____	3. _____
4. _____	4. _____

Your judgment of the quality of a question is a measure of face validity (that is, the extent to which a question, on the face of it, is a good predictor of shyness), but this is not the only possible measure of validity. Another criterion is to have some independent measure of a subject's shyness and correlate responses to each question with the measure. Presumably, if a question were a good predictor of shyness, it would correlate highly with this measure.

One such measure is a subject's response to question 21. This question directly asks subjects for their own assessment of whether they consider themselves to be shy. In order to determine how well each test question correlates with this self-assessment of shyness, sixty-nine subjects were given this questionnaire and correlations of each question with question 21 were calculated. They are presented in Table 1 below.

TABLE 1

Correlations of each question in the questionnaire with question 21. A low correlation (a positive or negative value close to 0) indicates that there is little relationship between the answer to that question and the answer to question 21; a high correlation (a value closer to −1 or +1) indicates a relationship between responses to that question and responses to question 21. For example, item 10 has a correlation of .42 with item 21. This means that subjects who tend to agree with the statement in question 10 tend to agree also with the statement in question 21. Likewise, subjects who tend to disagree with the statement in question 10, also tend to disagree with the statement in question 21. A negative correlation, such as in question 6, indicates that subjects who tend to agree with the statement in 6 tend to disagree with the statement in 21. Likewise, those who tend to disagree with the statement in 6 tend to agree with the one in 21 (note that even though a correlation is negative, it still means that there is a relationship between the two items in question, but a reverse relationship).

Question:	1	2	3	4	5	6	7	8	9	10
Correlation:	.23	.08	−.15	−.08	−.20	−.28	.38	−.24	−.24	.42

Question:	11	12	13	14	15	16	17	18	19	20
Correlation:	.29	−.22	−.20	−.27	.32	−.37	−.16	.17	.09	−.07

Compare your judgments of question quality against these correlations to see whether the ones you judged as good have either high positive or high negative values; also, check whether the questions you judged as poor have correlations near 0.

Another validity criterion that may be reasonable is the total score on the test. The logic of using this criterion is that individual questions may vary in how well they indicate shyness, but the test *as a whole* may be a much better indicator. If this were so, then it would be sensible to correlate scores on individual questions with those on the whole test to see which questions best predict the total test score. This was done for the same sixty-nine subjects as above; the correlations are presented in Table 2.

TABLE 2

Correlations of each question with the total test score. As in Table 1, a low value means little relationship of that question with the total test score, while a higher value (either positive or negative) means that there is some relationship. For example, the correlation of .55 for question 10 indicates that subjects who tend to agree with the statement in item 10 tend to have a high total score on the questionnaire, while subjects who tend to disagree with the statement in 10 tend to score low on the whole questionnaire. Another illustration is the correlation of −.49 for question 5. This means that subjects who tend to disagree with the statement in 5 tend to get a high total score, while subjects who tend to agree with the statement in 5 tend to have a low score.

Question:	1	2	3	4	5	6	7	8	9	10
Correlation:	.45	.41	−.54	.13	−.49	−.44	.46	.42	−.53	.55

Question:	11	12	13	14	15	16	17	18	19	20
Correlation:	.37	−.42	−.35	−.44	.40	−.46	−.27	.35	.25	−.01

Again, see how well your judgments of question quality are related to these correlations. Note also an interesting pattern in the two sets of correlations presented in Tables 1 and 2. Item 10 has both the highest absolute correlation with question 21 and the highest correlation with the total test score. Also, item 7 has very high correlations with both criterion measures. This consistency suggests that these two items may well be good, valid indices of shyness. How did you rate these items? Examine the items themselves to see if you can explain why they might be better than others.

Note also that two items, 4 and 20, have very low correlations with both criterion measures.

How did you judge these items? Why do you think they have such low correlations?

If we were to continue to develop a "shyness inventory," we might well try to use other validity criteria as well as the three described above. For example, we might try to use the inventory to predict some behavior that is characteristic of shy people. This would allow us to assess the predictive validity of the test. Whatever the criteria, though, the objective of test construction is to find questions that best predict that which you are trying to assess. This exercise should have given you some insight into the process by which this objective is reached.

CHAPTER 19

Psychopathology

Learning Objectives

1. Distinguish neurosis from psychosis.

DIFFERENT CONCEPTIONS OF MADNESS

Insanity as demonic possession
2. Give examples from historical sources of the treatment of madness as demonic possession.

Insanity as a disease
3. Describe the history of the treatment of insanity as a disease.
4. Describe the somatogenic view of mental illness, referring to the example of general paresis.
5. Define psychogenic disorders and explain the historical role of hysteria in clarifying the nature of these disorders.
6. Discuss the value of the psychogenic-somatogenic distinction.

THE PATHOLOGY MODEL

7. Explain the pathology model of mental illness.

Subcategories of the pathology model
8. Briefly describe the medical, psychoanalytic, and learning models as approaches to psychopathology.

Mental disorder as pathology
9. Discuss the role of pathology and deviance in the definition of mental illness.

Classifying mental disorders
10. Distinguish symptoms and syndromes. Indicate how mental illnesses are classified, referring to the changes in the latest taxonomy, DSM-III.

Explaining disorder: diathesis, stress, and pathology
11. Describe the diathesis-stress explanation of mental illness.
12. What does one have to know in order to explain fully a mental (or bodily) disorder?

SCHIZOPHRENIA

The symptoms
13. Describe the major symptoms of schizophrenia in the areas of thought, motivation, and behavior.

The search for the underlying pathology
14. Show how the assumption of a disorder in focus of activity can explain many of the symptoms of schizophrenia.
15. Review evidence for an organic basis for schizophrenia. Include results from cross-cultural, genetic, and drug studies.
16. Describe the dopamine hypothesis and indicate the types of evidence in favor of it. Suggest what types of experiments might prove it.

More remote causes of schizophrenia
17. Review the evidence for genetic factors in schizophrenia.
18. Describe the role of environmental effects in schizophrenia, including low social status and family pathology.
19. Evaluate the alternative possibilities that the environmental correlates of schizophrenia are caused by or are causes of schizophrenia.

The pathology model and schizophrenia
20. Review the symptoms, underlying pathology, and remote causes of schizophrenia. Apply the diathesis-stress model to this disorder.

AFFECTIVE DISORDERS

The symptom patterns

21. Compare and contrast mania and depression in terms of symptoms.

Organic factors

22. Review the evidence for a role for organic factors in affective disorders.

23. Explain the relation between hypotheses about neurotransmitter deficiencies in depression and the ways in which drugs act to relieve depression.

Psychogenic factors

24. Review the evidence for psychogenic factors in depression.

25. Describe the learned helplessness theory of depression, and summarize the evidence in favor of it that comes from both animal and human research.

26. Discuss whether affective or cognitive factors are primary in depression.

27. Indicate the adequacy of each theory of depression to account for the range of symptoms.

Affective disorders and the diathesis-stress conception

28. Apply the diathesis-stress conception to affective disorders.

ANXIETY DISORDERS

Phobias

29. Describe phobias, and explain how they can be accounted for in terms of conditioning or psychoanalytic concepts. What are the merits of each approach?

Generalized anxiety disorders

30. Describe generalized anxiety disorders, and both conditioning and psychoanalytic explanations for them.

Obsessive-compulsive disorders

31. Briefly describe the symptoms of obsessive-compulsive disorders.

Anxiety disorders and the pathology model

32. To what extent is it necessary to invoke anxiety as a cause of some neuroses? Evaluate the alternative that, at least sometimes, the symptom is the disease.

33. What is the role of learning in anxiety disorders?

CONVERSIONS AND DISSOCIATIVE DISORDERS

34. Contrast conversion and dissociative disorders with anxiety disorders.

Conversion disorders

35. What are conversion disorders, and what is the psychoanalytic explanation of them?

Dissociative disorders

36. Describe amnesia, fugue state, and multiple personality.

Factors that underlie conversions and dissociative conditions

37. Consider both anxiety defense and play-acting explanations of conversions and dissociative disorders. Evaluate the value of psychoanalytic and conditioning accounts of these disorders and the anxiety disorders.

PSYCHOPHYSIOLOGICAL DISORDERS

38. Define psychophysiological disorders. What is the critical difference between psychophysiological disorders and conversion disorders?

Essential hypertension

39. What is essential hypertension, and what is the role of stress and autonomic arousal in causing it?

The diathesis-stress concept and psychophysiological disorders

40. Apply the diathesis-stress model to psychophysiological disorders and to the issue of which type of disorder (e.g., essential hypertension, peptic ulcer) occurs in an individual.

A CATEGORIZING REVIEW

41. Explain how mental disorders can be classified according to the organic or mental basis of both the symptoms and the underlying pathology.

THE SOCIOLOGICAL CRITIQUE OF THE PATHOLOGY MODEL

What society does to those it calls mad

42. Describe the treatment of institutionalized people.

Whom does society call mad?

43. Describe the consequences of being labeled as mentally ill and of being institutionalized.

44. Discuss whether mental illness is almost exclusively defined by culture-specific factors.
45. Describe why labeling theory is inadequate to explain certain serious mental disorders, like schizophrenia.
46. Describe Laing's "romantic" view of schizophrenia and give arguments for and against it.

Social deviance
47. Discuss the distinctions between criminals and sociopaths.
48. Review the causes of sociopathy.

Some contributions of labeling theory
49. Evaluate the contribution of the sociological viewpoints and labeling theory, in particular, to the understanding of sociopathy and other forms of mental "illness." For what types of "illness" is this approach most convincing?

THE SCOPE OF PSYCHOPATHOLOGY

50. Discuss the problem of defining psychopathology and uncovering common principles underlying it.

Programmed Exercises

1. A group of milder psychopathologies in which a person maintains contact with reality is called the _____.

    neuroses

2. A more severe form of psychopathology in which there is loss of contact is called a _____.

    psychosis

DIFFERENT CONCEPTIONS OF MADNESS

3. A dominant early social response to insanity, which resulted in practices as varied as trephining the skull or the burning of witches, was based on the conception of insanity as

    _____ _____.

    demonic possession

4. The great physicians of antiquity assumed that the key to mental derangement was an imbalance between the main body fluids, or _____.

    humors

5. Prior to the 19th century, people with severe mental illness were treated more or less as we currently deal with _____.

    criminals (or prisoners)

6. The disappearance of the psychotic symptoms of _____

    _____ following administration of penicillin provides strong evidence for a view of mental illness as a disease.

    general paresis

    (or syphilis)

7. Mental symptoms which can be directly explained by malfunction at the organic level are called _____. Those, like hysteria, that are best explained at the psychological level are

    somatogenic

    called _____.

    psychogenic

THE PATHOLOGY MODEL

8. According to the _____ _____, a particular disease is considered as the underlying cause of specific mental symptoms.

    pathology model

9. According to the _____ model, mental illness has an organic basis, to be treated with somatic therapies. According to the

    medical

    _____ model, mental disorders are, in large part, the result

    learning

of maladaptive learning. According to the _____ model, mental illness results from psychogenic factors, of the sort described by Freud.

psychoanalytic

10. In the pathology model, the terms "psychopathology" and

"_____ _____" are not synonymous, since a mental illness with a clear pathological base may be quite common in a population.

abnormal psychology

11. A _____ is a pattern of symptoms that go together.

syndrome

12. In the most recent classification or taxonomy of mental illness,

called _____, more emphasis is placed on the description

DSM-III

of disorders, rather than on _____ about their cause.

theories

13. According to the _____ _____ conception, mental illness results from the interaction between a predisposition and some set of environmental events.

diathesis-stress

14. The analysis of mental disorders in the medical model includes

description of remote and immediate _____, which lead to

causes

the _____ of the disorder.

symptoms

SCHIZOPHRENIA

15. The incidence of schizophrenia is about one American out of

every _____.

hundred

16. Schizophrenic symptoms include disorders in thinking and

selective _____.

attention

17. Schizophrenic persons often lose contact with other people as

a result of social _____. This may lead to progressively worse problems, because they have few opportunities for real-

withdrawal

ity _____.

testing

18. Schizophrenic symptoms include elaboration of the private

world, such as _____ of persecution and hearing voices or

delusions

other _____.

hallucinations

19. Schizophrenics typically show either _____ or _____ affect.

apathy, inappropriate

20. Delusions are typical symptoms in the most common form of

schizophrenia, _____ schizophrenia.

paranoid

21. A cognitive theory of schizophrenia holds that many symptoms, especially the disturbances in language and thought, result from an inability to keep things in proper focus. This

results in an inability to hold on to one _____ of thought or action.

line (train)

22. One argument for a biological basis for schizophrenia is that

its incidence is about the same in many different _____.

cultures

23. One argument for an organic basis for schizophrenia is the effectiveness of a group of drugs called _____ in treatment.   phenothiazines

24. A current organic theory of schizophrenia holds that it results from too much brain activity caused by the catecholamine neurotransmitter _____, which may cause the overstimulation characteristic of schizophrenia.   dopamine

25. In accord with the theory that holds that neurons in the schizophrenic's brain are oversensitive to dopamine, a drug like _____, which enhances dopamine activity, makes schizophrenics worse and can induce a schizophrenic-like _____ in normals.   amphetamine

psychosis (syndrome)

26. Twin studies indicate that there is a significant _____ factor in the causation of schizophrenia.   genetic (hereditary)

27. Identical twins show a _____ of 44 percent for schizophrenia.   concordance

28. Studies indicate that schizophrenia is much more common in _____ classes and that class status is both a cause and effect of schizophrenia.   lower

29. The idea that schizophrenia is caused by faulty and contradictory communications from parents to their children is called the _____ _____ hypothesis.   double bind

30. In accord with the diathesis-stress model, the evidence for a genetic predisposition for schizophrenia corresponds to the _____, while the demonstrated role of environment events   diathesis

corresponds to the _____.   stress

AFFECTIVE DISORDERS

31. While schizophrenia can be regarded as essentially a disorder of thought, in the _____ disorders the dominant disturbance is one of mood.   affective

32. The two major types of affective disorders are _____ and   mania

_____.   depression

33. _____ _____ psychosis is a bipolar affective disorder.   Manic-depressive

34. Depression is associated with a high rate of _____.   suicide

35. Twin studies indicate a much higher role for genetic factors in _____ than in _____ affective disorders.   bipolar, unipolar

36. There is evidence that abnormal levels of either of two neurotransmitters, _____ and _____, may account for affective disorders. At high levels, these neurotransmitters may lead   serotonin, norepinephrine

to _____, while at low levels, they may lead to _____.   mania, depression

37. Two major types of antidepressant drugs are _____ _____   monoamine oxidase (MAO)

    _____ and _____. They operate, respectively, by pre-   inhibitors, tricyclics

    venting the _____ of transmitters or by preventing their   breakdown

    _____.   reuptake

38. According to a number of psychogenic approaches to depres-

    sion, the primary disorder is _____, which leads to changes   cognitive

    in _____.   affect (mood)

39. According to the _____ _____ theory of depression,   learned helplessness
    depression is caused by an expectation that one's actions will
    have no significant effects.

ANXIETY DISORDERS

40. An irrational and intense fear of an object or situation is

    called a _____.   phobia

41. According to a conditioning view, phobias expand by the pro-

    cess of _____.   generalization

42. According to the psychoanalytic approach, a phobia is the

    result of _____ of an unacceptable fear onto another ob-   displacement
    ject. If this view is correct, then removing a phobia should
    produce a new phobia, by the process of _____ _____.   symptom substitution

43. In phobias, anxiety is focused on a particular object or situa-

    tion. In _____ _____ disorders, it is all-pervasive, or   general anxiety

    _____ _____.   free-floating

44. In _____ _____ neurosis, anxiety is produced by persis-   obsessive-compulsive
    tent internal events (thoughts or wishes).

45. _____ are persistent thoughts. _____ are acts performed   Obsessions, Compulsions
    in an attempt to deal with these thoughts.

46. The success of _____ therapy suggests that, in at least some   behavior
    anxiety disorders, the symptom *is* the disease.

47. In _____ or _____ disorders, according to the psycho-   conversion, dissociative
    analytic view, the primary defense against anxiety is repression
    or denial.

48. In conversion disorders, the principal symptom is a _____   somatic (bodily)
    disorder, such as paralysis.

49. In dissociative disorders, a whole set of mental events are

    removed from ordinary _____. These disorders include   consciousness

    _____ _____ and _____ (cite two types).   fugue state, amnesia, or
                                                                          multiple personality

PSYCHOPHYSIOLOGICAL DISORDERS

50. In _____ disorders, organic damage is caused by psycho-physiological factors.

psychophysiological

51. Excessive and prolonged sympathetic arousal is thought to be

the cause of high blood pressure, or _____.

hypertension

52. It is believed that hypertension results from continual _____

sympathetic

arousal. This may be caused by excessive _____.

stress

53. In the face of continued stress, some people get peptic ulcers, some get essential hypertension, some get other psychophysiological disorders, and some show no obvious effects. These differences may be accounted for in terms of a preexisting

somatic _____.

diathesis (predisposition, susceptibility)

54. Psychophysiological disorders have primarily _____ symp-

organic

toms and primarily _____ underlying pathology.

mental

The SOCIOLOGICAL CRITIQUE OF THE PATHOLOGY MODEL

55. According to Szasz and others, at least some of the symptoms of mental illness result from the fact that a person is given a

specific diagnosis or _____ of some type of mental illness.

label

56. D. L. Rosenhan's study shows that people who lie about hav-

ing _____ _____ can be diagnosed as schizophrenic and may remain on a mental ward for some weeks, while behaving totally normally, because of this initial faked symptom.

auditory hallucinations

57. According to _____, schizophrenia is, not a pathological condition, but an attempt at mental rebirth.

R. D. Laing

58. Someone who behaves antisocially without signs of remorse is

called an antisocial personality, or _____.

sociopath

59. Szasz, Laing, and others have emphasized the stigmatizing

effect of being _____ as mentally ill and the dangers of

labeled

using _____ as a sole criterion for mental illness.

deviance

60. Certain groups of people traditionally placed in mental institutions primarily need physical care or help. Included in this group are older people with failing mental capacities, who

suffer from _____ _____.

senile dementia

Self Test

1. Treatment of "mental disorders" in the past by such procedures as trephination or burning at the stake is indicative of a conception of these disorders as caused by:

a. microorganisms
b. criminal impulses
c. degeneration
d. demonic possession

2. The discovery of a cure for general paresis gave support to the view of mental illness as:
   a. demonic possession
   b. akin to criminality
   c. a disease of society
   d. a disease, within the pathology model

3. The fundamental difference between a psychosis and a neurosis is:
   a. the psychosis involves more detachment from reality
   b. the neurosis is easier to cure
   c. all psychoses have a known biological cause
   d. b and c
   e. a and c

4. If a specific enzyme lack was pinned down as the case of a previously poorly understood severe mental illness, it would change its classification from _____ to _____.
   a. psychosis to neurosis
   b. neurosis to psychosis
   c. psychoanalytic to medical
   d. psychogenic to somatogenic
   e. minor to serious

5. Which of the following statements about the nature of mental disorders is true?
   a. all mental disorders are a product of society
   b. all mental disorders will eventually be treatable with drugs or chemicals, since they all have some sort of somatic base
   c. according to the medical model, illiteracy is a mental disease
   d. while serious disorders (psychoses) can be cured with drugs, neuroses cannot be so cured
   e. none of the above

6. Both the medical model and the psychoanalytic model:
   a. emphasize somatogenic disorders
   b. fail to explain conversion disorders
   c. are limited versions of the pathology model
   d. emphasize psychogenic disorders

7. It is probably true that most Swiss today are at least bilingual. Then a monolinguist Swiss would be deviant or abnormal. Classification of such a person as suffering from a mental disorder would depend, according to the pathology model, on:
   a. the establishment of the deviance

   b. demonstration that monolingualism seriously impairs functioning in Switzerland
   c. description of some underlying pathology that caused monolingualism
   d. b or c
   e. none of the above

8. Understanding of a disease includes knowledge of its symptoms, underlying pathology, remote causes, and:
   a. immediate cause
   b. psychogenicity
   c. psychoanalytic roots
   d. deviance

9. Certain types of color blindness occur, invariably, if a person inherits a particular gene or pair of genes from his or her parents. This "disorder" does not fit the diathesis-stress model, because:
   a. there is no diathesis
   b. there is no stress
   c. both diathesis and stress are present, but either is sufficient for manifestation of the disorder
   d. both diathesis and stress are present, but they do not interact
   e. c or d

10. The general idea that schizophrenics have difficulty distinguishing between personal (internal) and external events can be used to explain some of the symptoms of schizophrenia. Which of the following schizophrenic symptoms can be explained in this manner?
    a. delusions
    b. hallucinations
    c. catatonic immobility
    d. a and b
    e. all of the above

11. Delusions differ from hallucinations in that:
    a. delusions are associated with ideas of persecution
    b. delusions are based on interpretations of real events
    c. delusions are primarily visual while hallucinations are auditory
    d. delusions are associated with apathy
    e. delusions cause social withdrawal

12. The idea that the fundamental disorder in schizophrenia is a cognitive deficit having to do with failure to keep things in proper focus can explain all but one of the follow-

ing. Which feature of schizophrenia cannot be easily explained?
a. disconnected thought
b. rhyming associations
c. social withdrawal (as a consequence of overstimulation)
d. apathy

13. The fact that schizophrenic symptoms appear with about the same frequency in very different cultures can be taken to support a(n) _____ basis for schizophrenia.
a. psychogenic
b. abnormal
c. organic
d. cultural

14. Chlorpromazine is a drug in the phenothiazine family and is effective as therapy for schizophrenia. Phenothiazines are known to block the action of dopamine at the synapse. Dopamine is a neurotransmitter. Low levels of dopamine in animals lead to the neglect of stimulation. Taken together, these findings suggest:
a. that schizophrenia results from an excess of dopamine, leading to overstimulation or overload
b. that there is a strong, enzyme-based hereditary deficit in dopamine in schizophrenics
c. that schizophrenics have too little dopamine, leading to cognitive and affective symptoms
d. that there is probably no direct relation between dopamine levels and schizophrenia
e. that drugs should be given simpler names

15. Penicillin : general paresis :: _____ : schizophrenia
a. dopamine
b. amphetamine
c. phenothiazines
d. norepinephrine

16. The concordance rate among identical twins for schizophrenia is 44 percent, while the comparable figure for fraternal twins is 9 percent. These results suggest that:
a. genetic factors predominate as causes of schizophrenia
b. there is a very weak genetic component in the causation of schizophrenia
c. schizophrenia is essentially caused by environmental factors

d. the primary cause of schizophrenia is probably lack of a neurotransmitter, rather than a genetic effect
e. both genetic and environmental factors play important roles in the causation of schizophrenia

17. The incidence of schizophrenia is higher in the lower classes. This suggests that:
a. social class is a causal factor in schizophrenia
b. schizophrenics are lower in social class because they are schizophrenic
c. schizophrenia does not have a strong organic component
d. a and/or b
e. all of the above

18. According to some, family pathology is a cause of schizophrenia. It has been suggested that the critical problem is in self-contradictory communication to the child by the parents. This is called the _____ hypothesis.
a. dopamine
b. genetic
c. familial
d. double bind

19. There are some reports of poorer mental health in the *adoptive* parents of schizophrenics. This, along with studies of differences in the behaviors of mothers to their schizophrenic and normal children, suggests that:
a. pathological home environments cause schizophrenia
b. schizophrenic children can induce pathological behavior in parents
c. there is an organic basis for schizophrenia
d. there is a psychogenic basis for schizophrenia

20. The pathology model of schizophrenia presented in the text includes all but one of the following assumptions. Which assumption is not included?
a. family pathology leads to deficits in the function of brain neurotransmitters
b. some genetic factors contribute to pathology in the function of certain brain neurotransmitters
c. neurotransmitter deficits can lead to inability to focus in time or space

d. inability to focus in time or space can lead to social withdrawal

e. inability to focus in space and time can lead to inappropriate emotions

21. Manic disorders share with some forms of schizophrenia which of the following symptoms?

a. hallucinations

b. social withdrawal

c. shifting from one subject to another in conversation

d. blunted affect in response to stimuli that would normally elicit affective responses

e. enormous amounts of energy

22. A person shows little interest in the world around him. He shows little emotional response and has disconnected thoughts. On this basis, the most likely guess for a diagnosis would be:

a. mania

b. depression

c. bipolar affective disorder

d. schizophrenia

23. According to biochemical theories, high levels of norepinephrine or serotonin are causative factors in:

a. mania

b. depression

c. schizophrenia

d. a and b

e. a and c

24. All but one of the following provide evidence in favor of the theory that low levels of norepinephrine in the brain lead to depression. Which of these findings does not support this theory?

a. drugs that deplete norepinephrine cause depression in normals

b. helplessness training in animals depletes norepinephrine

c. drugs which increase the availability of norepinephrine are effective in therapy for depression

d. norepinephrine is involved with the systems in the brain that produce arousal and activation

e. dopamine, a neurotransmitter related to norepinephrine, is implicated in the causation of schizophrenia

25. In terms of the biochemical theory that holds that high levels of norepinephrine (or serotonin) cause mania, which of the fol-

lowing should be an effective therapy for mania?

a. tricyclics

b. MAO inhibitors

c. a drug that increases reuptake of norepinephrine

d. a drug that decreases the rate of breakdown of norepinephrine in the synaptic gap

e. a drug that increases the rate of synthesis of norepinephrine in the synaptic terminals

26. According to Seligman's helplessness views, the low affect of depression results from:

a. low levels of norepinephrine

b. negative cognitions that produce affective changes

c. a tendency towards suicidal thoughts

d. bipolar mood change

e. self-hatred

27. Which of the following symptoms of depression is particularly difficult to explain for both the biochemical and psychogenic (learned helplessness) theories?

a. negative affect

b. inactivity

c. responsiveness to antidepressant drugs

d. self-hatred

28. According to the learned helplessness theory of depression, which of the following would be the most relevant diathesis for depression?

a. depletion of norepinephrine or serotonin

b. past experiences in which a person could not control his/her environment

c. genetic factors

d. parents who gave the person too much responsibility as a child

e. c or d

29. Which of the following lists of disorders is arranged in order of *increasing* importance of psychogenic causative factors?

a. schizophrenia, depression, manic-depressive psychosis

b. schizophrenia, general paresis, phobias

c. phobias, depression, mental retardation

d. general paresis, depression, phobias

e. schizophrenia, phobias, general paresis

30. According to psychoanalysts, phobias represent:

a. displacement of a repressed fear onto a conceptually relaxed object

b. repression of infantile sexual urges, leading to excess fear

c. results of traumatic pairing of an object with a very negative stimulus

d. a form of stimulus generalization

e. a form of stimulus displacement

31. A critical feature of phobias is that they are:
  a. irrational fears
  b. any type of fears
  c. conditioned
  d. results of displacement disorder

32. One effective treatment for specific phobias is to expose the phobic person to weak instances of the phobic object while the subject relaxes. The strength of the stimulus is gradually increased. Under these conditions, many phobias disappear, and no undesirable symptoms seem to replace them. This therapeutic success is an argument in favor of:
  a. the conditioning view of phobias
  b. the psychoanalytic view of phobias
  c. a diathesis-stress model of phobias
  d. the importance of symptom substitution
  e. none of the above

33. A disorder in which anxiety is handled by repetitive and ritualistic acts is called:
  a. phobia
  b. fugue state
  c. obsessive-compulsive disorder
  d. conversion hysteria

34. Behavior therapists argue that the neurotic symptom _____ the disease.
  a. causes
  b. is
  c. can be separated from
  d. is one consequence of the underlying
  e. is a reaction to

35. Amnesia, fugue state, and multiple personality are all examples of:
  a. obsessive-compulsive neuroses
  b. psychoses
  c. conversion hysteria
  d. dissociative reactions

36. The fundamental distinction between anxiety disorders and conversion or dissociative disorders is that:
  a. anxiety disorders are more generalized
  b. anxiety is an explanation only for anxiety disorders
  c. organic factors are much more heavily involved in anxiety disorders
  d. in anxiety disorders, the anxiety is expressed more overtly
  e. a and b

37. Psychoanalysts and behavior therapists would probably agree that neuroses are:
  a. related to anxiety
  b. learned
  c. often related to prior trauma
  d. all of the above
  e. none of the above

38. Hypertension is believed to be caused by:
  a. thickening of artery walls
  b. higher sensitivity of artery muscles to stimuli
  c. increased autonomic responsiveness to stressful stimuli
  d. high levels of exposure to emotional stress
  e. all of the above

39. If a study found that, under the stress of threat of terrorism for a period of years, a group of 100 people developed a wide variety of psychophysiological disorders, including ulcers in some, hypertension in others, and asthma in still others, this would be evidence in favor of:
  a. a diathesis factor
  b. a stress factor
  c. a role for neurotransmitters
  d. an organic origin for psychophysiological disorders
  e. therapeutic use of the antibiotic terrormycin

40. A fundamental difference between a conversion disorder and a psychophysiological disorder is that:
  a. treatment of the organic "complaint" is much more likely to be effective in psychophysiological disorders
  b. psychophysiological disorders are much more likely to be accompanied by low levels of neurotransmitters
  c. conversion disorders are mental in origin
  d. anxiety is critically involved in the origin of almost all psychophysiological disorders
  e. psychophysiological disorders always involve the nervous system

41. In terms of the model of categorization of mental disorders in the text, diabetes : psychophysiological disorders :: schizophrenia : _____.
  a. general paresis
  b. bipolar affective disorders
  c. asthma
  d. sociopathy
  e. pneumonia

42. According to Szasz, in practice, people are
    treated as mentally ill simply because they
    are:
    a. self-destructive
    b. suffering some sort of organic disorder
    c. deviant
    d. from another culture
    e. taking drugs

43. Labeling theory predicts that mental disor-
    der is determined by what the culture labels
    as a disorder. Which of the following find-
    ings argues against this view?
    a. Rosenhan's study on being sane in in-
       sane places
    b. normal occurrence of behaviors in some
       cultures that are considered deviant in
       others
    c. roughly equal incidents of schizophrenia
       in different cultures
    d. the very high incidence of conversion
       disorders in Europe early in this century
    e. none of the above

44. The fact that "recovered" schizophrenics
    describe their inner experiences (during the
    period when they were diagnosed as schizo-
    phrenic) as very unpleasant argues against:
    a. Rosenhan's interpretation of mental ill-
       ness
    b. Laing's view of schizophrenia as mental
       rebirth
    c. the medical model view
    d. the neurotransmitter theory of schizo-
       phrenia
    e. none of the above

45. A person is apprehended after committing a
    series of crimes. The question is whether he
    should be treated as a criminal or a socio-
    path. All but one of the following charac-
    teristics suggest that he is a sociopath. Indi-
    cate the characteristic that suggests a crimi-
    nal, rather than sociopath, diagnosis:
    a. he is a loner
    b. he feels no guilt for the committed
       crimes
    c. he is anxious
    d. he is charming
    e. he is intelligent

46. Ironically, though labeling theory and other
    sociological views of mental illness were
    founded on an analysis of schizophrenia,
    they seem much better able to handle:
    a. depression
    b. sociopathy
    c. drug addiction
    d. b and c
    e. none of the above

Answer Key for Self Test

1. d pp. 638–39	24. e p. 662
2. d p. 642	25. c p. 662
3. a pp. 637–38	26. b pp. 663–64
4. d pp. 642–43	27. d p. 664
5. e pp. 642–44	28. b p. 664
6. c p. 645	29. d pp. 642–71
7. d pp. 645–46	30. a p. 667
8. a p. 647	31. a p. 665
9. b p. 647	32. a p. 666
10. d p. 651	33. c p. 668
11. b p. 651	34. b p. 669
12. d p. 651	35. d p. 670
13. c p. 653	36. d p. 670
14. a p. 654	37. d p. 671
15. c p. 654	38. e pp. 672–73
16. e p. 655	39. a pp. 673–74
17. d pp. 656–57	40. a p. 672
18. d p. 657	41. d p. 674
19. b p. 658	42. c p. 677
20. a pp. 658–59	43. c p. 677
21. c p. 660	44. b p. 679
22. d pp. 649–50	45. c pp. 680–81
23. a p. 662	46. d pp. 682–83

Investigating Psychological Phenomena

DEPRESSION AND NEGATIVE EXPERIENCES

Equipment: Pencil, paper, and stopwatch or
watch with second indicator
Number of subjects: One (yourself; you will need
the cooperation of a friend to serve as a timer for
about five minutes)
Time per subject: Twenty minutes
Time for experimenter: Twenty minutes

Depression is a very common disturbance. It can vary from almost universal "blue" moods to a serious, chronic, and incapacitating disorder. Because at least some of the characteristics of deep (psychotic) depression occur occasionally in most people, it is possible to study depression in a general population. In any population, there seems to be a more or less continuous distribution of people along a dimension running from depression to elation.

Severe depression is characterized by depressed mood, loss of interest in others and normally desirable things (such as food), feelings of hopelessness, helplessness, and worthlessness, and slowed down thought and motor activity. Many of these symptoms appear in mild forms in the general population. It is reasonable to expect that mildly depressed people will show some of the same bases or causes of their symptoms as severely depressed people.

A number of theories of depression are outlined in the text. These include biochemical explanations (e.g., depletion of norepinephrine), and psychological theories emphasizing hopelessness or learned helplessness. In this study we will explore a particularly simple additional theory: People are depressed because bad things happen to them. Clearly, some people get depressed in the face of success and others remain nondepressed following a series of adverse events. Nonetheless, it seems very reasonable that negative experiences would contribute to the causation of depression. We will test the hypothesis that people who are more depressed have had relatively more adverse experiences in the recent past.

A major purpose of this exercise is to illustrate some of the difficulties that arise in the scientific study of psychopathology. More than in previous studies in this manual, we want to make you aware of the problem of making definitive measurements that clearly support a particular hypothesis. We want you to appreciate the difficulty of research and at the same time realize that progress can be made.

The first problem that we face is this: How do we measure depression? A basic issue that arises is the matter of "subjective" or "objective" measurement. In the case of a "mood" disorder, one might be inclined to subjective measurement, and indeed, much of the diagnosis of depression is concerned with what people say about how they feel. More objective measurements would involve observation of people (facial expression, level of activity) or having them report on their own activities (how many hours they sleep each night, for example). In this study we look at a totally subjective measure, the subject's rating of his or her own mood. Remember that we are dealing with the range of depression and elation seen in the general population, and not with people actually diagnosed as depressed. In the case of diagnosis, interview and observation by an experienced clinician is involved, sometimes along with administration of a question inventory. We will use only self-ratings of mood and will collect two such ratings: one for the subject's momentary mood (how depressed he or she feels now) and the other for how depressed he has felt, in general, over the past year.

The second problem is this: How do we develop a measure of the incidence of negative and positive events in the recent life of each subject. We will use as our measure the subject's recall of negative and positive events over the past year. There are many problems and alternative interpretations of the results of this procedure. We will discuss them after you have served as a subject in this study.

Fill out the two rating scales below and enter your self-ratings on the answer sheet at the end of this section. Then continue to the recall task.

Rate what you judge to be your mood, right now. Circle the most appropriate number.

Extremely Depressed	Very Depressed	Moderately Depressed	Slightly Depressed	Neither Depressed Nor Happy
9	8	7	6	5

Slightly Happy	Moderately Happy	Very Happy	Extremely Happy
4	3	2	1

Rate what you judge to have been your mood, on the average, over the last twelve months.

Extremely Depressed	Very Depressed	Moderately Depressed	Slightly Depressed	Neither Depressed Nor Happy
9	8	7	6	5

Slightly Happy	Moderately Happy	Very Happy	Extremely Happy
4	3	2	1

RECALL OF NEGATIVE AND POSITIVE EVENTS

For this measure you will need the assistance of a friend who will time two separate two-minute intervals for you. No one but you will see what you write down.

You will go through two recall tasks, in order. Get a pen or pencil and sit at a table. When you are comfortable, ask a friend to say "Go" when the second hand of a watch crosses 12. When your friend says "go," turn to the next page, read the sentence at the top, and follow the instructions.

Ask your friend to say "stop" when two minutes have elapsed. You should then stop the task.

The next time the second hand passes 12 (i.e., a minute after you complete the first part of the task), have your friend time another two mintues. When he says "go," turn to the page after the one you had just written on, read the instructions, and follow them for two minutes.

Do not read on until you have completed the above task.

You are asked to perform the following task for exactly two minutes.

Someone will time the two minutes. When he says "go" read the sentence below and follow the instructions. Continue until you hear "stop" at two mintues.

List below all of the negative things that have happened to you in the last twelve months.

Don left
Karens Wedd canc.
Christmas
Wedd anniv.
Don & my arguments.
money problems
family (sisters unsupportve at times)
sisters interfere
mom mad at me
no sex life.
selling house
looking for new house

You are asked to perform the following task for exactly two minutes, following the performance of the "bad events" task.

Someone will time the two minutes. When he says "go", read the sentence below and follow the instructions. Continue until you hear "stop" at two minutes.

List below all of the positive things that have happened to you in the last twelve months.

friends great
3 kids wonderful
visits to Dr Kelly
affirmed ability to cope
raises at work
new friends
college course
looking inward
reaching out to friends in trouble
selected to teach STEP.

Add up the number of negative and the number of positive events that you remembered. Put these numbers on the answer sheet at the end of this section. Also enter the difference between the number of negative events and the number of positive events (# negative events minus # positive events), and the total # of events recalled (# negative events plus # positive events).

ANALYSIS OF DATA

We have obtained this same data (depression ratings and event scores) from sixty-four undergraduate students at the University of Michigan. We will present these data here. You will add your own results to theirs, and we will then discuss the results.

MEASURES OF DEPRESSION

We used two measures of depression: Rated mood now and rated mood over the last twelve months. You might expect that momentary and long-term mood would be related but that the two could sometimes be different. That, in fact, is just what our data show. Below is a scatter plot that presents the data from all sixty-four subjects (see the statistical appendix to the text to learn more about scatter plots). Each point on the plot represents the two mood scores for one subject. Enter your own data point.

There is a positive relation between the two measures of depression. All relations described in these results will be expressed as correlation coefficients (see the statistical appendix). A value of +1.00 indicates a perfect positive correlation; a value of −1.00 a perfect negative correlation, and a value of 0.00 indicates no relation at all.

Our measure of "mood now" correlates +.458 with the measure of "mood over one year."

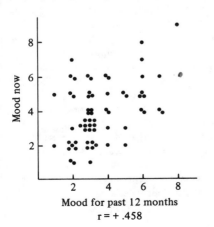

r = + .458

Looking at the scatter plot, you can see that there is some relation between the two mood measures. The general pattern of dots goes from lower left (happy on both scores) to upper right (depressed on both scores). But there are some exceptions: The correlation is positive, but far from perfect. Mark your point on the graph. Does your point fit in with the general pattern, or is it something of an exception? If an exception, can you explain this (e.g., it has been a very good year for you, but something unpleasant just happened to you)?

EVENT SCORES AND DEPRESSION

Before we test the major hypothesis (relatively more negative events in more depressed people), we can examine another prediction that can be made from the symptoms of seriously depressed people. Such people are characterized by a slowing down of action and thought. If this symptom also appears, in milder form, in the low levels of depression in the student population, we would expect a slowdown in memory search, along with other mental events. Therefore, we would expect that more depressed students would recall fewer events, positive or negative. (This type of finding would surely be true in a comparison of seriously depressed hospitalized patients versus "normal" subjects.) We can test for this possibility by computing the correlation between self-rated depression (mood now) and the total number of events recalled (positive plus negative events). Note that because high scores on the depression rating mean more depression and high scores also represent large numbers of events recalled, we would expect a negative correlation: High depression scores go with low event recall scores.

For our sixty-four subjects, the correlation between "mood now" and the total events is −.052: There is no evidence of any relation. Enter your score on these two measures in the scatter plot below. You can see by examining the scatter plot that the two measures do not seem to be related. The relations between "mood over one year" and total events is also small: The correlation is +.135 (this is very small, but also in the direction opposite to the direction we predicted). There are two possible interpretations of our result. One is that our sample is not representative of the population, and that there actually is a negative depression—total event relation. Given the data we have, there is no reason to believe this. Another interpretation is that there is no relation, but that there might well be such a relation if we looked at severely depressed people as well: That is, the slowdown of mental function may only be marked in severe depression.

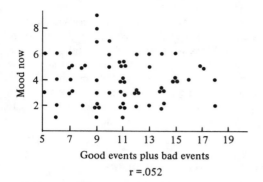

r =.052

We now ask whether increased depression goes with a higher relative incidence of negative events. If this was true, we would expect a positive correlation between either depression score and the difference between number of negative and number of positive events recalled. We present below the scatter plot for both depression scores. Enter your own points on each of these plots. Just by inspecting these scatter plots you should be able to see that there is a positive relation: Higher depression scores *tend* to go with higher negative minus positive event scores. In fact, the correlations are:

Mood now vs negative-positive events r = +.460
Mood over one year vs negative-positive events r = +.325

The relations are not overwhelming, but there is a clear relation. For example the .460 correlation is significant at more than the .001 level: This means that a correlation this high could come about less than one chance in 1000 if there was no relation between mood now and negative-positive events in the population (see the statistical appendix).

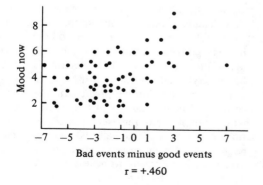

r = +.460

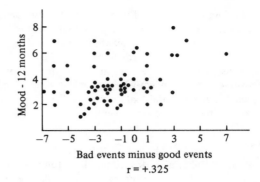

Bad events minus good events

r = +.325

DISCUSSION AND COMMENTS

Our hypothesis that in college populations, depression as measured by self-rating is positively related to relative recall of recent negative events, has been confirmed. We will now discuss a few problems in interpreting these results, in order to make you more aware of the type of thinking that must go into research in general, and especially in this area.

First, our measure of events can be interpreted in a number of ways. We did not actually measure the number of positive and negative events that our subjects experienced. We measured their *recall* for these events. A predominance of negative events could mean either that the subject experienced more of them or that the subject selectively remembers them . . . presumably because she is depressed. Remember that correlations show relations, but not causes (see the statistical appendix). Our hypothesis was that negative events cause depression. But the results of our study could be taken to indicate that in a relatively depressed mood, a person is more likely to remember negative events. The fact that the correlation was bigger between negative minus positive events and mood now, as opposed to mood over the last year, suggests that current mood may well influence what one thinks about. Of course, it is also possible that both effects exist: Negative events lead to depression and depression leads to selective memory for negative events. There is some evidence in the literature for both of these effects. Under further activities, we will discuss ways of finding out whether both of these effects actually occur.

Second, even if more negative events do occur in more depressed people, the events may not be a cause of depression. By virtue of being depressed, more negative events may occur to a person. For example, a depressed student will be less active, less inclined to study, and will probably not perform as well as he could in school.

Third, the same event that is evaluated as negative by someone who is depressed may not be considered negative by that same person when he is in a good mood (or by another person in a better mood). Many events may be both positive and negative (e.g., receiving a B in a course when one hoped for a A but did very little work and actually worried about getting a C, or the break-up of a relationship which had been unsatisfactory for some years). Read through your own events and decide how many could be seen as positive or negative.

We have just begun to scratch the surface, but we hope that you can appreciate the fact that a study like this would be just a beginning and that many more studies would have to be done to clarify the relation between negative events and depression. It should also be clear that whatever that relation is, there are many factors that influence depression. After all, the correlations we do have between depression and events are significant, but they are not that high. We might improve the correlations by getting better measures of depression and negative and positive events. But we also know from other studies, including those dealing with levels of catecholamines in the brain and specific types of past experiences (e.g., helplessness), that other factors are involved.

FURTHER ACTIVITIES

Try to think of some ways in which you could pull apart the effects of actual negative experiences and selective recall of them. After you decide on a few methods, read our suggestions below.

One approach is to get a more objective measure of the actual negative and positive events that a person has experienced. It is not practical to follow them around for a year. But one could get a fair measure by giving them a checklist of rather objective events, that are clearly negative or positive. Thus you could ask someone whether, over the past year:

A close relative or friend died
A course was failed
A job was lost
A favorite team had a disappointing season
A close relationship was broken

and so on, and of course, a set of positive events.

One could then compare the negative minus positive recall score to the results of the checklist. What would you administer first to the subjects: The free recall or the checklist? Why? You could try to make up an appropriate checklist for college students. It isn't easy.

A second approach is to test whether depressed people selectively remember negative events. For example, you could write a story that included a number of negative and positive events. It could be read to subjects and one could measure their recall for the story, say one hour later. One could look at whether people who are more depressed remember relatively more of the negative events.

Answer Sheet

(If your instructor collects the data, fill out the report sheet in Appendix B.)

Self-rating of mood now (enter number) ____6____

Self-rating of mood over last twelve months (enter number) ____8____

Number of negative events recalled ____12____

Number of positive events recalled ____10____

Negative minus positive events ____2____

Negative plus positive events ____22.____

CHAPTER 20

Treatment of Psychopathology

Learning Objectives

SOMATIC THERAPIES

1. Be aware of the two major approaches to the treatment of mental illness and their theoretical underpinnings.

Drug therapies

2. Know the main types of psychiatric drugs and their uses. What evidence is there that such drugs function specifically as antischizophrenic or antidepressant agents?
3. Evaluation of drug therapy is difficult. Be prepared to discuss necessary conditions for proper evaluation. Refer to control groups, the placebo effect, and the double blind technique in your discussion.
4. Know about the drawbacks of drug therapy.

Other somatic therapies

5. What is the rationale for the use of prefrontal lobotomy in the treatment of mental illness? What is the evidence on this technique?
6. Be aware of the role of electroconvulsive shock treatment (ECT). Know when such treatment is warranted.

PSYCHOTHERAPY

7. Be able to distinguish the four major branches of psychotherapy. Know what features characterize these schools.

Classical psychoanalysis

8. What investigative techniques are used in classical psychoanalysis? What can be said about the validity of psychoanalytic interpretations? Of what relevance is transference?

Modern versions of psychoanalysis

9. Know what variations on traditional psychoanalysis can be made by the neo-Freudians.

Behavior therapy

10. What basic assumptions are made by behavior therapists? How are these assumptions translated into treatment techniques?
11. How does systematic desensitization use response incompatibility in the eradication of phobias?
12. Compare and contrast systematic desensitization and flooding.
13. Describe aversive therapy.
14. How do cognitive therapies differ from traditional psychotherapy?
15. What techniques are used to improve the neurotic's interpersonal skills?

Humanistic therapies

16. How do humanistic therapies approach mental illness?

Some common themes

17. What common themes underlie the various therapeutic schools?

EVALUATING THERAPEUTIC OUTCOME

18. What extraneous factors should be considered in evaluating therapies?
19. What is the evidence concerning the effectiveness of psychotherapy?
20. Discuss Gordon Paul's study of therapeutic outcome in terms of both methodology and results.

EXTENSIONS ON PSYCHOTHERAPY

21. What extensions of psychotherapy are now common?
22. How effective are such therapies and how do

their goals compare to those of classical psychoanalysis?

23. Be familiar with the arguments for and against the effectiveness of psychotherapy.

Programmed Exercises

SOMATIC THERAPIES

1. Historically, proposed treatments for mental illness have fallen into one of two categories. One treats the illness at a(n)

   _____ level, while the other uses a(n) _____ approach.   biological, psychological

2. Attempting to restore the proper harmony among the bodily humors in order to reestablish the balance between bodily and

   mental functions was the purpose of early _____ _____   somatic therapies
   such as bloodletting.

3. A schizophrenic patient undergoing drug therapy has the

   greatest chance of being helped by the drug _____ .   chlorpromazine

4. It has been suggested that chlorpromazine acts merely as a(n)

   _____ , but the available evidence indicates that chlor-   sedative

   promazine and other antischizophrenic drugs have a _____   specific
   drug effect.

5. An individual feels extremely depressed most of the time. We

   would expect one of the _____ drugs to be most effective   tricyclic
   in relieving his symptoms.

6. Unlike other drug therapies, _____ seems to have preventa-   lithium
   tive powers in the treatment of manic-depression.

7. Simple "before-and-after" measurements are not adequate for evaluating the effectiveness of a drug because they don't take

   _____ _____ into account.   spontaneous improvement

8. A set of patients was given sugar pills and told that they were potent pain killers. Many of the patients reported that the "pain killer" was working. This illustrates the effect of a(n)

   _____ .   placebo

9. It is hypothesized that a new drug will alleviate symptoms of air sickness. One hundred volunteers received an injection of this colorless liquid, while another 100 volunteers received an injection of saline solution (a colorless and totally inert liquid). All 200 subjects took part in a simulated flight. Both subjective and objective indices of discomfort were recorded. Neither patient nor experimenter knew who received the drug. This

   study used a(n) _____ _____ technique to guard against   double blind
   any effects of expectations.

10. The biggest cost associated with drug therapy is the likelihood

    of _____ _____ _____ .   unpleasant side effects

11. In a prefrontal lobotomy, the connections between the _____   thalamus

    and the _____ lobes are severed.   frontal

12. Electroconvulsive shock treatment (ECT) is most effective in

    the treatment of _____ ; however, repeated shocks may   depression

    cause _____ _____ and _____ .   brain damage, amnesia

PSYCHOTHERAPY

13. According to the _____ school, neurotic ills stem from   psychoanalytic
    unconscious defenses against unacceptable urges.

14. A patient is asked to say whatever comes into his mind. This

    technique is known as _____ _____ .   free association

15. During a therapy session involving free association a patient
    repeatedly changed the subject or forgot what he was about to

    say. This patient was displaying _____ , an indication that   resistance
    he was about to remember something that he had previously
    tried to forget.

16. While Freud wanted patients to gain insight into their motives,

    he didn't want these insights to be merely _____ ; _____   intellectual, emotional
    involvement is necessary for genuine self-discovery.

17. Freud considered first _____ and then _____ as the   catharsis, transference
    means for producing emotional involvement.

18. The _____ _____ view emphasizes interpersonal and   neo-Freudian
    cultural factors rather than psychosexual development.

19. Behavior therapists hold that neurosis is caused by maladap-

    tive _____ which can be corrected through _____ .   learning, reeducation

20. The major goal of behavior therapists in treating phobias is to

    break the link between the _____ stimulus and the _____   conditioned, fear
    response.

21. Sequential tensing and relaxing of the major muscles produces
    muscular relaxation, which is considered incompatible with a
    fear response. Pairing the former with fear-evoking stimuli in

    order to eradicate phobias is part of the _____ _____   systematic desensitization
    paradigm.

22. Since fear-evoking stimuli can seldom be brought into the
    treatment room, systematic desensitization must depend on the

    patient's _____ of fear-evoking situations according to a(n)   imagination

    _____ _____ .   anxiety hierarchy

23. A man who is afraid of heights is asked to imagine that he is
    standing on the observation deck at the top of the Empire
    State Building and leaning over the edge. The therapist is try-

ing to _____ the patient with anxiety and _____ the link   flood, extinguish
between the stimulus and fear response.

24. In order to break compulsive fingernail biters of their habit,
we coat their nails with a harmless but extremely bitter liquid
so that they experience an unpleasant taste each time they bite

their nails. This is an example of _____ therapy.   aversive

25. In contrast to behavior therapists, some therapists dispense
with all conditioning techniques and, instead, help the patient
acquire more appropriate ways of thinking. This is known as

_____ therapy.   cognitive

26. In one type of cognitive therapy developed by Albert Ellis, the
patient is asked to discover the illogical phrases used in
anxiety-producing situations. This type of therapy is known as

_____ _____ psychotherapy.   rational-emotive

27. Once old, undesirable behavior patterns are eliminated, new
patterns must be developed. One technique employs "homework" assignments of increasing difficulty, called

_____ _____ _____.   graded task assignments

28. Unlike other forms of therapy, _____ therapists deal with   humanistic
the individual at a global level.

29. Rogers believes that people often dislike themselves. In his

_____ _____ therapy, an attempt is made to provide a   client-centered
situation in which personal growth can resume.

30. Humanistic therapy is characterized by its _____ nature, in   nondirective
which the therapist avoids advising or interpreting.

31. One common element of all therapists is _____ _____,   emotional defusing
as the patient is encouraged to rid himself of intense and
unrealistic fears.

32. An important part of therapy helps show the patient how he

reacts to others and is called _____ _____. This adds to   interpersonal learning

self-knowledge gained through _____.   insight

EVALUATING THERAPEUTIC OUTCOME

33. In general, a treatment group's scores on a test of emotional

well-being will be more _____ following treatment than will   variable

a control group's, indicating a _____ effect in addition to   deterioration
improvement.

34. In Gordon Paul's study of therapeutic outcome, results showed

that the _____ therapy and _____ therapy groups im-   insight, desensitization

proved relative to the _____ _____ control, but the   no treatment

_____ control also improved. Comparison of the various   placebo

improvements showed _____ therapy to be most effective.   desensitization

EXTENSIONS OF PSYCHOTHERAPY

35. _____ therapists are more interested in the relationships within the family as a unit than in the family members as individuals.

    Family

36. A group of people who get together to help each other manage a common difficulty is known as a _____ _____ group and is one form of group therapy.

    shared-problem

37. Those therapists who believe that many neuroses are a result of the patient's inability to endow life with meaning belong to the _____ school.

    existential

Self Test

1. Proposed remedies for mental disorders:
   a. are few in number
   b. can be divided into biological and psychological intervention
   c. all have a high success rate
   d. all of the above

2. Somatic therapies:
   a. involve getting the patient to imagine other people's feelings
   b. involve role playing and acting out of fears
   c. treat mental illness as a physical illness
   d. none of the above

3. The phenothiazines (especially chlorpromazine) reduce many symptoms of schizophrenia. Below are characterizations of five patients suffering from some form of mental illness. Which patients would be expected to improve with chlorpromazine treatment?

   i. this patient suffers from bizarre thoughts and beliefs
   ii. this patient is withdrawn and noncommunicative
   iii. this patient has frequent hallucinations
   iv. this patient is easily agitated
   v. this patient is deeply depressed

   a. all of the above
   b. i, ii, v
   c. ii, iii, v
   d. ii, iv, v
   e. i, ii, iii, iv

4. Depression is best treated (pharmaceutically) by:
   a. one of the tricyclics
   b. chlorpromazine
   c. amphetamines
   d. lithium carbonate

5. It has been suggested that lithium carbonate may:
   a. be a general cure for most forms of mental illness
   b. be totally useless, acting only as a placebo
   c. prevent future episodes of manic-depression
   d. have a general activation and arousal effect rather than a specific treatment effect

6. A researcher finds that after drinking nothing but milk for three months, three patients (out of nine) report that they no longer suffer from migraine headaches. The researcher proclaims the curative powers of milk. What critical questions cannot be answered due to the absence of a control group?
   a. what is the spontaneous recovery rate without treatment
   b. how did the milk cure the headaches
   c. why were only one-third of the patients cured
   d. can this finding be repeated

7. A motorist takes his car to the garage for a tune-up. Unbeknownst to him, the mechanic is dishonest and tells the motorist that he tuned the car when, in fact, he hadn't. The motorist feels that the car does run better. This is an example of:
   a. the placebo effect
   b. schizophrenia
   c. a double blind
   d. desensitization

8. A new drug is believed to alleviate the symptoms of manic-depression. The drug is tested in the following manner: One group of patients receives the drug in pill form, and another similar group receives a sugar pill. No patient knows which group he is in. A panel of psychiatrists evaluates each patient before and after the treatment period. The panel is not told whether a patient is getting the drug or the sugar pill. This is an example of:
   a. a placebo effect
   b. simultaneous control
   c. the double-blind technique
   d. transference

9. A treatment which was designed to liberate the patient's thoughts from his pathological emotions, but which produces ambiguous results and which may impair foresight and attention is:
   a. electroconvulsive shock treatment (ECT)
   b. prefrontal lobotomy
   c. lithium treatment
   d. catharsis

10. ECT was originally used to treat schizophrenia but was later found to be more effective in treating:
    a. depression
    b. mania
    c. compulsive behavior
    d. it is still most effective in treating schizophrenia

11. In contrast to pharmaceutical approaches to mental illness, psychotherapy
    a. is much more effective
    b. involves interpersonal interaction
    c. is more relevant to the nature of psychopathology
    d. none of the above

12. Orthodox (classical) psychoanalysis:
    a. states that illness is a result of unconscious defenses against unconscious urges
    b. states that most problems date back to childhood
    c. was developed by Freud
    d. all of the above

13. The cure for mental illness can be achieved by _____ according to the classical psychoanalysts:
    a. the victory of reason over passion
    b. a complete suppression of bad memories

c. a reenactment of the cause of the problem
   d. none of the above

14. When a patient is asked to say whatever comes into his mind, it is believed that sooner or later the memory relevant to the disorder should appear. This technique is known as:
    a. resistance
    b. repression
    c. free association
    d. role playing

15. Psychoanalysts believe the emotions are a principal part of therapy. One means for bringing emotions into play involves the relationship between the patient and therapist. The patient begins to behave as if the analyst were an important figure in his own life. This is known as:
    a. catharsis
    b. transference
    c. resistance
    d. intellectualization

16. In contrast to Freudians, the neo-Freudians emphasize:
    a. psychosexual development
    b. interpersonal and cultural factors
    c. intellectual rather than emotional insight into unconscious processes
    d. all of the above

17. Behavior therapists argue that:
    a. the theoretical notions of psychoanalysis are untestable
    b. the therapeutic effectiveness of psychoanalysis is unclear
    c. neurosis is caused by maladaptive learning
    d. all of the above

18. The behavior therapist tends to emphasize:
    a. giving the patient insight into the origins of his problems
    b. righting improper behavior patterns without regard for underlying causes
    c. curing the patient by a variety of means, including free association
    d. enabling the patient to reach a full realization of his human potentialities

19. For behavior therapists, fear:
    a. is a classically conditioned response
    b. has its roots in early childhood
    c. is a manifestation of emotional traumas
    d. is an operantly conditioned response

20. The use of muscular relaxation in the treatment of phobias is an example of:
 a. free association
 b. fear evocation
 c. humanistic therapy
 d. counterconditioning

21. In systematic desensitization, the patient first learns muscular relaxation and then constructs an anxiety hierarchy of fear-evoking situations. The next step is:
 a. to imagine the least fearful situation while relaxed
 b. to experience the least fearful situation while relaxed
 c. to imagine the most fearful situation and then relax as the conditioned link is extinguished
 d. to give the patient homework assignments involving exposure to fear-evoking stimuli

22. A patient who has a morbid fear of elevators is asked to imagine his most fear-producing situation. The therapist must be a proponent of:
 a. systematic desensitization
 b. a flooding procedure
 c. the placebo effect
 d. none of the above

23. The pairing of an unpleasant stimulus with an undesirable behavior is known as:
 a. paired associate learning
 b. cognitive therapy
 c. response-produced anxiety
 d. none of the above

24. Some patients' own thoughts become a fear-evoking stimulus. In such cases we say that the resulting anxiety is:
 a. response-produced
 b. a catharsis
 c. untreatable
 d. undetectable (except under unusual circumstances)

25. A therapist confronts a depressed patient with the irrationality of his belief that he cannot get a good job because he thinks he is incompetent despite evidence to the contrary. This therapist is most likely to be a proponent of:
 a. modeling
 b. cognitive theory
 c. desensitization
 d. could be any of the above

26. If and when irrational fears and beliefs are eliminated from a patient, new behavior patterns must be developed to achieve this. A therapist gives the patient a simple task to perform in his daily life. Once the patient masters this, the therapist gives him a slightly more difficult task, continuing in this way until normal behavior patterns emerge. This is the method of:
 a. modeling
 b. cognitive therapy
 c. graded task assignment
 d. assertiveness training

27. Modeling, assertiveness training, and role playing are all examples of:
 a. desensitization
 b. learning theory tools
 c. classical conditioning techniques
 d. techniques used in the development of normal interpersonal relations

28. In contrast to traditional psychoanalysis or behavior therapy, humanistic therapists:
 a. are interested in causes rather than effects
 b. deal with only one symptom at a time
 c. treat the individual at a global level
 d. believe that neuroses are a product of society

29. Psychoanalysis can be summarized by the word "unconscious" in the same way that behavior therapy can be represented by "conditioning." What two words best summarize humanistic therapy?
 a. cause, effect
 b. empathy, acceptance
 c. directive, interpretive
 d. rational, emotive

30. All of the following are common to the various therapeutic schools except:
 a. interpersonal learning
 b. insight
 c. emotional defusing
 d. therapy as an all-or-none process

31. Relative to an untreated control group's scores on a test of emotional well-being, the scores of a posttreatment group are:
 a. always at least slightly better
 b. seldom significantly different
 c. more variable
 d. less variable

32. A patient gets worse following therapy. This is known as:
    a. spontaneous remission
    b. the deterioration effect
    c. the placebo effect
    d. desensitization

33. Gordon Paul's work on stage fright demonstrated that desensitization:
    a. was not as effective as insight therapy
    b. is the best treatment for most mental illnesses
    c. did no better than a placebo control
    d. had the best results for this particular problem

34. In general, and in light of existing data, it appears that the most important factor in any treatment is that the patient:
    a. learns
    b. gains insight
    c. trusts the therapist
    d. no single factor is most important

35. In contrast to traditional psychotherapy, the goal of a shared-problem group is to _____ the problem that the members share.
    a. define
    b. cure
    c. discuss
    d. manage

36. The view that many emotional disorders result from a belief that everything is pointless characterizes the school of the:
    a. psychoanalysts
    b. nihilists
    c. existential therapists
    d. all of the above to some degree

37. According to the existential therapists, the primary method for initiating a cure involves:
    a. free association
    b. making the patient aware of the importance of free choice
    c. the recall of childhood memories
    d. lengthy philosophical discussions

Answer Key for Self Test

1. b p. 687		5. c p. 689
2. c p. 687		6. a p. 690
3. e p. 688		7. a p. 690
4. a p. 689		8. c p. 691

9. b p. 692	24. a p. 702
10. a p. 693	25. b p. 702
11. b pp. 693–94	26. c p. 703
12. d p. 695	27. d p. 703
13. a p. 695	28. c p. 703
14. c p. 695	29. b p. 704
15. b p. 696	30. d pp. 704–705
16. b p. 697	31. c p. 706
17. d pp. 698–99	32. b p. 706
18. b p. 699	33. d pp. 707–709
19. a p. 699	34. a p. 709
20. d p. 700	35. d p. 710
21. a p. 700	36. c p. 712
22. b p. 701	37. b p. 712
23. d p. 701	

Investigating Psychological Phenomena

DEMONSTRATION OF ROLE PLAYING

Equipment: None
Subjects: Yourself and one other
Time per subject: Thirty minutes
Time for experiment: Thirty minutes

As the author discusses in the text, role playing is one technique used by therapists to educate their patients about various aspects of interpersonal relations. This technique requires at least two people to assume the roles of individuals other than themselves in a particular social situation. In so doing, the hope of the treatment is that the participating individuals will gain some insight about the feelings, emotions, and cognitions of the persons whose roles are being played.

Although the technique sounds simple enough in principle, in actual practice it is a bit tricky. As the following quote illustrates, role playing participants frequently lapse back into their own personalities and have to be reminded about their role playing activities.

[The therapist] says "Tom, do you really care for me?" Tom says "I would say to her that I do, but she'd complain." Therapist: "Don't tell me what you *would* do. I'm Jane. Talk to me. Tom, do you really care for me?" Tom (turning away, looking slightly disgusted): "Yes." Therapist (still as Jane): "You don't say it like you mean it." Tom: "Yeah, that's what she says, and I usually . . ." Therapist (interrupting): "You're again telling me *about* what you'd say. I'm Jane. Tom, you don't say it like you mean it." Tom: "It's very hard for me to answer her when she says that." Therapist: "OK, I'm Jane. Tell me how you feel." Tom: "Jane, when you do that it really turns me off. Maybe if you didn't ask me so often I'd be able to say it spontaneously without feeling like a puppet . . . (then, in a tone that indicates he is now talking to the therapist as therapist) Gee, I wonder what would happen if I really said that to her" (Wachtel, 1977, pp. 234–35).

You can try role playing on your own to discover some of its features. Solicit the participation of a fellow student of the opposite sex from your introductory psychology class and set up the following situation.

The two of you are married and have just graduated from college. Each of you has very well-defined career plans, and you have each been skillful and lucky enough to have been offered very attractive first jobs that fit precisely the career lines that you have planned. The problem is that your job offers are in cities 1,000 miles apart. How do you decide what to do?

You should go through two sessions: first, have a discussion about this problem with your partner with each of you playing yourselves. Write down each of your responses on paper. Second, switch roles and try having the discussion again. In each case, put yourselves in the other's situation. Again, write your responses on paper.

After you have finished playing both roles, talk about differences in the conversations that resulted from your playing the male versus the female role. Compare the transcripts of each ses-

sion. Did this help you gain a different perspective on the problem?

At this point, you might want to try another role-playing exercise in which the two roles are quite different from one another. This will allow you to take two very different perspectives on a scene. Try out the following scene:

One of you should assume the role of an instructor for a course you are both taking (perhaps introductory psychology) while the other plays the role of a student. The issue is that the student has scored poorly on the midterm examination, but he feels that at least part of the reason for his poor performance is that he was graded unfairly by the instructor. In addition, the student was faced with taking four midterm exams within three days, so his performance was bound to suffer. Now imagine that the student has come in to talk with the instructor about these issues. The person playing the role of the instructor should really try to assume the personality and attitudes of the real instructor in the course as much as possible. After you have acted out a scene, switch roles. This time, to add some variety, have the student role be one of a very aggressive student who is determined not to leave the instructor's office without a change of grade. Again, after each scene, write down your impressions so that you can later discuss and evaluate them.

Having finished this scenario, think about some of the following questions: Was it more difficult to assume the role of the instructor or student? Was it difficult to stay in character without lapses? What insights have you gained about instructor-student relationships? Would this be a useful exercise for students and instructors to try in general? How was this role-playing exercise different from the first one?

Statistics: The Collection, Organization, and Interpretation of Data

Learning Objectives

1. What is the topic of statistics about? When are statistical tests needed in psychological research?

DESCRIBING THE DATA

2. What is scaling? Why is it important to understand the types of number scales?

Categorical and ordinal scales
3. Understand what categorical and ordinal scales are. Be able to describe the arithmetic operations permitted with each. Give examples of these scales.

Interval scales
4. What is the important feature of an interval scale? Give examples.

Ratio scales
5. What defines a ratio scale? What are some examples of ratio scales?
6. How do interval and ratio scales differ? What arithmetic operation is permitted with ratio scales?

COLLECTING THE DATA

The experiment
7. What are the essential ingredients of an experiment?

8. What is the difference between independent and dependent variables?

Observational studies
9. How do observational studies differ from experiments? How are they similar?
10. What are the advantages and disadvantages of observational studies?

The case study
11. What is the role of the case study in psychological research? When is it to be preferred over other methods?

SELECTING THE SUBJECTS

Sample and population
12. What is the difference between a sample and a population? When would you choose a sample?

Random and stratified samples
13. Understand some of the factors that must be taken into account in sampling.
14. What are the merits of random versus stratified sampling?
15. Why must one be careful in sampling responses?

ORGANIZING THE DATA: DESCRIPTIVE STATISTICS

Frequency distribution

16. How is a frequency distribution created from the raw scores in an experiment? To get practice in constructing a frequency distribution, plot one for the following heights (in inches) of males in a small class: 72, 72, 68, 66, 74, 73, 69, 69, 70, 67, 66, 73, 72.

Measures of central tendency

17. What is a measure of central tendency and why is it useful? Describe the three measures of central tendency that are commonly used. Calculate these three quantities for the scores given above.

Measures of variability

18. Describe what the range of a group of scores is, and describe why the range has limited utility. What is the range for the scores given above?

19. What is the variance of a set of scores? Why is it a useful measure of variability? Calculate the variance and standard deviation of the scores given above.

Converting scores to compare them

20. How are percentile ranks calculated, and how do they permit comparison of scores obtained from different tasks?

21. What is a z-score? Why is it useful for comparing scores from two distributions?

22. How are z-scores and percentile ranks similar?

The normal distribution

23. What are the characteristics of a normal distribution?

24. Be able to convert a z-score into a rank for a variable that has a normal distribution.

25. Understand the principle that can explain when a variable will be distributed normally. To do this you should roughly understand how a repeated binomial event will approximate a normal distribution.

DESCRIBING THE RELATION BETWEEN TWO VARIABLES: CORRELATION

Positive and negative correlation

26. What is the meaning of positive and negative correlation?

27. How is a scatter plot constructed? What does it show? What does a line-of-best-fit have to do with a scatter plot?

The correlation coefficient

28. Understand what various values of r mean.

29. How is a correlation coefficient computed? Do you understand the logic of this computation?

Interpreting and misinterpreting correlations

30. Give examples of cases for which a correlation cannot be interpreted in terms of one variable causing changes in another. What is the danger in interpreting correlations in terms of cause-effect?

INTERPRETING DATA: INFERENTIAL STATISTICS

Accounting for variability

31. What does it mean to account for variance?

32. Understand how variance is accounted for in actual experiments, such as the examples given in the text.

33. How does one account for variance in correlational data?

Hypothesis testing

34. What are null and alternative hypotheses? How do critical ratios allow us to rule out one of these hypotheses?

35. What trade-off is involved in the decision about where to set the cutoff for the critical ratio?

36. Be able to describe how hypotheses about differences between means can be tested using a critical ratio.

37. What is the relationship between a sample mean and a population mean?

38. What is a standard error, and what role does it play in testing hypotheses about sample means?

39. Be sure to follow the statistical analysis of the imagery experiment presented in the text.

40. Explain what it means to be reasonably confident that the mean of the population will fall within a specified interval.

Some implications of the hypothesis testing procedure

41. Explain how statistical conclusions are probabilistic. How does this affect these conclusions both about population means, and about individuals?

42. Why should statistical conclusions be conservatively drawn?

43. Based on your knowledge of how to compute a critical ratio, describe how sample size affects a statistical conclusion. When may statistical and psychological significance differ?

Programmed Exercises

1. The collection, organization, and interpretation of numerical

   data comprise the topic of _____.   statistics

DESCRIBING THE DATA

2. When all subjects in a group perform differently, or when the
   same subject performs differently on different occasions, we

   say that the data contain _____.   variability

3. Differences among subjects _____ groups and _____   between, within
   groups are the two sources of variability that are analyzed by
   statistical methods.

4. The assignment of numbers to events is called _____.   scaling

5. The type of _____ that numbers represent is defined by   scale
   which arithmetic operations are permitted on those numbers.

6. The assignment of the gears in a car to the categories 1st, 2nd,

   and 3rd involves the use of a (an) _____ scale.   categorical (nominal)

7. If you ask someone to rank order four cola drinks from most

   to least preferred, you would be using a (an) _____ scale.   ordinal

8. The Fahrenheit scale of temperature is a (an) _____ scale   interval
   as indicated by the fact that the difference between 30° and
   35° equals the difference between 75° and 80°.

9. The scale of length in feet is a (an) _____ scale; thus, we   ratio
   can say that a board of 4 feet is twice as long as a board of
   2 feet.

COLLECTING THE DATA

10. If an experimenter were interested in the effect of instructions
    to image on memory performance, he might run an experi-

    ment with a (an) _____ group given imagery instructions,   experimental

    and a (an) _____ group given standard memory instructions.   control

11. In the experiment referred to in question 10, the type of in-

    struction is the _____ variable, and a measure of recall   independent

    performance is the _____ variable.   dependent

12. An _____ _____ of the effects of city versus suburban   observational study
    living on rates of schizophrenia would involve selecting
    schizophrenic patients who had lived in urban or suburban
    environments.

13. The study of a particular aphasic subject intensively to reveal
    features of language behavior involves the use of a

    _____ _____ approach.   case study

SELECTING THE SUBJECTS

14. Psychologists are interested in drawing conclusions about

    _____ of subjects, but since it is frequently impractical to   populations

    test large numbers of people, they tend to test _____, then   samples
    generalize their conclusions.

15. A _____ sample is said to be unrepresentative of a   biased
    population.

16. A procedure for selecting subjects in which all individuals are

    equally likely to be selected is called a _____ _____.   random sample

17. _____ _____ is a technique for selecting subjects in   Stratified sampling
    which one tries to represent certain subgroups of a population
    in proportion to their size.

**ORGANIZING THE DATA:
DESCRIPTIVE STATISTICS**

18. A _____ _____ of birthweight could be represented by   frequency distribution

    a _____, a graph of the numbers of people in a sample   histogram
    who are born at various weights in the range to be studied.

19. There are three major measures of central tendency, the

    _____, _____, and _____.   mean, median, mode

20. The distribution of reaction times in an experiment is likely to

    be _____, since there will be none below 0, many short   skewed
    ones, and fewer and fewer long ones.

21. The _____ is a measure of variation that is defined as the   range
    difference between the highest and lowest scores.

22. The _____ is a measure of variation that takes account of   variance
    each score's deviation from the mean. Its square root is called

    the _____ _____.   standard deviation

23. The _____ _____ of a score is the percentage of scores   percentile rank
    that lie below it.

24. A _____ _____ expresses scores in terms of units of   z-score (standard score)
    standard deviations from a mean.

25. The heights of females in a population form a _____   normal

    _____, one in which there are equal frequencies of   distribution
    heights on both sides of the mean.

**DESCRIBING THE RELATION BETWEEN TWO
VARIABLES: CORRELATION**

26. If two dependent variables are related to one another, they are

    said to be _____.   correlated

27. If we ranked the top 10 runners in the world so that the top
    runner was ranked 1 and the 10th runner was ranked 10, and
    if we based these ranks on time to run the 1500 meter race,

there would by definition be a _____ correlation between rank and time.

positive

28. On the average, the faster one can complete each item on an aptitude test, the higher one's score assuming that one doesn't sacrifice accuracy. There is thus a _____ correlation between time per item and test score.

negative

29. Plotting two dependent variables, one on the abscissa and one on the ordinate yields a graph that shows the relationship between the variables. This is called a _____ _____.

scatter plot

30. A line fit to the points of the graph described in question 29 is called a _____.

line-of-best-fit

31. A _____ _____ of −1 indicates that there is a perfect _____ correlation between two variables.

correlation coefficient

negative

INTERPRETING DATA: INFERENTIAL STATISTICS

32. We say that we have _____ variance when we can attribute some of the variability in a set of scores to a particular factor.

explained (accounted for)

33. Squaring a correlation coefficient yields a proportion of _____ which is explained.

variance

34. For the experiment described in question 10, the _____ hypothesis is that there is no difference between the groups, while the _____ hypothesis is that the group with imagery instructions will recall more items.

null

alternative

35. The _____ _____ of a test statistic is usually set at 2 so that the probability of choosing the alternative hypothesis when the null hypothesis is, in fact, correct is quite small (one chance in twenty).

critical ratio

36. The standard deviation of a distribution of sample means is called the _____ _____.

standard error

37. The _____ _____ is the range within which we can be fairly confident the actual population mean will fall.

confidence interval

38. There are three important characteristics of statistical conclusions. They are affected by sample _____, they are _____, and they are _____.

size

probabilistic, conservative

Self Test

1. If there are 100 questions on a test, with each question worth one point, then the set of scores from 0 to 100 constitutes:
   a. a nominal scale
   b. an ordinal scale
   c. an interval scale
   d. a ratio scale

2. If we wanted to investigate the effect of cigarette smoking by mothers on birth defects in their children, we would likely:
   a. perform an experiment
   b. use correlations
   c. perform an observational study
   d. use a case study approach

3. An experimenter is interested in determining the effects of caffeine on sleeping behavior. He selects two groups of subjects to test his hypothesis that caffeine causes sleeplessness. Group 1 drinks regular coffee before bedtime while group 2 drinks decaffeinated coffee. The experimenter then measures the amount of time it takes subjects to fall asleep (as measured by an electroencephalogram). In this experiment:
   a. amount of sleep is the dependent variable and caffeine is the independent variable
   b. amount of sleep is the independent variable and caffeine is the dependent variable
   c. both are independent variables
   d. both are dependent variables

4. In the description of question 3:
   a. group 1 is the control group; group 2 is the experimental group
   b. group 1 is the experimental group; group 2 is the control group
   c. both groups are experimental; the experimenter has failed to include a control
   d. neither group is experimental; this is an observational study

5. If we test a randomly selected group of college students and then generalize our results to all college students, then:
   a. we are using a stratified sampling procedure
   b. we are making inappropriate inferences.
   c. we would need to correlate the results of our sample
   d. we are testing a sample in order to draw conclusions about a population

6. Suppose we wanted to know the size of the memory span (how many items a subject could hold in short-term memory) for all students in a particular school. To do this, we place all the names of all the students in a hat and draw out 100 for testing. This procedure is known as:
   a. stratified sampling
   b. biased sampling
   c. random sampling
   d. skewed sampling

7. If, in question 6, we had samples by grade in school, then we would have employed the technique of:

a. stratified sampling
b. biased sampling
c. random sampling
d. skewed sampling

8. The results of an examination are graphed so that each score is listed in order on the abscissa, and the number of students receiving that score is plotted on the ordinate. Such a graph:
   a. is a frequency distribution
   b. is a histogram of the scores
   c. is not a scattergram
   d. could be a normal distribution
   e. all of the above

9. Suppose the graph in question 8 turned out to look like the graph below. From this we could conclude that:

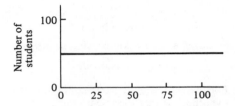

   a. the mean is greater than the median
   b. the mode is 50
   c. the variance is 0
   d. the test was statistically significant
   e. none of the above

10. Suppose the graph in question 8 turned out to look like the graph below. From this we could conclude that:

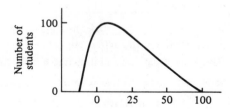

   a. the distribution is normal
   b. the median is lower than the mean
   c. the students with a score of 75 are in the 75th percentile
   d. the mode is 100
   e. none of the above

11. For the following five scores, 1, 2, 3, 4, 5:
   a. the median is 3
   b. the mean is 3

c. the variance is 2

d. all of the above

e. a and b but not c

12. Variability is to central tendency as variance is to:

a. correlation

b. z-score

c. mean

d. standard deviation

13. All of the following could be measures of variation in a set of scores except:

a. mean-median

b. highest score-lowest score

c. sum of (each score-mean)^2

d. average of highest two scores-average of lowest two scores

14. Consider two examinations: On one, the mean is 50, the standard deviation is 5, and your score is 65. On the other, the mean is 50, the standard deviation is 2, and your score is 60. Which of the following is true?

a. your percentile rank is higher on the second test

b. your z-score is higher on the second test

c. you can meaningfully compare your z-scores on the two tests

d. you cannot meaningfully compare your raw scores on the two tests

e. all of the above

15. If a set of scores on an exam has a mean of 75 and a standard deviation of 10, then:

a. the distribution must be normal

b. the distribution must be symmetric

c. a score of 50 corresponds to a z-score of −2.5

d. a z-score of 1.0 equals a test score of 75

16. If SAT scores have a mean of 500 and a standard deviation of 100, and if IQ scores have a mean of 100 and a standard deviation of 15, then with an SAT score of 650 and an IQ score of 115:

a. the z-score for IQ will be higher than the z-score for SAT

b. the percentile score for IQ will be higher than the percentile score for SAT

c. both of the above

d. the percentile score for IQ will be 84

e. the scores on the two tests will not be comparable since the tests differ

17. If we found a correlation coefficient of −.88 between reaction time and performance on a test of motor skill, we could conclude that:

a. a high score on the test of motor skill predicts a fast reaction time

b. a high score on the test of motor skill predicts a slow reaction time

c. motor skill causes people to have faster reaction times

d. reaction time and motor skill are largely unrelated

18. In the scatter plot shown below:

a. there is no relationship between x and y

b. the correlation coefficient is statistically significant

c. the correlation coefficient is close to 0

d. variable x is the independent variable

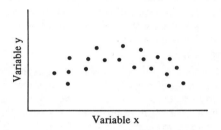

19. If a line-of-best-fit for a scatter plot were flat, then:

a. the correlation would be 1

b. the correlation would be 0

c. the correlation would not be significant

d. we know nothing about the correlation until we calculate it

20. Which of the following correlation coefficients shows the strongest inverse relationship between variables x and y?

a. .82

b. −.74

c. 0

d. −1.14

21. If the correlation between a parent's and his children's scores on a test of motor skills were .70, then we would know that:

a. seventy percent of the variability of the children's score is accounted for by the parents' scores

b. seventy percent of the variability in the parents' scores is accounted for by the children's scores

c. children's motor skills are caused by the skills of their parents

d. none of the above

22. An experiment is performed to determine whether eating breakfast improves one's test performance. Two groups are given tests,

one group after eating a good breakfast, one after no breakfast. Consider the following hypothesis: Eating breakfast has no effect on test performance. This hypothesis:

a. can only be evaluated probabilistically
b. is called the "alternative" hypothesis
c. cannot be evaluated in this experiment
d. is assessed by examining within-subject variability

23. In the experiment of question 22 which of the following would be necessary in order for us to believe that eating breakfast enhances test performance?

a. the sample must be normal
b. the sample must be statistically significant
c. the between-subject variance must be larger than the within-subject variance
d. all of the above
e. none of the above

24. Suppose you were to discover a hospital in which there were 8 new births each day, and you wished to test the hypothesis that this hospital had more births per day than the average hospital of its size. To do this we would need to know:

a. the correlations among births at all the hospitals in question
b. the mean, standard deviation, and number of hospitals in the comparison group
c. only the standard error of the births in the comparison group
d. none of the above

25. Two hospitals report 8 births per day average with a standard deviation of 10 births. For hospital A, this average was computed over 25 days; for hospital B, it was computed over 400 days. The standard errors of births in these hospitals:

a. are equal
b. are 2 in hospital A and .5 in hospital B
c. are not comparable because of the difference in number of days
d. none of the above

26. If a sample mean is 20, its standard deviation is 30, and the number of subjects in the sample is 9 then:

a. you can be fairly confident that the sample is normal
b. a subject with a score of 25 is in the fifth percentile
c. a score of 17 would be equal to a z-score of 1

d. you can be fairly sure that the population from which this sample was drawn has a mean greater than 0

27. Suppose you're trying to predict whether a Republican or Democratic candidate will win a particular senatorial race. You conduct a poll of the relevant voters and discover that 53% would vote for the Republican and 47% for the Democrat. Who do you think will win?

a. You can be reasonably confident that the Republican will win.
b. You can be reasonably confident that the Democrat will win.
c. Given the polling data, it's not clear who will win.
d. There isn't enough information to make a prediction one way or the other.

Answer Key for Self Test

1. d pp. A3–A4
2. c pp. A5–A6
3. a p. A5
4. b pp. A4–A5
5. d p. A6
6. c p. A7
7. a p. A7
8. e pp. A8–A14
9. e pp. A8–A11, A23
10. b p. A9
11. d pp. A9, A11
12. c pp. A10–A11
13. a pp. A9–A11
14. e pp. A12–A13
15. c pp. A12–A13
16. d p. A14
17. a pp. A16–A18
18. c pp. A15–A16
19. b p. A16
20. b pp. A16–A17
21. d pp. A17–A19
22. a p. A27
23. c p. A24
24. b pp. A25–A26
25. b p. A25–A26
26. d p. A26
27. d p. A27

Investigating Psychological Phenomena

This exercise provides an opportunity for you to apply some of the statistical concepts described in the text. Reconsider the experiment described on pp. A4–A5 of the text in which subjects are tested for recall performance on lists of twenty words with and without instructions to form images. Imagine that twenty subjects had been run in this experiment—the ten described in the text plus ten others. The data of all these subjects are presented in Table 1 below. In the first column are the recall scores with imagery instructions; the second column contains recall scores when no imagery instructions were provided; the third column is the difference between the first two, the amount of improvement. Finally, the fourth column contains the results of a test of imagery ability that was given to each of the subjects in this hypothetical experiment (scores on this test could range from 0 to 40). Using the data in this table, perform the following tabulations and analyses.

TABLE 1

Subject	Score with imagery	Score without imagery	Improvement	Test of imagery ability
Alphonse	20	5	15	30
Betsy	24	9	15	26
Cheryl	20	5	15	27
Davis	18	9	9	21
Earl	22	6	16	33
Fred	19	11	8	26
Germaine	20	8	12	32
Hortense	19	11	8	38
Imogene	17	7	10	30
Jerry	21	9	12	27
Kerry	17	8	9	29
Linda	20	16	4	24
Moe	20	10	10	26
Nicolas	16	12	4	22
Orry	24	7	17	36
Penelope	22	9	13	32
Quarton	25	21	4	23
Ronald	21	14	7	26
Steven	19	12	7	24
Terry	23	13	10	28

1. Create frequency histograms of the recall data on the two unlabeled sets of axes below. The left graph is for the recall scores with imagery instructions, and the right is for recall scores without imagery instructions. Note that you must decide what specific values to place on each axis for each graph.

Frequency histograms

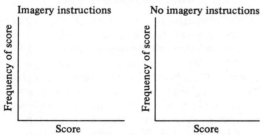

2. Calculate the mean, median, and mode of each of the distributions whose scores you have plotted above.

3. Calculate the range and standard deviation of each of these distributions.

4. Analyze the improvement scores to test the hypothesis that imagery instructions lead to better recall performance than no imagery instructions. To do this, you must compute a critical ratio that evaluates the sample mean of the improvement scores against the population mean for the null hypothesis (no improvement). Is this critical ratio larger than 2.0? If so, how do we interpret the improvement scores?

5. Examine the relationship between the improvement scores and performance on the test of imagery ability in two ways. First, create a scatter plot on the axes presented below. Second, compute a correlation coefficient between these sets of scores. Is there a relation between the variables? How would you interpret this relation psychologically?

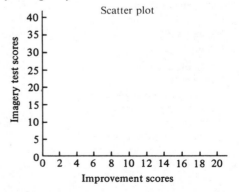

Now that you have completed your analyses, you should turn to the next page to examine the correct answers and compare them to your own answers.

Answers to Statistical Exercise

1.

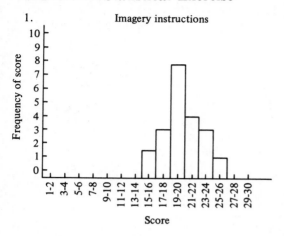

Imagery instructions

2. Imagery instructions
   Mean = 20.35
   Median = 20
   Mode = 20
   No imagery instructions
   Mean = 10.10
   Median = 9
   Mode = 9

3. Imagery instructions
   Range = 9
   Standard deviation = 2.46
   No imagery instructions
   Range = 16
   Standard deviation = 3.89

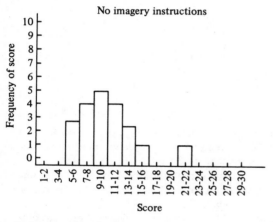

No imagery instructions

4. Critical ratio =

$$\frac{\text{sample mean} - \text{population mean by null hypothesis}}{\text{standard error of the mean}}$$

standard error of the mean

$$= \frac{\text{standard deviation}}{\sqrt{N}}$$

$$= \frac{4.05}{\sqrt{20}}$$

$$= .91$$

$$\text{critical ratio} = \frac{10.25 - 0}{.91}$$

$$= 11.26$$

This critical ratio is much larger than 2.0; therefore we may conclude that there is a statistically significant improvement in recall scores comparing no imagery to imagery instructions.

5. Scatter plot

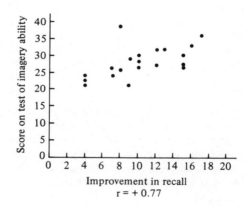

The correlation coefficient, r, is +0.77.

Both the scatter plot and the correlation coefficient indicate that there is substantial relationship between the variables. We might propose the following hypothesis to account for this relationship. Subjects with a better imagery ability are better able to form mental images in the memory task, and thus perform better. Our hypothesis must remain tentative, however, since we are not permitted to draw cause-effect conclusions from correlational data.

APPENDIX B

On the following pages you will find the report sheets for several of the experiments in the preceding chapters. If your instructor wants to collect the data for these experiments, use these reports sheets. You can cut them out and hand them in to your instructor.

Chapter 3

REPORT SHEET—HEART RATE

Data from Three Subjects (A, B, and C)

Instruction and time	A	B	C
"Begin and Relax"			
0:00–0:30			
0:45–1:15			
"Increase, physical activity"			
1:30–2:00			
2:15–2:45			
"Relax"			
3:00–3:30			
3:45–4:15			
"Increase, mental"			
4:30–5:00			
5:15–5:45			
"Relax"			
6:00–6:30			
6:45–7:15			

List for each subject the basic situation that they imagined in the "increase" minutes.

	Physical	Mental
A	_____	_____
B	_____	_____
C	_____	_____

Chapter 2

REPORT SHEET—NERVE IMPULSE

Practice   Trial 1 ankle = Time in seconds*

Part I   Trial 1 ankle = _____

Trial 2 ankle = _____

Trial 3 ankle = _____

Trial 4 ankle = _____

Trial 5 ankle = _____

Part II   Trial 1 upper arm = _____

Trial 2 upper arm = _____

Trial 3 upper arm = _____

Trial 4 upper arm = _____

Trial 5 upper arm = _____

Test

Part III   Trial 1 ankle time = _____

$\div 25 =$ _____ (a)

Trial 2 upper arm time = _____

$\div 25 =$ _____ (b)

Trial 3 upper arm time = _____

$\div 25 =$ _____ (c)

Trial 4 ankle time = _____

$\div 25 =$ _____ (d)

$\dfrac{a+d}{2} =$ _____ (average ankle time.)

$\dfrac{b+d}{2} =$ _____ (average upper arm time)

Average ankle time − average upper arm time = _____ (difference 1)

(1) Distance of ankle to brain (for third tallest person) = _____

(2) Distance of upper arm to brain (for third tallest person) = _____

Distance 1 − distance 2 = _____ (difference 2)

$\dfrac{\text{difference 2}}{\text{difference 1}} =$ _____ (speed of nerve impulse)

*Record time accurate to .1 second.

Chapter 4

REPORT SHEET—TASTE AVERSIONS

Number of subjects questioned _____

Number of subjects with aversions _____

Number of subjects who confirm Garcia's notions. _____

Summarize the results from all of your subjects below. You decide which questions are relevant to each feature of learned taste aversion, and summarize your results with respect to each of the features listed below.

BELONGINGNESS Relevant questions (Nos.)

_____

_____

_____

ONE TRIAL LEARNING Relevant questions (Nos.)

_____

_____

_____

LONG CS-UCS INTERVAL Relevant questions (Nos.)

_____

_____

_____

NOVELTY EFFECT Relevant questions (Nos.)

_____

_____

_____   _____

"IRRATIONALITY" Relevant questions (Nos.)

_____

_____

_____

OTHER INTERESTING RESULTS:

_____

_____

_____

Chapter 4

REPORT SHEET—MAZE LEARNING

Trial	Time	Number of errors
1	_____	_____
2	_____	_____
3	_____	_____
4	_____	_____
5	_____	_____

(using paper with cut-out hole)

Chapter 5

REPORT SHEET—MEASURING BRIGHTNESS CONTRAST

Background values:	1	3	4	5	7	10
matching value 1:	_____	_____	_____	_____	_____	_____
matching value 2:	_____	_____	_____	_____	_____	_____
matching value 3:	_____	_____	_____	_____	_____	_____
Total matching value:	_____	_____	_____	_____	_____	_____
Average matching value:	_____	_____	_____	_____	_____	_____

Chapter 7

REPORT SHEET—IMAGERY INSTRUCTIONS

Answer sheet for list 1   Answer sheet for list 2

1. _____	1. _____
2. _____	2. _____
3. _____	3. _____
4. _____	4. _____
5. _____	5. _____
6. _____	6. _____
7. _____	7. _____
8. _____	8. _____
9. _____	9. _____
10. _____	10. _____
11. _____	11. _____
12. _____	12. _____
13. _____	13. _____
14. _____	14. _____
15. _____	15. _____
16. _____	16. _____
17. _____	17. _____
18. _____	18. _____
19. _____	19. _____
20. _____	20. _____

Chapter 9

REPORT SHEET—LEXICAL RETRIEVAL TIME

Subject 1   Subject 2

List 1 _____	List 1 _____
List 2 _____	List 2 _____
List 3 _____	List 3 _____
List 4 _____	List 4 _____

Chapter 10

REPORT SHEET—PERSONAL SPACE

1 person elevator	Number of cases with subjects in predicted place (7 or 9)	_____/15
2 person elevator	Number of cases with subjects in predicted place (7 and 9)	_____/15
3 person elevator	Number of cases with subjects in noncontiguous squares	_____/15

Chapter 8

REPORT SHEET—THE STROOP EFFECT

Experiment 1

Color patch list	Letter string list
List 1 _____ sec. _____ errors	List 2 _____ sec. _____ errors
List 3 _____ sec. _____ errors	List 4 _____ sec. _____ errors
List 5 _____ sec. _____ errors	List 6 _____ sec. _____ errors
List 7 _____ sec. _____ errors	List 8 _____ sec. _____ errors
List 9 _____ sec. _____ errors	List 10 _____ sec. _____ errors
Average = _____ sec.	Average = _____ sec.
Total errors = _____	Total errors = _____

Experiment 2

Neutral words	Color words
List 1 _____ sec. _____ errors	List 2 _____ sec. _____ errors
List 3 _____ sec. _____ errors	List 4 _____ sec. _____ errors
List 5 _____ sec. _____ errors	List 6 _____ sec. _____ errors
List 7 _____ sec. _____ errors	List 8 _____ sec. _____ errors
List 9 _____ sec. _____ errors	List 10 _____ sec. _____ errors
Average = _____ sec.	Average = _____ sec.
Total errors = _____	Total errors = _____

Experiment 3

Neutral words	Color referent words
List 1 _____ sec. _____ errors	List 2 _____ sec. _____ errors
List 3 _____ sec. _____ errors	List 4 _____ sec. _____ errors
List 5 _____ sec. _____ errors	List 6 _____ sec. _____ errors
List 7 _____ sec. _____ errors	List 8 _____ sec. _____ errors
List 9 _____ sec. _____ errors	List 10 _____ sec. _____ errors
Average = _____ sec.	Average = _____ sec.
Total errors = _____	Total errors = _____

Chapter 11

REPORT SHEET—IMPRESSIONS

	Percent of subjects checking favorable adjective at left			
	Asch's Data		Your Data	
Adjective Pair	group A (24 students)	group B (34 students)	group A (__ students)	group B (__ students)
generous	24	10		
wise	18	17		
happy	32	5		
good-natured	18	0		
humorous	52	21		
sociable	56	27		
popular	35	14		
reliable	84	91		
good-looking	74	35		
serious	97	100		
restrained	64	9		
honest	80	79		

Chapter 15

REPORT SHEET—IMPLICIT LEARNING

1. _____	9. _____	17. _____
2. _____	10. _____	18. _____
3. _____	11. _____	19. _____
4. _____	12. _____	20. _____
5. _____	13. _____	21. _____
6. _____	14. _____	22. _____
7. _____	15. _____	23. _____
8. _____	16. _____	24. _____

Subject's statement of rule: _____

_____

_____

_____

_____

_____

_____

_____

_____

Number of correct responses out of 24: _____

Chapter 14

REPORT SHEET—CONSERVATION OF NUMBER

1. More blue _____ 5. More blue _____
   More red _____   More red _____
   Both equal _____   Both equal _____
2. More blue _____ 6. More blue _____
   More red _____   More red _____
   Both equal _____   Both equal _____
3. More blue _____ 7. More blue _____
   More red _____   More red _____
   Both equal _____   Both equal _____
4. More blue _____ 8. More blue _____
   More red _____   More red _____
   Both equal _____   Both equal _____

Chapter 19

REPORT SHEET—DEPRESSION

Self-rating of mood now (enter number) _____

Self-rating of mood over last twelve months
(enter number) _____

Number of negative events recalled _____

Number of positive events recalled _____

Negative minus positive events _____

Negative plus positive events _____

Chapter 16

REPORT SHEET—SEX DIFFERENCES

	Your data* (combined with classmate's data)			
	Males		Females	
Item	#	%	#	%
1. Killing cockroach	____	____	____	____
2. Queen Anne's lace (correct answer: flower)	____	____	____	____
3. Using word "shit" (less than 5 times)	____	____	____	____
4. Sew clothes	____	____	____	____
5. Intercourse only after spiritual love	____	____	____	____
6. Nude in locker room	____	____	____	____
7. Crying frequency (very often, often or only with good reason	____	____	____	____
8. Feel like smashing things	____	____	____	____
9. Chest measurement	____	____	____	____
10. Change tire	____	____	____	____
11. Playing radio	____	____	____	____
12. Prefer dominance in relationship	____	____	____	____
13. Overweight	____	____	____	____
14. Washing hair when depressed	____	____	____	____
15. Sleep in nude	____	____	____	____
16. Closest parent (mother)	____	____	____	____
17. Keep room neat	____	____	____	____

*Tabulate your results below in the following way. For the "yes" or "no" questions (e.g., item 1), add up the number of subjects who answered "yes." Then calculate what percentage answered "yes." For the "true" or "false" questions (e.g., item 8), record those who answer "true." For other items (e.g., item 2), add up the number of subjects whose answers are the same as those indicated in parentheses under "Item" (e.g., item 1—flower).

List the femaleness scores of all of your subjects:

Males: ____ ____ ____ ____ ____ ____ ____ ____ ____ ____

____ ____ ____ ____ ____ ____ ____ ____ ____ ____

Females: ____ ____ ____ ____ ____ ____ ____ ____ ____ ____

____ ____ ____ ____ ____ ____ ____ ____ ____ ____

Grateful acknowledgment is made to: F. Garb, A. Stunkard, and the *American Journal of Psychiatry* to adapt from Garb and Stunkard, "Taste aversions in man," *American Journal of Psychiatry* 131 (1974):1204–1207; W. Epstein, I. Rock, and the *American Journal of Psychology* to adapt from Epstein, W., and Rock, I., "Perceptual set as an artifact of recency," *American Journal of Psychology* 73 (1960):214–228; J. R. Stroop and the *Journal of Experimental Psychology* to adapt from J. R. Stroop, "Studies in interference in serial verbal reactions," *Journal of Experimental Psychology* 18 (1935):643–662; A. S. Reber and the *Journal of Verbal Learning and Verbal Behavior* to adapt from A. S. Reber, "Implicit learning of artificial grammars," *Journal of Verbal Learning and Verbal Behavior* 6 (1967):858–863; S. E. Asch and the *Journal of Abnormal and Social Psychology* to adapt from S. E. Asch, "Forming impressions of personality," *Journal of Abnormal and Social Psychology* 41 (1946): 258–290.

Illustrations

Page 3 Bugelski, B. R., and Alampay, D. A., "The role of frequency in developing perceptual sets," *Canadian Journal of Psychology* 15 (1961): 205–211. Adapted by permission of the Canadian Psychological Association.

Page 9 Katz, B., "The nerve impulse," *Scientific American* 187 (November 1952):164–165.

Page 12 Gray, G. W., "The great ravelled knot," *Scientific American* 179 (October 1948): 28–29.

Pages 13 and 31 Keeton, W. T., *Biological science*, 3rd edition. New York: W. W. Norton & Company, Inc., 1980. Copyright © 1980, 1979, 1972, 1967 by W. W. Norton & Company, Inc.

Pages 15 and 16 Hodgkin, A. L., and Huxley, A. F., "Action potentials recorded from inside nerve fibers," *Nature* 144 (1939):710–711. Adapted by permission.

Page 30 Nisbett, R. E., "Taste, deprivation and weight determinants of eating behavior," *Journal of Personality and Social Psychology* 10 (1968): 107–116. Copyright 1968 by the American Psychological Association. Reprinted by permission.

Page 32 Harlow, H. F., "Learning and satiation of response in intrinsically motivated complex puzzle performance in monkeys," *Journal of Comparative and Physiological Psychology* 43 (1950):289–294.

Page 43 Reproduced by permission of the publishers from Köhler, W., *The mentality of apes*. London, England: Routledge & Kegan Paul Ltd., 1976.

Page 44 *bottom* Pavlov, I. P., *Lectures on conditioned reflexes*, vol. I. New York: International Publishers, Co., Inc. 1928. Adapted by permission of International Publishers Co., Inc.

Page 45 From Spooner, A., and Kellogg, W. N., "The backward conditioning curve," *American Journal of Psychology* 60 (1947):321–334. Copyright © 1947 by The University of Illinois Press. Reprinted by permission of the publisher.

Page 46 Ralph Gerbrands Company, Inc., Arlington, Mass. Reprinted by permission.

Page 77 Gombrich, E. H., *Meditations on a hobby horse*. Oxford, England: Phaidon Press, 1963.

Page 81 From James J. Gibson, *The perception of the visible world*. Boston, Mass: Houghton Mifflin Co., 1950.

Page 82 Photograph by William Vandivert. From *Scientific American*, April 1960. Reprinted with permission of William Vandivert and *Scientific American*.

Page 83 Reprinted from *The formation of the perceptual world* by I. Köhler, by permission of International Universities Press. Copyright © 1964 by International Universities Press.

Pages 85 and 87 Boring, E. G., "A new ambiguous figure," *American Journal of Psychology* 42 (1930):444–445; and Leeper, R. W., "A study of a neglected portion of the field of learning: The development of sensory organization," *Journal of Genetic Psychology* 46 (1935):41–75.

Page 132 Tinbergen, N., *The study of instinct.* Oxford, England: Oxford University Press, 1951. Adapted by permission of the publishers.

Page 133 Reprinted from "Reproductive behaviors," by Etkin, E., in *Social behavior and organization among vertebrates* by Etkin, W., by permission of The University of Chicago Press. Copyright 1964 by The University of Chicago.

Page 147 Festinger, L., and Carlsmith, J. M., "Cognitive consequences of forced compliance," *Journal of Abnormal and Social Psychology* 58 (1959):203–210. Copyright 1959 by the American Psychological Association. Reprinted by permission.

Page 175 Nilsson, Lennart, *Behold man.* Boston: Little, Brown, and Company, 1974.